THE LANCE
AND THE SHIELD

ALSO BY ROBERT M. UTLEY

Custer and the Great Controversy:
Origin and Development of a Legend

The Last Days of the Sioux Nation

Frontiersmen in Blue:
The United States Army and the Indian, 1848–1865

Frontier Regulars;
The United States Army and the Indian, 1866–1891

The American Heritage History of the Indian Wars
(with Wilcomb Washburn)

The Indian Frontier of the American West,
1846–1890

If These Walls Could Speak:
Historic Forts of Texas

High Noon in Lincoln:
Violence on the Western Frontier

Cavalier in Buckskin:
George Armstrong Custer and the Western Military Frontier

Billy the Kid:
A Short and Violent Life

THE LANCE
AND THE SHIELD

The Life
and Times of Sitting Bull

ROBERT M. UTLEY

Ballantine Books • New York

This edition published by arrangement with Henry Holt and Company, Inc.

Library of Congress Catalog Card Number: 93-91086

ISBN: 0-345-38938-7

Maps designed by Jeffrey L. Ward

Cover design by Kathleen Lynch
Cover painting courtesy of Mr. and Mrs. David Blumberg

Manufactured in the United States of America

First Ballantine Books Edition: August 1994

10 9 8 7

For sons Don and Phil . . .
and daughter-in-law Susan

THE LANCE AND THE SHIELD

Sitting Bull treasured his lance and shield. His father presented them to him in ceremonies marking his passage to warrior rank, after his first coup at age fourteen. The shield, considered to possess sacred power, bore a design that came to Sitting Bull's father in a dream. The lance was decorated with beadwork crafted by his mother.

The lance was Sitting Bull's favorite weapon. An offensive weapon, it symbolized Sitting Bull's role among the Hunkpapa Sioux from 1864, following the Battle of Killdeer Mountain, until 1869, following the Treaty of 1868 and the split of the Lakota Sioux tribes into agency and nontreaty factions. During these years Sitting Bull became the Hunkpapas' most noted and effective warrior in raids against the whites, especially the soldiers in the forts along the upper Missouri River.

A defensive weapon, the shield symbolized Sitting Bull's role between 1869 and his surrender in 1881. As the principal leader of the nontreaty Lakotas, he defended his people and land against white aggression and encroachment. He had become the Lakota shield.

CONTENTS

PREFACE

FOR MORE THAN half a century, the standard biography of Sitting Bull has been Stanley Vestal's *Sitting Bull, Champion of the Sioux*. Others have come and gone but have been superficial or worse. Vestal, pen name for Walter Stanley Campbell, taught literature and creative writing at the University of Oklahoma until his death in 1957.

Perhaps it seems in poor taste that I should use Vestal's own research to challenge the domination of his biography. The explanation springs from my appraisal of each.

In preparation for his book, Vestal conducted exhaustive interviews with elderly Indians on the Sioux reservations of North and South Dakota. His field trips occurred in the late 1920s and early 1930s, when the young men of Sitting Bull's time were in their seventies and eighties but still mentally alert. He won the confidence of Sitting Bull's family and associates while they still could recount their experiences and impressions. In particular, White Bull and One Bull, Sitting Bull's nephews, were indispensable. There are questions I wish Vestal had pursued further and questions I wish he had thought to ask. I also wish he had kept a more meticulous record of his researches. But despite the flaws, his papers at the University of Oklahoma Library in Norman are invaluable. Neither his book nor mine could have been written without them.

Vestal's biography is another matter. First I must grant that Vestal's Sitting Bull and mine are essentially the same person. We reached our

destination, however, by altogether different routes. Vestal built his character more by literary than by historical method. I have built my character
by historical method.

The Vestal genre is not unique. He was one of a trio of scholars who
presented themselves as historians but viewed the Sioux through mainly
literary lenses. The other two were Mari Sandoz, biographer of Crazy
Horse, and John G. Neihardt, author of the classic *Black Elk Speaks*. Like
Vestal, they achieved ultimate truth in works that are good literature and
bad history.

I pay tribute to all three while noting their defects as I see them. In
particular, I salute Stanley Vestal for his research and for rescuing Sitting
Bull's memory from the ignominy that tainted it for a generation after his
death.

Vestal's interpretation of Sitting Bull came as a shock to many Indians
and whites identified with his final years. They remembered him as a
disgruntled troublemaker, obstinate, conceited, narrow-minded, obstructionist, a physical and moral coward, and pretender to high rank and power
that had never existed. Some, such as missionary Thomas L. Riggs,
complained that White Bull, One Bull, and others of the Sitting Bull
clique had duped Vestal by portraying a sainted but fictional forebear.

In historical truth, James McLaughlin, Sitting Bull's Indian agent
during the reservation years, duped everyone, white and Indian alike.
Finding Sitting Bull unpliable, too much the Indian of old to lend his
influence to government programs for transforming his people into imitation whites, McLaughlin created the false portrait that dominated
thoughts about Sitting Bull until Vestal reshaped it more truthfully. I have
discovered enough persuasive evidence in other sources to corroborate the
essence of the image recalled for Vestal by White Bull, One Bull, and
other Indians of the 1920s.

It is exceedingly difficult to write the biography of a person of another
culture, especially one that in its essentials no longer exists. I have tried
hard to look at Sitting Bull in terms of his cultural norms, not mine. Where
whites drew false conclusions because of ignorance of his culture, I have
sought to stress his perfectly rational underlying motives. Where I could
not fathom his motives, I have tried to avoid pronouncing judgments
according to my culture when his, if only I understood it better, might
have supplied a logical explanation. Yet Sitting Bull's claim to significance
beyond his own tribe rests on his role in the collision of two cultures, and I
have therefore had to view him from the white as wel¹ as the Indian
perspective.

I believe there are compensating advantages in looking through one set of cultural lenses at another and very different culture. Gary Wills gave me comfort when he wrote: "The great works of Parkman and Prescott gained by the fact that they were able to get partway outside both cultures they studied. As men of Protestant New England, they could be critical of French Jesuits and Spanish Friars as well as of the North and South Americans."*

---

* Gary Wills, "Man of the Year," *New York Review of Books* 38 (November 21, 1991): 18.

PROLOGUE

THE WHITE BUFFALO WOMAN gave the Lakotas the Sacred Calf
Pipe and with it all that made life meaningful. The people had wandered
the earth for countless generations, ever since emerging from the underworld in misty antiquity. Not until the wondrous appearance of the White
Buffalo Woman, however, were they truly Lakotas. "There was nothing
sacred before the pipe came," explained Left Heron. "There was no
social organization and the people ran around the prairie like so many wild
animals."[1]

She appeared first to two hunters. Approaching, they beheld a beautiful woman, garbed in white buckskin and carrying a bundle on her back.
So exquisite was she that in one of the men she stirred an evident lust. She
bade him to come forward. As he drew near, a cloud of mist enveloped
them both. When it dissipated, a pile of bones, writhing with horrid
serpents, lay at her feet.

The woman instructed the other hunter to return to his village and
give notice to prepare for her coming, that she bore a message of great
importance. In the village the people, informed of what had happened,
joined several tipis to form a large council lodge in which to receive the
mysterious visitor, and they dressed in their handsomest clothing.

When the woman arrived, she entered the lodge and faced the chief,
standing in front of a throng of expectant people. In her hands she held the
bundle that had been strapped to her back. After opening the wrapping,

1

she drew forth a round stone, which she placed on the ground. Then she removed a pipe. Its red stone bowl, she explained, stood for the earth. The buffalo calf carved on the bowl stood for all four-legged creatures. The wooden stem stood for all growing things. The twelve decorative feathers stood for the eagle and all other birds of the air.

This was the Sacred Calf Pipe, the woman declared. The person who smoked it achieved union with all peoples and all things of the universe—established communication, therefore, with *Wakantanka*, the Great Mystery.

"With this sacred pipe," she said, "you will walk upon the Earth; for the Earth is your grandmother and mother and She is sacred."

Touching the pipe to the stone at her feet, she continued: "With this pipe you will be bound to all your relatives: your grandfather and father, your grandmother and mother."

The stone, the woman pointed out, bore seven incised circles. Each represented a ceremony in which the pipe would be used and which expressed the sacred and social relationships that would henceforth order and uplift the lives of the people. She taught them the first, but reserved the remaining six for a future time.

After turning from the council lodge, the woman walked a few steps and sat down. She arose as a red-and-brown buffalo calf. Walking farther, the animal lay down and rolled, then got up as a white buffalo calf. Walking still farther, it turned into a black buffalo. On the brow of a hill, the black buffalo bowed to each of the four directions and vanished.

Because of the White Buffalo Woman and the Sacred Pipe, the Lakotas venerated their human kin. She established the relationships among kin and prescribed the manner in which they would be expressed. She enjoined peace—with friends and relatives, not enemies.

Because of the White Buffalo Woman and the Sacred Pipe, the Lakotas venerated the earth and the sky and all their contents, not alone for their material riches but for their sacred riches as well. All expressions of nature, animate and inanimate, singly and together, were sacred, the abode of *Wakantanka* in both single and multiple character.

Because of the White Buffalo Woman and the Sacred Pipe, the Lakotas enjoyed a rich spiritual and ceremonial life and a powerful bond, both tangible and mystical, to the world surrounding them.

Into this world, as the Lakotas neared the peak of cultural fulfillment, Sitting Bull was born.

1 YOUTH

"I WAS BORN on the Missouri River," said Sitting Bull to the first newspaper reporter to gain an interview with him. "At least I recollect that somebody told me so—I don't know who told me or where I was told of it."[1] Sitting Bull was similarly vague about the year of his birth, reflecting the relative unimportance of such matters in the Sioux scheme of life. The past took on significance only when relevant to the concerns of the present.

Thus the time and place of Sitting Bull's birth remain obscure. He may have been born in 1831, or 1832, or 1834, or 1837. He may have been born at Many Caches, a collection of Indian storage pits on the south side of Grand River almost directly across from where he met his death in 1890. Or he may have been born a hundred miles to the southeast, on Willow Creek, a tributary of the Bad (or Teton) River a few miles west of the Missouri River trading post of Fort Pierre. Many Caches in 1831 seems most likely.[2]

The youth destined for greatness as Sitting Bull was born into a distinguished Hunkpapa family. The Hunkpapas were but one small tribe of the Sioux confederacy. By the middle of the nineteenth century, the Sioux had divided into three groups of tribes. The location and way of life of each traced a century's history of migration and cultural adaptation as, pressed by Chippewas and drawn by the game-rich plains, the people spread westward from their original homes around the head of the Mississippi River.

Originally the Sioux consisted of seven autonomous but related groups. Although they had never assembled at one time and place, they claimed a unity born of shared culture, history, and language.

Especially language. In the dialect of the eastern tribes, they called themselves *Dakota*, or ally. In the dialect of the western tribes, the word became *Lakota*. Any peoples with whom peace had been formally concluded were allies and could come within the meaning of Dakota or Lakota. Any peoples with whom peace had not been formally concluded were automatically enemies. Whites called the Dakotas and Lakotas Sioux, a corruption of a Chippewa word signifying enemies. In time, Dakotas and Lakotas also answered to Sioux.[3]

The four eastern tribes, sometimes collectively labeled Santees, lived along the Minnesota River, the Dakota heartland in the early eighteenth century. They hunted the animals of the prairie and forest, fished the rivers, and harvested wild rice. They moved about mostly on foot and led a semisedentary existence.

The so-called middle tribes of Dakota, the Yankton and Yanktonai, had abandoned the woodlands for the prairies east of the Missouri River. They followed the buffalo on horseback but also retained many customs of their kinsmen to the east. They were a bridge between the Eastern and Western Sioux and shared the traits of both.

Still farther west, the seventh group in turn divided itself into seven tribes. Collectively known as Tetons as well as Lakotas, they spoke the Lakota dialect and by Sitting Bull's time had transformed themselves into true horse-and-buffalo Indians. The seven were Oglala ("Scatters Their Own"), Brule ("Burned Thighs"), Miniconjou ("Planters by Water"), Two Kettle ("Two Boilings"), Sans Arc ("Without Bows"), Hunkpapa ("Campers at the Opening of the Circle"), and Sihasapa ("Blackfeet"). The last were Blackfeet Sioux, not the Blackfeet tribe farther to the northwest.

The Lakota culture was hardly a generation old at the time of Sitting Bull's birth. Only around the beginning of the nineteenth century were the Lakotas fully transformed from pedestrians to mounted nomads. They occupied the high plains between the Missouri River and the Bighorn Mountains while ranging north to the Canadian prairies and south as far as the Platte and Republican rivers. Altogether, the Lakotas numbered between fifteen and twenty thousand people.

Each Lakota tribe claimed its own hunting grounds, although as kindred groups they did not jealously defend them against one another. The largest, the Oglala and Brule, centered on the North Platte River and ranged northward to the upper Powder River and eastward through the Black Hills to the Missouri. To their north, country bisected by the White and Cheyenne rivers, lived the Miniconjous and Two Kettles, overlapping on their north with the Hunkpapas (Sitting Bull's tribe), Blackfeet, and Sans Arcs. The last three, all small, appeared almost as one—often camping and traveling together and intermarrying extensively.

These Hunkpapas, Blackfeet, and Sans Arcs did not occupy a large homeland. Its heart lay in the grassy plains rolling west from the Missouri River below the mouth of the Yellowstone—Elk River to the Sioux. Relieved by a scattering of buttes and wooded plateaus, the prairies undulated from horizon to horizon, lush and green in spring, scorched and brown in summer. A system of rivers, parallel green troughs in the plains, flowed eastward into the Missouri.

For all its vast emptiness, this land supported bounteous if sometimes precarious life. Herds of buffalo blackened the plains, and elk, deer, antelope, bear, and smaller game afforded variety. Grouse and prairie chickens darted amid the sagebrush, while ducks and geese homed on lakes and river bottoms. Streams yielded trout, bass, and other fish. Edible roots, berries, and fruit rounded out a diet heavy on meat. The rich grasses of the high plains nourished the wild game as well as the domesticated horses that furnished the Hunkpapas their means of transportation. The narrow valleys, traced by groves of cottonwoods and willows, afforded water, firewood, grass, and shelter.

The climate of the northern Plains could be gentle and comforting but also deadly in its extremes. Winter storms dumped huge falls of snow, whipped the land with fierce gales, and dropped temperatures to depths that swiftly froze limbs and brought death. The summer sun blasted the plains with merciless heat, parched the grass, and dried the streams. Often it hid behind thunderheads that towered blackly before loosing sweeping downpours to send floods coursing down the valleys, or that turned suddenly icy and spewed forth storms of hail that stripped trees, shredded grass, and imperiled any creature caught without shelter.

AT THE TIME of Sitting Bull's birth in 1831, the family was headed by a father of the same name. Tatanka-Iyotanka, Sitting Bull, connoted a stubborn buffalo bull sitting on its haunches. The father did not at first name his son Sitting Bull but rather Jumping Badger, which all understood would be replaced with something more suitable at the appropriate time in his growth. No one called the boy Jumping Badger, however, for his willful and deliberate ways earned him the nickname Hunkesni, or "Slow."[4]

"My father and two uncles were chiefs," the son recalled years later. "My father was a very rich man, and owned a great many ponies in four colors." The oldest of three brothers, his younger brothers, Four Horns and Looks-for-Him-in-a-Tent, were also chiefs, with Four Horns destined to be remembered as one of the most revered in the history of the Hunkpapas.[5]

The family occupying the tipi that formed the boy's first world consisted of Chief Sitting Bull, his wife Her-Holy-Door, and a six-year-old sister, Good Feather. Later another sister was born to the family, named Brown-Shawl-Woman or Twin Woman. A half brother with the name Fool Dog, offspring of an earlier marriage, lived with his mother's people, the Arikaras.

Slow's earliest images were from the perspective of the cradleboard, in which he was tightly laced and released for cleaning only once or twice a day. They were chiefly of the tipi, the conical dwelling of buffalo skins stretched over a framework of lodgepole pines in which the family lived. It stood with other tipis of the band or, on occasion, several bands on the valley of some river or creek. In cold weather a fire burned in the center of the tipi's interior, its smoke drawn off by proper positioning of windflaps at the top attached to two poles, and a dewcloth hung from the inner wall near its base to provide insulation. In warm weather the cookfire burned outside the tipi, while the dewcloth came down and the wall went up a short distance from the pegs to admit cooling breezes. Sleeping robes and storage areas lined the circular base of the tipi. Backrests occupied the place of honor opposite the entrance. Here the father rested or smoked and talked with guests.

Outside, in good weather, the camp bustled with activity. Women scurried at their chores, laboring over smoky cook fires, laughing and gossiping among themselves. Men tended their ponies or sat smoking, making arrows, or mending weapons. Barking dogs darted among the tipis, snarling at one another and fighting over scraps of food.

In front of her tipi, Slow's mother labored at her own tasks. In a buffalo paunch or trade kettle slung from a tripod, she cooked meat and made soup, using stones fired to a white glow and dropped in the pot to keep the mixture boiling. When hunters returned, she cut up the meat. Much of it she sliced into thin sheets and hung from racks made of saplings to dry in the sun. For people on the move, it furnished a nourishing staple, either as simple dried meat or, mixed with tart berries and stored in skin parfleches, as pemmican. Other duties that occupied Her-Holy-Door included the laborious task of scraping and preparing buffalo hides and the skins of other animals; crafting clothing, containers, and utensils; and, when camp moved, dismantling and packing the tipi and all its contents on travois drawn by horses, then reversing the process at the destination. When this occurred—often in summer and autumn, infrequently in winter—Slow bounced along in his cradleboard, strapped to a travois or a horse's flank.

Like all Sioux parents, Sitting Bull and Her-Holy-Door doted on their children. "A child is the greatest gift from *Wakantanka*," the Great Mystery, a tribesman explained years later, sent "in response to many devout prayers, sacrifices, and promises."[6] As the tribe's future, children enjoyed outpourings of parental affection, indulgence, gentle but persistent instruction, and a complete absence of physical punishment.

That the Lakota mother performed all the hard labor did not imply inferior status in family or society. As one authority expressed it, "The simple fact is that woman had her own place and man his; they were not the same and neither inferior nor superior."[7] Far from a mere drudge, the Lakota mother in fact dominated tipi affairs. She, not the husband, owned the lodge and all the family belongings. She exerted the paramount authority over the children—daughters until wed and sons until their voices began to change.[8]

Her-Holy-Door exercised this influence on her son in his early years and also, as a widowed resident of his lodge, played an important part during most of his adult life. Her grandson remembered her as a very good woman, who taught her son much in his youth and who was a jolly sort who talked a lot and made people laugh.[9]

When finally freed from the cradleboard, however, Slow also came under the intense scrutiny and instruction of his father and, as customary, his uncles. Four Horns in particular, a stalwart warrior wise in the ways of his people, played a significant role in the boy's upbringing. These teachers passed long hours honing his riding and shooting skills. Success in the two basic roles of men in Sioux life—war and the hunt—depended on the ability to maneuver a speeding pony in tight circumstances and the swiftness and accuracy of launching arrows from a bow. Like all fathers, Sitting Bull reared his son to excel in both.

The life of the people was tied to the hunt. The economy depended overwhelmingly on the buffalo. Buffalo meat was the dietary staple. From the hide and fur came clothing, shelter, bedding, furniture, and containers. Sinews provided bowstrings and bindings for every purpose, from lashing together tipi coverings to stitching clothing and moccasins. Bones took shape as all manner of tools, utensils, and implements.

Because the economy centered on the buffalo, social and political organization and religious beliefs and practices also drew heavily on it. The migration of the herds governed the movements of the people and fixed the yearly cycle of life. The habits of the buffalo decisively influenced the form and function of the governing bodies of tribe and bands. Beginning with the wondrous appearance of the White Buffalo Woman, the buffalo inspired a rich spiritual and ceremonial life.

Even more than the hunt, war preoccupied the Hunkpapas. Alone and allied with friendly tribes such as the Northern Cheyenne and Northern Arapaho, they fought continually against enemy tribes. Where their range overlapped with that of others, they fought for control of hunting grounds. They fought in defense against the aggressions of others. They fought for plunder, chiefly the horses that comprised the prime measure of wealth. They fought for revenge, in retaliation for injuries real and fancied. They fought for glory and the strictly prescribed war honors that determined prestige and leadership. They fought because they had always fought and knew no other way.

Chief among tribal enemies of the Hunkpapas were the Crows to the west and the Assiniboines to the north. The Crows had conducted a fighting retreat against the westward thrust of the Sioux. By 1850, as Sitting Bull became a warrior of note, the Sioux and Crow hunting grounds merged in a zone of conflict roughly along Powder River, although war parties from each side made incursions deep into the other's territory. To the north, the Assiniboine frontier lay along the Missouri River north and west of the mouth of the Yellowstone. Sioux and Assiniboine—Hohes, as the Sioux called them—also struck far into each other's homeland.

Once a formidable foe, the sedentary Missouri River tribes of Arikara, Mandan, and Hidatsa (or Gros Ventres) had been so decimated by smallpox that they could no longer stand up to the Sioux. All three occupied earth-lodge villages scattered along the Missouri from the Knife River to the Grand—Hunkpapa-Blackfeet country.

Thus war and the hunt shaped the tribe's social organization and political institutions, which were loose and ever-changing in response to variations in game movement and population, the actions of friends and enemies, and the highly developed individualism of the people.

At the core of tribal society stood the band, or *tiyospaye*. This was an extended family group in which all were relatives by blood, marriage, or simply a declaration of kinship. Kinship, in fact, forged the unity not only of the band but of the Lakota people as a whole. Kinship ensured that everyone belonged—unless expelled because of some grave offense. Kinship decreed that no one should want so long as anything remained to be shared. Kinship established an intricate system of relationships, forms of address, and modes of behavior. Young Slow, for example, addressed all his father's brothers and cousins as "Father" and enjoyed with each reciprocal obligations and privileges well understood by all. "The ultimate aim of Dakota life," an authority has observed, "was quite simple: One must obey kinship rules; one must be a good relative."[10]

No chief commanded merely by virtue of his station. He led by example, by demonstrated wisdom, and above all with the advice of a council of elders. In the deliberations of the council, every decision represented consensus, not majority vote. When consensus could not be attained, decisions were deferred or simply not made. For important issues, such a failure could produce drift, paralysis, or acute factionalism.

No family felt bound by a council's decision or a chief's instructions. Dissenters could leave at any time, to join another band or wander alone on the plains. In certain circumstances, however, everyone must obey: in wartime, during a formal camp movement, in a communal buffalo hunt involving the entire village, or during some other event affecting the common welfare. In such undertakings, the chiefs relied heavily on men's societies. From these fraternal groups came the *akicita*, or policemen, who enforced the rules and regulations laid down by the leadership.

Likewise on the tribal level, a council of men experienced in war, the hunt, civil affairs, and spiritual matters discussed broad questions of policy, while four executive officers, "shirt wearers," carried out the policies and decisions of the council with the support of the *akicita*. For people who rarely came together as a tribe, these tribal officials, especially the shirt wearers, played an important role. They heightened awareness of tribal identity, provided a sense of tribal continuity, and dealt with increasingly difficult problems of relations with neighboring tribes.

Usually the bands assembled in tribal conclave only once a year, in June. This was for the annual sun dance, the great gathering of spiritual and social regeneration, the core event in the tribe's sacred life. After the sun dance, in late summer and autumn, the bands moved about singly or in company with others in search of the buffalo. Usually family groups hunted. When the need became acute or large herds were sighted, however, they organized a communal hunt, governed by rigid rules enforced by the *akicita*. With the onset of winter, bands scattered to sheltered valleys to sit out the cold, stormy months until the spring grasses revived the horses and again encouraged mobility. In early summer, most bands united once more as a tribe at a prearranged site for the sun dance.

BY HIS TENTH YEAR, Slow had absorbed the traditions and customs of war and the hunt, but like other boys he also engaged in the strenuous games that the Sioux loved because they were fun and because they instilled a competitive spirit in prospective warriors. Slow especially liked the hoop game, in which contending teams with sticks tried to roll a hoop into their opponents' zone. He won often, on occasion receiving prizes of knives, buckskin leggings, robes, arrows, and once ten buffalo hides. Sometimes he lost, but he was always a good loser.[11]

Slow also excelled at foot racing. In time he became the fastest runner in the Hunkpapa tribe. Only his friend Crawler, who was a year older, could give him a close race, and Crawler did not beat Slow often.[12]

As a youth, Slow cemented close friendships that carried into his adult years and figured importantly in Hunkpapa affairs. Since the Hunkpapas were a small tribe, with families numbered only in the hundreds, nearly everyone knew everyone else. Among the more important of Slow's companions were Red Feather, Black Bird, Thunder Hawk, Crawler, Bear's Rib, Crow, Gall, Crow King, Circling Hawk, and Strikes-the-Kettle.

Sitting Bull and Her-Holy-Door had done their work well. Slow rode expertly and shot arrows with superior accuracy. Already he gave evidence of developing traits of character admired by the Sioux.

In his tenth year an incident occurred that demonstrated Slow's skill with bow and arrow as well as some early stirrings of character. The band was camped in Grand River Valley, the tall cottonwoods, elms, and oaks leafing in spring green and attracting numerous birds. The boys practiced their marksmanship on the birds of the woods as well as rabbits and squirrels.

Village Center, a noted arrow maker, organized a contest, offering a bow and set of arrows as a prize to the boy who shot the prettiest bird. Slow's ambition was to kill an oriole, which looked like a ball of fire flying from one treetop to the next and was one of the hardest birds to hit with bow and arrow.

At the edge of the forest, Slow and his companions came on two other boys firing at a bird high in a cottonwood tree. One, a notorious bully, explained that he had shot an especially prized arrow, which had missed and, instead of falling to the ground, lodged on a tree limb. He offered one of his best arrows to the boy who could retrieve the arrow. When Slow's turn came, he took careful aim using a special arrow with a blunt point. It hit the lost arrow and knocked it to the ground, but also shattered it. Furious, the owner castigated Slow for destroying his arrow and demanded that he pay for it. The other boys rushed to Slow's defense, insisting that the promise be kept.

Slow ended the heated quarrel by saying to the aggrieved youth, "Here, take my blunt-point arrow that caused you so much grief. Keep it and get your bird."

In the evening, as all the boys laid out their trophies for Village Center's inspection, one of the boys spoke up. He had something to tell, he said, before the prize was awarded. Displaying the broken arrow, he explained that but for Slow's manly act in yielding his own prize arrow, serious trouble might have erupted from the quarrel.

"Give the bow and arrows to Slow," all said. "He has won the day."[13]

Not only birds fell before Slow's bow. Still ten, he killed his first buffalo, thus displaying his mastery of riding and shooting. "When I was ten years old," he later boasted, "I was famous as a hunter. My specialty was buffalo calves. I gave the calves that I killed to the poor that had no horses. I was considered a good man."[14] Good men were above all generous men, and giving away the fruits of his hunts foreshadowed one of Slow's most pronounced traits—generosity.

Generosity, in fact, was one of the four cardinal virtues that all Lakota men strove to cultivate and practice. The measure of achievement in these virtues determined the tangible wealth and honors one accumulated and the reputation and influence one enjoyed in the band or tribe. Inculcated from earliest childhood, the four virtues were bravery, fortitude, generosity, and wisdom.[15]

Bravery took first rank, and the system of war honors carefully calibrated and recognized degrees of bravery. Individual valor meant more than group victory, and the warrior who most fearlessly risked his life earned the admiration of all the people and received the most cherished honors. First coup—striking an enemy with a coup stick—showed more daring than slaying one from a distance. A man who had counted first coup, or second, third, or fourth, boasted of it, had it certified by witnesses, reveled in public acclaim, and wore an eagle feather in his hair as badge of the deed. Beginning as toddlers, Slow and other boys were encouraged to seize every opportunity to demonstrate their bravery and were warmly applauded when they did.

The second virtue, fortitude, assumed two faces. First was the capacity to endure physical pain and discomfort. The tortures of the sun dance, the scalding steam of the sweat lodge, the freezing temperatures of a northern Plains winter, the wounds of enemy arrows, the bone-shattering injuries of the buffalo hunt—all had to be borne without visible sign of distress.

The second dimension of fortitude was dignity and reserve, especially in emotional situations. Decorum ruled group gatherings as well as personal relationships, with a host of conventions ensuring that humor, affection, and excitement be kept in their proper place, not embarrassingly displayed to strangers.

Generosity reflected a true appreciation of the tribe's values. People were what counted, not property. Mere possession of property conferred no prestige, indeed could be viewed as disgraceful. The prestige came from giving away the property. An elaborate system of gift-giving, among individuals, families, bands, and even tribes, afforded constant opportunity for the practice of this virtue. As one Lakota observed, "A man must take pity on orphans, the crippled and the old. If you have more than one of anything, you should give it away to help those persons."[16] This imperative applied to the prime measure of wealth, the horse, and the prime staple of diet, the buffalo, as well as to all other possessions.

The final virtue, wisdom, grew out of excellence in the other three, out of the experience of age and maturity, and out of power and insight gained through an active and fruitful spiritual life. A man who possessed wisdom displayed superior judgment in matters of war and the hunt, of human and group relationships, of band or tribal policy, and of harmonious interaction with the natural and spiritual world. Among the Lakotas, the first three virtues were fairly common, for they could be developed with hard work and long practice. The fourth, however, was rare, and the few so endowed enjoyed great influence and positions of political or spiritual leadership.

For Sitting Bull and Her-Holy-Door, planting the seeds and nurturing the growth of the four virtues consumed much of the time and effort of child rearing. Slow's older sister, Good Feather, grew up to marry Chief Makes Room of the Miniconjou Sioux and pass on the four virtues in full measure to two accomplished sons, White Bull and One Bull. Slow grew up to become one of the finest exemplars of the four virtues in all the history of the Sioux. Few surpassed him in bravery, fortitude, or generosity, and none, so long as the old ways lasted, in wisdom. He represented the ideal to which all aspired.

In common with others who acquired wisdom, Slow mastered the intricacies of the spiritual world. Religion did not exist apart from everyday secular life, but consisted in achieving harmony with all the tangible and intangible manifestations of the natural world. A complicated scheme of deities resided everywhere—in sky, sun, moon, earth, and rock, in wind and lightning, in deer and buffalo—and held power for good or evil. With reverence and in awe, the people appealed to the benevolent and propitiated the malevolent. They approached them as individual deities possessing particular powers, but also in their corporate unity as one possessed of all-encompassing power—*Wakantanka*, the Great Mystery. The purpose of spiritual practices was to acquire the personal power needed to make one's way through life successfully.[17]

Amid all the verities, all the skills, all the rituals and practices, Slow and his comrades concentrated on war as the surest avenue to renown. Success in war opened the way to all else worth cherishing in Sioux life. Boys entering adolescence honed their talents and eagerly sought an opportunity to gain admission to the warriorhood. For Slow, the chance came at age fourteen.

2 WARRIOR

THE BAND CAMPED on Powder River, the frontiers of Crow territory. The year was 1845, Slow's fourteenth. One of the warriors organized a war party to strike westward in search of Crow horses and scalps. Ten men joined the group. Much against his parents' counsel, Slow insisted on going too. Unproven lads often accompanied war parties as errand boys, learning the ways of war without actually fighting.

On the third day out, crossing a divide, the party spotted a dozen mounted Crows gathered in conference beside a creek below. Whooping and shouting, the Sioux raced down the slope in a headlong charge. Startled, the Crows spread out to receive the attack. One Crow, however, spurred his horse to escape. Slow, mounted on a sturdy gray horse his father had given him, his naked body painted yellow from head to foot and hung with colorful strands of beads, shrieked a war cry and galloped in pursuit. The powerful gray swiftly overtook the quarry. Pulling abreast, Slow smashed his adversary with a tomahawk and knocked him from his mount. Another Hunkpapa hurried in to finish off the victim and count second coup.

In fierce fighting, the Sioux killed all but four of the Crows, who fled the field. The party returned to the camp on Powder River to proclaim victory and exult over Slow's first coup, which marked his elevation to the rank of warrior.

A proud Sitting Bull performed all the prescribed rituals. He gave a feast where he extolled the boy's exploit. He placed a white eagle feather upright in his hair, the symbol of a first coup. He presented the gray and many other horses to the needy in recognition of Slow's bravery. He substituted a fine bay for the gray, painted his son black from head to foot in token of victory, and led him around the camp so all could applaud.

As the ultimate accolade, the father conferred on Slow his own name. Henceforth he would be Tatanka-Iyotanka, Sitting Bull, and the father would be Jumping Bull. The name Sitting Bull, according to fellow tribesmen, suggested an animal possessed of great endurance, his build much admired by the people, and when brought to bay planted immovably on his haunches to fight on to the death.[1]

As a final tribute, Jumping Bull presented his son with a shield. Like the shield of every Sioux warrior, Sitting Bull's shield contained power far beyond the tough buffalo hide of which it was crafted. All shields claimed sacred origins and thus endowed their users with sacred power. The design on Sitting Bull's shield had appeared to his father in a vision. A specially skilled craftsman fashioned the shield, and a holy man painted the vision onto buckskin stretched over the cured hide. Colorfully painted in scarlet, green, dark blue, and brown, it featured a bold figure that may have been a bird or, according to One Bull, a manlike being that appeared in Jumping Bull's vision. Four eagle feathers hung from the circular frame, signifying success in all four of the cardinal directions.

Through all his years as a fighter, Sitting Bull carried his treasured shield. When he sketched his first pictographic autobiography, the shield appeared in nearly every representation of an encounter with an enemy.[2]

For the Sioux, counting first coup at an early age was a spectacular demonstration of bravery, the first and most important of the four cardinal virtues. Sitting Bull had leaped into manhood amid public acclaim that promised much and expected much.

Proudly, young Sitting Bull wore the single white eagle feather upright in his hair, the mark of his bravery in the fight with the Crows. Only a year later, in 1846, he added a red feather, to signify a wound.

His band camped on the Musselshell River, north of the Yellowstone and on the borders of enemy country. Scouts reported unknown Indians spying on the Sioux from hiding places in the hills around the village. Fifteen men went to investigate. As they probed the surrounding country, about twenty Flatheads burst from ambush in a ravine and charged. A volley broke the charge and caused the Flatheads to dismount, form a line behind their horses, and direct a heavy fire at their adversaries. Sitting Bull announced that he intended to dash the "daring line"—a gallop exposed to enemy fire that was a popular means of exhibiting bravery. As the others shouted encouragement, Sitting Bull guided his horse at a full run the length of the Flathead front. Bullets and arrows cut the air and ground around him, but he was hit only once, in the foot. Finally, after both sides had lost about half their number in killed or wounded, the Flatheads pulled off to the north, and the Sioux returned to camp in victory.

For a second time, at the age of fifteen, Sitting Bull was the focus of a victory celebration. To the white feather of first coup he added the red feather of a battlefield wound.[3]

The red feather and white feather testified to Sitting Bull's entry into one of the world's most highly developed warrior societies. By the middle of the nineteenth century, no tribes of the Great Plains boasted a prouder war record than the Lakotas. Little more than a century earlier, they had been prairie dwellers along the Minnesota River, where their Dakota kin still lived. Originally dependent on dogs and their own feet for movement, they acquired horses by theft and trade and evolved into the archetype of the mounted nomads of the plains. Those who led the westward advance developed into the Lakotas, and by the time of Sitting Bull's initiation as a warrior they had established their western border at the Bighorn Mountains and put the Missouri River to their rear. In one conquest after another, they had pushed aside Kiowas, Omahas, Poncas, Otos, Pawnees, Arikaras, Mandans, Hidatsas, Assiniboines, and Crows. A century of conquests had made them a proud, arrogant, and demanding people, and continuing hostilities with the dispossessed or the threatened kept them a finely tuned war machine.[4]

In combat, although quarter was sometimes granted on impulse, no one was immune. Men, women, and children of all ages expected to be killed if seized or cornered, their scalps and other parts of the body torn off as trophies, their remains hacked and disfigured as a permanent affliction in the spirit world.

For a young warrior bent on making a name for himself, exploits of war were not enough. He had to become active in one or more of the *akicita* societies. Fraternal, secret, and governed by intricate rites, the societies strengthened kinship's sense of belonging, afforded occasions for feasting, dancing, and camaraderie, and above all provided a forum for recording and recognizing feats of war. They traced their origins, traditions, and values to war and conferred their highest rewards on men successful in war.

Paradoxically, although absorbed with matters of war, the societies rarely fought as a group. Beyond celebrating the fighting prowess of their members, their formal importance to the tribe lay in the civil realm. From the societies, usually in rotation, the tribe's leaders drew the *akicita*, who enforced the rules and regulations laid down by the leadership. They wielded peremptory powers and could impose painful and costly punishment. Transgressors could be whipped or beaten, have their property destroyed or horses killed, and even in extreme cases be killed.

For all the plains tribes, the usual offensive measure was the war expedition. Anyone who wished to organize and lead such an expedition sought volunteers to join him. Much planning and preparation, and consultation with a holy man, preceded the departure, which took place at night and without public ceremony. If the party was large enough, *akicita* functioning as marshals regulated the march and enforced the rules. Their role was especially important in closing in on the enemy, for warriors eager for distinction often broke formation and ruined a carefully planned operation. When a fight appeared imminent, the men adorned themselves and their mounts with paint, feathers, and other ornamentation, for they wanted to look their best in battle and, if killed, in the spirit world. Often a holy man performed rites aimed at enhancing the attackers' power.

Almost always, the objectives of the war expedition were horses and scalps. Sometimes the enemy's location and strength were known. More often, the expedition simply rode forth in search of targets of opportunity.

If the warriors returned victorious with horses and scalps, they sent word ahead and made a grand ceremonial entrance. The people turned out to cheer, and the victors paraded about displaying their trophies. At night, sometimes even for four nights, the people staged the "Dance Until Morning Dance." Everyone feasted, while the women marched with the scalps taken by their men mounted on poles. The warriors, their faces painted black as the sign of victory, sang war songs and recounted their deeds of bravery.

By contrast, unsuccessful war expeditions crept into the village at night, cloaking their shame in the darkness.

Victorious or not, war parties frequently suffered casualties. The wounded sought treatment from medicine men. The dead, their remains always brought back if possible, set off paroxysms of mourning in their families. Those who had lost relatives in battle shrieked their grief, cut their bodies, and impoverished themselves by giving away nearly all their possessions.[5]

As Sitting Bull grew into early manhood, he participated in many war expeditions and performed many feats of bravery that won the applause of his people. His pictographic autobiographies record a dozen or more face-to-face encounters with Crow and Assiniboine warriors during the 1850s, all ending in victory. The details may not always have been remembered accurately, but these pictographs cannot be dismissed as imaginative inventions. Warriors boasted of their deeds, but never fabricated them. War honors rested on the testimony of witnesses and were not to be trifled with.[6]

Early in his career as a warrior, Sitting Bull gained membership in both the Kit Fox and Strong Heart societies. In the Strong Hearts, generally looked on as the most prestigious, he quickly won distinction. Among some forty to fifty members, he became one of two bonnet wearers, or sash bearers, who ranked immediately below the two leaders. The sash bearers carried a picket pin and rope, and in battle they were expected to stake themselves to the ground and stand until released by a comrade or killed by the enemy. In several pictographs of his war record of the 1850s and early 1860s, Sitting Bull portrayed himself in the Strong Heart sash and distinctive headdress, a skullcap with buffalo horns and a long trail of eagle feathers.

Sitting Bull also flourished in the Midnight Strong Heart Society, an elite within an elite that he and several other leading warriors founded. Among the cofounders were two destined for Hunkpapa leadership, Gall and Crow King.[7] This group took its name from late-night feasts and ceremonies. Sitting Bull's Midnight Strong Heart regalia consisted of a buffalo hat with four feathers in the back, a weasel skin, and a be-feathered lance. "Sitting Bull had the best," commented one of his followers.[8]

As Sitting Bull strove for excellence in everything he undertook, he became a noted hunter as well as warrior. In a communal or village hunt, he stood out conspicuously. He rode naked except for a breech cloth and tied his hair behind the ears to fall on his back. Liberal splashes of red paint marked him and his horse—his legs, arms, forehead, around his eyes, the small of the back, and the horse's legs. He used no saddle and fixed a coiled lariat to his waist on the right side. Bow and arrows completed the outfit. Only a few others painted themselves like this for the hunt. Sometimes, his horse might have an eagle feather between the ears and one at the tailbone.[9]

Sitting Bull loved horses and owned many. They were "wonderful fast horses," observed Little Soldier, as noted for speed as Sitting Bull himself was on foot. Indeed, he delighted in horse racing as much as foot racing and won many wagers on both.[10]

Sitting Bull's horsemanship in battle was faultless. Without saddle or bridle, he could lunge to one side or the other, flattening himself on his mount's flank, dodging arrows, and presenting a small target by gripping the horse's mane with his hands and the trunk with his legs. From this position he could fire a trade musket or pistol, though not a bow and arrow.[11]

Sitting Bull's fastest horse, a sorrel stolen from a white man about 1858, bore the name Bloated Jaw, or Lump on the Jaw. He always rode this mount into battle, and because he wanted to get there first he never tried to hold it in. As a result, he usually did get there first, and his name became well known to all the enemy tribes.[12]

Bloated Jaw also got Sitting Bull to a buffalo herd first. Even if twenty or thirty hunters dashed on a herd, Sitting Bull usually arrived first and often killed four or five buffalo before the herd scattered. In the hunt as in battle, therefore, Sitting Bull rode in the vanguard—"and so," White Bull marveled, "wherever he was and whatever he did his name was great everywhere."[13]

His name, in fact, struck alarm and fear in the hearts of enemy warriors. Observing this effect, his comrades sometimes disconcerted an enemy by shouting *"Tatanka-Iyotanka he miye"* ("Sitting Bull, I am he!"). Soon this battle cry gave way to another, equally dismaying to the enemy: *"Tatanka-Iyotanka tahoksila"* ("We are Sitting Bull's boys!").[14]

Expert with bow and arrow, knife, tomahawk, and war club, competent with firearms, Sitting Bull favored the lance above all weapons. Endowed with muscular arms and shoulders, he wielded it with deadly force. The lance came to him as a gift from his father, presented with the shield at the time of his first coup. The sturdy ash shaft was seven or eight feet long and tipped with an eight-inch notched iron blade. Blue and white beads, his mother's contribution, encircled the entire length, and an eagle feather fluttered from the base. When not in use, it was stored in its own special wrapping.[15]

As he matured, Sitting Bull took on his adult build. With a heavy, muscular frame, a big chest, and a large head, he impressed people as short and stocky, although he stood only two inches under six feet. His dark hair, often braided on one side with otter fur and allowed to hang loose on the other, reached to his shoulders. A severe part over the center of the scalp glistened with a heavy streak of crimson paint. A low forehead surmounted piercing eyes, a flat nose, and thin lips. Although dexterous afoot and superbly agile mounted, he appeared to some as awkward and even clumsy.

As Sitting Bull matured as a warrior, he acquired the robust sexual appetites characteristic of his class. Sioux mores exalted female chastity but also encouraged youths glorying in their manhood to work every wile and stratagem to violate it. Although not rampant, premarital sex was not uncommon either. Nor was adultery and "wife stealing," which produced enough fury, mayhem, and even murder to form a disruptive thread running throughout Lakota history. [16]

Sitting Bull's sexual life is likely to have been active, although of course undocumented. White Bull observed that "members of societies stole each other's wives, by approval," and as a leading member of numerous societies, Sitting Bull may well have indulged the practice. White Bull also declared that "Sitting Bull's wife was never stolen for intercourse, and he never got next to another." Then he contradicted himself by revealing that Sitting Bull stole one of the two wives of a man named Card and lived with her. [17]

Sitting Bull's early marital history is uncertain and confused, but he himself related the story of his first marriage, in 1851, to a woman One Bull identified as Pretty Door but whose name more likely was Light Hair. [18]

Shortly after the union, in a camp at the mouth of Powder River, the couple set forth on a hunting trip. With two riding mounts, a packhorse, and a horse-drawn travois, they moved up the Powder half a day's journey and camped in a heavy growth of cottonwoods beside the river. The next day Sitting Bull discovered a herd of buffalo and killed two with arrows in the flank. He and Light Hair skinned the carcasses, cut up the meat, and loaded it on the packhorses. On the way back to camp, they stirred a herd of antelope, and the hunter killed one.

For the next few days, the couple sliced and dried the meat and prepared for the return to the village. In the hunt, Sitting Bull had lost most of his best arrows, and while Light Hair worked with the meat he made new ones. She had a cook fire burning in the center of the tipi and was boiling cracked bones to render the fat. The tipi stood beneath a big cottonwood tree, and a limb angled over the open smoke vent. While skimming fat with a buffalo-horn spoon, she saw a reflection in a spoonful of fat. It was the face of a Crow warrior peering from the tree limb into the smoke opening.

"An enemy is spying us from above," she whispered. "Do something at once before he takes a shot at us."

Quickly Sitting Bull strung an arrow into his bow and without even aiming loosed it upward through the vent. He then lunged for the entrance and scrambled out, but stumbled and fell. By the time he regained his feet, the quarry had disappeared. Bloody footprints showed that the arrow had hit its mark. "We broke camp at once and returned home," Sitting Bull concluded.

In 1856, in an encounter with Crows, Sitting Bull gained another red feather and a wound that dogged him the rest of his life. High up the Yellowstone, where it turns east in a "big bend" after dropping out of the high country, the two forces fought over some horses the Sioux had stolen. The contenders had broken off combat and pulled back when one of the Crows, wearing the red shirt of a chief, turned and advanced to renew the fight. Sitting Bull accepted the challenge. Armed with trade muskets, the two approached each other on foot, Sitting Bull resplendent in his Strong Heart bonnet and sash and carrying the shield his father had given him. Face to face, the two crouched and fired. Sitting Bull's ball hit the Crow in the belly and killed him. The Crow's ball punched through Sitting Bull's shield and, ranging downward, struck his upturned foot, ripping a furrow from toe to heel. Sitting Bull limped over to his victim, removed the scalp, and then with the fortitude expected of a Sioux warrior calmly mounted his black horse and rode away. He could not dance in the victory dance, however, and had to watch from the sidelines. The wound did not heal properly, and to the end of his days he walked with a limp. Despite his lameness, however, he could still make a respectable showing in a foot race.[19]

Sitting Bull's middle twenties coincided with a period of rising tribal consciousness among the Hunkpapas. Until the 1850s, few purely tribal institutions existed in more than rudimentary form. When the bands united in tribal gatherings, a council of elders discussed tribal policy and left its execution to the chiefs and other officers of the bands. In 1851, however, the Hunkpapas instituted the office of "shirt wearer," a post that developed in all the Lakota tribes. In tribal affairs, four shirt wearers interposed between the council and the headmen and *akicita* who carried out tribal policy and decisions. The four shirt wearers chosen by the council in 1851 were noted band chiefs: Four Horns, Running Antelope, Red Horn, and Loud-Voiced-Hawk.[20] The most respected of these was Four Horns, Sitting Bull's uncle. Thirty-seven years old, tall, slim, with a light complexion, he was a quiet man but a wise man, one whom everyone liked.[21]

A noted band chief who never attained shirt-wearer status was Black Moon, a cousin of Sitting Bull's. The same age as Four Horns, he gained distinction as a wise and influential leader and accomplished holy man. His name figures more prominently in Hunkpapa affairs than all the shirt wearers except Four Horns.

As the tribal political institutions evolved, so did the institutions of war. The *akicita* societies expanded in numbers and importance, and war chiefs attained this station under authority of the tribe as well as of the band and the society. Sitting Bull's war record clearly entitled him to such recognition. In 1857 the Midnight Strong Heart Society made him a war chief, and in the same year he became a war chief of the Hunkpapa tribe.[22]

The tribal chieftainship came to Sitting Bull on nomination of four close friends and comrades in arms: Strikes-the-Kettle, Black Bird, Brave Thunder, and Gall. Strikes-the-Kettle and Black Bird would be with Sitting Bull on his last day.

Gall would also be close to Sitting Bull for the rest of his life. Stocky, powerfully built, with intense eyes, large flat nose, and thick lips, Gall could be abrupt and scornful as well as open and merry. "You can't help but feel very friendly when you see him," commented an acquaintance. "You are not afraid to talk to him. Sitting Bull was so reserved it was not easy to approach him like it was Gall."[23] Everyone admired Gall's war record, although men of principle thought him too ready to adjust his course to the exigencies of the moment.

These advocates presented Sitting Bull's name to a convention of warriors at a tribal gathering near the mouth of Grand River, not far from his birthplace. With this group's endorsement, they then placed his name before all the people, who gave their assent. In a confirmation ceremony, Sitting Bull smoked a pipe decorated with porcupine quills and the neck feathers of a mallard duck. He received a cup containing water and sweet grass. He sucked the sweet grass, which bound him always to tell the truth. He was then presented with a cane, which signified a long life, so long that walking would finally require a cane. The tribal chieftainship attested to Sitting Bull's achievements in war and elevated him to the top councils of the Hunkpapa people.[24]

Family events also marked this year of 1857. Sitting Bull's marriage to Light Hair had ended with her death in childbirth but had yielded a son. At the age of four, however, the boy died of disease. Grieving for the lost son, the father formally adopted his nephew, One Bull, a lad of the same age.[25] One Bull was the second son of Sitting Bull's sister, Good Feather, and Chief Makes Room of the Miniconjous. Sitting Bull reared One Bull as if he were his own son. One Bull's brother, White Bull, three years his senior, remained with the Miniconjous, although he often visited the Hunkpapas and rode with his uncle and brother on the warpath.

Shaped by their uncle's influence and guidance, both One Bull and White Bull developed into skilled warriors and hunters and accomplished practitioners of the cardinal virtues. Both were men of intellect and strong character, admired specimens of Hunkpapa manhood, and virile husbands who fathered many children by many wives. In old age, thanks to Stanley Vestal, they provided an indispensable foundation of source material for recapturing Sitting Bull's early years. One Bull in particular, who lived longer and more intimately with Sitting Bull than any other man, ensured that his uncle's memory would endure as a person rather than a mere name. The brothers lived nearly to the century mark and died within a month of each other in 1947.[26]

In 1857, besides One Bull, another boy also joined Sitting Bull's family. He was an Assiniboine youth of about thirteen who had been caught up in a sudden, fierce clash between his people and a Hunkpapa raiding party. The fight occurred in Hohe country, north of the Missouri. The Sioux chased the Hohes across a shallow lake, the horses half running, half swimming. Sitting Bull, clad in his Strong Heart regalia, counted two first coups, one in the water and one at the edge, before his horse was struck down. The surviving Hohes ran into dense timber and made good their escape. Several Hohes were killed along with eight Sioux.

As Sitting Bull made his way out of the lake on foot, he found that Swift Cloud had captured a Hohe boy. He had tried to defend himself, but his arrow had slipped from the bow string. As Swift Cloud and others prepared to kill their captive, he cried and turned to Sitting Bull, threw his arms around him, and called him "older brother." Touched, Sitting Bull declared that the boy should be spared. The captors balked at such a foolish notion, but Circling Hawk came to Sitting Bull's support, and they prevailed.

Sitting Bull took the boy into his tipi as an adopted brother. He had no brother of his own, and the loss of his son may also have influenced this uncharacteristic burst of compassion for an enemy. Good natured and reticent, yet with a keen sense of humor, the Hohe was of medium build and slightly fleshy. Under Sitting Bull's tutelage, he grew up to be a brave and skilled warrior, and loyal to his savior through all the years to the last tragic day on Grand River. People called him simply Hohe, or Stays Back, because he refused to return to his people when given the chance, or Kills Plenty, because he killed plenty of enemies. Whites later knew him as Little Assiniboine. But the name that finally overshadowed all others was Jumping Bull, a tribute to Sitting Bull's father.[27]

The youth received his new name in 1859, when Jumping Bull no longer needed it. In the spring, the Hunkpapas camped on the upper Cannonball River, near the base of two wooded promontories they called Rainy Buttes, because it always seemed to rain when they were there. The people had broken camp and were moving out to the north when a crowd of some fifty yipping Crows poured over a ridge and charged toward them. The attackers cut off two boys walking in front of the procession and killed one before the eyes of the startled Sioux. Quickly the Hunkpapa warriors assembled and counterattacked in two groups.

The fight spun out across the plains in individual encounters. Swift Hawk killed a Crow with a big wart on his chin and counted first coup. Sitting Crow, Grindstone, and Knife King chased another across a creek, where his horse stumbled and threw him. When he could not find his bow and arrows, he cried like a baby as his three pursuers closed in and killed him. Sitting Crow counted first coup.

Elsewhere on the field, a retreating Crow's horse gave out and he found himself on foot surrounded by angry Sioux.

"Leave him to me!" yelled Sitting Bull's father, dismounting and advancing on the enemy. He should not have done this, people later agreed; he was in his sixties and too old to be fighting like a young warrior. But Jumping Bull shouted that he had suffered a toothache all night and wished he had died, and now was his chance.

Drawing his knife, the Crow lunged at Jumping Bull, who went for his own knife but found that the sheath had slid behind his back, out of reach. As he fumbled for his weapon, the Crow thrust his knife blade into Jumping Bull's neck at the collarbone and slashed downward, splitting his breast. As the old man sank to his knees, the Crow recovered the knife and plunged it so deeply into the top of Jumping Bull's skull that the blade snapped from the handle.

As the Crow turned and ran, furious Hunkpapas gave chase. Someone had summoned Sitting Bull, who galloped to the scene, saw what had happened to his father, and joined in the pursuit. On overtaking the quarry, Sitting Bull hit him with his lance and knocked him from his feet. Other Sioux gathered around and riddled him with musket balls and arrows. In his rage, Sitting Bull flung himself from his horse and hacked the body into pieces, then dashed on to slay other Crows. Finally, judging him too recklessly exposed, comrades brought him back.

Meantime, Feather-on-Head and several others had spotted some Crow women and a child and taken them captive. That night word spread through the village that the prisoners would be put to death in revenge for the killing of Jumping Bull.

But Sitting Bull had cooled. "If you intend to do this for my sake," he told the people, "take good care of them and let them live. My father is a man and death is his."

At summer's end, the captives were sent back to their home. At that time Sitting Bull's adopted brother took the name Jumping Bull.[28]

3 WICHASHA WAKAN

SITTING BULL, testified his nephew White Bull, was a *Wichasha Wakan*. He had seen things in dreams and visions, and what he saw came true. He could prophesy.[1]

Literally, *wichasha* meant "man," but in association with *wakan* it had connotations of wisdom, leadership, and spirituality, and specifically a man who had performed certain sacred ceremonies that lay at the heart of Lakota ritual.[2] *Wakan* meant sacred and incomprehensible power. It resided everywhere, in *Wakantanka*, the Great Mystery, and in every component of the universe, from immense to tiny. In men, as White Bull noted, *wakan* came largely in dreams and visions, from which beneficiaries drew the insight and knowledge of their calling.

In varying numbers and ability, *Wichasha Wakan*, holy men, sat in the council of every Lakota band. How many were also war chiefs is unclear. Since sacred power underlay success in war, however, the combination would have represented an ideal even if not common. As both *Wichasha Wakan* and a war chief of the entire tribe, Sitting Bull embodied the aspirations of every Hunkpapa man.[3]

Mastery of the sacred world required mastery of the natural world, for the two were the same. Lakotas not only lived close to nature; they regarded themselves as an integral part of nature. Nature profoundly affected their everyday lives, and in turn, to the best of their ability, they tried to manipulate it for their benefit. This manipulation took the form of propitiating the deities that resided in every manifestation of nature, of reverencing them, fearing them, trying to understand them, and honoring or appeasing them with elaborate group ceremonies and numberless individual rites and taboos.

Lakotas did not compartmentalize religion, and had no word for it. Rather, they cherished a rich body of beliefs and rituals that functioned in all realms of life at all times.[4]

As a *Wichasha Wakan*, Sitting Bull understood these beliefs and rituals, but equally important, he understood the natural phenomena that gave rise to them. Hardly had he left the cradleboard when learning began, the lessons alternating with instruction in riding and shooting. Every living creature, especially the buffalo and the eagle; every tree, plant, bush, and blade of grass; the streams and lakes, even the rocks and the very soil itself; the sky and all its contents of sun, moon, stars, clouds, and the winds from the four directions—the form, cycle, and habits of all were studied and observed in infinite detail. Since all were *wakan*, the particular powers of each for good or evil were absorbed, together with the ways of eliciting the good and warding off the evil.

For his genius as a *Wichasha Wakan*, Sitting Bull owed a large debt to his teachers—Jumping Bull, Her-Holy-Door, and Four Horns. But even more the genius sprang from an intense spirituality that pervaded his entire being in his adult years and that fueled a constant quest for an understanding of the universe and of the ways in which he personally could bring its infinite powers to the benefit of his people.

His people were his obsession. He did not ignore or neglect individuals, who continued to rejoice in his kindness, generosity, and compassion. But he usually employed his talents for the welfare of all the people. "Sitting Bull's work was not for individuals," observed Robert Higheagle, who lived in his camp, "but for the whole tribe and therefore he did not cure the sick nor advise individuals."[5]

That Sitting Bull regarded himself as predestined to minister to and better the condition of his people he disclosed in his first interview with a journalist, in which the interpreter doubtless translated "*Wakantanka*" as "God":

I was still in my mother's insides when I began to study all about my people. God (waving his hand to express a great protecting Genius) gave me the power to see out of the womb. I studied there, in the womb, about many things. I studied about the smallpox, that was killing my people—the great sickness that was killing the women and children. I was so interested that I turned over on my side. The God Almighty must have told me at that time (and here Sitting Bull unconsciously revealed his secret) that I would be the man to be the judge of all the other Indians—a big man, to decide for them in all their ways.

"And you have since decided for them?" the reporter asked.

"I speak. It is enough," Sitting Bull replied.[6]

Although a holy man rather than a medicine man, Sitting Bull had mastered the techniques of healing. He knew which roots and herbs relieved which maladies, and he understood the role of ceremonies and incantations in driving out the malevolent spirits that caused physical distress. He was a doctor, White Bull testified, and carried roots for doctoring, but he did not regularly practice medicine.[7]

Wichasha Wakan were dreamers—men who had experienced dreams with sacred content or who had attained visions of powerful spiritual meaning. Not all dreamers were holy men, but all holy men were dreamers. One function of holy men was to help people interpret dreams, for they imposed obligations as binding as a personal vow, and to ignore their intent was to invite personal calamity. Rituals, ceremonies, and entire cults found their origin and meaning in dreams.

For many men, though not all or even most, the sacred aspect of life began in adolescence with the vision quest. Dreams occurred spontaneously, while the more intense vision normally had to be sought. The vision equipped the youth with some great guiding power to see him through life. Usually it appeared to him objectified in a patron animal or bird. Somewhere between the ages of ten and fourteen, the boy solicited counsel and instruction from a holy man, purified himself in a sweat lodge, and went to a remote hill to fast and struggle until the vision came. Afterward, the holy man interpreted the vision and helped devise a special fetish or design to summon the power when needed.

Surviving evidence is silent on Sitting Bull's vision quest. Robert Higheagle indicates that he had one,[8] and in light of his later history, especially his pronounced spirituality, it seems unlikely that Sitting Bull omitted this central experience in the making of a leader. The vision, however, was a profoundly personal possession, commonly shared only with the *Wichasha Wakan* who helped in the preparation and interpretation. Sitting Bull's vision doubtless remained a confidential matter between him, his advisor, and the source of his power as revealed in the vision. Whatever the content and meaning, the vision must have been intense and of lasting power, for success such as Sitting Bull attained usually depended on sacred underpinnings of formidable strength.

Men who had experienced similar dreams united in dream societies. Resembling the *akicita* societies, they performed certain functions in tribal ceremonies and had their own special songs, dances, rituals, and regalia. Dream societies brought together men who had dreamed of the buffalo, elk, bear, wolf, deer, and other animals. Not surprisingly in light of his name and his skill as a hunter, Sitting Bull had dreamed of the buffalo and thus belonged to the Buffalo Society.[9]

Sitting Bull also belonged to the exclusive fraternity of the Heyoka, those who had dreamed of thunder birds. *Wakantanka* conferred no greater honor than a thunder-bird dream nor no more fearsome obligation. Failure to perform the Heyoka ceremony attracted lightning strikes that could kill. The thunder-bird dreamer had to abase himself publicly through dress and behavior, inviting ridicule by acting the fool and conducting himself in ways the opposite of normal. Heyoka might dress for cold in summer and heat in winter, walk or ride backward, cry amid humor or laugh amid sadness. A regular feature of the ceremony, against the backdrop of special dances and songs, was to thrust hands and arms in a kettle of boiling soup and retrieve choice pieces of meat. A man performed the Heyoka ceremony but once, after he had dreamed of the thunder bird, but he participated in all subsequent ceremonies of others.[10]

"Sitting Bull must have had a dream of the thunder bird," declared Robert Higheagle, "because he painted his face with lightning. Only those who dreamed of the thunder birds . . . painted their faces with lightning." Therefore, he concluded, "Sitting Bull must have performed the ceremony of the thunder bird one time."[11]

One Bull, himself a Heyoka, recalled that Sitting Bull composed a thunder-bird song, which he once used in an attempt to end a drought. Alone on a hilltop through an entire night, he sang of thunder birds riding across the sky proclaiming: "Against the wind I am coming / Peace pipe I am seeking / Rain I am bringing as I am coming."[12]

As befitted a dreamer, Sitting Bull achieved great eminence as a singer and composer. Many of his songs were designed for particular spiritual purposes, such as the ceremonies of the *akicita* and dream societies to which he belonged, and to resolve tribal crises or achieve tribal purposes. Others had purely secular intent, such as a tribute to his mother or lament for a friend who had failed to return from the warpath. Still others reflected his love of children, to whom he was unfailingly kind and generous.[13]

Many songs revealed Sitting Bull's regard for animals and birds. Even as a child, he gave evidence of singular rapport with the animal world, and in manhood it bloomed as a widely admired talent.

Birds in particular absorbed him. One song was a celebration of the bob-o-link, which he composed one day while observing one with his young nephew One Bull. "He would imitate the songs of the birds," recalled Robert Higheagle. "He was said to understand what the meadowlarks say."[14]

Two Bulls recalled an incident when Sitting Bull interrupted a feast to succor a wounded meadowlark. When chided by others, he lectured them sternly on the meadowlark's special friendship for the Sioux and the sage counsel the little birds offered those wise enough to listen. "Let us teach our boys to be kind to all the birds," he concluded, "especially to our meadowlark friends that speak to us in our language."[15]

One song suggested the origins of his passion for birds. Sleeping beneath a tree, he dreamed that a beautiful bird watched over him from the hollow tree trunk. Suddenly he heard the noise of a beast crashing through the underbrush. The bird knocked on the trunk and told him to lie very still, like a dead man. Although fearful, he heeded the bird's warning. A great bear ambled by without noticing the man. When he disappeared, Sitting Bull awoke and saw a golden-winged woodpecker hammering on the tree trunk while also eyeing him. Extending his hands to the bird, he sang: "Pretty bird you have seen me and took pity on me / Amongst the tribes to live, you wish for me / Ye bird tribes from henceforth, always my relation shall be."

And they were.[16]

People recalled occasions on which Sitting Bull spoke to buffalo and wolves. He himself composed a song about an encounter with a wolf at the age of fifteen: "Alone in the wilderness I roam / With much hardships in the wilderness I roam / A wolf said this to me."

In the woods along Grand River one day, he had come across a wolf wounded by two arrows. "Boy," cried the animal, "if you will relieve me your name shall be great." Sitting Bull pulled out the arrows, washed and dressed the wounds, and sent the animal on his way. He dedicated the song to the wolf tribe.[17]

As a *Wichasha Wakan*, Sitting Bull treasured his peace pipe. All prominent men owned a pipe, but for holy men it was the most sacred of ceremonial objects. For them, the pipe was an essential medium for communing with *Wakantanka*.

All pipes imitated the Sacred Calf Pipe. It had been presented to the Sioux by the White Buffalo Woman, the beautiful apparition who laid the groundwork for the Lakotas' moral precepts and the ceremonies expressing them. With a polished red catlinite bowl and wooden stem sheathed in bird skins and ornamented with eagle feathers, the pipe passed from generation to generation of the same family, those specially designated as guardians on behalf of the people. Each day, wrapped in buffalo calf wool and red flannel, it hung from a tripod in front of the keeper's tipi, never to be taken out except on the most significant occasions.

"The Lakota should smoke the pipe first when considering any matter of importance," commented the holy man Sword.[18] Aside from invoking *Wakantanka*, smoking any of the replicas signified peace, truth, and mutual trust, whether among nations or among men. Smoking preceded all councils and figured in all ceremonies. Smoking accompanied sacred meditation and devotion. For holy men, smoking summoned the spirit of the White Buffalo Woman and opened communication with *Wakantanka*.

The White Buffalo Woman had charged the Sioux with performing seven ceremonies vital to their well-being. One was the vision quest. Another was the rite of purification by sweat bath, *inipi*. Other ceremonies dealt with such matters as peace making, puberty celebration, and honor to recently deceased family members. But by all measures the most important of the White Buffalo Woman's benefactions—the one that became crucial to the entire Sioux way of life—was the sun dance. The sun dance played no less a part in the life of Sitting Bull than in the life of the Sioux confederacy.

The sun dance was to the tribe what the vision quest was to the individual—a great outpouring of religious devotion and supplication aimed at securing tribal power and well-being. The sun dance honored and celebrated *Wi*, the sun, the all-powerful deity that reigned over the natural world, the underworld, and the spirit world, defender of the four cardinal virtues of bravery, fortitude, generosity, and wisdom. As it brought most of the bands together in tribal conclave, moreover, the sun dance afforded an occasion for visits, feasts, frolics, and all-around good times.

The sun dance took place in the moon of chokecherries, June, and lasted for twelve days. The first four days featured various ceremonies reinforcing the ideals and customs of the Sioux. For the women, fertility and chastity found expression in rituals. For the men, rites dramatized hunting, scouting, raiding, and victory over the enemy. The men's societies took in new members and staged their own ceremonies.

The second four days were devoted to instructing and preparing the dance candidates. These were men who had announced their intention to dance one of the six forms of the sun dance. They danced in fulfillment of a vow, usually made earlier in battle or some other critical situation, to give of their bodies in exchange for divine intervention. They danced to gain spiritual aid for others or for themselves. They danced to secure spiritual help in a vision quest. And prospective *Wichasha Wakan* danced as a vital measure of self-sacrifice in the making of a holy man.

In the first of the forms of self-sacrifice, the candidate merely danced and fasted while staring at the sun until exhausted. Although the least demanding of the forms, it still required exceptional fortitude. The second form involved laceration of the arms in a prescribed number of cuts or gashes ranging from ten to two hundred, depending on the vow. The remaining four forms required insertion of skewers beneath the chest or back muscles, or both, and dancing suspended or weighted by a buffalo skull, or both, until the flesh tore through and released the supplicant.

Torture of the body in the sun dance represented the highest form of self-sacrifice and carried heavy spiritual meaning. "I must give something that I really value to show that my whole being goes with the lesser gifts," explained Chased-by-Bears. "Therefore I promise to give my body."[19]

In the final four days, following fixed ritual and ceremony, the people prepared the dance circle, raised the dance pole, and staged the dances themselves. With this culminating event, charged with the fervor and wonder of religious rapture, the tribe ended on a peak of spiritual and social renewal, energized and rededicated as the bands turned to the summer and autumn hunts or mounted war expeditions against an enemy.

By accenting all the values of Lakota culture, by exerting enormous social and religious force on every individual, by strengthening the solidarity of the tribe, and by creating a sustained atmosphere charged with intense emotion, the sun dance occupied a place of incalculable importance in the life of the Lakota.[20]

And so it was in the life of Sitting Bull, who had to dance to become a *Wichasha Wakan*. This seems to have occurred when he was twenty-five, in 1856, when the Hunkpapas gathered on the east side of the Little Missouri River. Dreamer-of-the-Sun, the old holy man who had served as sun-dance leader for years, had died, and his mantle had fallen to Black Moon. Under his tutelage, Sitting Bull "pierced the heart"— skewered beneath both chest and back muscles—and hung suspended until he tore loose. While struggling and staring into the sun, he cried out appeals for his people to have good health and plenty of food. Amid his cries a voice came to him: "*Wakantanka* gives you what you ask for / *Wakantanka* will grant your wish." Afterward, concluded One Bull,

"Sitting Bull danced often. He wanted to learn to love his god and his people."[21]

Years later White Bull commented that his uncle had been pierced and had danced many times. He had given of his flesh so generously that White Bull vividly remembered his heavily scarred arms, back, and breast.[22]

Throughout Sitting Bull's adult years, the Hunkpapas marveled at the depth of his piety. He was, Robert Higheagle observed, "a man medicine seemed to surround."[23] He communed frequently with *Wakantanka*, invariably beginning with the pipe ceremony. As White Bull recalled, he filled and lit the pipe, then held it to the front, stem upright with his right hand on the bowl, and called on *Wakantanka* to aid the tribe through all troubles, promising in return to give buffalo hides, tobacco, and even his flesh in the sun dance. He then, according to One Bull, pointed the pipe toward each of the four winds, "and when he did, he could foretell anything."[24]

Nor was Sitting Bull remiss in fulfilling his vows. Occasionally on a buffalo hunt he would shoot a buffalo, pray, and then give the entire animal to *Wakantanka*—just leave the carcass on the ground.[25]

Sitting Bull's stature as a *Wichasha Wakan*, achieved in his late twenties after his first sun-dance sacrifice, coincided with the rounding out of his adult persona. He enjoyed acclaim as a warrior, hunter, and holy man, and in addition he drew wide admiration for his character. Among the most pronounced traits were kindness, generosity, and humility.

Sitting Bull's kindness, especially to children and old people, was a legend in his own time. He demonstrated it once shortly after his band had crossed the Yellowstone River and camped on the north bank. During the night cloudbursts transformed the river into a virtually impassable torrent. The next morning a young woman let out a wail as she discovered that her favorite riding horse had been left on the opposite side, where it could be seen neighing and pawing the ground. Several young men volunteered to try to retrieve the animal, but the people argued that the swift current made such an attempt too dangerous. Sitting Bull said nothing, but walked upstream half a mile and entered the river. As the people watched from the shore, he struggled to the south side.

After crawling from the stream exhausted but safe, he approached the skittish horse. "Grandchild," he said soothingly, "I have been sent to come to your rescue. Do not run away from me. Somebody is waiting for you on the other side."

Lengthening the short halter already on the horse with rope found in the old village site, Sitting Bull rested and gained his strength for another crossing. "Grandchild," he again addressed the horse, "do your best— permit me to guide you across. If you and I reach the other side safely, I shall have the tribe make a dance in your honor."

Together they plunged into the raging stream, Sitting Bull on the horse's back. The current carried them half a mile downriver, but they reached the north bank safely. The people rushed to greet him with cheers and songs of praise in honor of a man who had demonstrated not only kindness but bravery as well. And the people fulfilled his vow with what came to be known as the Sacred Horse Dance.[26]

One Bull retained bright memories of his uncle's kindness. He counseled One Bull always to be kind, even to people who hated him, to love the tribe, and to seek peace. If quarrels broke out in the camp, Sitting Bull worked to end them. He constantly gave meat to the needy, and even to dogs. If a hungry dog looked in the tipi while Sitting Bull was eating, One Bull recollected, he cut off a piece of meat and threw it to him.[27]

When One Bull was about six years old, Sitting Bull presented him with a handsome pinto pony. One Bull named the animal *Itanchan*, Chief, and lavished affectionate care on him. When Chief reached the age of two, One Bull trained him to be ridden. The boy never used a whip or harsh words or did anything to make the pony mean, and he developed into the swiftest runner in the camp, the envy of all and the object of many rejected offers of purchase.

Then one night Chief disappeared from the herd. One Bull searched desperately for three days, without success. Sitting Bull learned what had happened. He vowed to "leave no stone unturned" to find the missing pony. The stone he had in mind was a sacred stone. After preparing a sweat lodge, Sitting Bull invited other holy men of the village to participate in an *inipi* ceremony. Inside the dark lodge, amid suffocating steam, the men sang sacred-stone songs, while Sitting Bull prayed to his own sacred stone to aid in finding the pony. When the men emerged, Sitting Bull said the stone had told him that some covetous person had led Chief to a gulch four or five miles west of the village and pushed him over the side. He lay there now, alive but fatally injured. All ran to the place and there found the animal, broken but breathing. As One Bull wept, Chief neighed and died.

No effort was made to find the culprit, for success would have required retaliation and led to even more travail than the pony's death had already caused. To save further trouble, Sitting Bull gave One Bull another pinto pony.[28]

Generosity, in Sitting Bull a natural outgrowth of kindness, also drew strong sanction from one of the four cardinal virtues. Stories of Sitting Bull's generosity were legion. Bear Soldier told of a formal communal hunt in which the hunters wiped out an entire herd. Sitting Bull had dropped four of the beasts, as shown by the distinctive markings of his arrows. He summoned the hunt leader, his old friend Red Feather, and had him proclaim that Sitting Bull had more than he needed and would give a buffalo to anyone who had failed to score a kill. A man who had been thrown from his horse claimed the gift and thanked Sitting Bull. Then Red Feather repeated Sitting Bull's offer. An old man who had broken his bow at the outset came forward and received the second animal. "The example set by Sitting Bull," Bear Soldier testified, "was followed by other good hunters by their donations to the less fortunate ones."[29]

Humility expressed itself both in dress and in deportment. Except on special occasions, Sitting Bull dressed in common clothes, with nothing to betoken his status beyond one or two eagle feathers in his hair as emblems of first coups. Seldom, his friends agreed, could he be persuaded to "tog up." Although well off in the material evidences of success, his lifestyle suggested poverty rather than affluence. His one conspicuous indulgence was a large tipi on which were painted representations of his exploits of war.

Sitting Bull's manners matched his dress, with none of the arrogance or insolence that some chiefs assumed. In relations with fellow tribesmen, he behaved like a common Hunkpapa without rank or status and affected no superior airs. He talked freely at times, but not often. When he spoke, it was slowly and quietly, with great conviction and authority. He also listened intently, never interrupting a speaker. He possessed a keen sense of humor and occasionally laughed heartily. "Sitting Bull could take a joke on himself," said Robert Higheagle. "I have been in Sitting Bull's lodge many times and listened to the people cracking jokes." But he also periodically gave way to fits of depression, when he was somber and withdrawn.[30]

As Sitting Bull added honor after honor to his war record and achieved ever greater fame as a *Wichasha Wakan*, he emerged as the Hunkpapa incarnate, epitome of the four cardinal virtues of bravery, fortitude, generosity, and wisdom. As Robert Higheagle remarked, "There was something in Sitting Bull that everybody liked. Children liked him because he was kind, the women because he was kind to the family and liked to settle family troubles. Men liked him because he was brave. Medicine men liked him because they knew he was a man they could consider a leader."[31]

The portrait of Sitting Bull that takes shape as he neared the end of his twenties is notable on two scores.

First is the apparent contrasts, amounting in effect to three distinct personalities. One was the superlative warrior and huntsman, adept at all the techniques of war and the hunt, boastful of his deeds, laden with honors and ambitious for more, celebrated and rewarded with high rank by his people. Another personality was the holy man, suffused with reverence and mysticism, communing constantly with *Wakantanka* and all the constituent deities, dreaming sacred dreams and carrying out the rites and ceremonies they mandated, entreating for the welfare of his people, offering sacrifices ranging from a buffalo carcass to his own flesh. A third personality was the good tribesman, a man of kindness, generosity, and humility, unostentatious in dress and bearing, composer and singer of songs, friend of children and old people, peacemaker, sportsman, gentle humorist. The contrasts seem to verge on contradictions.

The second notable feature of this portrait is a question: Is it executed in colors too bright and appealing to ring true? Is this Sitting Bull an inflated caricature of the reality—a warrior too triumphant, a holy man too holy, a citizen too noble? Was he the paragon without blemish that he seems?

Probably not, in the eyes of some of his contemporaries. Factions and personal rivalries kept Sioux society in turmoil all the time, and certainly Sitting Bull had his detractors for whom this portrait would have invited ridicule. Yet he had even more admirers and devoted supporters, as attested by his known record and the affection with which many recalled him in later years. To be sure, the characterization is rooted in the memory of his immediate family and in the testimony of men looking back on their glory days from the nostalgic glow of old age. They probably embellished beyond the limits of strict accuracy.

Even allowing for such considerations, Sitting Bull emerges as a towering figure in his or any other culture. Within the context of Sioux culture, the seeming incongruities of his three personas are not implausible. They represent paragons that inspired imitation. In Sitting Bull they were simply three faces of the same personality. That he achieved all three is testimony to uncommon merit.

By Sitting Bull's late twenties or early thirties, in fact, all the Hunkpapas considered him a leader, whether they liked him or not. He attained this stature coincident with the rise of the gravest threat the Lakotas had ever faced. *Wasichus*, white people, had been part of the Lakota world ever since its beginnings in Minnesota, but never a dangerous or menacing part. Now, in the 1850s, the Lakotas perceived the *Wasichus* as a distinct and growing danger, and they were right. Besides embodying the Lakota virtues, Sitting Bull now came to embody the spirit of Lakota resistance to the *Wasichu* threat.

4 WASICHUS

"WORNOUT FENCES," Sitting Bull and his comrades called the place where they went to trade with the *Wasichus*—the white men.[1] Fort Pierre had stood on the west bank of the Missouri River three miles above the mouth of Bad River since 1832, and its rotting palisade and rundown log buildings did indeed resemble wornout fences.

The fort could defend itself if necessary. A protective stockade surrounded the interior, and corner bastions mounted cannon. The treeless river bottom extended westward for a mile or more before broken by bluffs gently rising to the plains, so no Indians could approach without detection. Usually, however, clusters of tipis carpeted the valley floor, sheltering Sioux who had come to trade rather than fight.

Fort Pierre afforded the Hunkpapas and their Lakota and Yanktonai neighbors their principal window on the white world. Originally an outpost of the American Fur Company, it now operated under the rubric of Pierre Chouteau and Company, a loose partnership that had bought out the Astor empire's Western Department in 1834. From the first, the fort had served as the company's chief trading outlet for the Missouri River Lakotas. There the Indians went to exchange buffalo robes for the trade goods that had become essential parts of their material culture.[2]

For the Hunkpapas, the people they observed at Fort Pierre were the only *Wasichus* they knew until others began to appear in mounting numbers during the 1850s. Largely French Canadians and mixed bloods of French and Indian parentage, the fort's complement hardly displayed the best face of white America. Sometimes the chief company agent boasted formal education and social graces, but for the most part the traders were an illiterate, volatile, hard-drinking set of roughnecks.

From his earliest years, Sitting Bull had regularly associated with white traders. He observed them during periodic trips to Fort Pierre, when his band raised tipis in the broad river bottom surrounding the fort and bartered buffalo robes for trade goods. And he grew familiar with them during their annual visits to his village beside one of the creeks or rivers flowing east toward the Missouri. Like all his people, Sitting Bull viewed these strange men with mixed feelings.

On the one hand, however evil, traders had become a necessary evil. The Indians had grown to depend on the goods they supplied, especially firearms and ammunition and metal tools, containers, and utensils. Life without them would be much more onerous, even fatal when confronting enemies equipped with firearms. For better or worse, trade goods had become necessities, and they could be obtained only from white men, directly or through Indian intermediaries.

On the other hand, the traders were a jarring and costly presence in the Indian world. They trespassed on Indian land. They felled timber in the river bottoms for their stockades, their cooking and heating fires, and the voracious fireboxes of their steamboats. Their stock ate the prairie grasses. Especially alarming, the westward retreat of the buffalo and the periodic scarcity of game could be blamed on the whites, even though the Indians themselves slaughtered more buffalo than they needed, to supply the traders' market for robes.

Finally, for those tribesmen who stayed around the fort, whiskey debauched and disease devastated. Epidemics of cholera, smallpox, influenza, measles, and other lethal pestilence periodically scourged the tribes.

On top of these alarming intrusions into the native world, white people simply did not behave as a Hunkpapa thought people should behave. They were eternally surprising, mystifying, and disgusting, to be tolerated because of the trade but scarcely to be emulated.

Pierre Chouteau and Company operated trading posts upriver from Fort Pierre, as did opposition firms that proved more transitory. Forts Clark and Berthold served Arikaras, Mandans, and Hidatsas (Gros Ventres), who lived in earth-lodge villages, grew corn, and also hunted buffalo. Fort Union, on the north bank of the Missouri just above the mouth of the Yellowstone, catered to Assiniboines, or Hohes, linguistic relatives of the Sioux but long their enemies.

Although the Hunkpapas rarely traded at Fort Union, they frequently visited Forts Clark and Berthold, both peacefully, to trade, and, belligerently, to fight. This behavior reflected their ambivalence toward the Arikaras. Longtime enemies, the two tribes raided each other incessantly. The Rees suffered the handicaps of a small population, the result of a smallpox epidemic, and a fixed village. Yet they fought splendidly and often bested their Sioux tormenters. Periodic truces interrupted this warfare, when the Sioux came to trade robes for corn and even engage in horse racing and other competitive games with their erstwhile enemies.

Likewise with the trading posts of Clark and Berthold. Sometimes the Sioux came with hostile intent, and exchanges of gunfire or other violence erupted. At other times they came to trade, the same as at Fort Pierre.

Another people who mingled with the Lakotas in uncertain relationships were the Slotas, the Sioux name for the Métis who radiated west and south from the Red River of the North, in the British possessions. These were mixed bloods of French and Indian descent whose squealing two-wheeled carts bore trade goods of every kind to the Indians. With the Slotas the Sioux exchanged robes and skins for powder, lead, and sometimes whiskey. With the Slotas too the Sioux frequently fought.

The few whites who had reached the upper Missouri conveyed nothing of the magnitude and complexity of the world from which they came and very little of its habits of behavior and thought. Yet within Sitting Bull's lifetime the white world would overwhelm the Hunkpapa world.

In 1831, the year of Sitting Bull's birth, the United States was composed of almost 11 million whites and more than 2 million nonwhites, compared with fewer than 3,000 Hunkpapas. The boundaries of the United States embraced 1.8 million square miles, the Hunkpapa domain scarcely 50,000.

When Sitting Bull entered the Hunkpapa world, whites in threatening numbers lived no closer than 500 miles to the southeast. In 1840 the frontier of white settlement, moving steadily west since the first English colonists set foot on the Atlantic shores, extended from the head of Lake Michigan southwest across Iowa, then turned south along the edge of the open prairies west of Missouri and Arkansas.

Most whites thought it would never go farther. Beyond lay the "Great American Desert," part of the United States thanks to President Thomas Jefferson's Louisiana Purchase but fit only for wandering Indians. The government erected a line of military posts to mark this "Permanent

= THE UPPER MISSOURI IN THE 1850s =

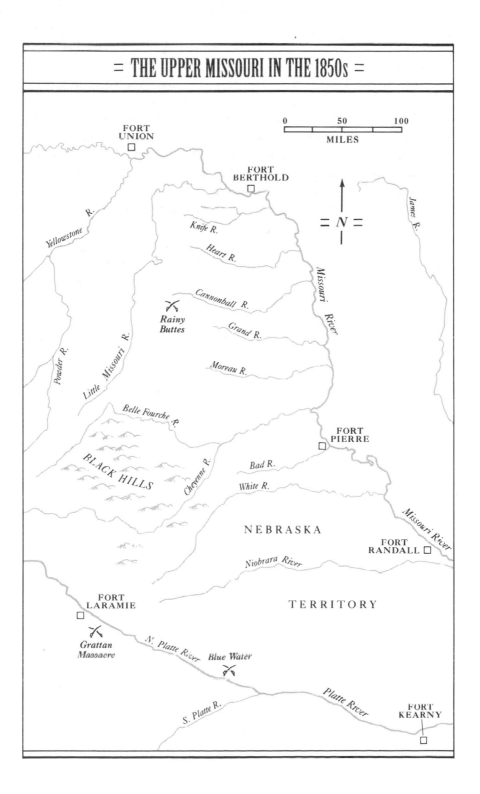

FORT
UNION

FORT
BERTHOLD

0   50   100

MILES

Yellowstone R.

Knife R.

Heart R.

= N =

James R.

Cannonball R.

*Rainy
Buttes*

Grand R.

Missouri River

Powder R.

Little Missouri R.

Moreau R.

Belle Fourche R.

FORT
PIERRE

Cheyenne R.

Bad R.

BLACK HILLS

White R.

Missouri River

NEBRASKA

FORT
RANDALL

Niobrara River

FORT
LARAMIE

TERRITORY

*Grattan
Massacre*

N. Platte River

Blue Water

Platte River

FORT
KEARNY

S. Platte R.

Indian Frontier." Reflecting a policy conceived by Jefferson but carried to ruthless extremes by President Andrew Jackson, tribes of eastern Indians that stood in the way of white settlement were coaxed or forced to migrate to new homes west of the Permanent Indian Frontier.

White attitudes toward Indians in the time of Andrew Jackson and the infant Sitting Bull centered on the idea of progress, a conception rooted in the Renaissance and the Enlightenment but given a distinctively American cast by the westward movement. Progress demanded the conquest of the wilderness, an imperative fortified by God's command to "be fruitful and multiply, and fill the earth and subdue it." Progress affected the Indians in two ways. Since they were a central feature of the wilderness, conquest of the wilderness required conquest of the Indians. And since the rise of humankind through history was seen in terms of progress from savagery to civilization, in the Indian whites saw their own distant ancestor and in themselves they saw what the Indian might one day become.

Conquest of the wilderness meant destruction of the Indians. About the means of destruction, however, there was disagreement. They could be either destroyed outright by killing or, consistent with the tenets of progress, elevated from savagery to civilization. In either event, since the generic Indian (like savagery and civilization) was a white conception, they ceased to exist.

This self-serving philosophy undergirded Andrew Jackson's "Indian Removal" as well as the policies that took shape later, after whites concluded that the Great American Desert might be made to bloom after all. Sitting Bull had not reached manhood when this happened. The Permanent Indian Frontier collapsed in the whirlwind of expansion associated with the Mexican-American War of 1846 to 1848. By Sitting Bull's twentieth birthday, 1851, the United States had flung its western boundary to the Pacific and swelled to a continental nation of 23.2 million people and 3 million square miles.

The Hunkpapa population and territory remained the same as in 1831, and the Hunkpapa people remained as ignorant of whites, and of impending catastrophe, as they had been in 1831.[3]

HARBINGERS OF THIS impending catastrophe appeared among the Lakotas in the 1850s, in the person of agents and other officials of the United States government. Before 1851, the Lakotas had scant awareness of the Indian agent. They had signed treaties with the United States in 1825, but these scraps of paper had involved no more than easily forgotten professions of friendship. A government agent came up the Missouri each year to deposit a modest heap of presents for them at Fort Pierre. He owed his position to the Chouteau company, bought the goods from the company, unloaded them from a company steamboat, and left them to be handed out by the company agent. Understandably, the recipients made little distinction between the government agent and the company agent.[4]

This situation changed abruptly after 1851. In September of that year, the government convened a grand gathering of tribes of the Great Plains at Fort Laramie, on the North Platte. The purpose of this treaty council grew out of the territorial gains of the war with Mexico and a diplomatic settlement with Great Britain that ended the Oregon boundary dispute. In long lines of covered wagons, emigrants toiled up the Platte River Road, bound for the rich farmlands of Oregon or the newly discovered goldfields of California. Indian hostilities, against whites and among themselves, threatened this westward migration. Officials believed that a treaty with the Plains tribes might lessen the danger.

The Fort Laramie treaty council attracted many of the Plains tribes, but not all. Represented were Sioux, Cheyennes, Arapahoes, Shoshones, Crows, Assiniboines, Arikaras, Mandans, and Hidatsas. How many upper Missouri Lakotas journeyed to Fort Laramie and participated in the council is uncertain. Official records made little distinction among Lakota tribes.[5]

The Fort Laramie Treaty of 1851 purported to establish peace between the United States and all the tribes, and it also bound the tribes to quit making war on one another. The government could build roads and military posts within Indian lands but promised to protect the Indians from the aggressions of white people. For each tribe, boundaries were described—the Sioux supposedly accepting a territory limited by the Heart, Missouri, White, and North Platte rivers and a line cutting north just west of the Black Hills. In return, the United States would provide $50,000 in annuities for fifty years—a paltry sum for so many Indians. In consenting to ratification, moreover, the Senate reduced the term of years to fifteen.[6]

The Fort Laramie Treaty caused much trouble and set the stage for other troublesome treaties to follow. In one serious flaw, the officials assumed that the signatory tribes understood and would abide by the stipulations of the treaty. The annual annuity issues were meant as rewards for compliance. Yet even if all Lakota chiefs had understood the promise, "touched the pen," and intended to try, they could not have ended intertribal warfare. It was too deeply embedded in the culture of every tribe.

And every chief did not sign the treaty. Of those selected, apparently on the advice of traders who had their own interests to serve, only six were Sioux—four Brules, one Two Kettle, and one Yankton. When officials set forth to gain assent to the Senate's amendment, they lined up another cast of signatories—three Yanktons, one Miniconjou, and one Sans Arc from the upper Missouri, five Brules and five Oglalas from the Platte. The Hunkpapas and Blackfeet may be pardoned for wondering when and how the Great Father thought they had promised to quit fighting the Arikaras, Assiniboines, and Crows. They did not quit, and each year they staged a stormy scene with the Indian agent come to distribute their goods and lecture them on their obligations under the treaty.[7]

The backwash from the Laramie Treaty stirred more than simple irritation at white officials. The Sioux could agree among themselves on few major issues, and when they disagreed they split into factions that quarreled heatedly and sometimes violently. Whether to take the treaty annuities, and assume the obligations that went with them, opened such schisms in all the Lakota tribes. Sitting Bull's people remained more unified in their opposition than the Miniconjous, Sans Arcs, and Two Kettles, but cracks appeared in the solidarity of even the Hunkpapas and Blackfeet.

The factionalism cut two ways, vertically and horizontally. The issue pitted band against band, although less at first among the Hunkpapas than their southern neighbors. More vehemently, it pitted youth against age. Older men dreamed of peace and did not object strenuously to taking the white man's presents. Young men had no patience with peace talk. War offered the only path to honor, status, and rank, and they saw no reason why they should not, as their fathers before them, gain recognition by accumulating Hohe scalps or stealing Crow ponies.

Sitting Bull is easy to picture among these hotheaded young men. Twenty-two in 1853, he was zealous for war honors, dedicated to excellence and success in whatever he undertook, and intent on achieving stature and influence among his people. If the old men prevailed, the traditional path to these rewards would be blocked. He had proved himself time and again in raids on the Crows and Hohes and possessed a clutch of eagle feathers and a sizable herd of stolen ponies to testify to his skill and bravery. Which of the repeated depredations around Fort Union and other trading posts he may have participated in cannot be known, but his drive and ambition leave little doubt that he rode in the forefront of many, if not most.

Nor is it likely that whites enjoyed any special exemption from his aggressions. If a hunter, herder, or packer for a trading company carelessly exposed himself, he risked his possessions and his life. The Hunkpapas and Blackfeet ruled their stretch of the upper Missouri, and any prey, Indian or white, who offered gain with little peril invited attack by young Sitting Bull and his comrades. As in the ambivalent relationship with the Rees, however, plundering or killing whites caught defenseless in the open did not preclude bartering with them in friendly fashion at trading posts bristling with rifles and cannon.

Thus matters might have simmered but for more tremors set off by events at Fort Laramie. On August 19, 1854, a green young army lieutenant, both ignorant and arrogant, marched into the Brule village of Conquering Bear and demanded the surrender of a Miniconjou visitor who had killed an oxen straying from an emigrant train. When the chief temporized, Lieutenant John L. Grattan ordered his thirty men to open fire with rifles and cannon. Conquering Bear fell, mortally wounded, but the enraged warriors swarmed over the soldiers and killed them all.[8]

The "Grattan Massacre," as the whites termed it, brought the Lakotas into armed conflict with white soldiers. In the spring of 1855, the government bought the "Wornout Fences" from the Chouteau company, and throughout the summer steamboats disgorged "walking soldiers" at the Fort Pierre landing. Other soldiers marched up the Platte to Fort Laramie, en route smashing the Brule village of Little Thunder, successor to the dead Conquering Bear, on Blue Water Creek. For the first time Sioux saw women and children cut down by American soldiers and many others taken captive. By late October this army had marched through the heart of Lakota country and established itself in winter quarters around Fort Pierre.

All the Lakotas stood in awe of the soldier chief who had whipped Little Thunder and marched defiantly through their country daring them to fight. General William S. Harney was a big, powerful man with personality and convictions to match, a veteran Indian fighter with a neat white beard. "The Big Chief of the soldiers is an awful man," one of the Lakota leaders declared, "when he speaks to us he makes us tremble." They named him "Mad Bear," for when turned loose among the Sioux, that is how he behaved.[9]

Harney planned a treaty conference. He did not invite the Lakotas, he summoned them. Among the chiefs who went were Four Horns and Makes Room, which means that Sitting Bull probably went too.

When the conference opened on March 1, 1856, Harney did not negotiate a treaty, he dictated it: (1) All Indians who had murdered whites or committed other depredations must be delivered to the commander of the nearest military post; (2) all stolen property must be turned in at a military post; (3) Indians must not "lurk" near any road used by whites or molest white travelers, and any violators must be surrendered to the army. In return, the United States would "protect the Sioux from imposition by whites," resume annuity issues, and restore the prisoners taken at the bloodletting on the Blue Water.[10]

Every Indian who listened to Harney knew that these harsh terms could not be met. What provoked the greatest alarm and the most dialogue, however, was his scheme for enforcing them. For each tribe, he would appoint a head chief and hold him responsible for compliance. If the chiefs could not compel obedience, "the General will assist them to enforce their commands. After this, it will be no excuse for a chief to say he is not able to make his band obey him."

Spokesman for the Hunkpapas at the Fort Pierre council was Bear's Rib. Of all the chiefs at the council, only he spoke up and tried to make Harney understand the impossibility of what he required. But Mad Bear had no tolerance for back talk. He made it plain that the only alternatives were strict obedience or the example of Little Thunder.

At the conclusion of the conference on March 5, Harney named a head chief for each tribe and presented each with his commission of office. For the Hunkpapas, the distinction fell to Bear's Rib. Harney also invited each head chief to nominate a series of subchiefs to help in governance. Bear's Rib named nine, of whom two were shirt wearers: Four Horns and Loud-Voiced-Hawk. Among the secondary chiefs proposed by the Miniconjou head chief Lone Horn was Makes Room, husband of Sitting Bull's sister Good Feather and father of White Bull and One Bull.

Almost certainly Sitting Bull, now twenty-six, stood by as General Harney presented Four Horns and Makes Room with their commissions of office. It would have been an instructive part of his education, fraught with lessons for future dealings with the *Wasichus*. More immediately, it would have been a mystifying, frustrating, and even infuriating experience. For a white soldier chief to be so ignorant of Indian ways yet so powerful that he could dictate a reordering of the Indian world seemed preposterous. One obvious conclusion: Avoid all dealings with white soldier chiefs.

As time passed, the Harney Treaty turned into little more than a bad memory, unenforced and unenforceable. From the government's standpoint, it had no legal force, for the Senate had failed to consent to ratification. Harney left the upper Missouri in the summer of 1856, and the soldiers themselves did not remain much longer. The army abandoned Fort Pierre, and in the spring of 1857 the garrison took new station at Fort Randall, 150 miles down the Missouri.

Other than the memory of Mad Bear, the principal legacy of the Harney Treaty was a squad of head chiefs and subchiefs bearing certifying scrolls from the general himself. In Indian practice, tribal head chiefs had never existed and, despite the ornate commissions, did not now. But government agents treated the Harney appointees as head chiefs, and gradually, because of government patronage, they acquired more prominence and even more power. Their rise, in turn, intensified the already serious factionalism in all the tribes over how to deal with the whites.

Throughout the 1850s, even during the time of Mad Bear, the young men raided their enemies. If whites got in the way, they suffered too. When the raids fell on tribes in the vicinity of such trading posts as Forts Union, Berthold, or Clark, the aggressions were likely to spill over onto the whites. Sometimes, if in a particularly bellicose mood, the Indians went directly after the whites.

A representative incident occurred at Fort Union on August 22, 1860. As the night watchman opened the gates at dawn, 250 Hunkpapa and Blackfeet warriors, resplendent in their war regalia, raced their ponies toward the entrance. After slamming the gates, the watchman gave the alarm, and the fort's complement gathered on the parapets. Fearing to antagonize their assailants further, the officers in charge withheld fire while the Indians indulged in a carnival of destruction outside. Some methodically slaughtered all the cattle grazing around the fort. Others fired haystacks, piles of firewood and building lumber, wagons, and outbuildings. They also tore up the vegetable garden. Still others set fire to two mackinaws at the landing and cast them adrift on the Missouri. After about four hours, a dozen warriors seized firebrands and advanced on the fort itself. As they brazenly worked to set the stockade ablaze, the chief trader ordered his men to open fire. One Indian fell dead at the northwest corner, and others were hit retreating. After a short conference, all vanished.[11]

Sitting Bull's part in these events reflects the ambivalence that settled over most of the Hunkpapas, torn between the old habits and the policies represented by Bear's Rib. Sitting Bull's pictographic autobiography shows no lessening of his warrior activity, and he may well have been among those who charged the gates of Fort Union. On the other hand, Four Horns drifted closer to Bear's Rib, probably because he had been appointed one of the government subchiefs by General Harney and pressed to work for peace. Sitting Bull often camped with his uncle at Fort Pierre.[12] This was a new Fort Pierre, erected by the Chouteau company less than two miles north of the ruins of the old.

Sitting Bull also, as he himself testified, worked for Pierre Garreau, a huge, utterly fearless trader at Fort Berthold, in the early 1860s. As a Garreau emissary to the Hunkpapas, Sitting Bull bought furs for the Chouteau firm. He was influential with his people, he later declared, and could make good trades. The relationship ended after two years, when Garreau failed to pay him the agreed amount, and Sitting Bull quit.[13]

ON MAY 27, 1862, Agent Samuel Latta arrived at Fort Pierre by steamboat with the annual annuities. Three thousand Brules, Hunkpapas, Blackfeet, Miniconjous, Sans Arcs, Two Kettles, and Yanktonais camped in the valley. Sitting Bull and his band were there, ready to receive their presents and live at peace with the whites as Bear's Rib urged.[14] That night the chiefs went aboard ship to partake of a feast hosted by Latta.

The next morning all assembled for the issue of annuities. Latta made the usual speech about the Fort Laramie Treaty. Then about ten or twelve chiefs replied, "in the most earnest and feeling manner." They said they were friends of the whites and wanted to live in peace but that the rest of their people, the majority, grew more and more hostile every year. General Harney had promised them protection, but no soldiers had come. Now they must break off relations with the government and rejoin their people. They could hold out no longer. Their lives and property were in danger if they accepted any more presents, and so they declined to receive Latta's annuities.

Bear's Rib rose to make his response. For eleven years he had been a friend of the whites and the government. Year after year he had relied on General Harney and the succession of Indian agents to send help, but none came. If he received the presents, he endangered his life and the lives of all other chiefs. Still, this one final time, since they were all stacked on the landing, he would accept them, but he wanted no more sent.[15]

After the issue, Latta proceeded upriver, while the Lakotas dispersed.

Bear's Rib's band headed for the Little Missouri to hunt buffalo, leaving the chief with seven or eight young men to follow in a few days. On June 5 a band of 150 Miniconjous and Sans Arcs arrived at Fort Pierre to trade. They asked where the friendly Indians were and bragged that they had come to kill the government chiefs.

Word of the boast reached Bear's Rib in his lodge, and the next morning, June 6, he called their bluff by appearing inside the stockade of Fort Pierre. Within the hour two Sans Arcs, Mouse and One-That-Limps, approached him. Mouse raised his musket and fired point blank, the ball plowing through Bear's Rib's left arm and hitting him in the chest. Instantly, as he crumpled, Bear's Rib blasted Mouse with a double-barreled shotgun. Both collapsed, dead. One-That-Limps died too, at the hands of Bear's Rib's vengeful young men.[16]

Six weeks after the slaying of Bear's Rib, some Indians delivered a written message to Pierre Garreau at Fort Berthold. Signed by ten Hunk-papa chiefs, it was addressed to the Indian agent for the upper Missouri. Amid all the verbiage, composed by someone with a literary talent rare in that time and place, several messages stood forth to represent the temper of the Hunkpapas:

> We notified the Bear's Rib yearly not to receive your goods; he had no ears, and we gave him ears by killing him. We now say to you, bring us no more goods; if any of our people receive any more from you we will give them ears as we did the Bear's Rib. . . . We have told all our agents the same thing, but they have paid no attention to what we have said. If you have no ears we will give you ears, and then your Father very likely will not send us any more goods or agent.
>
> We also say to you that we wish you to stop the whites from travelling through our country, and if you do not stop them, we will. If your whites have no ears we will give them ears.[17]

This letter expressed both old and new grievances. The issue of the Fort Laramie Treaty with its "obligations" and presents had angered the Lakotas for a decade. So to a lesser extent had white travelers, but they were so few as to constitute no more than a minor irritant. Now, however, in 1862, the trickle gave promise of swelling to a flood. Gold had been discovered in the Rocky Mountains, and the Missouri River was about to become a popular thoroughfare to the mines. Scarcely a month after the chiefs handed their letter to Garreau, moreover, their Dakota kinsmen in Minnesota rose in bloody revolt against encroaching white settlers. Together with the discovery of gold in the mountains, the aftermath of that uprising would have profound consequences for the Lakotas and for the Hunkpapa warrior and holy man Sitting Bull.

The assassination of Bear's Rib marked a watershed between two eras in the history of the Lakotas.

5 LONG KNIVES

BY 1862 THE LAKOTAS had regained their contempt for white soldiers. In the same letter that promised whites the fate of Bear's Rib if they did not get ears to hear, the Hunkpapas flung down a challenge. "The whites in this country have been threatening us with soldiers," they declared. "All we ask of you is to bring men, and not women dressed in soldiers' clothes."[1]

The Long Knives were soon to come, for in 1862–63 the upper Missouri took on new importance for the whites. Far to the west, around the headwaters of the Missouri River, prospectors discovered gold in the summer of 1862, and the news touched off a rush for the new diggings. Gold-seekers crowded the Choteau firm's steamers from St. Louis to Fort Benton, the Missouri's head of navigation. Argonauts from the upper Midwest trekked overland along a route that lay north of the Missouri River. By the autumn of 1862, between five and six hundred gold-seekers, both overlanders and river travelers, had passed through Fort Benton en route to the goldfields.[2]

Already incensed toward whites, the Lakotas reacted swiftly to the influx of travelers. In August 1862 they attacked a Chouteau steamer bound upriver filled with would-be miners. By autumn a veteran river captain declared that he had never seen the Indians so hostile toward whites.[3]

But the charge that finally propelled the Long Knives toward the upper Missouri exploded in Minnesota. In August 1862 grievances festering for years finally boiled over, and the Dakota Sioux rose against the settlers surrounding their reservation on the Minnesota River. Hundreds of whites died before Minnesota authorities scraped together an army to send against the rebels. Henry H. Sibley, a veteran Indian trader and the state's first governor, led the column up the Minnesota River Valley. On September 22 he won final victory on the battlefield of Wood Lake.

Sibley crushed the rebellion in Minnesota, but not in Dakota Territory. Dakota refugees fleeing his offensive spilled onto the Dakota prairies, mixing with Sissetons who had taken no part in the uprising, with Yanktonais, and even with Lakotas along the Missouri River. The influx of the Minnesota Indians not only added to the unrest of the resident Indians, who were still smarting over the summer's emigration to the mines, but so frightened the settlers edging up the Missouri into Dakota Territory that one-fourth of them abandoned their homesteads.[4]

And in the summer of 1863 the Long Knives once again arrived in Dakota. They were not the regulars of Harney's day but fresh young volunteers, recruited to fight for the Union on southern battlefields. Their mission was to complete the conquest of the Dakotas and to frighten the Lakotas into cooling their belligerence toward the emigrants traveling to the mines. General Sibley would lead one army northwest from Minnesota, while another under General Alfred Sully would ascend the Missouri to act in concert. The operations of Sibley and Sully marked the onset of warfare between the United States and the Lakotas, which would last nearly continuously until Sitting Bull's final surrender in 1881.[5]

For Sitting Bull and the Hunkpapas, the summer and fall of 1863 rocked with action and adventure. The backwash from Minnesota, the swelling emigration to still richer mines newly discovered in the mountains, and the invasion of their domain by nearly five thousand bluecoats stirred excitement surpassing even the uproar caused by Mad Bear Harney seven years earlier.

Hunting east of the Missouri River in July, Hunkpapas and Blackfeet became embroiled in Sibley's offensive against the Minnesota refugees. After a major battle at Big Mound on July 24, fleeing Dakotas tumbled into the Lakota camps. Covering the flight of their families, Hunkpapa and Blackfeet warriors joined with their eastern kin in the Battles of Dead Buffalo Lake on July 26 and Stony Lake on July 28. In each, Sibley's cavalry and artillery prevailed, sending the Indians in headlong retreat west to the Missouri River.

Sitting Bull most probably fought in these actions. In the midst of a brief, vicious fight at Dead Buffalo Lake, one warrior pulled ahead of the others and rode down the hill almost to the army's mule herd itself. It is tempting to speculate that this is the scene Sitting Bull reproduced in his pictographic autobiography that Stanley Vestal's informants identified as "Sitting Bull, facing a heavy fire, as shown by flying bullets, charges a mule-skinner armed with a blacksnake whip, counts *coup* on him, and makes off with a saddled mule."[6]

Dakotas and Lakotas together escaped across the Missouri River, and Sibley and his army turned back to Minnesota. For the Sioux, however, the winter meat stores lost during the retreat gave the buffalo east of the river renewed appeal. Once more they began to cross the Missouri. Most were Dakotas, but some Hunkpapas and Blackfeet went along.[7]

Whether Sitting Bull was among these Hunkpapas is not recorded. If he was, he fought in the Battle of Whitestone Hill on September 3, 1863. These Indians knew that General Sully's army had reached Fort Pierre about the same time that Sibley returned to Minnesota. Because severe drought had slowed his advance, however, they concluded that Sully did not pose much danger. He did, as they discovered to their surprise at Whitestone Hill, where the soldiers killed about 100 Indians and captured 156 while again destroying huge quantities of camp equipage, tipis, and dried buffalo meat.[8]

All those who escaped from the village at Whitestone Hill again fled to the Missouri River and crossed. The Lakotas remained in their own country, while the Dakotas returned to the east side for the winter.

The Hunkpapas moved north. It was autumn, harvest time for the Rees and thus a good occasion to seek a truce and trade robes for corn. On the Missouri below the mouth of the Little Missouri, the Hunkpapas chanced on a large camp of Rees returning from their fields to their permanent village at Fort Berthold. The two tribes warily raised their tipis about a quarter of a mile from each other and began bargaining.

With trading in progress in both villages, some of the men organized horse races. As usual, the races featured much rivalry and betting. One race was so close that the judges could not agree. The argument grew heated. A Ree struck a Hunkpapa judge, and a free-for-all broke out. As men raced for their weapons, the Rees seized as captives all the Sioux who were trading in their village, and the Hunkpapas retaliated by holding all the Rees who happened to be in their village.

Fighting flared but soon stopped as the Ree chief rode into the midst of the conflict and signaled a truce. The Rees, he said, wanted to see Sitting Bull in their camp at once. Sitting Bull went forward, mounted his horse, and allowed a Ree to lead it into their camp. Soon he returned, astride a beautiful Ree horse and clothed in a splendid war bonnet and other finery presented him by his hosts. When he reached his people, he ordered the Ree captives brought forward and released. The Ree chief reciprocated, and the crisis passed. Trading resumed. The incident disclosed how respected a leader Sitting Bull had become among his own people and how formidable was his reputation among enemy tribes.[9]

That the white soldiers would come again in 1864 seemed probable, especially since they had built a new fort on the east side of the Missouri a few miles below Fort Pierre. This outpost, Fort Sully, served notice that, for the first time since Harney's troops had garrisoned Fort Pierre, the soldiers had settled on the upper Missouri with every intention of staying. General Sully readied a new offensive for 1864.

Despite the reverses of the previous summer, the Lakotas still thought themselves invincible. Throughout the winter, they expressed their anger and defiance in bombastic threats sent through traders and Indians friendly to the whites and through sporadic raids on stock herds at Forts Pierre, Berthold, and Union. By June 1864 Lakotas, Yanktonais, and Dakotas were scattered in camps on the upper Grand and Heart and the lower Yellowstone, eager to fight the soldiers.

By the early days of July, the Sioux had no illusions about their adversary's intent. Word spread through the camps of a gruesome act that gave notice of resolve. On June 27, as the army marched up the east bank of the Missouri, an engineer officer riding in advance blundered into an ambush set up by three Dakota warriors. No sooner had he fallen than a cavalry unit galloped to the scene, cornered the killers in a buffalo wallow, and shot them down. One soldier cut off their heads with a butcher knife and carried them to the evening's camp. The next morning, as a sergeant recalled, "Gen. Sully directed me to hang the heads on poles on the highest hill near the camp as a warning to all Indians who might travel that way."[10]

Although scarcely above such a deed themselves, the Sioux felt shock and outrage at the white general's barbarism. To give him the fight he sought, they began to consolidate their villages on the Knife River. By July 19, when Sully started up the Cannonball River with nearly three thousand soldiers (and an unwelcome train of emigrants bound for the mines), as many as fourteen hundred lodges of Hunkpapas, Blackfeet, Miniconjous, Sans Arcs, Yanktonais, and Dakotas had assembled. Among several thousand warriors were Chief Four Horns and his nephew Sitting

Bull, now a mature thirty-three. Also in the camp was Sitting Bull's elder nephew White Bull, fourteen and about to fight in his first battle.[11]

As scouting parties brought word of Sully's approach, the chiefs moved the big village a day's journey north to the edge of a low range of rugged, wooded mountains that fell away on the north to the tumbled badlands of the Little Missouri River. A series of buttes and ridges, separated by steep ravines and gorges choked with brush and stunted timber, rose stairlike to the dominating mountain mass. In the natural fortress formed by these foothills, near a pleasant spring flowing with clear water, the Indians laid out their camp, fully four miles in length. This area was a favorite hunting ground, and the Lakotas called it *Tahchakuty*—"the place where they killed the deer."[12]

Like most days in the summer of 1864, July 28 dawned clear and hot. The sun blasted the rolling plains to the south, now reduced to thin dry grass, prickly pear, and dust, the few water holes little more than muddy alkali sinks. Two days earlier thirty warriors had tangled with Sully's Winnebago Indian scouts, riding far in front of his column. Now, as White Bull watered his horses at the spring, word came that the soldiers, all on horseback, were rapidly approaching across the parched plains. The village stirred with excitement as warriors painted and dressed for battle. White Bull seized his bow and arrows and joined Four Horns and Sitting Bull as they rode forth with hundreds of other men to fight the soldiers. Confident in their numbers, they did not order the lodges packed and the village moved. The women, children, and old men, in fact, gathered on a high hill to watch.[13]

About five miles out, the Indian force confronted the soldiers, who now numbered twenty-two hundred; the rest guarded the emigrants at a corral on Heart River. Already alerted by his scouts to the location of the village, Sully had judged the terrain too broken for mounted action and had dismounted to advance on a broad front of skirmishers, horseholders behind the footmen, wagons and artillery still farther to the rear. Resplendent in paint and war costume, the warriors sat their ponies in little clusters on every hill and ridge facing the blue lines and curling around the flanks. The Lakotas made up the right segment of the force, the Yanktonais and Dakotas under Inkpaduta the left. Warily each side sized up the other.

The Hunkpapa Lone Dog opened the fray. He would go close to the soldiers, he said, and if they shot at him the Indians would all open fire. Lone Dog, explained White Bull, "was with a ghost and it was hard to shoot at him—he had a charm." Lone Dog rode to a hill within rifle range of the blue skirmish line, brandished a big, elaborately ornamented war club, and shouted at the soldiers. Soon three bullets zipped around him, and he quickly rode behind the hill. Once again Lone Dog displayed himself, this time accompanied by White Bull, but by now the battle had begun.[14]

For five miles the fighting roiled northward toward the village at the foot of the Killdeer Mountains. The Indians fought in typical fashion, warriors singly and in knots galloping to and fro, stabbing suddenly toward the soldiers to loose arrows or musket balls, withdrawing quickly, sometimes gathering in large groups for a daring thrust aimed at piercing the enemy lines.

At one point a party of about one hundred, returning from a sweep in search of the soldiers, blundered into the rear of Sully's command, threatening the wagon train and horses. Artillery galloped to the scene and quickly dispersed the attackers.

Despite their unusual strength, the Sioux could not slow the steady advance of the soldiers. Bow and arrows and trade muskets proved no match for long-range rifles and cannon, which swung into action with bursting shells whenever a warrior force grew too bold. Swift and agile on their ponies, the Indians fell back with only a few casualties. No soldier was hit.

As the fighting neared the village, warriors took cover behind hills and in thickets of the ravines. Noncombatants hastened to strike camp and flee.

On the east, Inkpaduta's Yanktonais and Dakotas concentrated for a lunge at Sully's right. A battalion of Minnesota cavalry drew sabers and charged, down a slope, across a rocky ravine, and up the other side into the Indians. The warriors stood firm, resisting desperately in hand-to-hand combats and releasing arrows from the cover of brush. For a mile and a half they conducted a stubborn withdrawal, to the base of a steep butte. There the fray intensified, but the soldiers dismounted and directed a heavy carbine fire at the defenders, who finally broke and scattered. In this action, the Indians lost twenty-seven killed, the soldiers two.[15]

Meanwhile, on the Lakota side of the battlefield, the men tried vainly to hold back soldiers swinging their left flank in an arc directly at the village. Artillery wrought carnage, clearing hilltops and lobbing explosives into ravines where the Indians sought cover. Most of the Indian casualties occurred there.

In the midst of this action, a Hunkpapa came out from the village singing and leading a horse pulling a drag bearing a crippled man named Bear's Heart, or Man-Who-Never-Walked. This man, about forty years of age, said that he had been useless all his life and now wanted to die in battle. Men pointed the horse toward the soldiers and lashed him into a run. Rifle fire brought down the horse, and as the drag collapsed, bullets smashed fatally into Bear's Heart.

Mounted on a fast sorrel and armed with musket and bow and arrows, Sitting Bull had fought with his usual bravery throughout the day. Now, as the soldiers launched a final assault from the west aimed at the village itself, he saw a bullet slam into Four Horns's back.

"I am shot," his uncle yelled, clinging grimly to his mount.

Sitting Bull dashed to the rescue, seized the horse's bridle, and, as White Bull steadied the injured man, led the way into a sheltering thicket. There Sitting Bull gave Four Horns water to drink, applied medicine to the wound, and bandaged it. The bullet remained inside, Four Horns said; he could feel it and it hurt. (The chief recovered and later explained that the bullet had dropped into his stomach and never bothered him again.)

While Sitting Bull doctored his uncle, the soldiers won final victory, scattering men, women, and children into the mountains and seizing the village. The women had taken down a few of the lodges, but most remained intact. They had also thrown meat into the ravines, hoping to return and retrieve it. But the soldiers methodically destroyed everything that could benefit the Indians. Lodges, meat, robes, utensils—all went up in flames the next day.

For Indians who had taunted the Great Father to send real soldiers, not women dressed as soldiers, Killdeer Mountain was a stunning defeat. The Sioux had fought bravely, but their feeble weapons were overwhelmed by the soldiers' rifles, cannon, and six-shooters. The troops counted more than a hundred bodies left on the battlefield. How many dead and wounded were carried away is not known. The loss of the village and all its contents, moreover, was a grievous blow.

For their part, the soldiers had lost only two killed and ten wounded—the dead and all but two of the wounded in the cavalry charge on Inkpaduta. The Sioux kept close watch on their enemies, however, and on the night of July 29, as the army camped on the way back to the Heart River corral, a hundred vengeful warriors cut off a picket post and filled two soldiers with more than a dozen arrows each.

On the night of July 28, the Sioux had thwarted further pursuit by scattering through the western foothills of the Killdeer Mountains and losing themselves in the tangled terrain of the Little Missouri Badlands, where the cavalry could not catch them. Within a week, without tipis and bereft of nearly all other possessions, they had journeyed some sixty miles to the southwest, crossed the Little Missouri, and established a makeshift camp on the western edge of the Badlands nearly opposite the head of Heart River. Their scouts kept Sully under observation and reported his march west up the Heart, aiming toward the Yellowstone. Reinforced in their new campsite by more Miniconjous and Sans Arcs, Brules, and even some Cheyennes coming north from the Black Hills, they meant to give battle again. The wild tumble of the Badlands, which the army would have to cross, offered an ideal setting for the Indian style of ambuscade warfare.

Once more, however, Sully's stubborn persistence and superior fire power prevailed. For three days, August 7 to 9, 1864, hundreds of Sioux and Cheyenne warriors thronged the maze of treeless, grassless buttes, cones, turrets, pinnacles, and ridges crowding both sides of the river. Sully's pioneers hacked narrow passages through the web of steep-sided ravines and gorges while in single file his army and supply train and the emigrant wagons, enveloped in clouds of choking dust, threaded the frightful labyrinth. Alert skirmishers and well-handled artillery kept the Indians beyond the range of their muskets and bows and arrows, and they inflicted little damage. At the same time, artillery rounds added scores of casualties to those already killed or maimed at Killdeer Mountain. Occasionally, at dusk or dawn, the Indians struck suddenly at a stock herd or tried to surprise an advance party or rear guard. These sallies usually exploded in a brief, violent collision at close quarters before the Indians had to scatter.

Although at first eager, Sitting Bull quickly lost heart for this fight. The Sioux had inferior arms and needed ammunition. Having lost their food stores at Killdeer, they were also hungry. Four Horns's wound may have discouraged Sitting Bull, as did the death of a cousin in the fighting.

"Let them go and we will go home," he urged his comrades, but they would not listen.

On the last night of the fighting, August 8, a shouted dialogue between the Indians on either side took place. One of Sully's Indian scouts opened the exchange.

"We are about thirsty to death and want to know what Indians are you," he yelled.

Sitting Bull answered for the Sioux. "Hunkpapas, Sans Arcs, Yanktonais, and others. Who are you?"

"Some Indians with the soldiers," came the reply, "and one Indian badly shot through the arm." The soldiers were hungry and thirsty, he added, "so just stay around and they will be dead."

Sitting Bull shouted back asking why the Indians came with the soldiers. "You have no business with the soldiers," he declared. "The Indians here have no fight with the whites. Why is it the whites come to fight with the Indians?" Now, he said, "we have to kill you and you dry to death."[16]

Although the Lakotas had passed the winter daring the white soldiers to come and fight, Sitting Bull was not indulging in mere bombast. He voiced the truth as he saw it, and as he and his followers would consistently see it for the next decade and a half. They indeed had no quarrel with the whites—so long as the whites cleared out of Sioux country and left it to the undisturbed possession of its native owners. However inconsistent with the dynamics of the white westward movement, this was hardly an unreasonable point of view. In all its simplicity, it would dominate Sitting Bull's thinking for the rest of his life.

Whether Sitting Bull's persuasion or Sully's firepower decided the issue, by noon on August 9, as the military column began to crawl up from the Badlands to the plains beyond, the Sioux gave up the contest. With the soldiers once again drawing near their campsite, they pulled off to the southeast and lost themselves in the Badlands. That afternoon the column passed through the abandoned camp, which was three miles long and three-fourths of a mile wide. "Their fires were yet burning," observed an officer, "and many of their effects, including the undisposed-of bodies of dead warriors, were left in the camp to tell of the hasty and unexpected flight."[17]

After crossing the Little Missouri to the east, the coalition of tribes broke up and scattered. Sitting Bull, probably with Four Horns's band and possibly other Hunkpapa bands, drifted southeast, trailing a buffalo herd. At the end of August, on the low divide between the creeks heading Grand River on the east and the Little Missouri Badlands on the west, these Hunkpapas spotted another force of invading whites—an emigrant train of nearly 100 wagons and more than 150 people bound for the mines. It was in the charge of Captain James L. Fisk, an army officer who had wangled a political commission to open overland routes to the mines. The emigrants had reached the Missouri after Sully's departure, but the officer left behind to build still another fort had provided an escort of fifty soldiers. Warriors from the Hunkpapa village tracked the procession for several days, awaiting an opportunity to pounce.

It came on September 2. A steep gulch barring the descent to Deep Creek halted the train while the men cut down the banks and forced a passage. As the train threaded the defile, one of the wagons turned over. A second wagon pulled out of line, and three emigrants and nine soldiers stopped to repair the damage and right the wagon.

The train had covered scarcely a mile when about one hundred Hunkpapas led by Sitting Bull charged the little party of whites. Mounted on a fast horse, Sitting Bull reached the objective first. He bore down on a soldier astride a horse and grappled with him, attempting to throw him to the ground. The soldier drew his revolver and fired. The ball struck Sitting Bull in the left hip and came out the small of his back. Throwing himself on the opposite side of his mount to guard against another hit, Sitting Bull pulled out of the fight. White Bull and Jumping Bull (or Little Assiniboine, Sitting Bull's adopted Hohe brother), together with a third man, spurred to the rescue. Holding the wounded chief on his horse, they guided him to safety. Jumping Bull, now twenty years of age, had mastered some medical techniques. When far enough from the battlefield, the three men helped Sitting Bull to the ground, where Jumping Bull stopped the bleeding and bandaged the wound. They then took him to the village about six miles distant.[18]

Sitting Bull thus missed the rest of the fight. This time superior firearms gave the defenders no advantage, for the Sioux achieved complete surprise. In a sharp, furious clash at close quarters, the warriors cut down the whites with arrows, tomahawks, and knives. Ahead, the train corraled, and about fifty men, both emigrants and soldiers, ran back to the rescue. One, mounted, galloped in advance and charged into the midst of the Indians, cutting down six with carbine and six-shooter before turning and racing back to his own lines. He reached safety, but with three arrows in his back that would soon take his life. His comrades on foot lost still more men to arrows and knives. In all, six soldiers and two teamsters were killed, while three men were never found.

After three days of march slowed by Indian harassment, the emigrants forted up. Forming the wagons in a circle, they erected defensive ramparts of sod, which they named Fort Dilts, in honor of Jefferson Dilts, the bold scout who had charged alone into the Indians on the first day. A howitzer kept the Indians at bay.

The Hunkpapa village contained a white woman, Fanny Kelly. She had been seized on July 12 by Oglalas in a raid on a wagon train on the Platte, then carried north and, on the eve of the Killdeer fight, traded to a Hunkpapa, Brings Plenty. Now the Sioux forced her to write a message to

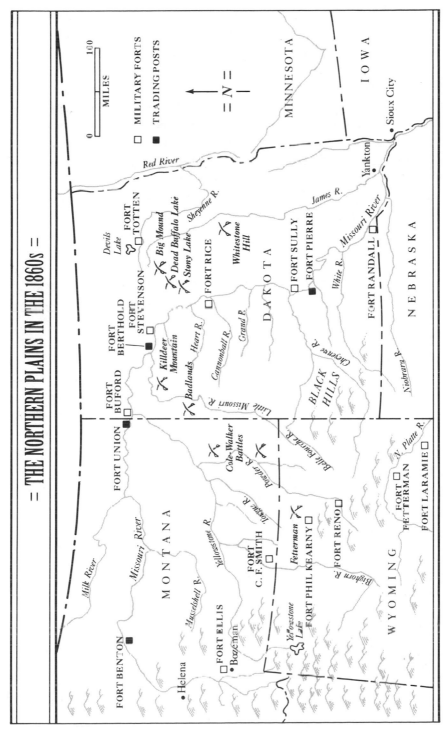

= THE NORTHERN PLAINS IN THE 1860s =

the chief of the emigrants using the point of a lead bullet. Under a white flag, Porcupine and two others carried the paper to a hillside within view of Fort Dilts and left it fastened to a stake pushed into the ground.

The paper opened negotiations. The whites could see Mrs. Kelly through binoculars and tried to buy her release. Fisk yielded some flour, sugar, coffee, and three horses as a token of good faith, but the Indians demanded four wagons loaded with food before giving up the captive. The bargaining broke down in mutual distrust.[19]

After several days, the Indians tired of the standoff and set forth to find buffalo, which the booming of the howitzer had scattered. Already couriers had slipped out of Fort Dilts under cover of night and ridden for the Missouri. On September 20 a relief expedition reached the emigrants and escorted them east to safety.

FOR THE UPPER MISSOURI LAKOTAS, General Sully had left a large and troubling legacy. Twice he had decisively defeated them in open battle and so swiftly routed them that they abandoned their villages. The soldiers had destroyed tipis, large quantities of camp equipage, and, most crippling, winter food stores.

More lasting and more alarming still, Sully had planted garrisons deep in the heart of their homeland. Supply problems forced him to give up his purpose of building a fort on the lower Yellowstone, but he left units at the trading posts of Forts Union and Berthold, and he erected a large permanent installation, Fort Rice, on the west bank of the Missouri ten miles above the mouth of the Cannonball. From Fort Sully, established only a year earlier, the military frontier had leaped more than three hundred miles up the Missouri to the mouth of the Yellowstone.

Another part of Sully's legacy was a sharpening of factionalism. Voices of moderation, muted during two years of bombast stirred by the fallout from Minnesota, the emigration to the mines, and the invasions of the white soldiers, once more asserted themselves. On October 23, hardly a month after the clash at Fort Dilts, two hundred Hunkpapas and Blackfeet parleyed with General Sully's adjutant general, Captain John H. Pell, at Fort Sully. Speaking for both tribes was the younger Bear's Rib, son of the elder Bear's Rib murdered in 1862. Although lacking the wisdom and force of his father, Bear's Rib emerged as the new spokesman for the Hunkpapa peace faction.

Contrite, Bear's Rib told the army officer how foolish the Sioux had been to make war and how sad they felt over the outcome.

"We used to laugh when they said the whites were going to try and go through our country to fight us," he conceded. Sully and Sibley, however, had demonstrated how wrong they were.

"We realize that the whites go wherever they want to, that nothing can stop them. That where they want to stay we can no more drive them away than we can a wall of solid rock."

Captain Pell spoke sternly, warning of more expeditions and more forts so long as the Sioux misbehaved. In particular, he said, before the army would even think of calling off the war, the Indians must bring in the captive white woman, Fanny Kelly. Although "much cast down," six of the chiefs promised to try.[20]

It is questionable how accurately Bear's Rib voiced the feelings of other Hunkpapa and Blackfeet chiefs, even those who sat silent during his speech at Fort Sully. The summer's setbacks had doubtless roused peace yearnings in some while producing an opposite effect in others. Judging by Sitting Bull's actions over the next four years, he did not share the sentiments of Bear's Rib, or if he did it was a matter of temporary expediency during a hungry winter.

Whatever Sitting Bull's attitude toward larger issues, he took a personal interest in the fate of Fanny Kelly. When chiefs who wished to appease the white soldiers at Fort Sully offered horses in ransom, Brings Plenty declined to bargain. Twice Sitting Bull pressed Brings Plenty to give in, but he stubbornly refused. At length, Sitting Bull and his friend Crawler confronted Brings Plenty in his tipi, with the woman present.

"My friend," said Sitting Bull, "I sent for this woman to be brought to me at my tipi and you would not give her up."

Cowed by the implicit menace, Brings Plenty said nothing. Crawler motioned to Mrs. Kelly, who quickly joined her saviors, and the three withdrew.[21]

On December 9, 1864, a delegation of Blackfeet Sioux rode into Fort Sully and delivered Mrs. Kelly, bundled in buffalo robes, to the army.

"My God, am I a free woman!" she exclaimed as the gate slammed behind her.

After four months of captivity, she was, thanks chiefly to Sitting Bull.

"She is out of our way," he observed. Although named "Real Woman," a tribute, she had different ways, he said. He could see by her face that she was homesick, "so I sent her back."[22]

THE CAMPAIGNS OF Generals Sibley and Sully in 1863 and 1864 gave Sitting Bull his first taste of battle with the Long Knives. They did not, he discovered, fight like Indians, who indulged all manner of individual escapades to demonstrate bravery and who followed a leader only so long as it suited their convenience or inclination. The whites fought in organized groups, obedient to the commands of their officers, and brought overwhelming firepower to bear. Their cannon in particular were frightening and deadly. Here was a new challenge for a war chief such as Sitting Bull, accustomed only to battling enemies who fought as he did.

The lessons were clear: acquire better firearms; avoid open battle with the Long Knives and rely instead on the hit-and-run tactics at which the Sioux excelled. Sitting Bull's record suggests that he fully grasped the first lesson, only partly the second.

With the fighting of 1863–64, furthermore, Sitting Bull's ambivalence toward white people, especially the Long Knives, began to fade. He would continue to do business—not always amicably—with white traders at Forts Pierre, Berthold, and Union, as also with the wandering Red River Métis, the Slota, from the Grandmother's country to the north. They were the source of manufactures on which the Sioux depended, most importantly powder, lead, and muskets, and finally repeating rifles and metallic ammunition. They had to be tolerated.

Not the white soldiers or other representatives of the Great Father, or the white travelers bound for the mines, or the white farmers inching up the Missouri from the south. Their effect on the game, the timber, and the grass had long been ominously plain. Sitting Bull preferred that all of these whites simply get out of Sioux country and stay out. If they would not, he would fight. No threats of military punishment, no bribes of annuities or rations, no overtures to talk, no peace blandishments could sway him from a fixed purpose to fight for his land and its resources, his people and their way of life. Chiefs like the younger Bear's Rib might temporize, vacillate, or surrender, but not Sitting Bull. For the next seventeen years, he remained distant and aloof from all whites except traders, uncompromisingly true to his principles, his culture, and his purpose of resisting the white advance.

6 LANCE

BY 1865 SITTING BULL had been a tribal war chief of the Hunkpapas for eight years. He combined a superlative war record with a hard-line attitude toward the white invasion. Except for the traders, in his view, the *Wasichus* must all get out of Lakota domain and quit traveling through it. If they would not go peaceably, they must be driven out. Since they gave no sign of leaving, Hunkpapa militants pressed the war chief to take the lead in driving them out.[1]

Sitting Bull accepted the charge, and for the next four years he led the Hunkpapa offensive against the whites. In this aggressive war he wielded his favorite attack weapon, the lance, which now came to symbolize his role as the offensive arm of the Hunkpapa tribe.

Not all the Hunkpapas agreed with the militants' program. Although no less alarmed and angered by the white presence, the moderates increasingly perceived the futility of contesting the issue. As Bear's Rib conceded, General Sully's easy victories at Killdeer and Badlands shattered the vision of invincibility that had brought the Lakota tribes together in the summer of 1864. Now, in 1865, Sully was coming again, and a growing peace bloc wanted to talk with him instead of fight with him.

The younger Bear's Rib and other stay-around-the-fort chiefs were not alone in feeling this way. Some chiefs who passed most of their time in what the whites termed the "hostile" camps did too. Most conspicuous was Lone Horn, principal chief of the Miniconjous whose status General Harney had confirmed in 1856.

Among the Hunkpapas the most prestigious of the fence-straddlers was Running Antelope, eleven years Sitting Bull's senior and one of the tribe's four shirt wearers. Brave warrior, accomplished diplomat, stirring orator, a man of high principle and independent thought, he gradually came to believe that the whites could not be expelled and that his people's survival lay in seeking the best accommodation possible with the invaders. As the uncompromising Sitting Bull watched the spirit of compromise take hold of Running Antelope, the two drifted apart. Less overtly, even Four Horns may have wavered as the bullet in his back—which he believed had now dropped into his stomach—reminded him of the quick and complete rout the tribe had suffered at Killdeer Mountain.

Driving the vigorous war sentiment of Sitting Bull and his faction was news that flashed from tribe to tribe during the winter. In November 1864 Colorado militia under Colonel John M. Chivington had brutally massacred Black Kettle's band of Southern Cheyennes. Most of this tribe had then fled north to spread outrage among Sioux and Cheyenne alike and call for a united quest for revenge. Along the Platte Road and to the very outskirts of Denver, warriors had killed travelers, plundered ranches and trains, outfought soldiers, and even sacked Julesburg. These successes, combined with a memory of Sand Creek that continued to burn hotly, stirred a nearly universal war fever among the tribes as they slowly withdrew northward into the Powder River country. Of the Lakotas, the Oglalas took the lead, following the redoubtable Man-Afraid-of-His-Horses and the rising war leader Red Cloud. Their wrath quickly leaped to the Missouri to add to the ferment among Hunkpapa extremists.

Further incensing all the tribes, the army launched fresh initiatives on a broad front. In April 1865 Appomattox freed many soldiers who could be shipped to the West before their terms of service expired. In the summer General Sully would again lead a force up the Missouri River. Based on the Platte, General Patrick Edward Connor would maneuver three columns in the Black Hills and Powder River country.

By sun-dance time in June 1865, a big village similar to the one at Killdeer a year earlier had come together on the upper Heart River, near the site of Sully's wagon corral of 1864. Present were Hunkpapas, Blackfeet, Miniconjous, Sans Arcs, and even some Cheyennes. Runners had brought invitations to come to Fort Rice to talk with General Sully, and controversy rocked all the camp circles. The war faction ruled, and groups that wanted to heed the invitation had to steal away at night to avoid "soldiering" by the *akicita* societies.

Fort Rice had replaced Fort Sully as the army's principal bulwark on the upper Missouri. Located on the west bank of the river about ten miles above the mouth of the Cannonball, it occupied a grassy flat less than a mile wide, bordered on the east by the river and on all other sides by low hills webbed by ravines that afforded excellent cover for Indians who wanted to approach unseen. A palisade with blockhouses enclosed rude structures fashioned from green cottonwood. The soldiers assigned there held Fort Rice in scarcely more affection than the Sioux.

Lakota raiding parties tormented Fort Rice throughout the spring of 1865, repeatedly hitting the stock herds or wood cutters near the post. Although devastated by a winter of scurvy, the troops held their own with verve and skill. They were "galvanized Yankees"—Confederate prisoners of war who preferred fighting Indians to rotting in a Union prison camp. Their energetic young colonel, Charles A. R. Dimon, drew to his cause the Hunkpapa and Yanktonai warriors of Bear's Rib and Two Bears, who had camped near the fort. In exchange for rations, they rushed to aid the soldiers when the post came under attack. Thus bitter factionalism pitted Hunkpapa against Hunkpapa in open combat.[2]

Despite the threat of *akicita* soldiering, by the time Sully's army reached the east bank of the Missouri opposite Fort Rice on July 13, about 250 Hunkpapa, Blackfeet, and Yanktonai tipis dotted the river bottom and low bordering hills, and more were said to be approaching. All the Indians, acutely apprehensive of both General Sully and Fort Rice, stood ready to stampede on the slightest pretext.

One occurred almost immediately. As a ferry bore the commanding general from his camp on the east bank of the river to the fort on the west bank, the proper young colonel fired his artillery in salute. The Hunkpapa and Blackfeet camps exploded in pandemonium. Officers finally persuaded the chiefs that another Sand Creek was not intended, but 130 lodges on the way in turned back in panic with lurid visions of butchery.[3]

One of those lodges belonged to Sitting Bull, General Sully revealed in the first known document penned by a white to mention him by name. "At one time the feeling was very strong to come in and surrender," Sully reported on August 8, relaying what his runners had told him of happenings in the Indian camps. But "a chief (who wishes to lead the war party) called Sitting Bull, hearing this on his return to camp, went through the different villages cutting himself with a knife and crying out that he was just from Fort Rice; that all those that had come in and given themselves up I had killed, and calling on the nation to avenge the murder."[4]

After enlisting some three hundred warriors of several tribes in a revenge expedition, Sitting Bull set out for the fort. The raiders struck early in the morning of July 28. Vividly painted and bedecked warriors bore down on the fort from north, west, and south, aiming for clusters of stock, tended by soldiers or civilians, grazing in the river bottoms.

The fight opened on the north, as Sitting Bull and six warriors spurred their mounts toward two horses belonging to the post trader. Sitting Bull, possibly on swift Bloated Jaw, rode far in front of the other six. Nearly naked and splashed with red paint, according to a watching soldier, "he wore a headdress of feathers and plumes that fell half way over his back." The handful of men seized the horses and pulled back as the garrison turned out to meet the attack.

"Indians never fought so gallantly before," conceded one of the soldiers. Time and again warrior forces charged, even closing in hand-to-hand combat, only to be driven back by steady infantry fire. Sully had sent the mercurial Colonel Dimon home on furlough and substituted Lieutenant Colonel John Pattee, a cool, experienced plainsman who handled his troops with great skill. By late morning, with howitzers lobbing explosives at concentrations of Indians, the fighting tapered off into long-range sniping. By noon the Sioux had withdrawn completely.[5]

The fighting cost the troops only one killed and four severely wounded by arrows. How many casualties the attackers suffered is unknown, but, because of the tenacity of the assault and the superiority of the army firearms, doubtless they lost many more than the defenders.

Sitting Bull's reputation was not enhanced by this fight. A delegation of Hunkpapas who visited Fort Rice two months later, including Sitting Bull's old friend Grindstone, told of the role of their war chief. He and another had indeed led the opening charge, but then they had guided the two captured animals away and taken no further part in the battle. According to the informants, this so incensed others of the war expedition that, back in camp, they whipped Sitting Bull and killed the two horses.[6]

Whatever the explanation for Sitting Bull's conduct, he had temporarily blocked the peace movement. Supposing that the Battle of Fort Rice had canceled General Sully's willingness to talk peace, the chiefs of the big Lakota village west of Fort Berthold struck their tipis and hastened still farther west, across the Little Missouri Badlands and down toward the Powder.[7]

There the Sioux chanced on more soldiers—two of General Connor's columns under Colonel Nelson Cole and Lieutenant Colonel Samuel Walker. They had joined forces north of the Black Hills and, fully two thousand strong, had struggled across the sun-blasted plains while their horses and mules gave out and their rations dwindled. Early in September, verging on collapse, the columns stirred up the Lakotas. For three days about three hundred Hunkpapa, Blackfeet, Miniconjou, and Sans Arc warriors snapped at the military columns as they moved down the Powder toward the Yellowstone, then turned back up the valley.

The Indians gained some broken-down horses and felled a few soldiers, but weather inflicted almost fatal calamity on the invaders. On the night of September 2, the prolonged drought that had dried the water holes and seared the grass yielded to a driving storm, with sleet and plunging temperatures. The next day 225 horses and mules died, and most of the supply wagons had to be abandoned.

On September 5, from both sides of the Powder Valley, the Sioux launched concerted attacks on the soldiers. Artillery and repeating Spencer carbines kept the Indians at a distance. When one company charged, however, warriors suddenly got in its midst and cut down four men before the cavalry could withdraw.

Mounted on a sorrel horse and armed with rifle and bow and arrows, Sitting Bull fought in this battle. He wore war paint and two feathers in his hair and carried the shield his father had given him. With White Bull, Jumping Bull, Black Moon, and other Hunkpapas, Sitting Bull rode with the force of warriors attacking from the east. But he was not one of the heroes of the day; that honor belonged to Bull Head, Stand-Looking-Back, and Bull Eagle, the daring men who had plunged into the midst of the charging cavalry. (Bull Head was destined to quarrel with Sitting Bull and finally, on the last day of life for both, command the police expedition that burst into the chief's cabin.)

As Cole and Walker struggled up the Powder Valley, their assailants gave up the fight. Farther up the valley, however, lay the Oglala and Cheyenne villages of Red Cloud and Little Wolf. After sending couriers to alert them to the approach of the columns, the Hunkpapas returned to their villages. Thus Cole and Walker had to fight their way through even larger gatherings of Indians before finally reaching safety. By the time their ordeal ended, they had come to the very threshold of complete disaster.[8]

As at Fort Rice, however, Sitting Bull had not contributed much to the discomfiture of Cole and Walker. His pictographic autobiography shows him running off several horses belonging to these soldiers, one of which he gave to Jumping Bull, another to a sister. But in the fighting itself, as White Bull gently put it, Sitting Bull was "sort of a coward."[9]

The reflections on his valor must have stung Sitting Bull. For a war chief to be thought wanting in bravery was a grave threat to his reputation. Any number of factors could have accounted for his behavior at Fort Rice and on the Powder, ranging from mere impulse to the edicts of *Wakantanka*.

Domestic concerns were a distraction, if nothing more, for in 1865 long-simmering discord finally made Sitting Bull's tipi a difficult place to live. Since the death of Light Hair, he had taken two wives, Snow-on-Her (or Blizzard) and Red Woman. By Snow-on-Her, the eldest, he had two daughters, by Red Woman a son, all infants or small children. Also living with Sitting Bull were his widowed mother, his sister, and her son One Bull. Under the best of circumstances, such an aggregation of family, even when split between two lodges, contained potential for dissension. But the two wives harbored an abiding jealousy for each other and bickered constantly.

Sitting Bull's widowed mother, Her-Holy-Door, also may have influenced his battlefield conduct. By 1865 Sitting Bull was thirty-four years old; he may have begun to lose his zeal for combat and war honors and to think of leaving the fighting to younger men.

"You must hang back in war time," his mother counseled him. If he got killed, the burden of caring for his children would fall on her and his two sisters. "So you must be careful how you act in war."[10]

Doubtless Sitting Bull heeded the last part of his mother's injunction, but despite the shadow of Fort Rice, his record in the next few years contains no hint of hanging back. His preeminent stature in the war faction remained intact, and his role as a leader of repeated war expeditions against the white soldiers endured unchallenged.

The government's aggressive war offensive coincided with still another rise of peace sentiment. Once again, even as the Lakotas fought Cole and Walker, runners bore them invitations to go to the Missouri and talk with government emissaries. Between October 10 and 28, at Fort Sully, the commissioners concluded a series of treaties with representatives of the Hunkpapas, Miniconjous, Sans Arcs, Blackfeet, Lower Brules, Two Kettles, Upper and Lower Yanktonais, and even Oglalas. All contained essentially the same language binding the parties to peace, including peace among tribes; but the key provision pledged annual government annuities in exchange for the Indians' promise to withdraw from all white travel routes, both existing and as established in the future.[11]

Sitting Bull and the Hunkpapa war faction had scorned to meet the peace commissioners and in the spring of 1866 renewed their war against Fort Rice. In Hunkpapa reckoning, however, Fort Rice soon yielded to another fort, even more detested, that the army began building in the summer of 1866. The token force General Sully placed at Fort Union in 1864 had seemed only a temporary irritant. Now, two miles down the Missouri and opposite the mouth of the Yellowstone, a company of regulars set to work on the permanent post of Fort Buford. Like Fort Rice, it occupied a flat river bottom with low bordering hills and was at first designed with stockade and blockhouses for defense. But Fort Buford represented a spear thrust deep into the Hunkpapa world, the most alarming military intrusion yet. From the first, the Hunkpapas hated it like no other, and for four years Sitting Bull centered his offensive on this detested emblem of the white invasion.

Sitting Bull's offensive on the upper Missouri paralleled an even more determined offensive in the Powder River country, and over the same issues. Gold-seekers had found that the Platte corridor opened better routes to the Montana mines than did the Missouri, and in 1864 John M. Bozeman pioneered a shortcut that linked the Platte with the diggings. The Bozeman Trail angled northwest from Fort Laramie, crossed the upper Powder, ran along the eastern base of the Bighorn Mountains, and ended in the western settlements of newly created Montana Territory. In the summer of 1866 the army built three posts along the Bozeman Trail: Forts Reno, Phil Kearny, and C. F. Smith.

For the Powder River Lakotas, here were the same grievances of travel routes and forts that had inflamed their brethren on the Missouri. Spearheaded by Red Cloud's Oglalas, the Lakotas fought back with a persistence and effectiveness that overshadowed Sitting Bull's similar efforts at the same time. On December 21, 1866, they decoyed Captain William J. Fetterman and eighty soldiers out of Fort Phil Kearny and slaughtered them to a man. Stunned whites called this the Fetterman Massacre, while the Indians knew it as the Hundred-Soldiers-Killed Fight. A few Hunkpapas took part, including Sitting Bull's nephew White Bull, but the main force consisted of Oglalas, Miniconjous, and Cheyennes. Leading the decoy party was a brooding, mystical young Oglala warrior named Crazy Horse.[12]

The campaign against Fort Buford began in August 1866. Logging details, herders, and travelers bound for the mines sporadically ran afoul of war parties prowling in the vicinity of the construction site. By December, as one of the bitterest winters in memory set in, Sitting Bull tightened the noose. From a village located in the Yellowstone bottom about ten miles above the river's mouth, he organized a sustained offensive.

The hardest blow fell on December 23. Sitting Bull and a war party crossed the Missouri on the ice and seized the sawmill and icehouse near the riverbank some five hundred yards from the newly completed stockade and bastions. From there they kept up a desultory fire at the fort until artillery drove them off.

The next morning, before daybreak, they occupied the same positions. Intent on setting them ablaze, four men spurred their horses toward the fort's haystacks, but drew musket fire and turned back, with one man hit. At the sawmill Sitting Bull, with a wry sense of humor, beat time on a large circular saw blade and sang lustily in accompaniment.

Soon, however, the soldiers emerged from the fort and attacked. For a time the Indians vigorously defended their positions, shouting insults and challenges while loosing a barrage of arrows. This ended when the blue cannoneers got the proper range. Two Indians were killed by exploding shells, and others caught fragments of grape or were hit by musket balls as the infantry stormed the sawmill and icehouse. Quickly the warriors took refuge in gullies and under the riverbanks. Some then set ablaze the stacks of firewood the soldiers had spent months cutting and splitting, while the rest disappeared upstream toward Fort Union.[13]

At Fort Union Sitting Bull approached the stockade waving a white flag and asking to see the chief trader, David Pease, whom the Indians called "Beans." Pease put some provisions outside the fort and engaged in a long-distance parley. Sitting Bull shouted that he intended to kill every soldier at Fort Buford and wanted Pease to give him a red shirt so that the defenders could identify him. In battle, he promised, he would throw off his robe so all could see the shirt. Pease obliged, then sent word to Fort Buford, where the soldiers were all ordered to concentrate their fire on the Indian wearing the red shirt.[14]

If Sitting Bull ever exposed his red shirt, no soldier at the fort reported it. But throughout the terrible winter of 1866–67 the Hunkpapas kept vigil, cutting off all communication with the outside world and giving rise to breathless newspaper reports that the entire garrison had been massacred. Spring and summer brought no relief, although in the summer reinforcements and improved breech-loading rifles made the place more dangerous for the Sioux. "Messages from Sitting Bull continued to be received from time to time," the post surgeon noted, "announcing that at no distant day Fort Buford was to be destroyed from the face of the earth."[15]

Sometime during 1867 Sitting Bull talked with another Fort Union trader, Charles Larpenteur. His recollection of the conversation reveals Sitting Bull's state of mind as he pressed the war against the white soldiers.

"I have killed, robbed, and injured too many white men to believe in a good peace," he asserted. "They are medicine [*wakan*], and I would eventually die a lingering death. I had rather die on the field of battle."

As for Indians who made peace with the whites and took their presents, they had better do as he did—go to the buffalo country, eat plenty of meat, and when they needed a horse go to some fort and steal one.

"Look at me," he challenged some listening Assiniboines. "See if I am poor, or my people either. The whites may get me at last, as you say, but I will have good times till then. You are fools to make yourselves slaves to a piece of fat bacon, some hard-tack, and a little sugar and coffee."

Such would be his creed until, as he foresaw, the whites got him at last.[16]

In this year of 1867, furthermore, the army provided still other targets for Sitting Bull. Troops arrived at a site downstream from Fort Berthold and began building Fort Stevenson. Like Fort Berthold, it was on the east side of the river, which made it more difficult to get at. But labor details cutting trees for lumber on the west bank came under repeated attack. Moreover, with the establishment in 1867 of Fort Totten at Devils Lake, the mail route linking it and Stevenson fell under the scrutiny of Sitting Bull's wide-ranging patrols, and careless mail parties paid with their lives.[17]

The army banned trade in arms and ammunition with the Hunkpapas, but the ban took effect only at the military posts themselves. Since the "hostiles" dared not attempt to trade there, they usually went to Fort Berthold. The custom was to camp about ten miles out, on the west side of the Missouri, and send in word that they wanted to trade. The traders then took out a stock of goods and put them on display in a tipi that had been erected for the purpose. During these sessions, the Indians took pains to remain on good behavior, with the *akicita* enforcing honesty and decorum and ensuring that the robes were well prepared. Among the regular customers in this barter, testified one of the traders, were Sitting Bull and Gall.[18]

Sometimes the Hunkpapas went to the fort itself. On one such occasion, Sitting Bull and trader Fred Gerard tested each other's strength and will. As remembered by Gerard, "The cause was a dispute about the price of some Iroquois shells. Sitting Bull got them in his possession and was going to set his own price on them, after turning over to me some buffalo hides. The result was that I took the shells from him forcibly. He pulled up his double-barrelled gun and I seized him and the gun being cocked, I slipped the caps off [the hammers] with my thumb."

A Ree, Son-of-the-Star, stepped forward and cocked his revolver. "What do you say?" he asked Gerard.

Because a large Hunkpapa camp stood nearby, Gerard signaled Son-of-the-Star not to shoot Sitting Bull.

The encounter produced sequels extending over many years. Sitting Bull sent word to Fort Berthold that he had an arrow in his quiver for Gerard. "I sent word back that I had a rifle that could speak true and if he ever came back he would hear it speak." Several years later two Hunkpapas arrived at Berthold with a gift of two horses and a pipe. Sitting Bull wanted to come in peacefully and trade with the Rees. Gerard consulted the Rees and assented.

The obligations of gift-giving now bound Gerard to reciprocate, which he failed to do. Sitting Bull never forgot. Years later, on the reservation, he happened to see a black stallion belonging to Gerard. Fittingly, it was the horse Gerard had ridden as a scout for General Custer in the Battle of the Little Bighorn. Doubtless with a sense of humor betrayed only by a twinkle in his eye, Sitting Bull simply mounted the horse and rode off, remarking as he went, "Now I have one of the horses that Gerard owes me."[19]

Gall did not fare so well in one of his trading visits to Fort Berthold. There a long-simmering enmity with a prominent Ree finally boiled over and nearly cost Gall his life.

The Ree was an able young man in his early twenties named Bloody Knife. Born of a Hunkpapa father and a Ree mother, he had been reared a Hunkpapa, but when about twelve had accompanied his mother when she decided to return to her own people. Ever since, Bloody Knife had been a Ree. Feuds dating from childhood, reinforced during a later visit to his father's tribe, kindled in Bloody Knife a deep hatred for both Gall and Sitting Bull. Beginning with General Sully, Bloody Knife pursued his vendetta by making himself useful to a succession of Long Knife chiefs.

When Gall and a few followers camped near Fort Berthold in December 1865, Bloody Knife at once alerted the officer commanding the company of troops left by General Sully at the post during that winter. Guided by Bloody Knife, a lieutenant and a detail of soldiers surrounded

Gall's lodge. As he emerged from the flap, they shot him, knocked him down, and pinned him to the ground with a bayonet. The officer pronounced him dead, but Bloody Knife intended to make sure. After placing his shotgun against Gall's head, he fired both barrels. The officer, however, kicked the muzzle aside and the charges only tore up the snow-covered ground. Gall's wife took him to an old woman renowned for treating gunshot wounds, and her expert doctoring, coupled with his iron constitution, wrought a miraculous recovery.[20]

Throughout 1867, while Sitting Bull's Hunkpapas annoyed Forts Buford and Stevenson, their neighboring kin to the west beleaguered Forts Phil Kearny and C. F. Smith. No traffic moved on the Bozeman Trail without military escort. In August, dropping their hit-and-run tactics, the Indians massed against the two forts. In the Wagon Box and Hayfield Fights, they assaulted soldiers in fixed defensive positions and suffered severe casualties from new breech-loading rifles. Even so, the Sioux and Cheyennes remained stubbornly committed to a war that could be ended only by the abandonment of the Bozeman Trail and its three guardian forts.

Sitting Bull doubtless followed the progress of Red Cloud's war with an interest born of the tribal affinity with his Lakota brethren. The Bozeman Trail did not cross Hunkpapa territory, however, and he would have perceived it as affecting his interests only in the general sense of bringing soldiers close to his homeland from another direction. In fact, Red Cloud's war, inspiring still another peace offensive, set off a chain reaction destined to have profound consequences for Sitting Bull and his people.

The new peace initiative would touch Sitting Bull for the first time but leave him as inflexible as ever on the basic issue of the white presence in his domain. Not so Red Cloud. His victory set him on a different course altogether, one of compromise, and one finally that personalized, in Red Cloud and Sitting Bull, two powerful magnetic poles of leadership.

7 HEAD CHIEF

AS THE OFFICIALS of the Indian Office well knew, the Jesuit missionary Pierre-Jean De Smet enjoyed unrivaled credibility with many of the tribes of the American West. Where no other white man dared venture, the beloved Black Robe found welcome. Secure in the righteousness of his faith, trusting to God's protection, he went fearlessly among even the most remote groups, speaking kindly and gently, urging universal peace, and calling on them to embrace the Christian God. Few could resist his charm and grace, and few found grounds for dispute in the principles he espoused.

The Sioux, regardless of faction, proved as receptive as other tribes. They too professed to want universal peace. After all, it was an ideal proclaimed by the White Buffalo Woman herself—although within the Lakota confederation and with the admonition to war ruthlessly on all enemies. Peace could be had readily, therefore, if the whites and the enemy tribes simply cleared out of lands claimed by the Sioux.

Nor did the priest's theology trouble the Sioux, so long as it did not undermine the elaborate body of belief and ritual that centered on *Wakantanka*. A crucifix might provide as much protection as a sacred bundle, the holy waters of baptism match the *wakan* powers of a sacred stone.

As had occurred often in the past, in 1867 the Indian Office enlisted Father De Smet in the latest peace movement. This shift in policy sprang from the bitter and costly Indian wars of 1864–65 and from the moral indignation of easterners over the butchery at Sand Creek. It sprang also from a fresh surge of the westward movement that dramatized the continuing need, from the white viewpoint, for a solution to the "Indian problem."

The end of the Civil War released the enormous national energies generated by the war for a renewed assault on the economic potential of the western territories. Emigrants by the thousands moved west, seeking fortune or adventure in the new towns and cities, the newly opened mines, the unfenced grasslands awaiting cattle and sheep, the prairie sod inviting the plow, and all the related opportunities of a booming frontier. Up the Platte Road, crowded with stagecoaches and wagon trains, advanced the rails of the Union Pacific, aiming for a meeting with the Central Pacific building east from California. To the south, the Kansas Pacific struck up the Smoky Hill toward Denver. As never before, white people crowded into the Indian hunting grounds, aggravating the problems that had always divided the two races.

To government theorists, a better solution to the problems than war seemed attainable. If only the Indians were treated kindly and fairly, ran the argument, a just settlement responsive to the needs of both sides could be worked out. From such thinking grew the comprehensive peace effort of 1867–68. It focused on the central Plains, where the conflict of interests and peoples was most acute. But conflict troubled the upper Missouri too, and in addition the Indians there were linked by tribal kinship to those opposing the whites farther south. Thus the upper Missouri Lakotas found themselves on the margins of the peace offensive, and the particular concern of the Jesuit Black Robe from St. Louis.

Aside from making peace, the main purpose of the peace commission of 1867–68 was to clear all Indians away from the principal overland travel routes—the Platte Road and Union Pacific Railway, the Smoky Hill Trail and Kansas Pacific Railway, and the Santa Fe Trail. Two huge reservations, one north of Nebraska and the other south of Kansas, would be set aside for all the tribes of the Great Plains. In October 1867, in the Medicine Lodge treaties, the negotiators persuaded the southern Plains tribes to promise to settle on the reservation south of Kansas, in the Indian Territory.

In 1868 the peace commission turned to the northern Plains, where the central issue was not Sitting Bull's remote guerrilla war against Forts Buford and Stevenson but Red Cloud's headline-grabbing war against Forts Phil Kearny and C. F. Smith. With the government now ready to give up the Bozeman Trail in exchange for peace, the Oglala and Miniconjou chiefs gathered at Fort Laramie to touch the pen. Red Cloud had won his war.

It remained, however, to persuade the upper Missouri Lakotas to sign the Fort Laramie Treaty. Leaders of the peace faction presented no problem, but leaders of the war faction had to be coaxed into council before there could even be talk of signing. To carry out this mission, the commissioners looked to Father De Smet.

Even as the missionary prepared for the dangerous journey to the warring camps, Sitting Bull kept his eye fixed on the hated forts, ignoring the vaporous talk of peace that always drifted through the Lakota villages. Well aware that commissioners wanted to meet with him and his fellow chiefs, he answered, in May 1868, with a war expedition.

Sitting Bull led his warriors first to the favorite objective, Fort Buford. At the fort's hay field they found two civilian laborers loading a wagon with hay. The military patrol sent to search for them that night discovered both bodies, "horribly mutilated, stripped of clothing, scalped, and pierced and pinned to the ground with 27 barbed arrows." The feathers identified the arrows as Hunkpapa.[1]

From Fort Buford, the war party rode down to Fort Stevenson but, finding the garrison alert, headed northeast to Fort Totten, on Devils Lake. En route the warriors cut down two mail riders, then ran off with four mules from the Totten herd. On May 24 they seized two replacement mail riders sent out from Fort Stevenson. Sitting Bull judged them to be mixed bloods, so he spared their lives. After relieving them of their clothing, arms, horses, and other equipment, he instructed them to serve notice on the army commanders that he, Black Moon, Four Horns, and Red Horn did not intend to meet with the peace commissioners but rather would keep on killing white men until all left the Indian country.[2]

Hostility toward white people, however, did not demand rudeness toward so revered a white person as Father De Smet. The chiefs had known of his plan to visit them for nearly a year. Through Running Antelope, Bear's Rib, and other chiefs along the Missouri, trader Charles Galpin had been putting out feelers all winter. His wife Matilda, Eagle Woman, offspring of a Hunkpapa–Two Kettle union, helped give Galpin high credibility with the Sioux. Without compromising their grievances or their demands, therefore, the militants could extend traditional Lakota hospitality, listen politely, and utter sentiments calculated to please the Black Robe.

Sitting Bull had been home from the raid against Forts Buford, Stevenson, and Totten for only a few days when Father De Smet's entourage

approached. The Hunkpapa village lay on the south side of the Yellowstone River a few miles above the mouth of the Powder. It consisted of
about six hundred lodges of several bands, including those of Black
Moon, Four Horns, and Red Horn. Among the war chiefs were Sitting
Bull, Gall, and No Neck.

De Smet had organized his expedition at Fort Rice, where the local
Sioux, fearful for his scalp, had looked on the journey incredulously. The
party consisted of about eighty Lakota and Yanktonai tribesmen, including such prominent chiefs as Running Antelope, Two Bears, and Bear's
Rib. Charles and Matilda Galpin went along as interpreters.[3]

On June 19, 1868, amid great excitement, the Black Robe entered the
Hunkpapa village. Four Horns had dispatched scores of colorfully painted
and clothed warriors to meet the procession in the valley of the Powder. As
the cavalcade advanced on the village, the entire population turned out to
shout greetings and participate in the welcome. De Smet's "standard of
peace," displaying an image of the Virgin Mary surrounded by gilt stars,
floated in the vanguard as the parade drew up at Sitting Bull's lodge in the
center of the village.

Rigid security measures betrayed the apprehension of the tribal leadership for the guests' safety. During the march from Powder River, twenty
akicita had surrounded the Black Robe and his party. At the village, as
throngs of people pressed in from all sides, Black Moon ordered the *akicita*
to disperse the crowd, and Sitting Bull had the priest's baggage carried
into his own tipi. *Akicita* escorted De Smet and the Galpins into the
lodge, brought food and water, and stood guard outside while they rested.
Others tended the horses. At sundown Sitting Bull, Black Moon, Four
Horns, and No Neck entered the tipi. De Smet awoke from a nap to find
Sitting Bull crouched beside him.

Galpin translated as Sitting Bull spoke, and De Smet later set it down
in Jesuitical language scarcely faithful to the Hunkpapa idiom. Even so,
the meaning remains clear:

> Black-robe, I hardly sustain myself beneath the weight of white
> men's blood that I have shed. The whites provoked the war; their
> injustices, their indignities to our families, the cruel, unheard of
> and wholly unprovoked massacre at Fort Lyon [Sand Creek, in
> Colorado] . . . shook all the veins which bind and support me. I
> rose, tomahawk in hand, and I have done all the hurt to the whites
> that I could. To-day thou art amongst us, and in thy presence my
> arms stretch to the ground as if dead. I will listen to thy good

words, and as bad as I have been to the whites, just so good am I
ready to become toward them.[4]

And doubtless he was, with the usual caveats about complete white
withdrawal from Lakota country.

The council took place the next day, June 20. Ten tipis had been
joined to form a single huge council lodge. De Smet's banner had been
hoisted in the center, near buffalo robes spread on the ground as seats. At
noon *akicita* ushered the priest and the Galpins to the robes and seated
them facing Black Moon and Four Horns, the principal spiritual and
political leaders of the village. Behind them, the lodge partly uncovered
to expose the interior, five hundred tribesmen had arranged themselves
according to the several bands composing the village. In their front,
behind Black Moon and Four Horns, sat the war chiefs—Sitting Bull,
White Gut, No Neck, and Gall. Pressing the warriors from the rear, with
order imposed by *akicita*, the old men, women, and children formed a
dense mass of absorbed spectators.

Four Horns opened the council by lighting his pipe. After extending it
to the sky, the earth, and the four directions, he handed it to Father De
Smet. From him, with each taking several puffs, it descended from chief
to chief in order of rank. Black Moon then invited Father De Smet to
speak.

As the priest stood, complete silence prevailed. He had come only as
an advisor, De Smet said, to urge the Sioux to meet with the Great
Father's commissioners at Fort Rice and "end this cruel and unfortunate
bloodshed." What he asked—"beseeched"—was a Christian forgiveness
and forbearance alien to the concept of vengeance so deeply embedded in
the Lakota way—"to bury all your bitterness toward the whites, forget
the past, and accept the hand of peace which is extended to you."
Gesturing toward his flag, he declared that he would leave this "holy
emblem of peace" in the possession of the chiefs, "a token of my sincerity
and good wisdom for the welfare of the Sioux Nation."

After passing the pipe once again, Black Moon responded. Conceding
the Black Robe's words to be "good and full of truth and meaning," he
nevertheless chronicled the "many sores in our bosoms to be healed."
There were the forts, the travel routes, the slaughtered buffalo and other
game, the ravaged stands of timber, and all over the land red spots on the
ground that were not from slain buffalo but from humans, red and white,
killed by one another. "We have been cruelly treated and often treach-

erously deceived." He hoped these were all things of the past, and "we will try and forget them from this day."

Repeating the pipe ritual, Sitting Bull, as tribal war chief, spoke on behalf of the warriors. His speech was clearly inferior to Black Moon's. It seemed designed less to convey his true feelings than to ingratiate himself with the Black Robe. After invoking the aid of the Great Spirit, he conceded that for four years he had led his warriors in "bad deeds," but only because "they pushed me forward." Now he welcomed the Black Robe and hoped he succeeded in his quest for peace. Hunkpapa emissaries would return with De Smet to meet with the white commissioners. Whatever they agreed in council, Sitting Bull concluded, "I will accept and remain hereafter a friend of the whites."

After shaking hands with Father De Smet and both Charles and Matilda Galpin—the latter a mark of high respect for Eagle Woman—Sitting Bull returned to his seat. No sooner had he sat down, however, than he sprang up and said he had forgotten a few things. He then poured out an afterthought that all but wiped out his formal speech. He wanted all to know that he did not propose to sell any part of his country; that the whites must quit cutting his timber along the Missouri River; and that the forts of the white soldiers must be abandoned, "as there was no greater source of grievance to his people."

Whereupon, as De Smet noted, "with cheers from all, he resumed his seat."[5]

Once again De Smet and the Galpins slept in Sitting Bull's lodge, with all the chiefs present and *akicita* outside. At daybreak on June 21 the caravan began the return journey to Fort Rice. Sitting Bull and a contingent of *akicita* rode escort as far as Powder River, where he delivered a brief address recalling the pledges made the day before, then shook hands and turned back.

That neither Four Horns nor Black Moon, still less the war leader Sitting Bull, intended to go to Fort Rice reveals that they regarded the prospects for peace on acceptable terms as not likely. To accommodate the respected Black Robe, however, they sent a delegation of lesser chiefs headed by Gall.

Patiently waiting at Fort Rice were the three commissioners designated to carry the Fort Laramie Treaty to the upper Missouri Lakotas. On July 2 Hunkpapas, Blackfeet, and Yanktonais assembled for the council and heard the treaty read. The agenda called for each chief to make a speech, then sign the treaty already negotiated with the Lakotas at Fort

Laramie. The proceedings dramatized the fantasy world in which Indian treaties were concocted.

Gall (identified as Man-that-Goes-in-the-Middle) spoke first. His speech contained no hint of an understanding that the commissioners expected him simply to sign a document that had already been worked out, no hint even that he fathomed the nature of a treaty. "The whites ruin our country," he declared. "If we make peace, the military posts on this river must be removed and the steamboats stopped from coming up here."[6]

Having set his own conditions for a treaty, Gall sat patiently while twenty other chiefs made their speeches. Then, with the treaty laid on the table, he marched to the front and touched the pen. Of all the Indians who signed at Fort Rice on July 2, Gall's mark appeared first.

The treaty that Gall had so innocently signed addressed no fundamental grievances of the Hunkpapas. The government had agreed to abandon the Bozeman Trail forts, a matter of interest to the Hunkpapas but hardly vital. Altogether ignored were the detested forts on the upper Missouri, the steamboats, and whites in general. In blustering language, Gall had asserted that all must go or there could be no peace. Yet he signed a treaty of peace that said nothing about any.

Though silent on Hunkpapa complaints, the Fort Laramie Treaty spelled out provisions of breathtaking portent for all the Lakotas. Obscured by technical jargon that even white officials had trouble understanding was a sweeping blueprint for the future of the Sioux that no chief who signed could have even dimly comprehended.

The treaty created a "Great Sioux Reservation"—all of what later became the state of South Dakota lying west of the Missouri River. Except along the northern fringes, this was not even part of the traditional Hunkpapa range. There the government would establish an agency, issue clothing and rations for thirty years, build schools and educate the Indians, and teach them how to support themselves by farming.

Since Red Cloud's war had been fought over the Bozeman Trail, the treaty contained a vaguely worded article labeling as "unceded Indian territory" the Powder River country west of the Great Sioux Reservation as far as the summit of the Bighorn Mountains. By inference at least, Indians who wished to live by the chase rather than by government dole might continue to reside in this tract. That neatly postponed a dispute over going to the reservation, but white officials confidently looked to the day when the extinction of the buffalo would eliminate the issue.

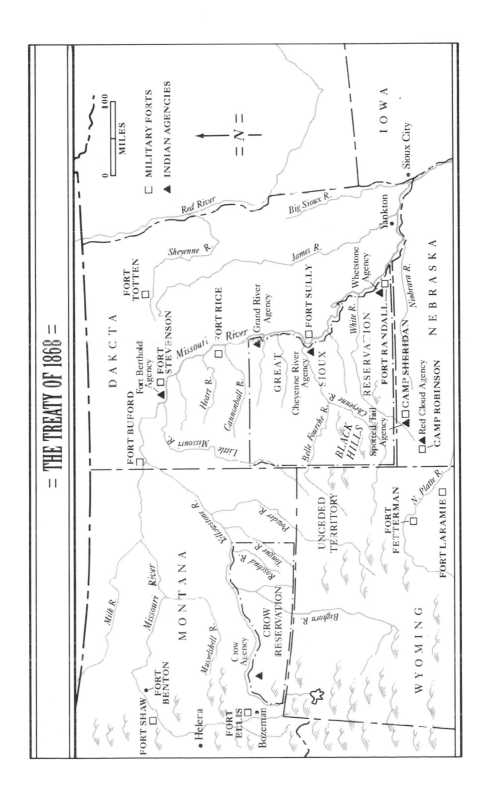

At that point another article would govern. It bound the signatories to "relinquish all right to occupy permanently the territory outside their reservation as herein defined." That, at least in the legal framework of the white people, shrank Lakota domain to the limits of the Great Sioux Reservation. On the reservation, moreover, railroads and wagon roads could be constructed only after damages had been assessed—a backhanded way of opening even the reservation to the hated travel routes.[7]

All these legalisms were bewildering enough to white officials. Gall can hardly be reproached for not perceiving that he had bound the Hunkpapas not only to end their war against the whites but ultimately to settle on and remain on a reservation, there to give up the chase, obey the dictates of a white agent, dress like white people, live like white people, and learn to farm like white people.

Sitting Bull probably had less understanding of the treaty than Gall, or even interest in its contents. That in only a few years it would be cited as proof of his broken promises and justification for war against him would have struck him as nonsense. But government officials could read the treaty and find evidence that he had promised not to make war on whites or other Indians, not to oppose a railroad up the Yellowstone River, and ultimately even to live within the confines of the Great Sioux Reservation. He of course had agreed to nothing, and the proposition that Running Antelope, Bear's Rib, or even Gall could agree to on his behalf would have struck him as still greater nonsense.

Testifying to Sitting Bull's view of the De Smet mission, less than two months after Gall signed the treaty, Sitting Bull led another devastating raid on Fort Buford. With 150 yipping warriors, he bore down on the fort's beef herd, made off with 250 head, and left three soldiers dead and three grievously wounded.[8]

AS SITTING BULL rose to ever higher levels of influence, his uncle Four Horns remained the most respected Hunkpapa leader, chief of a prestigious band and since 1851 one of the four tribal shirt wearers. Tall and light-skinned, quiet and unassuming, he spoke gently but wisely. In council he led rather than dominated. He seems to have understood the long-term implications of the white advance, but finally, after some indecision, he resolved to remain true to the old ways and not seek compromise with the government officials.

As Four Horns grew older, however, he worried that the Hunkpapa leadership was weakening. Although still in his fifties, he felt his own powers as a band chief declining with advancing years, and he observed sadly that the other three shirt wearers had brought themselves into disrepute. Running Antelope had eloped with another man's wife, Red Horn had stolen two wives from Bear Skinned, and Loud-Voiced-Hawk had stabbed another Hunkpapa. Four Horns persuaded his fellow shirt wearers that, with white encroachment growing daily more critical, some radical new measure was needed to recharge the tribe's leadership.[9]

The conditions created by the Treaty of 1868 patterned the setting in which Four Horns conceived his plan. The Sioux could surrender most of what made them Sioux, settle on the Great Sioux Reservation, and yield their independence to white officials. Or they could try to keep a foot in each world, following the herds in the unceded territory but also exploiting the agency system to whatever limits the government would tolerate. Or, like Sitting Bull, they could fiercely reject all relations with whites (except traders, of course), hold to the old ways as distant from whites as possible, and meet any further white encroachments with force.

A hard core of each tribe, possibly one-third of the total Lakota population, chose the last course. To these holdouts the Hunkpapas contributed the largest proportionate share, perhaps one-half or more of the tribe.

These nonreservation bands were the object of Four Horns's plan. He aimed to give the Hunkpapas strong leadership and bring the other tribes under Hunkpapa sway as far as possible. Unity of action had never been a Lakota strength, but Four Horns now concocted a truly sweeping scheme, one that extended well beyond the Hunkpapa tribe. He proposed not only to abdicate his own band chieftainship to his nephew, but to elevate him to nothing less than a supreme chieftainship of all the Lakota tribes, with the Yanktonais included as well. The post of supreme chief would embrace all matters of concern to the people, and specifically it would involve a separate identity as head war chief, or "chief soldier," with authority over all decisions of war and peace.[10]

No precedent for such an office existed. It ran counter to basic tenets of Sioux life. Individuals, bands, and tribes gloried in their independence and fiercely guarded their freedom to do just as they pleased, constrained only by social conventions and the obligations of kinship. They responded to authority only as it sprang from consensus or a chief highly respected for wisdom, and even then some people had to be "soldiered" into obedience by the *akicita*. With every tribe composed of virtually autonomous bands and crosscut by feuding factions, Four Horns could not have seriously believed that all the Lakota tribes, and the Yanktonais too, would agree to such a revolutionary proposition.

As the sagacious shirt wearer may have sensed, however, in Sitting Bull the man and his times intersected. The Treaty of 1868 accelerated trends that had been forming for a decade or more, creating historical forces that, to Four Horns at least, exposed a leadership hierarchy inadequate either in structure or personality. Even if alien to traditional ways, his idea made sense when viewed against the backdrop of the conditions engendered by the treaty.

Sitting Bull possessed the qualifications for such a role. Now thirty-eight and long in the highest councils of the tribe, he combined the dynamism and drive of relative youth with experience in war, the hunt, and the political and spiritual leadership of his people. His war record against enemy tribes ranked with the best. Against the whites, it surpassed all, for in the sustained war against Fort Buford he had truly acted as the Hunkpapa lance, thrusting repeatedly at the soldiers intruding into his homeland. He had been a tribal war chief since 1857 and was active in the men's societies. Of his bravery, despite several troubling episodes, there could be no doubt, nor of the other cardinal virtues either.

Sitting Bull appealed in particular to youth. His record represented everything youth aspired to. His stubborn opposition to the white man's brand of peace, moreover, gave ambitious young men a clear alternative to elders who would block the paths to glory by yielding the principal means by which men rose to honor and status in the tribe. Peace was not for young warriors, and they probably contributed more support to Four Horns's strategy, and his candidate, than any other element of the population. Later they formed Sitting Bull's strongest constituency.

Other tribes included chiefs of high stature and ability too: Lone Horn of the Miniconjous, Spotted Tail of the Brules, Red Cloud and Man-Afraid-of-His-Horses of the Oglalas. Measured by inflexible opposition to whites, however, only Red Cloud could match Sitting Bull, and he was already gravitating toward the reservation.

Another Oglala of high merit and dazzling future was Crazy Horse. Seven years younger than Sitting Bull, Crazy Horse had risen rapidly in the appraisal of his tribe. A quiet loner, eccentric in dress and unpredictable in behavior, a mystic and introvert, he yearned only to excel in war. He had gained shirt-wearer rank in the Oglala tribe in 1865, but he wore the mantle uncomfortably. He rarely attended leadership councils and then never spoke. In 1870, following an attempt to steal another man's wife that gained him a pistol bullet in the face, he had to give up the shirt of office. Thereafter he devoted himself exclusively to war. In December 1866 Crazy Horse had led the decoy party that lured Captain Fetterman out of Fort Phil Kearny to disaster, and he amassed countless war honors in fights with Crows, Shoshones, Flatheads, and other enemy tribes. He was the greatest Lakota warrior.[11]

In the stepped-up mingling of the nonreservation factions of the Lakota tribes in the Powder River country, Sitting Bull became well acquainted with Crazy Horse. The two respected each other's qualities and shared the same grim determination to hold aloof from the white world. Crazy Horse would become Sitting Bull's staunchest ally outside the Hunkpapa tribe.

Most likely on the middle Rosebud Creek, probably in 1869, Sitting Bull's supporters contrived a ceremony to anoint him as supreme chief of the Sioux confederation.[12] Present in the camp were Hunkpapas, Blackfeet, Miniconjous, Sans Arcs, Oglalas, and Cheyennes. Promoting Sitting Bull's candidacy among the Hunkpapas were Four Horns, Black Moon, Red Horn, Loud-Voiced-Hawk, and even Running Antelope, already eclipsing the younger Bear's Rib as the leading reservation chief. Makes Room and Lame Deer proclaimed Miniconjou support. Spotted Eagle and others indicated Sans Arc backing. Other tribes gave their blessing.

Four Horns presided. He conducted a formal election, eliciting the vote of all the concurring chiefs in each tribe. He then turned to Sitting Bull.

"For your bravery on the battlefields and as the greatest warrior of our bands," Four Horns intoned, "we have elected you as our war chief, leader of the entire Sioux nation. When you tell us to fight, we shall fight, when you tell us to make peace, we shall make peace."[13]

With Sitting Bull in the vanguard, a triumphal cavalcade wended its way through the village, the new supreme leader singing: "Ye tribes behold me / The chiefs are no more [that is, the four shirt wearers had stepped down] / Myself shall take courage [as their successor, that is, he pledged leadership]."[14]

The designation of Sitting Bull as supreme chief was an astute political move. A faction likely representing no more than minorities of varying size within each tribe lifted him to an office that had never existed and that was alien to Sioux thinking about political organization. It could be viewed as a tainted power play, driven by factional and family self-interest, and large segments of the nontreaty tribes did not accept it. But the deed had been done, and as the authors well knew, its success now depended on Sitting Bull's ability to convert an office of doubtful legitimacy into one that functioned in practice as its designers intended.

And that is what he did. Throughout the first half of the 1870s, with the firm backing of Black Moon, Four Horns, and Crazy Horse, Sitting Bull carried the banner around which all true Lakotas rallied. These were the "hunting bands," the "northern Indians," the "hostiles" who remained in the unceded territory year around. Some drifted into agencies to visit relatives and make trouble for the agent, as Gall did on occasion. But most, imitating Sitting Bull and Crazy Horse, never went near an agency.

During these years, as the hunting bands followed the buffalo in the unceded territory, the agency culture took root and bloomed. The two factions drifted even farther apart, separated not only by distance but by thought, habit, relationship to the government, and above all by patterns born of dependence and independence. The principal leaders of the reservation people were Red Cloud and Spotted Tail, watching over their Oglalas and Brules at agencies in northwestern Nebraska, just off the reservation. For the Hunkpapas, the dominant leaders were Running Antelope, Thunder Hawk, and, increasingly in eclipse, the younger Bear's Rib. On the upper Missouri, Grand River Agency ministered to the Hunkpapas, Blackfeet, and Yanktonais, Cheyenne River Agency to the Miniconjous and Sans Arcs.

Although not embraced as head chief by everyone, Sitting Bull came as close to fulfilling Four Horns's vision as Sioux political organization allowed. To him more than any other falls the distinction of holding together the coalition of tribes that stood firm against the United States for seven years.

The tribes never came together all at once. Each summer portions united in more or less strength to stage a sun dance and conduct tribal hunts. In times of special white menace, more joined in the concentration than in times of quiet. And always during the warm months their numbers swelled with visitors from the agencies, then with the approach of winter dropped as these visitors returned to their homes.

In the perception of the white world, Sitting Bull emerged as *the* chief of these hunting bands. They were usually identified in official reports and the newspapers as "Sitting Bull's followers" or "the hostiles under Sitting Bull." No Indian commanded others, as whites persisted in believing, but Sitting Bull came to exert an influence beyond his own tribe without parallel in the history of his people.

At the same time, his authority can be exaggerated. However extraordinary, it could not transcend limits imposed by notions of political leadership deeply ingrained in Sioux thought and practice. Its true nature was best captured by a Northern Cheyenne, Wooden Leg, whose people fell under Sitting Bull's spell. Alluding to the governance of the village when more than one tribe came together, he explained:

> These councils of chiefs of all of the tribal circles were held sometimes at one camp circle and sometimes at another. In each case, heralds announced the meeting and told where it would be held. Each tribe operated its own internal government, the same as if it were entirely separated from the others. The chiefs of the different tribes met together as equals. There was only one who was considered as being above all the others. This was Sitting Bull. He was recognized as the one old man chief of all the camps combined. [15]

Red Cloud competed with Sitting Bull for the allegiance of the Lakotas. The task Red Cloud set for himself was much more complex and demanding, and he pursued it successfully for a generation. It was to find a tolerable life on the reservation, one that took as much as possible from the whites, especially rations, without surrendering any more than imperative of the old ways, especially freedom. [16]

Sitting Bull and Red Cloud, each in his own way, labored for the welfare of their people. At first glance, Sitting Bull seems the more admirable, the altruist who never, to his dying day, conceded that a Lakota should be anything but a pure Lakota of old, and who tried to surround his world with impenetrable walls that would bar all whites except traders. Red Cloud, by contrast, was the appeaser, the chief Lakota interface with the white world, the man who compromised the old ways in an attempt to carve out a new life fitted to new conditions. The new life turned out to be a disaster, but at least it was life. The old life that Sitting Bull pursued found its doom in historical forces beyond his control or comprehension. In the end, all the Lakotas had to go the way of Red Cloud. In the end, Sitting Bull was the patriot, Red Cloud the statesman.

8 SHIELD

IN THE SUMMER of 1870 the firm of Durfee and Peck, traders at Fort Buford, won a contract to supply wood to the post. They established a wood camp in a grove of timber about two miles above Fort Union, now falling into ruin since its abandonment in 1867. Throughout the summer Sioux raiders harassed the axmen and the teamsters hauling wood down the valley to the fort.

At daybreak on September 25, 1870, about two hundred Hunkpapas, Miniconjous, and Cheyennes struck suddenly. They kept a safe distance from the defenders, strongly posted in their camp, and concentrated instead on the party's cattle herd. But they cut off Charles Teck, driving eight yoke of oxen some five hundred yards from camp, and quickly surrounded him. Teck pumped out five rounds from his Winchester and felled five warriors, but the rifle jammed on the sixth. Swinging the weapon as a club, he finally went down under a shower of blows from knife-pointed war clubs. Beyond range from the wood camp, the Indians methodically butchered cattle until a relief detachment from Fort Buford drove them off.

As a parting gesture, warriors appeared on a nearby bluff and defiantly waved Teck's scalp. His desperate, futile fight impressed them. "I have helped to kill a great many white people along this river," the Hunkpapa Red Shirt observed, "but I never saw one fight so well or die so bravely as that boy at the mouth of the Yellowstone."

Once again Sitting Bull had thrust his lance at the hated Fort Buford. There could be no doubt that he had led the war expedition, the defenders agreed, for several of the old Buford hands clearly recognized him.[1]

It was the last time. Never again, until his surrender eleven years later, did anyone record seeing Sitting Bull near Fort Buford or any of the other military stations on the river below the fort. The war begun in 1865 at Fort Rice and expanded in 1866–67 to include Buford, Stevenson, and Totten ended abruptly in 1870. Ambitious young warriors ranging beyond the control of their chiefs might harry these forts and other white targets, but Sitting Bull had shifted his personal course, and the direction of his leadership, from the offensive to the defensive.

"Be a little against fighting," Four Horns counseled his nephew, "but when anyone shoots be ready to fight." This was now Sitting Bull's creed. Henceforth he would be the shield of his people rather than the lance. Crazy Horse, the like-minded Oglala war chief, wholeheartedly endorsed this policy.[2]

THE NEW POLICY coincided with a shift westward of the Lakota range, in part dictated by changing patterns of buffalo migration but also because this was the course Sioux conquest had taken for the past two decades. In the 1850s the Hunkpapas considered the Powder River their western frontier, beyond which they had to watch constantly for Crows. By the 1870s the Crows had been pressed westward, and the Lakota hunting bands now looked on the territory west of the Powder as their own heartland. Now their western frontier lay along the Bighorn River.

Lakota domain also embraced the plains north of the Yellowstone to the Montana stretch of the Missouri River as far west as the Musselshell. In the early 1870s plentiful buffalo drew the Hunkpapas and the Blackfeet, Miniconjou, and Sans Arc bands that frequently traveled with them to the north. Increasingly, the Hunkpapas wintered on the Big Dry or the Red Water, streams that drained northward into the Missouri from the low divide separating it from the Yellowstone. Summer, however, usually found them south of the Yellowstone, with the Oglalas and Brules.

Only along its fringes did the Lakota world rub against the white world, and there not too abrasively. The issue that did bring the two into irreconcilable conflict was the Northern Pacific Railway. Projected to connect St. Paul, Minnesota, with Seattle, Washington, the Northern Pacific would run up the Yellowstone Valley, the very heart of the country occupied by the Lakota hunting bands.

White lawyers could argue to one another's satisfaction that the Northern Pacific did not violate the Treaty of 1868. The treaty bound the Indians not to oppose railroads anywhere on the plains, and even permitted them on the Great Sioux Reservation itself if the Indians were compensated. But whether the Yellowstone fell within the "unceded Indian territory" provided for in the treaty could be debated, for its northern limits were not specified. If the western boundary, the summits of the Bighorn Mountains, governed the northern boundary, then the unceded territory fell well south of the Yellowstone, for the Bighorns did not extend as far north as the Yellowstone. Anyway, the treaty required consultation with the Indians only for railways or roads within the reservation itself.

Sitting Bull and his followers cared nothing for these legalisms, and knew nothing of them. Except for Gall, the chiefs of the hunting bands had not signed the treaty, and they had only the vaguest notion of its contents. They knew simply, beyond dispute, that the Yellowstone and its tributaries belonged to them. They had only recently wrested this land from the Crows. Railroads frightened away the buffalo and brought in white people. They could not be tolerated in the midst of Indian country. The Northern Pacific meant war—the very kind of defensive war Sitting Bull and Crazy Horse had agreed they would wage against white intrusion.

White officials also knew that the railroad meant war, but the generals were not ready. With one exception, infantry alone manned all the forts of Montana and Dakota. They could defend their own parade grounds but could not fight an offensive war against the highly mobile Plains horsemen.

A pragmatic executive in the nation's capital already had an answer: a policy of expediency applying to the entire West, not just the Sioux. It mirrored the Peace Policy that President Ulysses S. Grant had inaugurated toward the Indians on moving into the White House early in 1869.

"Temporizing as an expedient in government may be either a sign of weakness and folly," Commissioner of Indian Affairs Francis A. Walker wrote, "or it may be a proof of the highest wisdom." When an evil such as the Indians was self-destructing anyway, "temporizing may be the highest statesmanship."

Walker therefore advocated buying time by buying Indians. A liberal feeding policy, he thought, would buy time for the army to prepare for war and the other forces of westward expansion to work their effect. From this reasoning sprang a major government overture to Sitting Bull and the other chiefs of the hunting bands.[3]

The initiative centered not at the Lakota agencies on the Missouri in Dakota but at the Milk River Agency in Montana. Located north of the Missouri at the trading post of Fort Browning, this agency served Assiniboines, River Crows, and Gros Ventres of the Prairie (no kin of the Hidatsas at Fort Berthold, also known as Gros Ventres).

Milk River had already provided a testing ground for Walker's policy. In the spring of 1871, more than six thousand Yanktonais and Dakotas, the latter refugees from the Minnesota uprising of 1862, arrived at the agency, drawn by plentiful buffalo. Their chiefs announced that they had come to stay. Their old country east of the Missouri in Dakota was dead, barren of buffalo, and they intended to settle on Milk River and receive rations from the Great Father. They had been killing and plundering whites for years, Agent Andrew J. Simmons pointed out, and would return to that pastime if their demands were not met. In the spirit of the temporizing policy, their demands were met. The resident Indians, long-standing enemies of the newcomers, promptly fled, but Simmons persuaded Durfee and Peck to build a trading post, Fort Belknap, farther up Milk River to house a subagency that could care for these tribes.

Also attracted by the buffalo, several hundred Lakota lodges trailed the Yanktonais and Dakotas up the Milk River and learned of the government's generosity. The Dakotas explained to the white officials that these were nontreaty tribes from the south. Once they had followed Red Cloud, but the whites had put medicine in his eyes and now they acknowledged no other chief but Sitting Bull. Here, it seemed, was a chance to temporize with the very people causing so much worry over the Northern Pacific. Montana Indian superintendent Jasper A. Viall gained authority to try to open negotiations with Sitting Bull.[4]

Sitting Bull seems to have been receptive, at least temporarily. For one thing, chiefs were supposed to try to make peace, and he had a precise set of conditions for peace that he may have felt called on to present to the white officials. For another, he wanted better trading arrangements. A ban he had imposed on all trade between his people and white traders had proved self-defeating. Slotas could provide arms, ammunition, and other goods, but they were nomadic and offered a less certain source than fixed trading posts. Durfee and Peck's Fort Peck, on the Missouri at the mouth of Milk River, enjoyed a lively trade with Yanktonais, Dakotas, and Lakotas, and Sitting Bull resolved to cement a trading relationship there.

A third factor influencing Sitting Bull may have been a new source of informed advice about white people. He was a swarthy mixed blood of twenty-one, half white and half Polynesian, named Frank Grouard. Fathered by a Mormon missionary, Benjamin F. Grouard, he had been adopted by another missionary, Addison Pratt, and brought to Utah. Mormon life proved too tame for the youth of fifteen, and in 1865 he ran away to Montana. Freighting, mail riding, and escapades beyond the pale of the law occupied him until he wound up in Sitting Bull's tipi.[5]

How and when this happened is unclear. At some point between 1867 and 1871, he either freely joined the Hunkpapas or was taken prisoner. Whichever, his own account of his subsequent adoption by Sitting Bull seems valid. Repeating an impulse such as had led to his rescue and adoption of the Hohe Jumping Bull, Sitting Bull decided to throw his protection around Grouard. Gall and No Neck urged that Grouard be put to death. Pointing to the acclaimed precedent of Jumping Bull, however, Sitting Bull prevailed. Grouard became his savior's adopted brother, named Standing Bear, but better known as the Grabber, the descriptive term for a standing bear struggling with an opponent.[6]

Sitting Bull's patronage did not win the Grabber immediate freedom. For months he lived as a prisoner, closely guarded by Jumping Bull and White Eagle, Sitting Bull's cousin. Gradually they became friends and companions, as did Sitting Bull's sister, who had helped to rear Jumping Bull and who now exerted great influence in transforming Grouard into an acculturated Sioux. As he learned Sioux language and ways, he earned the trust of his captors and the liberty of the camp.[7]

As an adopted brother of Sitting Bull, Grouard surely provided information and advice about dealing with the white world that gained thoughtful consideration. His counsel probably influenced the decision to open trade with Fort Peck and at least listen to what the officials at Milk River Agency had to say.

After nightfall on September 8, 1871, Sitting Bull and a small party appeared outside the Fort Peck stockade. He called out his name and stated that he came as a friend. In talks with the trader, he said he wanted to open trade and to meet with a government agent about making peace. In the meantime, he promised, he would prevent any raids on whites. For a month his people came and went in small trading parties, and Sitting Bull himself paid another visit on October 12. During that time, the trader reported, a war party had organized at his village but had been called off after severe soldiering by the *akicita*.

The peace conference took place at Fort Peck during three weeks in November 1871. Agent Simmons represented the government. Sitting Bull did not attend, either because at the last moment he could not bring himself to sit down with white officials, or because, as he sent word, he was dealing with the troubles caused by his soldiering of the war party. Black Moon and the chiefs and headmen of two hundred lodges spoke for the Lakotas.

Black Moon declared that both he and Sitting Bull wanted peace. If the Great Father wanted peace too, he must stop the Northern Pacific, expel all white soldiers and citizens from the Indian country, and abandon Fort Buford and the settlement at the mouth of the Musselshell. This country belonged to the Lakotas. They had taken it away from the Crows and Gros Ventres, and now, if necessary, the young men would throw their lives away fighting the soldiers. They did not want the white man's civilization, such as their brethren were having forced on them at the lower agencies; what they wanted was "just something to eat."[8]

Something to eat was probably the largest factor in moving the hunting bands to meet with Simmons at Fort Peck. With the usual long and hungry winter in prospect, the people may have been so envious of the rations being handed out to the Yanktonais and Dakotas that Black Moon and Sitting Bull had to swallow their loathing of white officials and explore whether their followers could share in the largess. In fact, these two chiefs and some seven hundred lodges spent the winter of 1871–72 in the neighborhood of Fort Peck and periodically received rations. At the same time, Gall and Red Horn took their bands into Grand River Agency to live on government dole for six months before, with the greening of the grass, heading west to the Yellowstone.[9]

So encouraging did the temporizing policy appear in neutralizing the Sitting Bull bands that Washington officials hurried to formalize it. At Commissioner Walker's urging, Congress included an item in the appropriations bill enacted in May 1872 providing $500,000 for providing subsistence and clothing to the Lakota Sioux near Fort Peck.[10] Armed with this tantalizing bait, a prestigious commission headed by Assistant Secretary of the Interior Benjamin R. Cowen set out for Fort Peck to persuade Sitting Bull and his fellow chiefs to journey to Washington and settle their differences with the Great Father himself.

Only a handful of minor Lakota chiefs showed up at Fort Peck in August 1872 to meet with the commission. The snow and cold that

fostered winter hunger had given way to green grass and abundant buffalo. Secretary Cowen counted 453 lodges of Lakotas pitched near the
fort, only sixty-nine of which were Hunkpapa. Of the residents of all,
moreover, two-thirds were children under fourteen. The men and their
chiefs were down on the Yellowstone, hunting buffalo, raiding Crows,
and, as it turned out, fighting with white soldiers.

To speak for him, Sitting Bull sent his brother-in-law His-Horse-
Looking, husband of his younger sister, Twin Woman. Sitting Bull, this
man reported, had instructed him "to go, and whenever he found a white
man who would tell the truth, to return, and he would go to see him."
His-Horse-Looking did not, Cowen added wryly, "tell us whether his
search had been successful."

From His-Horse-Looking and others who talked with the commissioners, Cowen gained revealing insights into the character of the men
who opposed the Northern Pacific. Of Black Moon and Sitting Bull he
wrote:

That these chiefs have great influence among the Lakotas . . . is
undoubted, notwithstanding some of the chiefs from the lower
agencies affect to consider Sitting Bull as a mean-spirited sort of
fellow, with but little or no influence, and very small following.
The Indians whom we met of the Tetons consider him the leading
man of their people, and their speeches at the council sufficiently
indicated their fear of and respect for him. When he has visited the
post [Fort Peck] his control of his braves is said to have been more
complete than is usual among Indians, and other chiefs showed
their respect for him by removing their koo [coup] feathers from
their heads in his presence.[11]

Although the Cowen mission could be viewed as an embarrassing
failure, the underlying policy of temporizing had its effect on the
Lakotas. Five hundred thousand dollars in food and clothing dangled a
powerful lure as another winter approached. It turned out to be one of
unusual severity. By the end of December 1872, more than eight hundred
Lakota tipis, mostly Hunkpapa, had been raised in the Missouri Valley
around Fort Peck.

Rations created severe divisions among the hunting bands and, for the
winter at least, almost entirely isolated Sitting Bull from his people. Even
Black Moon went to Fort Peck, together with Long Dog, a Hunkpapa war
leader gaining increasing notoriety as a ruthless fighter. Sitting Bull re-

mained stubbornly absent, wintering on the Red Water and Big Dry with only fourteen lodges of diehard followers.[12]

Temporizing seemed to be working so well that the government decided to institutionalize it at Fort Peck. In December 1872 the Interior Department authorized the abandonment of Fort Browning as headquarters of Milk River Agency and the consolidation of all Sioux—Yanktonai, Dakota, and Lakota—at Fort Peck. Fort Belknap would continue to function as a subagency responsible for Assiniboines, River Crows, and Gros Ventres.[13]

The Milk River Agency at Fort Peck, flaunting the promise of rations and clothing for "friendly bands" of Lakotas, continued to incite factional conflicts—more in times of want than in times of plenty. As a delaying tactic, however, it failed. War came just as quickly as if no Lakotas had ever been coaxed into Fort Peck. Accepting the Great Father's rations did not bind a Sioux to look the other way as the railroad approached, however much government officials believed it should. No one who listened to the Lakotas, "hostiles" and "friendlies" alike, could doubt that the hunting bands would never drop their antagonism to a railroad in the Yellowstone Valley.

The government's temporizing initiative undoubtedly tested Sitting Bull's leadership severely. It spawned divisions and factional squabbles through all the bands that gave him allegiance. On occasion, when hunger overwhelmed the spirit of independence and the abhorrence of government officials, it drained away all but a handful of devoted adherents. But sooner or later full bellies subverted the policy and replenished his following.

EVEN AS THE white threat loomed over the Lakotas, warfare with the Crows continued unabated. Neither the momentous issues spawned by the Treaty of 1868 nor the approach of the Northern Pacific Railroad distracted the Lakota leadership from seeking to outwit their historic enemies, or the young men from the more appealing pastime of harvesting Crow ponies and Crow scalps.

For the Sioux, the most memorable encounter with the Crows took place in the winter of 1869–70, amid the first painful adjustments to the Treaty of 1868. They remembered it as the Thirty-Crows-Killed battle.

Sitting Bull's band wintered that year along the Missouri River and on Big Dry Creek. They thus edged into hunting grounds also frequented by River Crows, the northern kin of the Mountain Crows the Sioux contended with on the upper Yellowstone.

In the middle of the winter, amid bitter cold and deep snow, two Hunkpapa boys were returning from a day of hunting when a party of thirty River Crows cut their trail in the snow. Except for two men mounted on one pony, the Crows were afoot. The two hurried to overtake the boys and succeeded in killing one. Wounded, the other escaped to carry word to the Hunkpapa village.

At once Sitting Bull organized a revenge expedition of about one hundred warriors. His two uncles, Four Horns and Looks-for-Him-in-a-Tent, went along, as did Jumping Bull. Before leaving camp, Sitting Bull performed a pipe ceremony and vowed to offer tobacco, buffalo hides, and even some of his flesh if *Wakantanka* would favor the movement. Guided by the surviving boy, the men rode through the winter darkness to the scene of the killing, then followed the Crow trail in the snow to the head of Big Dry Creek. On a rocky promontory rising from the surrounding plains, the Sioux found their enemies posted behind rock breastworks.

As dawn broke, the Hunkpapas charged without even pausing to reconnoiter. A few on each side had firearms, but most had only bow and arrows. The Sioux fought in typical fashion, each man for himself, each striving for deeds of bravery and the coups that added to war honors. Singly, they dashed on the fortifications, fired at the Crows, and pulled away, only to repeat the rush from another direction. Well protected and steady in their own bravery, the Crows sold their lives dearly.

Astride a bay horse, Sitting Bull urged his men to battle with songs of bravery. He and his adopted brother Jumping Bull both distinguished themselves. Jumping Bull guided his pony in close to the fort and rode a complete circle around it, drawing heavy fire and causing the Crows to exhaust their ammunition. Sitting Bull darted to the breastworks and reached across with his bow to count three coups, one first and two second, on warriors downed by others.

Although outnumbered more than three to one, the Crows enjoyed the advantages of defense from fortified positions, and they exacted heavy casualties. Of the one hundred Sioux warriors, thirteen died on the battlefield and seventeen limped off with serious wounds. Among the dead was Sitting Bull's uncle Looks-for-Him-in-a-Tent, cut down on the rock parapet by a Crow bullet in the breast.

As the morning hours slipped by, the individual lunges of the Hunkpapa warriors gradually depleted the defending ranks. Like his warriors, Sitting Bull charged as chance presented and retreated when the fire grew too hot. Finally, as noon approached, Sitting Bull and his men surged forward in a body, leaped the walls, and in desperate hand-to-hand fighting killed the last of the Crows.

Back in the village, the victors staged a scalp dance. But this was also a time of mourning. Sioux did not often risk lives in such bold frontal charges, and the cost of victory had been unusually high. Grieving for his uncle, Sitting Bull cut his hair, avoided paint and smeared himself with mud, and went about the wintry camp without leggings or moccasins. He had borne the body of Looks-for-Him-in-a-Tent back to the village and installed it in a tipi. When the camp moved, the tipi and its contents remained.[14]

The following summer, 1870, Sitting Bull's band joined a big Lakota camp on the Yellowstone below the mouth of the Rosebud. Present were Hunkpapas, Oglalas, Miniconjous, and Sans Arcs. There Sitting Bull gave a striking demonstration of his powers as a *Wichasha Wakan*.

One day, with a crowd gathered for some occasion, Sitting Bull arose and announced that he must withdraw to give force to a vision. He walked away from the people and sang. As he sang, he saw a ball of fire approaching, but it vanished immediately before reaching him. On returning to the village, he performed the pipe ceremony and declared that in the smoke he saw a battle with enemy Indians in two days, with many enemies killed and some Sioux as well. Doubters, he said, should simply wait two days and see for themselves. The next morning another holy man went out and in another vision saw an enemy camp to the north. Scouts probed northward and discovered a Flathead camp in the valley of the Musselshell River.

At the head of four hundred warriors representing all the tribes in the village, Sitting Bull rode forth to fulfill his prophecy. After reaching the objective, he revealed his plan of attack—the familiar decoy stratagem. A small party would openly advance to draw out the enemy while the rest of the warriors would quietly surround the village and spring the trap.

The decoy rarely worked because some eager warrior usually charged prematurely and gave away the ruse. Now the decoys, forty-three in number, watched as a Flathead led some horses out from his village. Before the main force could get into position, the decoys charged. They captured seven horses, but the man raced back to the village and gave the alarm. A hundred Flatheads rode out to give battle.

The main force of Sioux drew up to receive the Flathead attack. After a brief skirmish, with light casualties on both sides, the Flatheads scampered back to their village. A Miniconjou chief galloped to the front and shouted that enough had been hit, it was time to withdraw.

Most of the Sioux left the field, but a few remained, among them Sitting Bull, White Bull, and Jumping Bull. They watched as a party of Flatheads came out to retrieve their dead. With a whoop, the Sioux opened fire and charged. The enemy hastily withdrew, but one had to dismount before reaching safety. Sitting Bull, intent on seizing the man's horse, galloped toward him. The Flathead raised his rifle and fired. The bullet smashed into Sitting Bull's left forearm, and he turned back. Comrades brought him off the field.

Although scarcely a glorious triumph, the event had verified Sitting Bull's prophecy. A battle had in fact occurred in two days, and the ball of fire in his vision stood for the Flathead bullet that had won him still another red feather. The arm healed quickly.[15]

Fights such as the Thirty-Crows-Killed battle and the Flathead encounter flashed around the Lakota frontiers throughout the early 1870s. This was a time of rising white menace. But for the Lakotas, tribal enemies of old, not the white newcomers, remained the central preoccupation.

AS SITTING BULL turned forty he embarked on yet another major change in his domestic status. Sometime in the late 1860s, he lost patience with the constant bickering between his two wives, Snow-on-Her and Red Woman. Judging the former largely at fault, he threw her out of the tipi. In 1871 Red Woman died of sickness, leaving him with a young son by her as well as the two daughters by Snow-on-Her. Good Feather, who had joined her brother's family when he adopted her son One Bull in 1857, moved into his tipi to care for the children. His mother, Her-Holy-Door, also remained a formidable presence in his lodge.

A chief of Sitting Bull's stature, however, badly needed a wife, and in the spring of 1872 he moved to acquire one. A woman named Four Robes caught his eye. She was a sister of Gray Eagle, with whom Sitting Bull bargained for her hand. He offered some of his best horses, and the match was consummated.

Four Robes had an older sister, Seen-by-the-Nation. She was a widow with two sons, Little Soldier and Blue Mountain, the latter a deaf-mute. Seen-by-the-Nation told Four Robes she wanted to live in the same tipi with her. Four Robes asked Sitting Bull to marry her too, and in late summer of 1872 he again approached Gray Eagle. A war party was then forming, and Sitting Bull knew Gray Eagle needed a good horse. He therefore offered his prized sorrel Bloated Jaw in exchange for Seen-by-the-Nation.

Thus did Sitting Bull add two wives to his family, together with two stepsons whom he adopted. Both sisters were of jolly disposition, kind to everyone, and never jealous of each other. The arrangement seems to have pleased all parties and endured until Sitting Bull's death.[16]

SITTING BULL'S RISE in the estimation of his people owed much to his leadership in the men's societies. These were both the *akicita*, such as the Strong Hearts, and the dream societies, such as the Buffalo and the Heyoka. In middle age still others absorbed his energies and loyalties, most notably the Silent Eaters and White Horse Riders.

Organized about 1869, possibly in response to the stresses growing out of the Fort Laramie Treaty, the Silent Eaters dedicated themselves to the welfare of the tribe rather than the benefit of individual members of the society—an objective mirroring Sitting Bull's own self-imposed purpose in life. Rarely did more than twenty men belong, and they came from the sagest and above all the bravest segments of the warrior fraternity.

The Silent Eaters were a secret group. The herald, Crawler, announced meetings by going quietly from member to member. They gathered at midnight in the lodge of one of the members, the place changing from time to time. They feasted on the finest cuts of buffalo and dog, but never sang or danced as in the festivities of other societies. Hence the name Silent Eaters. Instead the men recounted war deeds and talked about problems of concern to the entire tribe. Rarely did the tribal leadership fail to heed their counsel. The meetings always ended with a pipe ceremony, led by a designated pipe bearer.

In time the Silent Eaters became more closely identified with Sitting Bull than any other society. If not one of the founders, he quickly ascended to supremacy. His preeminent position sprang not only from his character and sagacity but from his positions as band chief, tribal war chief, and supreme chief of the Sioux, however qualified the last distinction.[17]

In contrast to the secret, late-night meetings of the Silent Eaters, the activities of the White Horse Riders were highly visible. Sitting Bull founded the society in 1875 or early 1876 and presided as its chief. Members staged colorful parades for entertainment, but like other *akicita*

societies they performed police duties too. Indeed, Sitting Bull may well
have organized the White Horse Riders as a kind of personal police force
to fortify his authority as head chief of the Sioux.[18]

GRADUALLY, in the 1870s, the Sioux began to acquire rifles and pistols
that fired metallic cartridges. Any improved firearm was a treasure, but
Winchester and Henry repeating rifles were especially prized.

For Sitting Bull's people, obtaining arms superior to the old trade
muskets, which fired powder and ball and lacked accuracy and hitting
power, was a difficult undertaking. And for the proud owner of such a
piece, assuring a continuous supply of ammunition was difficult and
uncertain. Men therefore husbanded their cartridges and reloaded ex-
pended ones. Without practice, and frequently firing inexpertly reloaded
shells, most Sioux were indifferent marksmen, better with bow and arrow
than with firearms. But war with well-armed whites and enemy tribes
demanded equivalent weapons.

Despite obstacles, the hunting bands found arms sources. Traders at
the military forts and Indian agencies feared losing their government
license by violating the ban on selling arms to "hostiles." But sometimes
they took the risk, and often, as they well knew, "friendlies" bought arms
from them to trade to their kin in the hunting bands. Unsupervised
traders at Missouri River posts in Montana offered another source, as did
itinerant merchants working out of Helena and Fort Benton. Presenting
still another opportunity were the Slotas, the Red River Métis who wandered the plains north and east of the Missouri.[19]

The Slotas had long traded with the Lakotas intermittently, but in the
summer of 1872 Sitting Bull decided to establish a firm connection. The
conflict with the whites had grown more threatening, and his men needed
rifles and cartridges. Journeying to one of the Slota camps north of the
Missouri, he entered into his own version of a treaty, in which the Slotas
agreed to bring a caravan of trade goods to the Hunkpapa camp.

Deep in the following winter, the Slotas arrived with a caravan of
sleighs loaded with merchandise. This was the winter when most of the
Hunkpapas clustered around Fort Peck drawing rations, but Sitting Bull
and his small following camped at the head of the Big Dry. Ominously,
five of the Slota sleighs contained whiskey, and many in the camp embarked on a prolonged binge. Pandemonium reigned, with fights, maim-
ings, and even killings dominating the trading and accentuating factional
divisions. The Slotas disposed of firearms and other trade goods—White

Bull bought a breech-loading rifle—but their whiskey made a shambles of Sitting Bull's trade treaty.

"The French half-breeds left after they saw what they had started," related Frank Grouard, who was there. "They pulled up stakes and left in the night and took what whiskey was left with them."[20]

Only a few months later, in April 1873, the Hunkpapas had another encounter with Slotas, this one even more violent. Some two to three hundred Slotas had crossed the Yellowstone and moved south up the Rosebud. They had thus penetrated deep into Sioux hunting grounds, and the Sioux looked on them as interlopers, far from their rightful territory and probably prospecting for gold. His people had never fought the Slotas before, observed Old Bull, but they were trespassing. These also may have been the same Slotas whose whiskey had caused so much trouble recently, which would have made them even less welcome south of the Yellowstone.[21]

The Hunkpapas were camped on the middle Rosebud when a scouting party ran across a Slota rider. In an exchange of shots, one of the Hunkpapas was fatally hit. Back in the village, Sitting Bull got up an expedition of about one hundred warriors and rode forth to do battle. At daybreak the next morning, near the head of the Rosebud, the Sioux found the quarry.

The Slotas were waiting. They had corraled their wagons, bunched their stock in the center, and thrown up earthen embankments. Expert marksmen armed with repeating rifles and even a cannon, they calmly awaited the Sioux onslaught.

White Bull opened the fight with a dash on the corral. He rode swiftly around it without drawing fire or seeing defenders, then returned to the main body. All the warriors then charged. The Slotas loosed a hot fire that hurt no one but promptly sent their assailants back to cover. Herding their horses into a draw, the Sioux took positions from which to snipe at the corral. After several hours, they had shot down most of the animals inside it.

A few warriors crept to firing positions within fifty yards of the Slota corral. One, His Knife, caught a bullet in the forehead. White Bull rushed out and dragged his body to safety. Two Crow, an old man, took His Knife's place but was also killed.

Cleverly, the Slotas released a pinto pony and drove it into the open. Cloud Man mounted and galloped in pursuit. Slota fire dropped both him and his horse. He got up and ran after the animal on foot. The Slotas shot him in the back and, as White Bull put it, also "shot his prick off." Sitting

Bull, without feathers and armed with a rifle and a sword presented him by the Strong Hearts, sprinted out and retrieved Cloud Man's body.

Even before Sitting Bull returned to the Sioux position, the Slotas suddenly poured out of their defenses and charged.

"They are coming," White Bull shouted. "To your horses."

The Slota attack, combined with the rush of warriors for their mounts, stampeded the herd and scattered Sioux in all directions. So sudden was the assault that it caught some old men and young boys sitting under a tree watching the fight, and three men were slain before they could get out of the way.

At least eight Hunkpapas died in the futile assault on the Slota position. Individually the men fought bravely. None, of course, had been more daring than Cloud Man. White Bull had also distinguished himself, and Sitting Bull and Jumping Bull were both mentioned admiringly. But the Slota fight again highlighted the flaws in the Sioux style of combat against a well-armed and disciplined foe. As Old Bull said, "Sioux were scared. They could do nothing. Terrible."

After retrieving Cloud Man, therefore, Sitting Bull sought out his warriors and announced, "We have fought enough, let us go home."

This was the kind of warfare Sitting Bull and his people understood— the honor of coups and ponies, the satisfaction of killing traditional enemies, the sense of tribal power that came from seizing and holding hunting grounds and serving notice on all peoples that the buffalo belonged only to the Sioux and their friends. Men could flaunt their bravery, inflict damage on the enemy, and when they tired of fighting simply call off the battle and go home. If they had clearly lost, they crept back in shame. If they had merely fallen short of decisive victory, they could still revel in the scalps and coups and stage victory dances to celebrate individual feats of bravery.

When as old men the warriors of this time recounted the battles of their youth, they remembered mainly who were the bravest, who counted the coups, and who died. The details of battlefield movements, even of individual deeds, blurred in the shadow of the honor roll. When pressed, they would talk about their battles with the white soldiers, but they plainly preferred to recall the glories of war with enemy tribes. That was real war, war understood by both sides, war that conferred honor and prestige without threatening tribal survival.

That threat came from the white people. They fought a different kind of war, a serious, unremitting war not confined to the battlefield, one that the Sioux never really understood. As the Lakota hunting bands traded thrusts with the Crows and Flatheads in the early 1870s, they found themselves confronted ever more menacingly with white soldiers. That conflict, given the purpose to which Sitting Bull and his followers had dedicated themselves, was irreconcilable by any means short of decisive war.

9 WASICHUS ON ELK RIVER

THE LAKOTAS CALLED the Yellowstone Elk River. Few rivers in their homeland meant more to them. It watered a broad, grassy valley spotted with groves of cottonwoods and willows. On either side bluffs rose to rolling plains, green with nutritious grass in spring, brown and parched in summer, wind- and snow-swept in winter, and often teeming with buffalo and other game. On the south the Powder, Tongue, Rosebud, and Bighorn rivers drained snowmelt from the Bighorn peaks and emptied into Elk River, which in turn, born in a huge lake high in the Rockies, carried its own spring rush of snowmelt. Although but recently Crow domain, Elk River and its tributaries were treasured Lakota possessions. They defined the Lakota heartland, and they had been gained at the cost of Lakota blood.

As Lakotas of every tribe had repeatedly told white officials, the valley of Elk River could never be yielded to a railroad.

Long Knives first appeared in the Yellowstone Valley in the autumn of 1871, escorting surveyors of the Northern Pacific. Sioux watched with suspicion, but made no move to interfere. Instead, delegations went to the Grand River and Cheyenne River agencies to ask whether the whites meant to build a railroad. That they asked before shooting testifies to the defensive policy on which Sitting Bull and Crazy Horse had decided.[1]

Of their resolve to shoot, however, there could be no doubt. This became abundantly plain in personal terms early in April 1872, when

Spotted Eagle and 150 lodges of Sans Arcs appeared at Cheyenne River Agency. He was a young chief, hardly more than thirty, tall, energetic, and thoughtful, and destined to become one of Sitting Bull's closest associates. In council with Colonel David S. Stanley, he spoke calmly but bluntly. He knew the whites intended to build the railroad, he stated, as the expeditions of the previous autumn had forecast. Neither he nor any other Sioux had ever given consent to this and never would, nor would they even listen to such a proposition. "He then said," reported Stanley, "that he would fight the rail road people as long as he lived, would tear up the road and kill its builders."[2]

As Spotted Eagle and his people turned back to the west, having steadfastly refused to accept any rations or other presents from the agent, the army planned further operations. Northern Pacific engineers wanted to follow up on the preliminary surveys of 1871, and the army assigned formidable forces to make certain they worked in safety. Stanley himself would lead an expedition of six hundred soldiers west from Fort Rice, while Major Eugene M. Baker, with nearly five hundred, would push down the Yellowstone Valley from Fort Ellis, in the Gallatin Valley near the town of Bozeman.

By midsummer Spotted Eagle and his people had joined with bands from other Lakota tribes to form a huge camp of about two thousand lodges at the so-called big bend of Powder River about 125 miles above its mouth. After a sun dance, the combined tribes decided to mount a war expedition against the Crows. As many as a thousand warriors may have ridden on this foray. As they penetrated Crow territory in the Yellowstone Valley above the Bighorn, scouts brought word of soldiers on the north side of the river.

This was Major Baker's command, shepherding an engineering party of twenty railroad employees. On August 12, 1872, they established a base camp on the north bank of the Yellowstone nearly opposite the mouth of Arrow Creek. An abandoned riverbed, traced by a ragged line of brush and stunted timber, formed a large horseshoe circling the camp on three sides, with the river on the fourth.

On the night of August 13 the chiefs met in council to decide whether to drop the incursion against the Crows and attack the soldiers instead. Before they could reach a decision, however, parties of eager young men slipped out of camp and embarked on their own independent expeditions against the soldiers. Despite a screen of *akicita* deployed to prevent just such premature movements, some Brules and Hunkpapas crept up on the soldiers. White Bull set forth alone, eluding the *akicita* who accosted him by professing to have to "pass water," then stalling until they had moved on. Before reaching his destination, however, he met Crawler and two comrades leading stock they had stolen from the soldier camp. The Brules proved less stealthy and triggered a wild exchange of fire in the darkness as the soldiers and civilians scrambled into defensive positions.[3]

Enough Indians had slipped by the *akicita* to form a strong force in the wooded slough, and in the darkness they posed a dangerous threat to the defenders. On the east an attacking group succeeded in overrunning the tents of a party of civilians and capturing their contents. In the firing there, the Hunkpapa Plenty Lice was shot from his horse and killed and his body was left within the military lines.

As often happened, impetuous young men had settled the question their chiefs were debating. By daybreak, all the fighting men had crossed to the north bank of the Yellowstone and gathered in front of the military position. A counterattack by the soldiers had driven the night's attackers out of the arc of brush and timber, and now Indians covered the bluffs rising from the flat valley beyond. The troops established their defensive line in the thickets and behind the natural parapet of the old riverbank. From the heights warriors aimed a plunging fire into the military line and camp. Others raced back and forth on a "daring line" in the valley below, firing from horseback and performing fearless deeds. From a high promontory on the east, Sitting Bull and Crazy Horse oversaw the battle.

As the sun rose on the battlefield, all eyes turned in wonder on Sitting Bull as he staged a spectacle of bravery so imaginative that it surpassed all others that day. After getting his pipe and tobacco pouch from his horse, he walked from the bluffs out into the open valley to within view of the soldier lines. He wore a shirt, leggings, and two feathers in his hair, and he also carried his bow, quiver of arrows, and a rifle.

Seating himself on the ground, he shouted, "Who other Indians wish to smoke with me come."

As Sitting Bull calmly and with studied deliberation filled the bowl with tobacco, White Bull, Gets-the-Best-Of, and two Cheyennes ventured into the open and seated themselves beside the chief.

The "smoking party," as White Bull termed it, was a terrifying experience. After kindling the tobacco, Sitting Bull puffed placidly, then passed the pipe to his companions. With pounding hearts, each puffed vigorously and passed it quickly down the line. Throughout Sitting Bull said nothing, just looked around and smoked quietly as soldier bullets kicked up dirt and sang through the air. When all the tobacco had burned, Sitting Bull picked up a stick and thoroughly cleaned the bowl, stowed the pipe in its pouch, rose to his feet, and slowly walked back to the admiring knots of fellow tribesmen. The other smokers ran back, Gets-the-Best-Of so hastily that he left his bow and arrows on the ground. As a further display of his own bravery, White Bull returned to retrieve the weapons.

This ingenious exhibition, so captivating to people who placed great emphasis on daring, added to Sitting Bull's long list of valorous feats, reinforced his reputation for bravery, and answered those who, in the worsening factionalism of the early 1870s, mocked his pretensions. In addition, it did no harm to his asserted authority as head chief of the Lakotas. It was, White Bull remembered, "the bravest deed possible."

"That's enough," Sitting Bull shouted, "we must quit, that's enough." After his courageous exhibition, no one argued.

But Crazy Horse insisted on one more dash along the daring line, and he asked White Bull to accompany him. Without feathers, wearing a white shirt, his hair flying loose behind, and armed only with a lance, Crazy Horse charged the length of the line, White Bull galloping behind. When nearly back to the Indians, a bullet hit Crazy Horse's mount and tumbled him to the ground. Regaining his feet, the Oglala ran the rest of the way to safety.

Such was the Battle of Arrow Creek, the first overt challenge to the Northern Pacific. If it fell short of Spotted Eagle's threat to tear up the road and kill all its builders, it nonetheless reassured the Sioux that they had backed their rhetoric with action. Spotted Eagle, in fact, sent a message into Cheyenne River Agency asking all to be informed that he had stood up in front of the soldiers to fight and that now, whenever he met whites, he would fight them.[4]

And however inconclusive, Arrow Creek so shook the Baker Expedition that the company's engineers refused to go any lower down the Yellowstone. Instead, they redirected their survey to the Musselshell River, then hurried back to the safety of Fort Ellis. They had lost one soldier killed and two wounded, and one civilian mortally wounded, together with a few mules and horses and all sixteen of their beef cattle. The Indians lost two killed and half a dozen wounded.

What the Lakotas remembered most vividly about Arrow Creek, however, was not the casualties or even Sitting Bull's exhibition of bravery. It was the fate of Plenty Lice. As they watched from the bluffs, four soldiers seized the arms and legs of the dead Hunkpapa and threw him on a campfire. Later his relatives visited the battlesite and retrieved the scorched bones of their kinsman.

The Battle of Arrow Creek had hardly ended and the large aggregation of warriors scattered than a courier reached Sitting Bull with word of more Long Knives approaching from the east. The messenger came from Gall, who with about twenty or thirty men had discovered Colonel Stanley's expedition from Fort Rice.

Just before daybreak on August 16, only two days after Arrow Creek, Gall's little party took station in some timber on the east edge of the military camp on O'Fallon's Creek. A crashing volley of rifle fire turned the soldiers out of their bedrolls, and they scrambled to form a defensive perimeter as some twenty warriors raced toward the stock herd, held inside a corral of wagons and tents. The infantrymen thwarted the attempt to stampede the animals, but the Hunkpapas galloped yipping and firing through the very center of the army bivouac.[5]

Down O'Fallon's Creek and up the Yellowstone, Gall kept the soldiers and engineers on constant alert. At the mouth of the Powder, where Stanley expected to meet Major Baker, the engineers erected their initial mound for a survey back toward the Missouri. Cannoneers fired their pieces in the vain hope of signaling Baker, whose engineers were already serving notice that they wanted to turn north from the Yellowstone. At this moment Gall struck again.

One of the engineers had wandered into the hills looking for agates, only to discover galloping warriors bearing down on him. He ran into the valley shouting for help, and his comrades hastily mounted and raced the Indians for the prize. The whites won, and the man was saved. After a brief exchange of fire, the Hunkpapas withdrew to the west side of the Powder.

Soon Gall himself walked down to the riverbank, laid his rifle on the ground, and shouted that he wanted to talk with the soldier chief. Stanley dropped his pistol and holster and went to the opposite bank. Gall refused an invitation to meet on a sandbar in the middle of the stream, and the loud conversation, conducted through an interpreter, accomplished little. Gall asked what the soldiers were doing in Sioux country. When told, he asked how much they intended to pay for the privilege of building a railroad. Finally, as Stanley noted, "he threatened to bring all the bands and give us a big fight."

Observing warriors gathering menacingly in the woods behind Gall, Stanley promptly broke off the talk and turned back. He had gone only a few paces when the Indians opened fire. Soldiers fired back, hitting two.

Shortly after this episode, Sitting Bull arrived on the scene, not with "all the bands," as Gall had promised, but with enough to keep the soldiers occupied. As they traced their way back up O'Fallon's Creek on the return march, Sitting Bull made a threatening demonstration on the evening of August 21 and a more aggressive move the next morning.

The command had no sooner broken camp on August 22 than a large force of warriors pressed from the rear, and some two hundred others fired from positions on the bluffs edging the valley on the west. The wagon train corraled, the engineers halted work, and the infantry deployed in skirmish formation around the train. Stanley sent two companies to dislodge the Indians from the bluffs.

Sitting Bull himself conducted the defense against the infantrymen slipping, sliding, and scrambling up the craggy precipice while dodging rifle bullets. In the midst of the firing, he dismounted and took position behind a large rock on a promontory commanding the battlefield. Shouting that he was Sitting Bull, he launched into a long harangue. If the railroad came through, he declared, "there would be no more Indians." He had therefore sent for all the tribes. "After a while" they would come and wipe out the soldiers and the railroad workers.[6]

As Sitting Bull orated, the soldiers worked their way up the bluffs and gradually forced the Sioux out of their firing positions. No soldier was hit, but one Hunkpapa got too close and was killed with a bullet in the head.[7]

Although Sitting Bull and Gall had both vowed to summon large forces to destroy Stanley, they could not make good their threat. Instead they shadowed the expedition back across the Little Missouri Badlands and down Heart River, exacting in bushwhacking what they could not in open battle. Two officers and Colonel Stanley's black servant, straying from the command, forfeited their lives.

Sitting Bull and Crazy Horse had done little more than add a dash of adventure to the Stanley and Baker expeditions. Their performance at Arrow and O'Fallon's creeks had failed to match their bombast. In both encounters they had fought in the traditional Indian way—exciting, colorful, and bold, but not effective against military units posted in defensive positions, especially infantry armed with long-range rifles. They could cut off and kill careless stragglers and steal horses, mules, and beef cattle. But only occasionally could they raise more than a harassing opposition to so formidable an undertaking as a transcontinental railroad.

"This railroad is a national enterprise," General William Tecumseh Sherman told Congress in March 1873, "and we are forced to protect the men during its survey and construction, through, probably, the most warlike nation of Indians on this continent, who will fight for every foot of the line."[8] He had already moved to strengthen the military forces on the upper Missouri. That summer the Northern Pacific's railhead touched the river, and the town of Bismarck sprang up on the east bank. Across the river a fine new post, Fort Abraham Lincoln, rose from a valley five miles downstream. It would shelter part of the mounted troops the army had finally decided to send up the Missouri. They were the Seventh Cavalry, commanded by Lieutenant Colonel George Armstrong Custer. Noting his red-gold hair falling almost to his shoulders, the Indians called him Long Hair.

Long Hair's soldiers formed part of still another survey expedition, again commanded by Colonel Stanley. They pushed west from Fort Rice on June 20, 1873.[9]

The Sioux did not spot the invaders until they reached the Yellowstone early in August and began to march up the north bank toward the mouth of the Tongue. Some four hundred lodges of Hunkpapas and Miniconjous, with Sitting Bull in residence, were camped in the very path of the military column. Alerted to the approach of soldiers, they contrived a more serious attack than the previous summer. On August 4 a decoy party of about one hundred warriors made themselves known to two companies of cavalry scouting far in advance of the main column. Custer himself commanded. He allowed himself to be drawn almost, but not quite, into the trap, then withdrew into a grove of timber and held off his assailants until Stanley came to the rescue.

Fearful of a cavalry attack on their village, the Hunkpapas and Miniconjous moved hastily up the valley. Frank Grouard, the Grabber, was in the camp. "The soldiers expected to fight," Grouard remembered, "and we were making preparations to protect the women and children if they should attack. I could distinctly hear the band playing. It was years since I had heard a band. They were playing Custer's favorite battle tune. That was 'Garry Owen.' "[10]

The Sioux outran the cavalry, even though Custer pushed his men in a forced march of thirty-six hours. Near the mouth of the Bighorn the Indians packed their belongings into bull boats, circular frames of willow covered with buffalo hide, and swam their horses across the Yellowstone. They did this expertly, even though the river ran swift and deep. When their pursuers arrived on the riverbank on August 10, they tried to follow but could not reach the other side.

After recruiting more Miniconjous, Oglalas, Sans Arcs, and Cheyennes from a large camp on the lower Bighorn, Sitting Bull and his men returned to the Yellowstone the next day, August 11. Posting themselves in the timber on the south bank opposite the cavalry bivouac, they

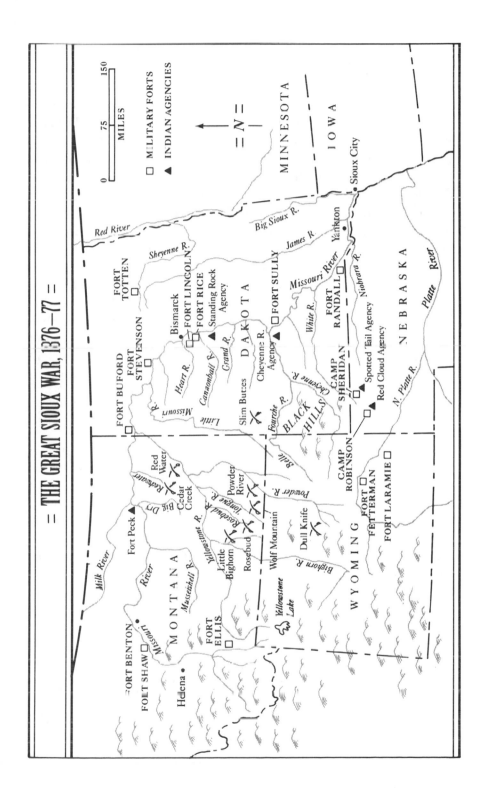

== THE GREAT SIOUX WAR, 1876—77 ==

opened a blistering fire on the enemy. The troopers fired back, and the exchange dragged on through most of the day. In the afternoon, parties of Sioux crossed the river above and below the soldiers' position. Mounted cavalry advanced to meet them and fought sharp skirmishes until the Indians fell back. Again they could hear the music the Grabber later identified as "Garry Owen."

When Stanley's infantry arrived on the scene, he had cannon run close to the shore and trained on the timber across the river. Exploding shells flushed the sharpshooters posted there, and the battle drew to a close.[11]

Both Sitting Bull and White Bull watched the fight from the heights on the south side of the Yellowstone. They were "in reserve" that day, explained White Bull, so they did not cross the river and take part in the fighting.[12]

After the Battle of the Yellowstone, the Hunkpapas pulled off to the south, up the Bighorn, and lost touch with the soldiers. A few warriors, however, watched the expedition move on up the Yellowstone and then turn north to the Musselshell. On August 16 six of them spotted a group of infantrymen frolicking in the Yellowstone. Riding down to the riverbank, the Sioux fired a volley that splashed the water harmlessly and scattered naked soldiers up the opposite bank.

On that note the Lakotas ended their latest encounter with the railroad builders and their blue-clad guardians. It turned out to be their last encounter, for the Northern Pacific Railroad abruptly ceased to be a pressing issue. The Panic of 1873 stopped the rails at Bismarck, on the Missouri's east bank. Not until six years later, long after clashes over other issues swept the Yellowstone Valley free of all Sioux, did the company revive, bridge the Missouri, and point west across Dakota to Montana.

The Northern Pacific quickly faded from the Lakotas' list of grievances. They had vowed to fight the railroad, and in four inconclusive battles and a few skirmishes they had. So far as a single chief embodied the spirit of resistance to the railroad, Sitting Bull merited the distinction. He had fought Baker, Stanley, and Custer and shared conspicuously in the verbal bravado that so alarmed white officialdom. That the Indians' battlefield performance failed to measure up to the rhetoric or the alarm occurred to neither side.

The Indian resolve, however, was never put to a fair test. Financial buccaneering on Wall Street rather than a few feeble Indian attacks threw the Northern Pacific into its six-year paralysis. How the Indians might have responded to grades, ties, and rails befouling the Yellowstone Valley while they still ruled may be glimpsed in the events of 1876. The warlike nation that General Sherman foresaw contesting every foot of the line would doubtless have reacted instantly, and open war would have come two years earlier than it did.

Sitting Bull's highly visible part in the fights with Baker, Stanley, and Custer gave him further prominence in the white world. More than ever he was seen as the leading "hostile" chief. No longer, after the fights of 1873, did white officials talk of coaxing Sitting Bull in and making a treaty with him.

PAHA SAPA, "Hills that are Black," the Sioux called the dark mountain mass that rose four thousand feet above the yellow plains in the western third of the Great Sioux Reservation. They esteemed the hills as a "Meat Pack," rich in small game, with sheltered valleys and abundant firewood, ideal for winter camping. Blanketed with thick stands of lodgepole pine, the hills also offered an excellent source of fine tipi poles.

In talks with white officials, Lakotas left no doubt that they placed high value on the Black Hills. Aside from their utilitarian attractions, a vague mystique hung over them. Some tribesmen hinted at a mild dread of the region, others at a sacred character residing in its craggy recesses. Usually the Sioux entered the Black Hills in family groups or small bands. Rarely did large numbers camp there. While the open plains and their wooded stream bottoms remained the favored location for band and tribal gatherings, that did not diminish the keen sense of possession with which the Sioux looked on *Paha Sapa*.

For his part, Sitting Bull regarded the Black Hills as a kind of reserve storehouse, to be tapped in times of want. As the Oglala Standing Elk remembered, "I heard Sitting Bull say that the Black Hills was just like a food pack and therefore the Indians should stick to it." Standing Elk, fifteen in 1875, puzzled over Sitting Bull's meaning until it came to him: "Indians would rove all around, but when they were in need of something they could just go in there and get it."[13]

Rumors of gold in the Black Hills had periodically tantalized white Americans and stirred boomlets in frontier towns. But the region remained unexplored and unknown, the haunt of Indians who turned aside all comers or made certain none who entered succeeded in leaving.

By the 1870s, however, whites had come to look covetously on the Black Hills. Dakota Territory had been organized in 1861, with immigrants settling in the extreme southeastern corner around Yankton and at Bismarck on the upper Missouri. Iowans and Nebraskans added their demands. Along the eastern and southern rims of the Great Sioux Reservation, "Dakota promoters" trumpeted the Black Hills as essential to the territory's prosperity, and the legislature petitioned the federal government for a geological survey to investigate the persistent rumors.

In July 1874 Long Hair Custer led his Long Knives out of Fort Abraham Lincoln and struck southwest to explore the Black Hills. The ostensible purpose of the expedition was to locate a suitable site for a fort to watch over the Indians at the Red Cloud and Spotted Tail agencies. But Custer took along a pair of "practical miners" and a bevy of newspaper correspondents whose presence suggested another purpose as well. As soldiers had appeared on Elk River three years earlier, so now they appeared in the very heart of *Paha Sapa*.[14]

The Custer Expedition remained in the field for almost two months. But even before the cavalrymen returned to Fort Abraham Lincoln, a courier had ridden out of the hills with news of the discovery of gold. "From the grass roots down it was 'pay dirt,' " cheered the *Chicago Inter-Ocean*.

Men ruined by the depression rushed to jumping-off points on the Missouri and the Platte rivers. Companies organized to hurry to the mineral district, others to outfit them. One party actually reached the hills during the autumn of 1874 and threw up a stockade to sit out the winter. Bismarck, Yankton, Sioux City, Omaha, and other frontier towns vied with one another in boosterism.

Predictably, the Sioux complained bitterly about Long Hair's soldiers in *Paha Sapa*. Most of the protests came from the agency Indians, who were closer to the event and more familiar with the Treaty of 1868. The hunting bands reacted more slowly, but ultimately with nearly as much vehemence.[15]

OUT ON THE Yellowstone and far up the Missouri, the hunting bands, while angry over the Black Hills, nursed other concerns as well. Topping the list, not surprisingly, were the Crows. Even before the railroad threat receded, Crows engrossed Sitting Bull more than whites.

Along the Bighorn River frontier, actually inside the Crow reservation defined by the Treaty of 1868, Sioux and Crow battled repeatedly in large-scale collisions. At the same time, raiding parties thrust deep into each other's territory in quest of coups, scalps, and ponies.

This intertribal warfare, however, no longer involved only the Sioux and the Crows. Now it occasionally spilled over onto whites—at the Crow

Agency; among the scattering of wolfers, trappers, and traders filtering into the upper Yellowstone Valley; and even around the farming community of Bozeman in the Gallatin Valley.

Sitting Bull could rationalize the activities of his warriors on the upper Yellowstone with his defensive policy. Raids against the Crows were an integral part of Sioux ways and had been as long as anyone could remember. If whites exposed themselves by building and operating an agency for the Crows, or even by trapping or trading on the edges of Crow territory, they could not expect young men on a war expedition to give much thought to exemptions. And if on occasion the raiders pushed beyond Crow country and ran off stock from the Gallatin Valley, that was an unfortunate violation of policy, but young men had always defied the wishes of their elders.

For the Lakotas, the lightning rod was the Crow Agency. A succession of agents called repeatedly for soldiers to defend it. But the army protested that the small garrison at Fort Ellis could not spare the men and thought, anyway, that the Crows themselves ought to furnish protection. "The Indians seem determined to take the place," the agent reported in July 1874, after two weeks of daily harassment. "We will do all we can to hold it."[16]

The problem grew still more pressing in June 1875. To detach the Crows from the pernicious influence of whiskey shops on the Yellowstone River, the agent moved the agency to a site fourteen miles south of the Yellowstone at the forks of the Stillwater River and Rosebud Creek (not the Rosebud east of the Bighorn). Now ninety miles instead of forty from Fort Ellis, but still within Crow territory and the Crow Reservation, the new agency stood as an even greater temptation to the Lakotas. Throughout the summer war parties from Sitting Bull's camp struck at the construction site and the trains hauling building materials. Two white men lost their lives, and the agency lost all its beef cattle and draft animals.[17]

Sioux depredations on the upper Yellowstone spread alarm through the Gallatin Valley settlements. Cavalry patrols from Fort Ellis watched the mountain passes during the raiding season, and only once did a sizable war party slip through to justify the alarm by running off some horses near Bozeman. East of the mountains, however, scarcely twenty-five miles from Bozeman, whites increasingly lost stock and occasionally their lives to Sioux raiders. This kept tension high in Bozeman and inspired enough citizen petitions for more military protection to activate the volatile and voluble governor of Montana Territory, Benjamin F. Potts.

In letter after strident letter to Washington authorities, Governor Potts complained about Sioux aggressions against the Crow Agency, the scattering of white settlement on the upper Yellowstone, and the farmers of the Gallatin Valley. The government's defensive policy, he lectured the Commissioner of Indian Affairs in August 1874, "places the lives and property of our people at the mercy of 'Sitting Bull' and his band of murdering robbers who have never acknowledged the authority of the government over them or observed the stipulation of any treaty." Imperative, he believed, was an offensive campaign to follow Sitting Bull to his village and punish him and his people severely. A year later he was still bombarding Washington with appeals for decisive action.[18]

If Sitting Bull sometimes stretched his defensive policy with aggressions along the margins of Lakota territory, he could point to continuing white intrusions into the very heart of that territory. With the bankruptcy of the Northern Pacific Railroad, soldiers no longer came to protect surveyors. But in 1874 and 1875 white citizens mounted two formidable invasions of the lands Sitting Bull had vowed with Crazy Horse to defend.

The first was the Yellowstone Wagon Road and Prospecting Expedition, a thinly disguised effort to find gold. It consisted of 150 men, mostly seasoned frontiersmen, armed with repeating rifles and two cannons, one an ancient smoothbore with canister rounds improvised from oyster tins, the other a brass howitzer with ammunition supplied by Governor Potts from the territorial arsenal. During late February 1874 "The Boys," as they called themselves, worked their way down the Yellowstone and, below the mouth of the Bighorn, crossed the river on the ice.[19]

The whites could hardly have conceived a more blatant provocation of the Sioux than this trespass. Sitting Bull's Hunkpapas, camped with Miniconjous of Makes Room and Flying By, sighted the procession as it cut across country from the Yellowstone to the lower Rosebud. Before daybreak on April 4, about thirty-two miles upstream from the mouth of the Rosebud, Sitting Bull led several hundred men to the attack.

In three battles during April, the Sioux attempted to destroy the interlopers, whose stock, firearms, and camp gear would have made prized possessions. In each, they suffered casualties and abandoned the field under the force of counterattacks. The first occurred on the Rosebud at the mouth of Greenleaf Creek, the second at the head of Sundance (later Reno) Creek, an eastern affluent of the Little Bighorn, and the third on Lodge Grass Creek, a western tributary of the Little Bighorn. In the last two, Hump's Miniconjous and Crazy Horse's Oglalas, attracted to the area by a large buffalo herd, joined the fray. In all, the Indians succeeded in killing one of the whites, thinning their stock herds, and finally, with material aid from foul spring weather, in so discouraging them that they went back to Bozeman. But the Sioux had paid heavily in dead and wounded.

These whites were more deadly adversaries than the soldiers. They were daring fighters and good shots, and they were clever. Many were wolfers or trappers, and after the first battle they left the campsite strewn with pemmican, biscuits, and beans laced with strychnine. But as No Flesh remembered, the Indians were suspicious and did not touch the food.

Not so the trap discovered in a camp on the Little Bighorn. The whites faked a grave, complete with grave board. A lanyard ran underground from the board to the friction primer of a howitzer shell, in turn blanketed with a layer of nails and bolts. When the Sioux moved in, a crowd gathered around the grave as High Bear, an Oglala, began to dig. Someone said the whites might have put something on the body that would fume and stifle the Indians, and they had better stand back. As they shuffled back, High Bear found the lanyard and, supposing it attached to a body, pulled. The grave exploded in a great cloud of dirt and debris, recalled Red Hawk, "knocking High Bear about two rods and filling all our eyes with dust." The bomb, said No Flesh, badly frightened everyone but killed no one.

The second intrusion sprang from another fanciful enterprise hatched in Bozeman. Fellows D. Pease, a veteran trader and former agent for the Crows, thought he could make peace between the Sioux and the Crows and tap the commerce of both at a trading post near the mouth of the Bighorn. Pease and forty-five followers selected a site on the north side of the Yellowstone almost on Custer's battleground of 1873, and in July 1875 they built several log huts connected by a palisade.

Pease should have known that the Sioux and the Crows were unlikely to meet in harmony on the neutral ground of his trading post. Indeed, at the very time his men labored to erect the buildings of Fort Pease, the two tribes (the Crows bolstered by Nez Perces from Idaho) fought another of the large-scale battles that were becoming increasingly common. This clash featured two days of sniping at each other across the Yellowstone River, followed by close combat on the south side scarcely five miles downstream from the fort. The Crows won, but the experience so unnerved them that they hastened off to the north. Sioux pursued, forcing another battle in which a leading Crow chief, Long Horse, was slain.[20]

For the Sioux, Fort Pease, flaunting its American flag above the stockade, represented another insulting trespass, this one apparently intended as permanent. They reacted as they had to Baker, Stanley, and Custer, to the Slotas of 1873, and to the Bozeman prospectors of 1874. Well into the winter of 1875–76, they held the post under close siege, killing six men and wounding eight in a series of incidents in the vicinity. Gradually the garrison dispersed, but a remnant hung on, and Fort Pease continued as an abrasive irritant in the midst of Lakota country.[21]

FOR MORE THAN five years Sitting Bull and the hunting bands that scorned the Treaty of 1868 had furnished just enough provocation to confirm the generals in their confident predictions of full-scale war. The fights with Baker, Stanley, and Custer seemed to validate General Sherman's prophesy that the Sioux would fight for every foot of the Northern Pacific's line. Even after the railroad subsided as an issue, the depredations on the upper Yellowstone kept tensions high. The adventures of the Bozeman prospectors and the builders of Fort Pease gave continuing emphasis to the hunting bands' hostility.

And yet the provocation owed more to verbal superlatives than actual performance. Governor Potts's appeals for help exaggerated the danger to the Gallatin Valley and the upper Yellowstone. The warnings of army officers at posts all around the Sioux country magnified both the intent and the capability of the Indians to make good their threats.

For their part, the Indian threats surpassed in rhetoric the diatribes of Governor Potts. The armed resistance actually offered to the Northern Pacific was a pale reflection of Spotted Eagle's vow to kill every railroad worker, or Sitting Bull's shouted promise at O'Fallon's Creek to bring together all the tribes of the northern Plains and wipe out the Stanley Expedition. After the danger of the railroad abated, the hunting bands reacted with vigor to the flagrant intrusions of the Bozeman prospectors and Fort Pease, but their attacks on the fringes of their territory, although inspiring sensational newspaper copy, were scattered and sporadic. In truth, even at the height of the Northern Pacific crisis, the Sioux, as always, were more preoccupied with Crows than with whites.

The Sioux had also indulged much rhetoric over soldiers in *Paha Sapa*. There too they had not backed their protests with action. The gold-seekers who defied the government's ban and slipped into the Black Hills encountered even less Indian menace than the Gallatin Valley settlers.

Moreover, the depredations that for years made travel on the Platte Road hazardous to life and property had almost ceased.

Yet because of rhetoric on both sides, fortified by enough violent incidents in Montana to provide a shaky credibility, both civil and military officials expected open war with the Sioux. The deepening dilemma of the Black Hills, lashing the government with political imperatives irreconcilable with moral imperatives, finally made the expectation self-fulfilling.

10 WAR

THE SIOUX and the Cheyennes hunted together and fought together, and they maintained a relationship intimate enough to allow the Lakotas to consider the Cheyennes Lakota. This affinity existed, however, mainly between the Cheyennes and the Miniconjous and Oglalas. "We never had associated closely with the Uncpapas," the Cheyenne Wooden Leg recalled. "They were almost strangers to us. We knew of them only by hearsay from the Ogallalas and the Minneconjoux."[1]

In the summer of 1875 Sitting Bull moved to close the gap. The rising white pressures on the Sioux and Cheyenne ranges suggested the need for more unity. While all the hunting bands still were preoccupied with the Crows and other enemy tribes, white soldiers had probed their lands too often to be forgotten. The Black Hills, explored by soldiers and now invaded by miners despite the government's ban, remained an open sore. The chiefs decided to join in one great sun dance to forge bonds between the Hunkpapas and the Northern Cheyennes.

The participants laid out four tribal circles on the middle Rosebud at the mouth of Muddy Creek. Present were Hunkpapas of Sitting Bull, Oglalas of Black Twin and Crazy Horse, Sans Arcs of Spotted Eagle, Miniconjous, and the Northern Cheyennes of Little Wolf and the holy man Ice (or White Bull).[2]

After the sun-dance lodge had been raised, Sitting Bull performed a special dance, full of holy symbolism and resonating with the themes of intertribal unity and triumphant conquest. It represented Sitting Bull at the peak of his political, military, and spiritual powers.[3]

Sitting Bull approached the sun-dance lodge astride a magnificent black war horse Ice had presented to him. Jagged streaks of white clay ran from the animal's rump down the right hip and leg, and from the root of each ear to the corners of the mouth. From the shoulders back to the rider's legs clustered white dots, representing hail.

Clad only in breechcloth, moccasins, and war bonnet, Sitting Bull was painted over his entire body with brilliant yellow clay. Black paint covered the lower half of his face, supporting a broad black streak that touched the corners of his eyes and ran across the forehead. Black bands circled his wrists and ankles. A round black disk on his chest represented the sun, a black crescent on his right shoulder blade the moon.

Dismounting but leading his horse, Sitting Bull danced into the lodge and around the circle to the back, then forward to the center pole and back to the rear. He called out, "I wish my friends to fill one pipe and I wish my people to fill one pipe."

This meant that the Cheyennes and Hunkpapas should fill pipes and smoke together in token of a pledge to act together. Black Crane, a Cheyenne, filled one pipe, a Hunkpapa another. Sitting Bull took Black Crane's pipe in his right hand and the Hunkpapa's in his left and motioned each to stand beside him. While the people in the lodge sang, Sitting Bull extended the two pipes toward the pole and, still holding his horse, danced forward to the pole, then back to the rear, the horse following. This he repeated several times as he made motions representing an approach on an enemy.

Now and then he spoke. Once he said, "I have nearly got them," meaning his enemies. On three successive approaches he pantomimed drawing his enemies toward him, but each time he retreated. On the fourth approach he swept his arms through the air and closed them over his chest. He had surrounded his enemies and had them in his power. Lifting the two pipes to the sky in offering to *Wakantanka*, he declared, "We have them. The Great Spirit has given our enemy into our power."

A song and dance of triumph and thanksgiving ended the ceremony. Sitting Bull intoned: "The Great Spirit has given our enemies to us. We are to destroy them. We do not know who they are. They may be soldiers."

And as Ice observed too, "No one then knew who the enemy were—of what tribe."

The identity of the enemy grew clearer within a few weeks. The village had moved south across the Wolf Mountains to the upper Tongue River. There, in August 1875, a delegation of one hundred agency Indians, accompanied by two mixed-blood government employees, rode in with an invitation to go down to Red Cloud Agency and talk with commissioners of the Great Father about selling the Black Hills.

To Sitting Bull's surprise, one of the delegation was none other than Frank Grouard, the Grabber, whom he had not seen for two years.

The brotherhood of Sitting Bull with Grouard had proved less enduring than that with Jumping Bull. In the spring of 1873 Grouard told Sitting Bull he was going on a horse-stealing foray, then instead paid a visit to the Fort Peck trading post before returning to camp. Sitting Bull learned of the deception and in his fury vowed to kill Grouard. Neither the support of factions opposed to Sitting Bull nor the peace-making efforts of Good Feather and Her-Holy-Door appeased the chief's wrath. The conflict festered for several months, with the threat of death hanging constantly over the Grabber. Finally, in the autumn of 1873, he slipped out of Sitting Bull's village and took refuge with the Oglalas.

For nearly two years Grouard served the Oglala chiefs as he had Sitting Bull, as an able warrior and loyal counselor on the mysterious ways of the whites. The village contained most of the Oglala stalwarts, including Crazy Horse. With him Grouard formed a close and sympathetic relationship. As the months went by, he became more and more acculturated as a Lakota warrior, and more and more an expert on the customs and personalities of his adoptive people.

But the old ties to the white world tugged. In the autumn of 1874 the Grabber rode down to Red Cloud Agency to look around. He spent the winter with the Oglalas but in the spring returned to the agency. Still undecided about his future, he joined the delegation, headed by Man-Afraid-of-His-Horses, the agent sent to coax the hunting bands in for a talk, which would be held in September 1875 at Red Cloud.[4]

As soon as Sitting Bull learned of the Grabber's presence in the village, he sent for him. Wisely, Grouard brought Crazy Horse along to make certain Sitting Bull did not try to settle old scores.

In a series of questions, Sitting Bull sought to learn what lay behind the invitation to the council at Red Cloud. "I told him just what I came for and informed him that the best thing he could do was to go in and see what they wanted at Red Cloud Agency," Grouard recalled. "You will hear what I have to say at the council," declared Sitting Bull, ending the meeting.

The next morning all the men formed a great circle in the center of the village, and all who wished to speak gave their views. Big Breast spoke first, averring that he would not go in and would never sell his land. "All those that are in favor of selling their land from their children," he concluded, "let them go."

> Sitting Bull then got up and made a long speech [remembered Grouard]. It had the same purport. He said he would not sell his land. He said he had never been to an agency and was not going in. He was no agency Indian. He told me to go out and tell the white men at Red Cloud that he declared open war and would fight them wherever he met them from that time on. His entire harangue was an open declaration of war.

Crazy Horse and his fellow chiefs also refused to go in. In fact, very few from the village joined the delegates, possibly in fear of the *akicita*. And apparently with good reason, for either the *akicita* or a less formal faction schemed to kill the delegates and any defectors who joined them in their camp across the river. But Crazy Horse learned of the plot, summoned the leaders, and served notice that when men came with the tobacco of peace, they must be received hospitably. "My friends," he said, "whoever attempts to murder these people will have to fight me, too."[5]

FOR THE GOVERNMENT, the council at Red Cloud Agency climaxed a year of confusion, controversy, and indecision over the Black Hills. Throughout the winter of 1874–75, military patrols had sought to keep prospectors out of the hills. They enjoyed some success, but clearly their hearts were not in the mission.

Meanwhile, the government tried to "extinguish Indian title" to the Black Hills. The effort concentrated on the agency chiefs, for the hunting bands had no contact with white officials. Even the tenuous connections with Black Moon and Sitting Bull based on Milk River Agency at Fort Peck had collapsed by 1875.

That the hunting bands did not talk to white officials did not mean they lacked influence with the chiefs who did, as the members of the Allison Commission who gathered at Red Cloud Agency in September 1875 discovered. Despite the resistance of Sitting Bull and Crazy Horse, about four hundred "northern Indians" finally came down for the council. Amid ten thousand agency Indians, they formed a small minority, but a rowdy one. On September 23 Little-Big-Man, an Oglala shirt wearer from Crazy Horse's camp, led a mock charge of warriors toward the commission. Stripped and painted, yipping and firing rifles in the air, they badly frightened everyone, whites and Indians alike. Little-Big-Man also blustered that he had been sent by Sitting Bull to prevent the loss of the Black Hills and would shoot anyone who signed an agreement.[6]

After the council in which he rejected the invitation to go to Red Cloud Agency, Sitting Bull and the Hunkpapas moved to the mouth of the Powder. There he received old Lone Horn of the Miniconjous. Lone Horn had attended the council at Red Cloud and, as the people gathered to listen, told about the commissioners' effort to talk the people into parting with the Black Hills. Red Cloud and Spotted Tail, Lone Horn said, had been willing, but he had scolded them.

"Don't you know there are more people out than here?" he asked, referring to the absent hunting bands. They should take part in the decision. In any event, he added, ridiculing the terms on which the agency chiefs stood ready to sign, "you are very cheap."

"How!" Sitting Bull responded. "Brother, it is well that you have said that; these hills are a treasure to us Indians. That is the food pack of the people and when the poor have nothing to eat we can all go there and have something to eat, and it is well that you have said this."[7]

The reply highlighted the growing divergence of values between the agency chiefs and the hunting band leaders. At Red Cloud, the negotiators had argued over how much the Indians should be paid for the gold in the Black Hills. Sitting Bull cared nothing for gold. The "food pack"— and the land itself—gave the hills their value.

From the Hunkpapa camp, Lone Horn made his way to Cheyenne River Agency. Of all the Lakota chiefs, he had been the most successful in leading a double life. In 1856 General Harney had recognized his true status by appointing him head chief of the Miniconjous, and ever since he had represented his people in deliberations with white officials. At the same time, he had frequently lived with the hunting bands and shared fully in their activities, including war. Their chiefs accorded him high respect. That winter the venerable old man died—of grief over the Black Hills, his people said.

Frustrated and angry, the Allison commissioners returned to Washington bristling with antagonism. In their report they urged Congress to fix a fair value for the Black Hills and "then notify the Sioux Nation of its conclusions," which should be "presented to the Indians as a finality." The four years of rations and annuities provided by the Treaty of 1868 had expired; if the Indians balked, therefore, all issues should be cut off. Moreover, thought the commissioners, no settlement seemed likely until the Sioux felt the power of the United States.

With the failure of the Allison Commission, the Grant administration faced an impossible dilemma. The electorate demanded the opening of the Black Hills, and close to fifteen thousand miners were already working the diggings. The army had no stomach for keeping them out and made only token efforts. Yet in every legal and moral sense the Sioux owned the Black Hills, and no white man had a right to be there. The Allison Commission had failed to "extinguish Indian title," and political imperatives allowed no time for another attempt. The nation's honor demanded that treaty promises be kept or their violation rationalized.

In a rare concert of opinion, all elements of government agreed on the solution—war. On November 3, 1875, senior generals and Indian officials met secretly with President Grant at the White House and worked out a plan. The meeting produced two presidential decisions. First, although the orders to bar miners from the Black Hills would remain in effect, the army would no longer enforce them. Second, the troublesome hunting bands would be compelled to abandon the unceded territory and settle on the reservation. Both decisions attacked the stubborn issue of title, the first by filling up the Black Hills with white settlers, the second by curbing the independence of the Sitting Bull bands and thus their power to obstruct the sale of the hills.

Ostensibly the war against the hunting bands had nothing to do with the Black Hills. It was justified by the greatly overstated depredations against Montanans on the upper Yellowstone and in raids on friendly Indians such as the Crows and Rees. These violations of the Treaty of 1868 legitimized war against people who had never subscribed to that treaty. Even if they had, the treaty sanctioned their indefinite residence in the unceded territory and contained no warrant for forcing them out.

Six days after the White House meeting, an Indian inspector recently returned from the upper Missouri submitted a report that provided the basis for carrying out the presidential decision. Characterizing the Sitting Bull bands as wild, hostile, lofty, independent, arrogant, defiant, and contemptuous of government authority, he alluded to their raids on white settlers and peaceful Indians and concluded: "The true policy, in my judgment, is to send troops against them in winter, the sooner the better, and *whip* them into subjection." The "true policy," of course, had just been decided by the president, and without much question this document was fashioned as the instrument for launching that policy.[8]

The basic war aim was to neutralize the independent "hostiles" by merging them with their dependent brethren on the Great Sioux Reservation. To soften the appearance of naked aggression, Indian Office authorities decided that, before unleashing the military, they should notify the hunting bands to report to their agencies. On December 6, therefore, the Commissioner of Indian Affairs directed the Sioux agents to send runners to the winter camps in the unceded territory with an ultimatum: Come to an agency by January 31, 1876, or the soldiers would march against them.

OUT IN THE Yellowstone country, oblivious to the forces gathering against them, the objects of these bureaucratic machinations pursued their usual winter routine. Sitting Bull and the Hunkpapas wintered on the Yellowstone near the mouth of the Powder, his people visiting and trading at Forts Peck and Berthold. Miniconjous, Sans Arcs, and Cheyennes wintered farther west, on Tongue River, and kept up the pressure on Fort Pease, the beleagured trading post opposite the mouth of the Bighorn. The fort's residents had given up all pretense of trading with Indians, and it served as a base for wolfers. By February 1876 the Sioux investment had so strangled the fort that appeals were sent to Bozeman for a military rescue. Major James Brisbin led a column of cavalry down the Yellowstone from Fort Ellis, reaching Fort Pease on March 4 to find nineteen of the original forty-six men cowering inside the stockade. Turning back upriver, he left behind an empty post, its flag defiantly flapping from the flag staff, to guard the north bank of the Yellowstone.[9]

The Miniconjous and Cheyennes who had besieged Fort Pease moved east to the Powder. By early March 1876 all the hunting bands were scattered in small camps along the Powder and its eastern tributaries.[10]

Most had already learned of the government's ultimatum to go to the agencies. Probably it puzzled more than angered the tribes. Except for Fort Pease, none of the chiefs had plans for war against anyone but Crows. They had no sense of impending war with the whites and thus did not understand the ultimatum as portending war. In Indian conceptions of time, moreover, a deadline such as January 31, 1876, carried no urgency and indeed no meaning. In truth, the chiefs simply did not know what to make of this missive, delivered at such peril by couriers braving deep snow and bitter cold.

Few of the runners brought back an answer from the hunting bands. One who did gave a report that suggests a typical reaction. The Indians, he said, received the message in good spirit and without ill feeling. They said they were now hunting buffalo and could not conveniently accept the invitation. Early in the spring, however, they would come in to trade their robes, and at that time their future could be thoroughly discussed. They were peaceful, they contended, and had no intention of going to war with the whites.[11]

Almost certainly this represented the thinking of the hunting bands as they pondered the message brought by the couriers in the dead of winter. They were a free and independent people, following their way of life as they had for generations. That any alien power could presume to enforce such an order, or had any reason to issue such an order, would have struck them as preposterous. Instead they looked on it as an invitation, one such as had sought their presence at Red Cloud for the Allison Commission, or at Fort Rice to talk with peace commissioners. They would heed the invitation when and if convenient.

Mixed signals came from Sitting Bull. A visitor to his camp in February reported him talking of making war as long as he lived and vowing to "die on a good American horse, fighting the whites." But this was characteristic rhetoric, meaningful only in terms of the defensive war he and Crazy Horse had agreed to conduct against intrusions such as Fort Pease. A more accurate reflection of his state of mind was reported by a Hidatsa who visited him in March. Sitting Bull betrayed no apprehension of hostilities with the government and said he had been peaceable all winter. He wanted to go to trade with the Berthold Indians and sent in five Hunkpapas to see if he would be received in safety.[12]

ONE OF THE winter camps lay on the west bank of the Powder about 140 miles above its mouth, only a few miles from the Wyoming border. More than a hundred tipis rose from the snow-covered river bottom. A tangle of bluffs and hogbacks lifted steeply from the valley on the west. The village consisted of about sixty lodges of Northern Cheyennes, the bands of Old Bear, Box Elder, and Black Eagle. The rest were He Dog's Oglalas and some Miniconjous. Altogether, the camp contained about 735 people, including 210 fighting men.[13]

At daybreak on March 17, 1876, with the temperature forty to fifty degrees below zero and a thick ice fog hanging over the valley, soldiers on white horses stormed into the village, pistols popping. Indians worked frantically to free themselves from tipis fastened tightly against the cold. Some even cut their way out with knives. Just from their sleeping robes and scantily clad, men, women, and children ran in all directions trying to escape the horsemen. Men grabbed their weapons and ran to secure their horses, only to find that other soldiers had already seized half the herd.

The warriors quickly rallied and took station among the rugged breaks on the west edge of the village. From there they sent a deadly fire among the tipis as the soldiers tried to burn all the Indians' possessions. Shortly after noon, with four dead and six wounded, the troops pulled out of the smoldering village.

The Indians had suffered only light casualties—one Sioux and one Cheyenne dead and several wounded. A blind old woman had been left in her tipi, but the soldiers, after questioning her, left her unharmed. A grievous loss, half the pony herd, turned out to be no loss at all, for that night warriors following the retreating column found the captured animals unguarded and recovered nearly all.

The true loss lay in the destruction of about half the village, casting the Indians destitute on the snowy land in bitter cold. Short on food, clothing, and shelter, they struggled down the Powder, seeking relief first with Crazy Horse, then Sitting Bull. After terrible hardship and suffering, they found with Sitting Bull a generous welcome that they never forgot.

The soldier attack on the Powder River village stunned the hunting bands. Even if they fully understood the government's ultimatum, they had not taken it seriously. They thought they were at peace, but now, unmistakably, the soldiers had declared war.

A Miniconjou who left Sitting Bull's camp on April 9 brought word to Cheyenne River Agency of the mood among the hunting bands. They were thoroughly roused, he said, and talked of striking the whites in an attack as complete as the one that had caught them on Powder River. Chiefs previously opposed to war now harangued their young men to attack undefended trading posts and obtain the arms and ammunition needed to wage all-out war.[14]

For Sitting Bull there was a special irony in the Powder River affair. The soldiers had reached the village by a night march on an Indian trail so faint that only one of the civilian scouts could follow it. But for him, all agreed, the soldiers probably would not have found their objective. He was Frank Grouard, the Grabber.

"One time that man should have been killed and I kept him," said Sitting Bull, "and now he has joined the soldiers. He is no good and should be killed."

As White Bull commented, Grouard was the only white man who ever fooled Sitting Bull, and he fooled the whole tribe.[15]

11 SOLDIERS UPSIDE DOWN

AT POWDER RIVER military leaders thought they had struck a blow at Crazy Horse himself. They had not done even that, and almost nothing else about the Battle of Powder River pleased them. General George Crook commanded the expedition, but he had entrusted the night march and dawn attack to Colonel Joseph J. Reynolds, an aged warrior who did not stand up to the rigors of winter campaigning. Reflecting his weak leadership, subordinates failed to perform well, and when the command pulled out of the village shortly after noon on March 17, 1876, no one felt victorious. The loss of the captured pony herd that night was a final humiliation. Dejected, the column turned back to Fort Fetterman, on the North Platte River.

The war against the hunting bands had been launched on February 1, 1876, the day after the Indian Office's ultimatum expired. General Philip H. Sheridan oversaw the offensive from his Chicago headquarters, but its execution fell to subordinate generals, George Crook in Omaha and Alfred H. Terry in St. Paul. Crook, his base at Fort Fetterman close to the Union Pacific Railway, marched, as planned, while winter still lay on the plains. On March 26, however, after the fiasco at Powder River, his ravaged command limped back into Fort Fetterman to refit. For his part, Terry could not be ready until spring thawed the Missouri River and opened the Northern Pacific. Sheridan's winter campaign turned into a spring campaign. Soon it would become a summer campaign.[1]

With Crook moving from the south, Terry planned to converge on the Yellowstone Basin from east and west. Colonel John Gibbon would lead the western column, based at Fort Ellis. The main thrust would originate at Fort Abraham Lincoln, with Custer in command. But the flamboyant cavalier got into political trouble that spring and nearly missed the campaign altogether. In the end, as directed by President Grant himself, Terry had to command the Fort Lincoln column in person, with Custer accompanying him in a subordinate capacity. Not until May 17 did this force get away. And not until May 29 did Crook complete the refitting of his expedition and again march north from Fort Fetterman.

AS APRIL BEGAN, winter still gripped the Powder Valley, although a thaw several days after the soldiers declared war had turned the blanket of snow to mud and melted the ice in the streams. Another storm had followed at the end of March.

Sitting Bull's village stood at the head of Spring Creek near the foot of Chalk Butte, an elevation on the divide between the Powder and the Little Missouri. One hundred lodges sheltered Hunkpapas and Miniconjous. They had passed most of the winter near the mouth of the Powder and only recently had moved eighty miles upriver. Some had turned east to trade at Fort Berthold.

About April 1 the victims of the soldiers' dawn attack sixty miles farther up the Powder reached Sitting Bull's village. They had found some relief with Crazy Horse on a branch of the Little Powder, but his village numbered no more than thirty lodges and could not meet all their wants. Alarmed at the soldiers' invasion, Crazy Horse's Oglala followers and a few Cheyennes who camped with him struck their tipis and joined the refugees in seeking Sitting Bull. Their advent swelled his village to 235 lodges.[2]

Sitting Bull's Hunkpapas more than lived up to the cardinal virtue of generosity. No sooner had the procession from the south been sighted than the women set kettles of meat to boiling. The men raised two large lodges in the center of the camp and arranged the newcomers in a circle around the inner walls. Women brought pot after pot of meat until the guests could eat no more. Other people came bearing gifts—robes, blankets, clothing, cooking utensils, horses, tipis. "Oh, what good hearts they had!" recalled Wooden Leg. "I never can forget the generosity of Sitting Bull's Uncpapa Sioux on that day."[3]

The chiefs met in council to decide what to do. There could not have been much debate. "At this great council, such as I have only seen once," related Cheyenne war chief Two Moons, "all agreed to stay together and fight."[4]

Here was exactly the condition foreseen when Sitting Bull and Crazy Horse agreed to fight only defensive war. The soldiers had started a war, and surely they would return to continue it. In unity lay strength, and all the hunting bands must gather to present the strongest defense.

There were not many people in these bands—far fewer than the whites, given to exaggeration, supposed. In all the unceded territory, the number of Lakotas and Cheyennes who rarely or never went to an agency did not exceed 3,400 people, including possibly 1,000 fighting men, in about 500 lodges. With 154 lodges, the Hunkpapas were the most numerous, followed by 100 Cheyennes, 70 Oglalas, 55 each of Sans Arcs and Miniconjous, and a few Blackfeet and Brules. Also in the unceded territory were the ubiquitous Dakota refugees from Minnesota, still defiant and still following the lead of the intractable Inkpaduta. A handful of like-minded Yanktonais usually traveled with him.

For both Sitting Bull and his adversaries, the big unknown in the equation was how many agency Indians would come out for the summer. Regardless of the number, they could not arrive until the spring grasses were high enough to nourish the ponies.

Meanwhile, the hunting bands would hang together and pull in the scattered winter camps. The migration of the buffalo would govern the direction of the march, which at this time of the year usually drew the Indians west, up the Yellowstone. The larger the village grew, the more often it would have to move, for grass, firewood, and game could not sustain large numbers in one place for long.

Sitting Bull assumed a commanding role, with Crazy Horse firmly backing him. This was the first time since they had formulated their defensive policy five years earlier that the soldiers had mounted an offensive directly threatening the Sioux and Cheyennes in their homeland. Earlier encounters had centered on the Northern Pacific Railroad. Powder River made unmistakably plain that the soldiers aimed at no mere railroad line but the people themselves. All looked to Sitting Bull for leadership.

Wooden Leg explained why:

He had come now into admiration by all Indians as a man whose medicine was good—that is, as a man having a kind heart and good judgment as to the best course of conduct. He was considered as being altogether brave, but peaceable. He was strong in religion—the Indian religion. He made medicine many times. He prayed and fasted and whipped his flesh into submission to the will of the Great Medicine. So, in attaching ourselves to the Uncpapas we other tribes were not moved by a desire to fight. They had not invited us. They simply welcomed us. We supposed that the combined camps would frighten off the soldiers. We hoped thus to be freed from their annoyance. Then we could separate again into the tribal bands and resume our quiet wandering and hunting.[5]

Throughout April and May the hunting bands gathered. By the middle of April, the village numbered 360 lodges. By mid-May more Hunkpapas and Cheyennes had joined, together with some Blackfeet and Inkpaduta's 15 lodges of Dakotas and Yanktonais, swelling the camp to 431 lodges. By early June it numbered 461.

By this time the village had crossed the Powder and Tongue to the lower Rosebud. It traveled in six separate tribal circles, each laid out with an opening to the east, each with its arc of tipis all opening to the east. By agreement of the council of chiefs, the Cheyennes invariably led the procession, selected the camping place, and planted their circle at the leading end of the village. With 100 lodges, they were second in strength only to the Hunkpapas, and they looked to an array of distinguished chiefs, including Box Elder, Old Bear, Black Eagle, Lame-White-Man, and Dirty Moccasins. The Hunkpapas of Black Moon and Sitting Bull, with 154 lodges, always brought up the rear and camped at the trailing end of the village. Between these two positions of greatest responsibility and danger, the other tribes pitched their tipis in tribal circles located irregularly to conform to the terrain: 70 Oglala lodges of Big Road and Crazy Horse; 55 Miniconjous of Lame Deer, Fast Bull, and Hump; another 55 Sans Arcs of Spotted Eagle; and 12 Blackfeet of Kill Eagle. Inkpaduta's followers formed part of the Hunkpapa circle.[6]

At each campsite, the village remained for two to five days, until grass and firewood had been consumed. Then the chiefs met in council and, on the basis of reports of buffalo brought by scouts, moved to another location. From the camps on both the Tongue and the Rosebud, hunters attacked the herds the scouts discovered and came back with stores of meat that turned the hunger of winter into the feasting of summer. Women prepared robes for trade and fashioned new lodge poles from the timber on the divides between the rivers.

As late as mid-June, well up the Rosebud, the village still consisted largely of year-round hunting bands. Some agency people had arrived, but not many. The number of summer visitors remained uncertain. The first hint of green grass did not appear until the last week of April, and not until the end of May did the prairies blossom enough to allow normal travel. The few lodges that joined from the agencies balanced the few that broke off to trade at Fort Peck or Berthold. The village held steady at more or less 460 lodges, housing about 3,000 people, including about 800 fighting men.

Consistent with the policy of Sitting Bull and Crazy Horse, the chiefs in council had agreed not to look for a fight. The soldiers had declared war, but the Indians would fight only if directly assailed. Sitting Bull did not want to fight, White Bull declared, but would if attacked. Generally chiefs counseled against fighting unless the enemy threatened the women and children, he said. Then they would fight to the death. "Our combination of camps was simply for defense," explained Wooden Leg. "The chiefs and old men all urged us to keep away from the white men."[7]

But as Wooden Leg added, "Many young men were anxious to go for fighting the soldiers." As usually happened, the young men heeded different instincts than their leaders.

Early in May the young men had their first chance, when scouts—"wolves," they were called—discovered soldiers on the north side of the Yellowstone opposite the mouth of the Bighorn, where abandoned Fort Pease still flew a tattered American flag. This was Colonel Gibbon's command. His twenty-five Crow scouts, enlisted at the new agency on the Stillwater, had yet to find any trace of Sioux. But their thirty-three ponies, grazing on an island in the Yellowstone, made a tempting prize. On the night of May 2 fifty Sioux warriors invaded the island and quietly made off with every animal. "We have found the Sioux," the scout commander wrote in his diary, "or rather, they have found us. . . . The Crows had a good cry over their loss, standing together in a row and shedding copious tears."[8]

Hardly two weeks later, early in June, a Cheyenne hunting party spotted more soldiers far to the south, on the head streams of the Tongue. After sampling some rain-soaked hardtack in an abandoned camp, they raced back to the village on the Rosebud and alerted the people to still other soldiers advancing from the south—General Crook, once more on the march. Thinking to steal some horses, another Cheyenne party, probably no more than a dozen men, led by Little Hawk, rode up the Tongue. On June 9 they tried to stampede the cavalry horses but failed. The officers judged they had been attacked by Crazy Horse himself, at the head of warriors ranging in their estimates from fifty to nine hundred.[9]

These brushes with soldiers to the north and soldiers to the south plainly told that Powder River was no mere isolated event. The soldiers had come firmly intent on making war on any Sioux or Cheyennes they could find. They had not come to guard railroad builders or explore the country. They had come, as Powder River served notice, to kill Indians.

Never had the Sioux and Cheyenne hunting bands felt so incensed against the government, the white people, and especially the white soldiers. Never had they felt their cause so just. Never, with almost all gathered in a single village, had they felt so unified, so powerful, and so ready to fight if attacked. Never had they felt so confident of victory if war came to their lodges.

As the plentiful buffalo banished want and the greening grasses fattened the ponies, these emotions intensified. In Sitting Bull they played on all the chords of his being as a holy man and produced a series of fervent religious experiences unusual even for him. Expressing his perfect harmony with all the elements of *Wakantanka*, his mastery of the sacred ceremonies, his powers of prophecy, and his dedication to the welfare of his tribe, they further catalyzed the mystical sense of potency and solidarity that had taken hold of the village as spring gave way to summer.

The first experience occurred while the village lay on the Rosebud seven miles above its mouth, May 21 to 24. An insistent force drew Sitting Bull to the top of a nearby butte to commune with *Wakantanka*. Seated on a moss-covered rock, praying and meditating, he fell asleep and dreamed. He saw a great dust storm propelled by high winds approaching from the east. Sailing smoothly in the opposite direction was a white cloud resembling an Indian village at the foot of snowcapped mountains. Fiercely the gale charged toward the cloud, and behind the storm Sitting Bull could see rank on rank of soldiers, their weapons and horse trimmings glinting in the sun. The tempest smashed into the cloud. Thunder pealed, lightning crackled, and great sheets of rain poured. Then the storm died out and the dust dissipated, leaving the cloud intact. It drifted serenely to the east and north before passing from sight.

Back in the village, Sitting Bull summoned the other chiefs and described his dream. The storm, he said, represented soldiers, the cloud the Sioux and Cheyenne village. The soldiers were coming to wipe out the Indians, he predicted, but they would fail. The Indians would win a great victory. The council instructed the standing scouts, the wolves, to watch with special care for an army approaching from the east.[10]

About the end of May, while the people camped on the Rosebud near the mouth of Greenleaf Creek, Sitting Bull summoned White Bull, Jumping Bull, and a son of Black Moon. He wanted them to go with him to a hilltop and listen to a prayer. He was attired in ordinary dress, without paint or feathers, and wore his hair loose. He carried his pipe, wrapped in sage. After a prolonged pipe ceremony in which all four participated, Sitting Bull rose, faced the afternoon sun, and prayed:

> *Wakantanka*, save me and give me all my wild game animals and have them close enough so my people will have enough food this winter, and also the good men on earth will have more power so their tribes get along better and be of good nature so all the Sioux nations get along well. If you do this for me I will sun dance two days and two nights and will give you a whole buffalo.

After concluding the ceremony, he wiped his face with sage. Once again, here were the themes close to his heart: peace and plenty for his people, sacrifice for *Wakantanka*.[11]

As he pledged in his prayer, Sitting Bull organized a sun dance. It took place as the village lay in the Rosebud Valley forty-five miles above the Yellowstone and eight miles below the mouth of Muddy Creek. The Hunkpapa tipis stood on the east side of the Rosebud, the Cheyenne on a plateau west of the stream. The move to this site occurred on June 4, and the village remained there until June 8.

Despite rain on the sixth, dance activities extended over the entire stay. The dance was entirely a Hunkpapa event, but people from the other tribes gathered to watch. The dance circle with its soaring pole rose from the valley floor a quarter of a mile north of the Hunkpapa camp circle, which occupied its usual position at the north, or trailing, end of the village.[12]

The sun dance afforded an appropriate occasion for Sitting Bull to fulfill another vow, previously made, to give flesh. Following purification in a sweat lodge, Sitting Bull entered the dance circle. The dancers assembled to watch as he performed a pipe ceremony, then sat with back resting against the dance pole, his legs extended, and his arms resting on the ground against his thighs. Buffalo robes hung from the pole and surrounded him on the ground—gifts to *Wakantanka*. Later he also made good his promise to give a whole buffalo carcass to *Wakantanka*.

White Bull sat nearby while Jumping Bull performed the operation.

Beginning at the bottom of Sitting Bull's left arm, Jumping Bull inserted an awl beneath the skin and removed a bit of flesh the size of a match head. Upward he worked, until fifty pieces had been gouged from the arm. Then he began on the right arm and repeated the process, for a total of one hundred. Blood flowed copiously, forerunner of painful swelling, while Sitting Bull cried out in sacrifice and supplication to *Wakantanka*. The entire rite consumed half an hour.[13]

As vowed in his prayer, Sitting Bull danced. He did not dance pierced and suspended, although scars on his bare chest and back testified to previous piercings. Instead he danced the first form, around the pole while fasting and gazing at the sun. After many hours, suddenly he stopped and, as the onlookers supposed, fainted, although he did not drop. They knew something profound had happened as he stood immobile peering upward at the sun. They gathered around and gently eased him to the ground. Some brought water to sprinkle on him.

When he opened his eyes, Sitting Bull described for Black Moon the vision that had come to him as he stood motionless staring intently at the sun. Black Moon in turn relayed it to the assembled throng. A voice had bade Sitting Bull to fix his sight on an image just below the sun. There he had observed, numerous as grasshoppers, soldiers and horses bearing down on an Indian village below. They came, men and animals both, upside down, their feet in the sky, their heads to the earth with hats falling off. Some Indians below too he saw were upside down.

"These soldiers do not possess ears," the voice proclaimed. "They are to die, but you are not supposed to take their spoils."[14]

It was a thrilling, uplifting image. Despite all the Indians had said about their desire for peace, the soldiers were coming anyway. They had no ears. They would attack the Indians in their village and try to kill them. Some would be killed, as shown by the Indians upside down. But all the soldiers would be killed, as made dramatically clear by their inversion in the vision. The people would win a great victory, but in return they must not, as enjoined by the voice, plunder the bodies of their enemies.

The prophecy, born of a vision in the emotionally charged atmosphere of the sun-dance lodge, gave new force to the mood of outrage and invincibility that had been gathering ever since the victims of Powder River had descended on Crazy Horse and Sitting Bull. With soldiers known to be approaching from the north and south, and with Sitting Bull's vision of two weeks earlier picturing still more coming from the east, the prophecy also carried compelling immediacy. The day could not be far distant when soldiers would fall upside down into the village.

THE INDIANS CALLED General George Crook "Three Stars." Perhaps they had observed three stars on his uniform, one on each shoulder and one on his hat. Even in his Omaha office at the headquarters of the Department of the Platte, however, he rarely wore a uniform, and never in the field. Instead he affected a canvas suit and cork helmet, preferred a mule to a horse, and wove his forked blond beard into braids tied behind his neck. Taciturn, reticent, he almost never told anyone what was on his mind.

Crook's formidable army of more than a thousand men tarried on the upper Tongue for a week while awaiting Indian auxiliaries, and it was there, on June 9, that Little Hawk's wolves tried to run off the cavalry horses. With the arrival of 175 Crow and 86 Shoshone warriors on June 15, Crook prepared to advance.

The Sioux and Cheyenne village, meanwhile, continued its leisurely progress up the Rosebud Valley. On June 8, after the memorable sun dance, it moved twelve miles to a site near the mouth of Muddy Creek for a rainy three days. A move on June 12 took it another twelve miles to the mouth of a western tributary of the Rosebud, usually dry, that rose in a gap in the Wolf Mountains, the divide between the drainages of the Rosebud and the river the Sioux called the Greasy Grass. The gap opened an easy passage to the head of a westward-flowing stream, Sundance Creek, that dropped gently to the Greasy Grass. Still tracking the buffalo herds, the chiefs' council decided to cross to the Greasy Grass. On white-man maps, these three streams came to be labeled Davis Creek, Reno Creek, and the Little Bighorn River.

On June 15 the Indians packed their lodges and headed up Davis Creek, leaving the Rosebud behind. Pausing for one sleep at a dry camp on the summit of the divide, on June 16 they resumed the march. That night they stopped at the upper fork of Reno Creek, twenty-one miles from the final Rosebud camp, and reestablished the village in the usual pattern. The Cheyenne circle occupied a plateau west of the valley, the Hunkpapa in the valley two miles upstream.

The day before, while crossing the divide from the Rosebud, Little Hawk and his handful of Cheyenne wolves had set forth again to spy on the soldiers to the south.[15] Near the head of the Rosebud, while the group roasted parts of a freshly killed buffalo, some of the men climbed a hill to scan the country. To the south they beheld an army of soldiers on the march, making for the Rosebud.

After a swift ride across the mountains, Little Hawk's wolves reached Reno Creek as the women were erecting the tipis. Howling like wolves to alert the people to important news, they dashed into the camp. Heralds rode through each camp circle spreading word of soldiers at the head of the Rosebud. "Get all the young men ready, and let us set out," shouted Little Hawk.[16]

The camp circles erupted with excitement and action. Some women, fearful of a soldier attack similar to Powder River, began to take down the tipis in preparation for flight. Young men painted and clothed themselves for battle, checked their arms, and secured their best horses.

The chiefs met in council to chart a course of action. Heralds announced their decision: "Young men, leave the soldiers alone unless they attack us."[17]

Once again the policy of Sitting Bull and Crazy Horse had prevailed, but once again the young men did as they pleased. "As darkness came on we slipped away," recalled Wooden Leg. "Many bands of Cheyenne and Sioux young men, with some older ones, rode out up the south fork [of Reno Creek] toward the head of the Rosebud. Warriors came from every camp circle." Altogether, about five hundred men rode into the darkness.[18]

The chiefs backed down. Both Sitting Bull and Crazy Horse prepared themselves for battle. When the sun rose over the big bend of the Rosebud on June 17, 1876, both rode with their young men.

Three Stars had roused his troops early that morning and marched two hours before halting for a rest at the big bend about eight o'clock. This was the very place, the Hunkpapas later noted, where they had fought the Slotas three years earlier. The men unsaddled, and no one, even though in Sioux country, thought to take the usual precautions against surprise. The general played whist with some of his officers while his soldiers made coffee. Crows and Shoshones, sensing the enemy nearby, ranged down the valley to the north.

The Sioux and Cheyennes raced up the valley and piled into the Crows scouting in advance. In desperate fighting, Crook's allies spoiled the charge and held the attackers to a line of broken ridges overlooking the troop bivouac. Thus saved from disaster, the soldiers scrambled to form a line and counter the assault.

White Bull and Sitting Bull plunged into the fight on the east flank of the contending lines. Astride a roan horse painted with jagged lightning streaks, White Bull became separated from his uncle and did not see him again during the battle. Sitting Bull, his arms swollen and all but useless from the flesh-giving of a week earlier, did not fight. Instead he ranged the lines exhorting others to have courage.[19]

The battle flamed all morning and into the afternoon. It was a confused melee, hard for anyone to make sense of. "Until the sun went far toward the west there were charges back and forth," recalled Wooden Leg. "Our Indians fought and ran away, fought and ran away. The soldiers and their Indians scouts did the same. Sometimes we chased them, sometimes they chased us."[20]

But this was not the usual sparring gamesmanship. Indians exhibited the expected individual daring and bravery, but they pressed the battle with a ferocity that astonished and disconcerted the soldiers and tested the skill of their officers. Repeatedly repulsed by superior discipline and firepower, the warriors kept returning to the attack. For one thing, they confronted their mortal enemies, the Crows and Shoshones. But more significant, they confronted the soldiers who had attacked their women and children at Powder River, and they battled with all the confident sense of power reflected in Sitting Bull's sun-dance vision.

"It was a hard fight," declared White Bull, "a really big battle. I lived up to my good name and counted five coups." Two Moons of the Cheyennes agreed. "It was a great fight," he declared, "much smoke and dust."[21]

As the afternoon waned, the attackers called off the fight and left for home. They had ridden most of the night and fought all the day. They were exhausted and hungry. The Sioux lost thirteen scalps to Crow or Shoshone opponents and mourned another seven killed in addition, as well as many wounded. The Cheyennes bore away several badly wounded men, one mortally. The soldiers lost nine killed and twenty-three wounded, their Indian allies one killed and seven wounded.

"The command finally drove the Indians back in great confusion," Crook reported, and, retaining possession of the field, he could declare the battle a victory for the soldiers. The next morning, however, he marched back to his base camp at the head of the Tongue. He had carried rations for only four days, the result of a false report of an enemy village located on the upper Rosebud, within easy striking distance. The wounded, moreover, needed treatment.

Despite Crook's claims, the true victory, both tactical and strategic, lay with the Indians. They had attacked a force twice as large as or larger than their own, kept it off balance and largely reactive for a day, inflicted serious casualties, and sent it in stunned retreat back to the security of the base camp. More significant than the Indians could know, their repeated thrusts and bold tenacity in close combat so unnerved Three Stars that he would not venture from his defenses until heavily reinforced. That counted him out of the strategic equation for six weeks, by which time the crucial events of the campaign had run their course.[22]

The Indians knew they had won. On the way back to their village, while mournfully burying their dead, they also feasted in triumph. The same emotions stirred the village—sorrow over the dead, elation over the victory.

The celebration, however, could not be staged in the village of death. The next morning, June 18, the women took down the tipis. One remained, in the Sans Arc circle, as a burial lodge for a man slain on the Rosebud. By evening the tribes had journeyed down Reno Creek almost to its mouth, angled across the low benches to the southwest, and relocated in the valley of the Greasy Grass—the Little Bighorn.

There in the familiar layout of the village, the six circles reverberated in joyous festival. It lasted for six days. Dancing, feasting, and recital of war deeds glorified the achievements of the Rosebud and reinforced the creed of invincibility rooted in unity. The allied tribes had thrashed the soldiers and, as scouts reported, sent them skulking off to the south, thwarted in their design to destroy the village. But this was not the great victory foreseen by Sitting Bull. His sun-dance vision pictured soldiers falling right into the village, and so that remained in the future.

Another cause fed and prolonged the festivities. At last the agency people had begun to arrive in significant numbers. On the back trail from the Rosebud down Reno Creek, and down the Little Bighorn itself, the newcomers converged on their destination. They came in small groups and large, trailing on the ground behind them, in a chaos of size, direction, and age, the marks of their progress. Over the span of only six days, the village more than doubled, from 450 to 1,000 lodges, from 3,000 to 7,000 people, from 800 to 1,800 fighting men. Here indeed was occasion for feasting and dancing, and for renewed confidence in the coalition's ability to defend itself.[23]

In quest of buffalo, the chiefs' council had planned to move even farther up the Little Bighorn, toward the Bighorn Mountains. Scouts, however, brought word of antelope herds to the north and west, beyond

After his surrender in 1881, Sitting Bull sat for many portraits. In this characteristic pose, taken in about 1885 when he was fifty-four, he wears a crucifix reputed to have been presented to him by Father De Smet at the peacemaking council of 1868. NATIONAL ARCHIVES

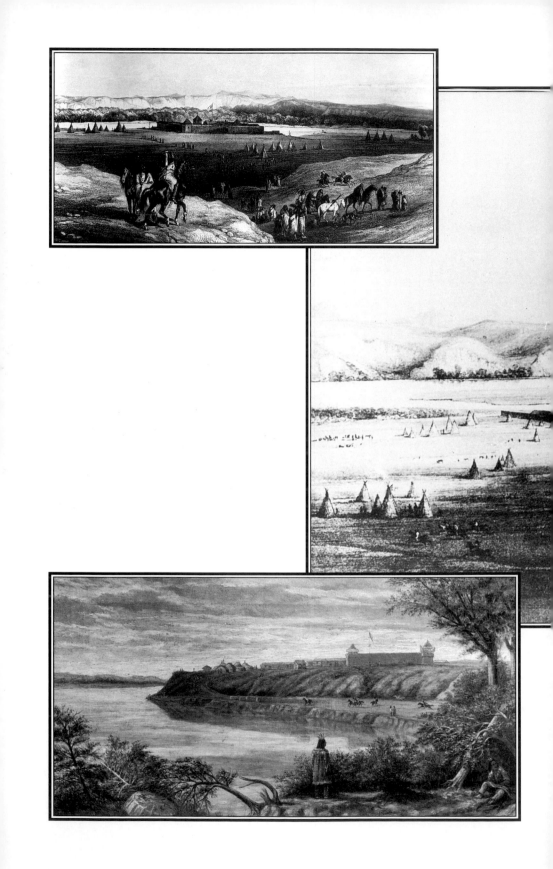

Principal trading outlet for Sitting Bull and the Hunkpapas in the 1840s and 1850s was Fort Pierre, seen above in Karl Bodmer's painting, which looks toward the Missouri River from the west. Forts Union and Berthold, opposite top and bottom, served enemy tribes; even so, Sitting Bull often went there to trade or to raid. Fort Union, also by Bodmer, was the post for the Assiniboines at the mouth of the Yellowstone River; Fort Berthold, the post for Arikaras, Mandans, and Hidatsas, was painted in 1867 by Colonel Philippe Régis de Trobriand, commander of nearby Fort Stevenson. SOUTH DAKOTA HISTORICAL SOCIETY; MONTANA HISTORICAL SOCIETY; NORTH DAKOTA HISTORICAL SOCIETY

General William S. Harney. Called "Mad Bear," he terrorized the upper Missouri Lakotas in 1856, leaving a legacy of "government chiefs" to complicate tribal politics.

Sitting Bull's visual autobiography. As a gift for Jumping Bull, Sitting Bull executed a series of forty-one pictographs in the 1860s to represent feats of bravery. Four Horns made two copies, one of which fell into the hands of an army surgeon at Fort Buford. Two significant exploits pictured: counting first coup at age fourteen, above, and, below, slaying the Crow warrior who killed his father at Rainy Buttes in 1859. Each is signed with the glyph, a sitting buffalo bull, that was Sitting Bull's signature before he learned to write his name. The shield is the one his father gave him. SMITHSONIAN INSTITUTION

*S*on of artist Thomas Sully,
Captain Alfred Sully painted a
camp of Lakotas at Fort Pierre
in 1857, above. In 1863-65 he
returned as a general. In this
painting of the Battle of
Killdeer Mountain, July 28,
1864, opposite, Lakota
warriors fan out to screen their
lodges from Sully's skirmishers,
advancing in a huge hollow
square. With aid from his
artillery (far right), Sully
scattered the Indians and
destroyed their village.

Typical Lakota camp scene before tipis were replaced with dank log cabins. MONTANA
HISTORICAL SOCIETY

*The Hunkpapas detested the
military forts along the upper
Missouri. General Sully
built Fort Rice in 1864, top
right, painted by Seth Eastman; Fort Buford, bottom
right, followed in 1866, to
arouse Sitting Bull's especial
ire. Ironically, his final
surrender took place at Fort
Buford in 1881. Rows of
stacked firewood—the winter
supply—were burned by
Sitting Bull's warriors in
1866 in an attack on the fort.*
LIBRARY OF CONGRESS;
NORTH DAKOTA
HISTORICAL SOCIETY

In 1868 Father Pierre-Jean De Smet, the bold Jesuit missionary, right, entered the Hunkpapa camp to confer with Sitting Bull and other chiefs in an effort to win their adherence to the Fort Laramie Treaty. In the watercolor below, prepared for the publication of De Smet's writings, the priest and his entourage meet the Hunkpapas on Powder River. NORTH DAKOTA HISTORICAL SOCIETY; JESUIT MISSOURI PROVINCE ARCHIVES, ST. LOUIS

In 1873 George Armstrong Custer, right, and the Seventh Cavalry were stationed at Fort Abraham Lincoln. "Long Hair" met the Lakotas in battle on the Yellowstone, then blazed the infamous "Thieves' Road" into the Black Hills. Custer's legendary "last stand" on the Little Bighorn, above, is by Richard Lorenze.

NATIONAL ARCHIVES, LITTLE BIGHORN BATTLEFIELD NATIONAL MONUMENT

Although "Long Hair" Custer is forever connected with Sitting Bull, Nelson A. Miles, right, and George Crook, below, played more consequential parts in his life. "Three Stars" Crook joined with "Bear Coat" Miles in forcing the final surrender of Sitting Bull and the hunting bands. Crook later headed the land commission that reduced the Great Sioux Reservation. Miles commanded military forces sent to the Sioux reservations during the Ghost Dance troubles of 1890.
MONTANA HISTORICAL SOCIETY;
ARIZONA HISTORICAL SOCIETY

Fort Walsh, above, head-
quarters of the North-
West Mounted Police in
Canada's Cypress Hills.
Through most of his
Canadian exile, 1877-81,
Sitting Bull dealt mainly
with Major James M.
Walsh, "Long Lance,"
left. A mutual respect
and friendship developed
between the two men.
GLENBOW ARCHIVES,
CALGARY, ALBERTA;
NATIONAL ARCHIVES
OF CANADA

Sitting Bull's council with Mounted Police officers, June 2, 1877, below, as sketched by police surgeon Richard Nevitt. On his field draft of this drawing, Nevitt included a hasty portrait of Sitting Bull, right, probably the first likeness of the chief ever committed to paper.
GLENBOW ARCHIVES, CALGARY, ALBERTA

New York Graphic's *rendition of the Terry Commission meeting with Lakota chiefs at Fort Walsh, Canada, October 17, 1877. Sitting Bull ordered Terry not to say two more words, to go home and leave the Sioux with their redcoated friends.*

SITTING BULL.

Harpers Weekly *devoted the front page of the issue of December 8, 1877, to sketches of Jerome Stillson, artist-correspondent of the* New York Herald, *who accompanied the Terry Commission to Fort Walsh. Stillson's likeness of Sitting Bull was the first to appear in public print.*

the Bighorn. On June 24, therefore, the Cheyennes led out in a reverse movement, down the river to the north.

The new location, eight miles below the old, afforded an appealing setting. The upper end of the camp, the Hunkpapa circle, lay about two miles below the mouth of Reno Creek. For nearly three miles downstream, the tribal circles sprawled across the valley floor west of the river. On the west the valley ended in low grassy hills and benches where the huge pony herd grazed. On the eastern edge of the valley the river, cold and brimming with the spring runoff from the Bighorn Mountains, meandered among thickets of shady cottonwood trees. A series of ragged bluffs rose steeply from the east bank of the river to a height of some three hundred feet.

There in the valley of the pretty stream the Indians called the Greasy Grass lay a village of unusual size. So many people and animals consumed immense quantities of game, forage, and firewood that they could not remain long in one place, or even together in one village. It had come together in this strength only in the few days preceding, and it could stay together for more than a few days or a week only through luck, frequent moves, and constant labor. White apologists, seeking to explain the disaster this alliance of tribes wrought, would later greatly overestimate its size. Still, it was big by all standards of the time, and it was more than twice as big as any of the army officers looking for it had anticipated.

Equally significant, the village contained a people basking proudly in the fullness of tribal power. Contrary to the mindset of army planners (except Three Stars, who had learned better), the Indians felt little inclination to avoid conflict. Their grievances united them in a determination to fight against those who would steal the Black Hills and send soldiers to attack their families and force them out of the unceded territory, where even the white people's paper conceded their right to live.

SITTING BULL'S TIPI stood on the southern margin of the Hunkpapa circle, opening east toward towering cottonwoods that marked the course of the Little Bighorn. At this point, the extreme upper end of the village, the river snaked halfway across the valley, away from the steep bluffs on the other side. Two sweeping river bends almost cradled the Hunkpapa circle, the southern partly masking the lodges from the valley above.

Thirteen people crowded Sitting Bull's lodge: his two wives, his mother, his two adolescent daughters by the discarded Snow-on-Her, his young son by the dead Red Woman, his two stepsons, his sister Good Feather (mother of White Bull and One Bull), and twin sons born to Four Robes only three weeks earlier. In addition, Gray Eagle, brother of his two wives, temporarily lived with Sitting Bull. One Bull, reared in Sitting Bull's tipi, had recently taken a wife and erected his own lodge next to his uncle's.[24]

As the great village bustled with evening chores on that hot June Saturday, the mystical sense of pivotal events bearing down on his people continued to grip Sitting Bull. Bidding One Bull to accompany him, he climbed a high ridge across the river, opposite the Cheyenne circle at the lower end of the village. The ridge commanded a sweeping view of the Little Bighorn Valley, carpeted in the foreground with tipis, the river snaking from the south, where the snowy peaks of the Bighorn Mountains formed a backdrop. As the sun sank on the chain of mountains, casting long shadows on the ravine-wrinkled slope of the ridge, Sitting Bull performed a ceremony of offering.

Heavily painted, he stood on the ridge crest and formally presented his offerings to *Wakantanka*. They included a buffalo robe, a ceremonial pipe, and bits of tobacco wrapped in buckskin and tied to carved cherry sticks. After each had been humbly presented, he prayed:

> *Wakantanka*, pity me. In the name of the tribe I offer you this peace-pipe. Wherever the sun, the moon, the earth, the four points of the wind, there you are always. Father, save the tribe, I beg you. Pity me. We want to live. Guard us against all misfortunes or calamities. Pity me.

After leaving his offerings on the ground at the top of the ridge, Sitting Bull and One Bull returned to the village.

Later on this very site the white people erected a monument, not to commemorate Sitting Bull's sacrifice and appeal for the well-being of his people but to pay homage to another chieftain and his people who made their own sacrifice on this hilltop the next day. The base of the monument bears this inscription: "In memory of the officers and soldiers who fell near this place fighting with the 7th United States Cavalry against Sioux Indians on the 25th and 26th of June, A.D. 1876."[25]

12 LONG HAIR

IF THEY HAD never actually seen him, the Hunkpapas had all heard of "Long Hair" Custer, *Pehin Hanska*, whose red-gold locks reached almost to the collar of the fringed buckskin jacket that he usually wore in the field. His headquarters, Fort Abraham Lincoln, lay only fifty miles up the Missouri from the Hunkpapa agency at Standing Rock—the new site and name for the old Grand River Agency, relocated in 1873. The Indians knew *Pehin Hanska* as the soldier chief they had fought on the Yellowstone in 1873 and as the man who had blazed the "Thieves' Road" into the Black Hills in 1874.

Long Hair gave the Sitting Bull people less concern than Three Stars, especially his Crow and Shoshone warriors who had fought so bravely at the Rosebud. Although scouts had followed Crook back to his base camp, the people in the great village along the Little Bighorn worried that the soldiers might attack at any time. So far as they thought about soldier chiefs at all, they thought about Three Stars. The threat, however, came not from the whipped Three Stars but from the confident Long Hair.

On May 17, 1876, Custer led his entire regiment, the Seventh Cavalry, out of Fort Abraham Lincoln. With 750 men, the Seventh formed the bulk of General Terry's force of 1,000. The rest were infantry, to guard the long wagon train and the supply base from which Terry expected to operate.

Also riding with the cavalry were thirty-seven Ree scouts, including

Bloody Knife. Ever since 1865, when he had almost killed Gall, Bloody Knife had sought revenge against Gall, Sitting Bull, and other Hunkpapas for indignities inflicted during his years as a child among the Hunkpapas. A succession of army officers paid tribute to Bloody Knife's skill as a scout and guide, and in the past three years he had become Custer's favorite. The Rees' longtime trader at Fort Berthold, Fred Gerard, went along as an interpreter.[1]

On June 21, Terry's column having met Gibbon's, Terry, Gibbon, and Custer met aboard the supply steamer *Far West*, tied to the bank of the Yellowstone at the mouth of the Rosebud, and laid plans for smashing Sitting Bull's village. As Terry had intended from the first, Custer would strike the blow. Although not confirmed by reconnaissance, the planners believed the Indian trail Gibbon's scouts had found on the Rosebud would turn west to the Little Bighorn. At the head of the Seventh Cavalry, Custer would push up the Rosebud, find the village, and attack. Terry would join Gibbon's command, which included slow-moving infantry, to march up the Yellowstone and the Bighorn to the mouth of the Little Bighorn, where they could block the northward flight of Indians giving way before Custer's offensive.

To strengthen his scouting capability, Custer borrowed six Crows from Gibbon. They knew the country intimately, as the Rees did not. Indeed, the Rosebud and Little Bighorn, which the Sioux defended as their territory, lay within the Crow Reservation as marked out by the Treaty of 1868.

For three days, June 22 to 24, the Seventh Cavalry made its way up the Rosebud, examining each successive village site. On the morning of the third day the officers prowled amid the ruins of the sun-dance lodge where Sitting Bull had looked at the sun and seen soldiers falling upside down into his village. The scalp of a white man hung from the frame. The Ree scouts, sensing themselves in the presence of powerful medicine, grew restive.

Later that day the command suddenly confronted a mystifying transformation in the Indian trail. Hitherto of uniform size and age, it now abruptly turned larger and fresher. Lodgepole marks cross-hatched the valley in all directions, disturbing older markings and testifying to a sequence of puzzling activity extending to recent days. Some of the pony droppings were no more than two days old, which meant that some Indians, at least, were as close as thirty miles. The officers seem not to have guessed the explanation—the sudden influx of agency Indians that over the past week had more than doubled the size of Sitting Bull's village while also disfiguring the original trail.

As expected, the Indian trail turned from the Rosebud up Davis Creek. A night march carried the regiment up the creek nearly to the divide. Custer intended to use the next day, June 25, to rest his men on the other side of the divide and send out scouting parties to find the village. He would then move into position for a dawn attack on June 26.

June 25 was another hot and cloudless day. From a peak in the Wolf Mountains south of the divide between Davis and Reno creeks, Crow and Ree scouts tried to point out for Custer evidence of the Indian village in the distant haze. Campfire smoke rose over the Little Bighorn Valley, fifteen miles to the west, they said, and the pony herd could be seen on the bench beyond. Custer could not see what they saw, but he had every reason to believe them.

Closer at hand, moreover, his worst fears seemed confirmed. Several parties of Indians could be glimpsed threading the hillocks on both sides of the divide. There could be only one conclusion. The soldiers had been discovered. The village would explode in all directions, leaving a hundred trails to follow and no one to fight.

At once Custer revised his plan. Forgoing a dawn attack with a rested command, he would have to find the village and destroy it on this day instead of the next. He would have to reconnoiter and advance in one movement—a reconnaissance in force. The plan of attack would have to unfold as information about terrain and objective unfolded.

In the bivouac at the head of Davis Creek, where coffee boiled in alkali water, the first bugle call in three days split the late-morning silence.

THE DIVIDE BETWEEN the heads of Reno and Davis creeks was a busy place that morning of June 25, 1876. Affording an easy passage of the Wolf Mountains between the Rosebud and the Little Bighorn, it held appeal for Indians as well as cavalry, no matter which direction they traveled. Both Oglalas and Cheyennes were there, some headed back to the agencies, others bound for Sitting Bull's village. Had Long Hair waited another day as planned, some one of these would surely have alerted the village to soldiers only fifteen miles away. If the Indian response to Three Stars's advance a week earlier afforded a precedent, what might have happened next may be guessed.[2]

The village drowsed into the hot afternoon. Women pursued domestic chores at their tipis. Others combed through the river bottom digging wild turnips and picking berries. Still others, with many children, splashed in the cool waters of the river. Weary from dancing and feasting that had rocked all the camp circles until dawn, men slept in their lodges or beneath the cottonwoods shading the riverbank. Many tended their ponies on the bench to the west or in the valley north of the Cheyenne circle. Reflecting the pervasive apprehension that something was about to happen, some tethered ponies at their lodges, as did the *akicita* on police duty. For most men, however, their mounts remained beyond easy retrieval.

At midafternoon a stir ran through the village and spread to the people along the riverbank. In each circle heralds took up and repeated the cry: "They are charging, the chargers are coming. Where the tipi is they say the chargers are coming."[3]

Women on the bluffs east of the river had sighted the cavalry on Reno Creek, where the lone burial lodge marked the village site of June 17, when the warriors had fought Three Stars. By the time the cry ran through the village, however, soldiers had already reached the Little Bighorn and begun to cross to the open valley beyond.

All the circles exploded in pandemonium. Men rushed to paint for battle and secure their ponies, either at their tipis or on the bench. Some took time to hurry family members to the western hills or the north end of the village. Women and children swarmed from the river to strike lodges and pack travois for flight.

"I heard a terrific volley of carbines," related Moving-Robe-Woman, daughter of Sitting Bull's friend Crawler. "The bullets shattered the tipi poles. Women and children were running away from the gunfire. In the tumult I heard old men and women singing death songs for their warriors who were now ready to attack the soldiers."[4]

CUSTER'S RECONNAISSANCE in force had finally uncovered the location of the village his scouts had seen in the distance at dawn. By now, however, he had fragmented the regiment. First he had sent a battalion under Captain Frederick W. Benteen to scout south along the foot of the Wolf Mountains to ensure that no tipis could be seen in the upper Little Bighorn Valley—where, in fact, they had been from June 18 to 24. Next, at the lower fork of Reno Creek, Custer had ordered Major Marcus A. Reno and a battalion of 175 men, including Bloody Knife and fifteen Ree

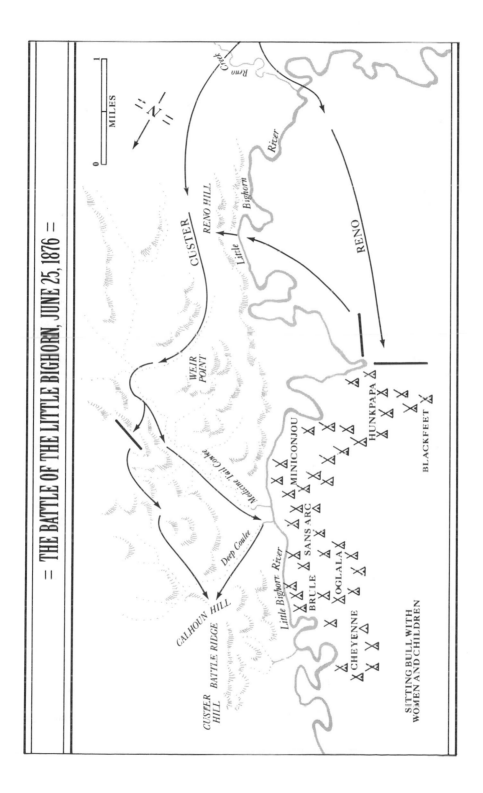

= THE BATTLE OF THE LITTLE BIGHORN, JUNE 25, 1876 =

scouts, to cross the Little Bighorn and advance on the enemy, whose location was now disclosed by a dust cloud rising from behind the bluffs blocking his view to the northwest. Although he had led Reno to expect direct support from the rear, Custer now turned the remaining battalion of about 210 men under his personal command to the right, toward the dust cloud. Benteen followed somewhere in the rear, as did the mule train with one company in escort.

HURRYING TO ESCAPE or attack, people and animals churned up great clouds of dust that rose over the village. The blue horsemen charging down the valley raised their own dust. Everyone shouted. Some sang death songs. Women sounded their distinctive warbling tremolo in encouragement of their men.

Through the dust the Hunkpapas could make out the hazy blue figures bearing down on the village from the south. The Hunkpapa lodges lay first in the line of attack.

Fortuitously, just as the alarm sounded, One Bull and Gray Eagle had returned from the bench with a remuda of horses. One Bull mounted and pulled his mother up behind him, while Sitting Bull did the same for his mother and his other sister. Leaving the rest of the family to fend for themselves, the two galloped into the hills, dropped the women, and returned.[5]

Meanwhile, the two wives and the children had made good their escape. Four Robes was so frightened that she grabbed only one of the infant twins. In the hills someone asked where the other was. Chagrined, she left the child with a friend and ran back to the tipi to retrieve the other.[6]

As the first bullets rattled through the tipi tops, Sitting Bull darted into his lodge to get his war paraphernalia. After emerging with his treasured shield, he placed it over One Bull's shoulder and also presented him with bow and arrows and a war club. The shield's sacred power would guard his nephew and adopted son from harm. In turn, One Bull handed Sitting Bull a Winchester repeating rifle and a six-shooter pistol.

"Go right ahead," Sitting Bull exclaimed. "Don't be afraid, go right on." After mounting his pony, One Bull galloped through the dust toward the gunfire.[7]

As One Bull left, his brother White Bull reined in his horse at Sitting Bull's lodge. He had spent the morning tending his herd, then returned to his tipi in the Sans Arc circle, where he lived with his Sans Arc wife. He noted that his uncle had not taken the time to prepare for battle. He wore no feathers, only the shirt and leggings he had donned in the morning, and he carried a repeating rifle and a revolver.

Mounted on a black horse, he was shouting to his gathering warriors: "Brave up, boys, it will be a hard time. Brave up."[8]

A shallow draw cut across the valley on the southern edge of the village, and there the first warriors collected to make a stand against the soldiers. But the soldiers did not get that far. Instead of charging among the tipis, they halted just short of the tip of the first river bend. Dismounting, some herded the horses into the shelter of the timber while the rest formed a thin skirmish line extending across the valley from the timber almost to the foothills.

A few Ree scouts rode to the left, forward of the soldier line. From there they fired into the Hunkpapa tipis, killing some women and children, then hastily withdrew. Among the dead were Gall's two wives and three children. "It made my heart bad," he later observed.[9]

Through the dust and the smoke of exploding carbines, the soldier line could be glimpsed spurting fire into the murk, three guidons flapping from staffs planted in the ground.[10] White Bull and Sitting Bull rode into the shallow draw to join with others, including old Four Horns, in holding back the soldiers. This was "standstill shooting," as White Bull called it, with some Indians mounted, others afoot, and all exchanging fire with the soldiers. Sitting Bull and White Bull were on the east, near the timber. They were "not standing around looking but shooting," White Bull explained.[11]

The blue line pushed forward about one hundred yards, and the soldiers dropped to their stomachs to fire.

"Who is a brave man will get that flag," shouted White Bull. But no one tried.[12]

Instead, the mounted men bunched in the draw and launched a charge against the line. Heavy fire deflected them to the west, toward the bench. That proved fortunate, for they rode around the left flank of the soldiers and got in their rear. The soldiers quickly rose to their feet and filed to their right, into the timber. So close did the warriors press that the soldiers on the left had to deploy at right angles to the old line to cover the movement. At the timber's edge, behind an old riverbank, a new line formed facing west toward the charging Indians. The soldiers had held their position in the open no longer than fifteen minutes.[13]

White Bull rode in the charge, and he and Sitting Bull became separated. Sitting Bull probably remained in the gully near the timber, firing at the soldiers. No one expected chiefs to expose themselves recklessly if there were enough young men to handle the task.

"Crazy Horse is coming!" The cry rippled through the fighters to the sound of pounding hooves, eagle-bone whistles, and the tremolos of women watching from the western hills. Scores of mounted Oglalas piled into the fray, lending momentum to the attack already under way by the Hunkpapas. Warriors still afoot moved against the right of the new line, while mounted warriors, the initiative clearly theirs, stabbed at its front and reached for its left and rear. Once again, with Indians about to get behind them, the soldiers fell back, to a clearing deep in the timber.[14]

The battle lost coherence. Indians filtered into the edges of the timber on all sides of the soldiers, firing steadily but largely blindly. Indians even gathered on the east side of the river to fire into the timber. The soldiers' formation broke up also, and in little bunches they hid behind trees and in the thick brush to return the fire. For half an hour this ragged contest sputtered inconclusively.

Having taken part in the mounted charge, One Bull and three companions dismounted and led their horses into the timber. As they worked their way through the brush, One Bull saw Good-Bear-Boy drop with a bullet in his leg. Going to his friend's aid, One Bull hoisted him to the back of his own mount, then, keeping it between him and the soldiers, backed out of the woods.

Once in the open, One Bull saw that the soldiers were also emerging from their hidden positions. They gathered at the timber's edge to the east and south and were mounting and forming for some new move. One Bull turned his horse to climb on behind Good-Bear-Boy. A bullet smashed into the horse's hip, but One Bull jumped on and headed for camp. The horse limped so badly, however, that he had to dismount and walk. Leaving Good-Bear-Boy in safety, One Bull secured another horse and returned to the fight.[15]

It had taken a spectacular turn. Soldiers galloped their horses in full retreat across the open valley to the southeast. Mounted Indians pressed from both flanks and the rear and even mingled with the terrified troopers, knocking them from their horses with tomahawks, rifles, and quirts. One Bull spurred to the chase.

"Indians covered the flat," Two Moons remembered. "They began to drive the soldiers all mixed up—Sioux, then soldiers, then more Sioux, and all shooting. The air was full of smoke and dust. I saw the soldiers fall back and drop into the river-bed like buffalo fleeing."[16]

For the troopers, the river crossing proved a deadly obstacle. They jumped their horses over the steep bank and floundered in the swift current. "With my captured rifle as a club I knocked two of them into the flood waters," said Wooden Leg. One Bull killed two there also, and one on the other side. "I saw boys pull men from their horses and kill them on the ground," related a watching Hunkpapa woman.[17]

The fortunate survivors scaled the high bluffs on the east side of the river and assembled on a flat hilltop overlooking the valley. Of 175 men, 40 had been slain, 13 wounded, and 16 left in the timber below.

Sitting Bull had lagged behind as the young men cut down the stampeding soldiers. Astride his black horse, he rode slowly across the valley floor viewing the carnage. Women and young boys moved about on foot, finishing off the wounded, stripping, plundering, and mutilating the dead. In the clearing in the timber, some of these found Bloody Knife, his skull smashed by a bullet (which had splattered Major Reno with blood and brains and set off the demoralized flight from the timber). Two women cut off the head and paraded it on a pole through the village, where their mother recognized it as the head of her brother.[18]

Sitting Bull had long regarded Bloody Knife as a traitor to his people and could have applied the same logic to another casualty discovered in the valley. This was Isaiah Dorman, "Custer's black white man," who was married to a Hunkpapa and known to the Sioux as Teat. A wood chopper near Fort Rice, he had signed on with Custer as an interpreter. Two Bulls, Shoots Walking, and several others gathered around Teat, badly wounded by a gunshot to the breast. "My friends," he said, "you have already killed me, don't count coup on me."

Sitting Bull rode up and said, "Don't kill that man, he is a friend of mine." Dismounting, Sitting Bull poured water into a buffalo-horn cup and gave it to the black man, then crossed the river and joined the Indians surrounding the soldiers on the hilltop.[19]

Others displayed no such compassion for Teat. A Hunkpapa woman, Eagle Robe, killed him with a rifle shot, and others made certain he would not look well in the spirit world. They slashed all parts of his body with knives, riddled it with arrows, nailed him to the ground with an iron picket pin driven through his testicles, and, the ultimate degradation, cut off his penis and stuffed it in his mouth.[20]

On the east side of the river, Sitting Bull spurred his horse up one of the deep ravines that scored the bluffs. Indians prowled the ravines shooting at straggling troopers trying to reach their comrades above. Others had taken firing positions to loose an occasional shot at the crowd on top.

One Bull joined his uncle. "Sitting Bull was back on the hill on the edge of the battlefield sort of directing things," One Bull remembered, "though he himself did not go into the fight at all."

Heavily smeared with blood, One Bull appeared to be badly wounded. Go back to the village and fight no more, Sitting Bull told him. But One Bull explained that he had not been hit at all. The blood was that of the wounded friend he had borne back to the village.

One Bull started to rejoin the fight. Let them go, Sitting Bull counseled, so they could tell the whites what had happened. One Bull left anyway, pursuing four soldiers climbing the bluffs.[21]

The victorious Indians did not press the attack, not because Sitting Bull advised against it but because of another threat to the women and children from other soldiers approaching the village to the north. One Bull caught a glimpse of blue on a northern ridge. On the lower skirts of the bluffs, near the river, White Bull also saw blue downriver. "The word passed among the Indians like a whirlwind," said Red Horse, "and they all started to attack this new party, leaving the troops on the hill."[22]

Reuniting, Sitting Bull and One Bull followed the ridgetops northward. From slopes overlooking the broad coulee that would be named Medicine Tail, they saw the soldiers, some riding down the coulee toward the river, others on a high ridge beyond. Warriors converged from everywhere, many fording the river at the mouth of the coulee, others sweeping around the foothills of the high ridges to the west.

In the coulee Sitting Bull and One Bull met a large force of warriors. Go on and fight, he told them. "He was not a leader," observed Gray Whirlwind, one of these men. One Bull started to go too, but Sitting Bull said no, there were plenty of warriors to hold back these soldiers. Now men were needed to protect the women and children. Other soldiers might appear and threaten them. But One Bull plunged into the fight anyway.[23]

Sitting Bull proceeded down the coulee and forded the Little Bighorn to the village. The Miniconjou and Oglala circles teemed with fighting men who had not made it into the first battle. Alerted by the sight of blue columns on the ridges east of the river, they streamed across the Little Bighorn at the mouth of the coulee while others forded in little knots downstream wherever a ravine opened a way to the heights beyond.

Sitting Bull rode around the edge of the Cheyenne circle. There, on the far western side of the valley, a large number of women and children had collected. With other men, he took station to make certain no body of soldiers as yet undetected harmed the families. Later, as urged by his uncle, One Bull joined these guardians.

From this place Sitting Bull and his comrades could plainly see the dust and smoke of battle roll northward along the high ridge on the other side of the river. At its northern end, the ridge rose to a hilltop.

CUSTER HAD ORDERED Major Reno to cross the Little Bighorn and attack the Indians, whose location was identified by dust rising from behind the bluffs. With the remaining five companies, Custer had then turned north, toward the ridges overlooking the valley. Probably, troubled by the dust cloud, he imagined the Indians fleeing in panic, and he hoped to cut them off. From the blufftops he saw the village for the first time and watched Major Reno open the battle at the upper end. Then Custer led his men down a ravine that opened on upper Medicine Tail Coulee.

The village was big, as Custer had observed from the heights. He needed his entire command. A messenger galloped on the back trail with orders for Benteen and the packmules to hasten forward.

On reaching Medicine Tail, Custer posted three companies in positions on the north slope commanding the ravine he had just descended. Benteen would approach by the same route. Stalling for time, Custer dispatched two companies down Medicine Tail to threaten the village and hold the ford.

Benteen did not come, but warriors in large numbers did. At exactly the right moment, Reno's retreat had freed all the Indian fighters to concentrate on Custer. The two companies on lower Medicine Tail fell back up another coulee draining the ridges to the northeast, while the three companies with Custer fought a delaying action northward across the high country to a reunion of all five companies.

This action occurred on a long flat hill that formed the southern end of the ridge that Sitting Bull watched from across the valley.[24]

ON THAT RIDGE White Bull excelled in the first of the Hunkpapa cardinal virtues, bravery. His experience traced the course of the fighting the full length of the ridge to its climax in what the white people called the "last stand."

White Bull rode with one of many groups of warriors making their way up the north branch of Medicine Tail toward the south end of the battle ridge. There the soldiers made an organized stand. Three companies dismounted, deployed, and for a short time steadfastly held off the Indians pressing from the south.

In this fighting White Bull made a "center run"—a daring dash directly at the enemy. After returning unhurt, he worked around to the east and joined more Indians to strike at the rear of the dismounted soldiers. Horseholders gripped the mounts of those fighting on foot. White Bull and some companions charged again. One shot a mounted soldier, who fell from his saddle. Swiftly White Bull dismounted, counted coup, took the dead man's pistol and ammunition belt, and rejoined the charge.[25]

The charge stampeded the cavalry's horses, which poured over the ridgetop and galloped toward the river. As Gall described this action: "They fought on foot. One man held the horses while the others shot the guns. We tried to kill the holders, and then by waving blankets and shooting we scared the horses down that coulee, where the Cheyenne women caught them."[26]

The saddlebags yielded ammunition for army carbines already falling into Indian hands.

After that, the soldiers lost organized cohesion. Of the action along the sharp spine running north half a mile to end in a hilltop, an Oglala woman observed, "The Indians acted just like they were driving buffalo to a good place where they could be easily slaughtered."[27] It was an apt metaphor. The soldiers behaved just like a herd of buffalo shattered into panicked bunches by a force of yipping, shooting Indian hunters. Like buffalo, the soldiers fell by the dozen and then by the score. Rolling northward, the battle spun out clusters of smaller battles that flashed in the rear.

In one such fight, White Bull counted another first coup. A mounted soldier tried to shoot him with a carbine, but White Bull struck him with his coup stick, then jerked him from his horse and killed him. Another Indian sprang from his horse and counted second coup. It was Crazy Horse, just arrived on the field. His presence braced all who saw him with new courage.

With Crazy Horse and many others, White Bull remained east of the battle ridge, firing from behind a parallel but lower ridge at soldiers concentrated on the east slope. Crazy Horse challenged White Bull to a daring run through these soldiers. With Crazy Horse in the lead, the two made the dash, White Bull hugging the flank of his horse. They galloped right through the soldiers and over the battle ridge beyond.

"The soldiers all fired at once," related Red Feather, watching Crazy

Horse, "but didn't hit him. The Indians got the idea the soldiers' guns were empty and charged immediately on the soldiers. They charged right over the hill." At close quarters, with pistols and in hand-to-hand combat, this group of soldiers went down on the hillside.[28]

According to He Dog, Crazy Horse's charge "broke through and split up the soldiers into two bunches."[29] Those to the south fought to the end singly and in little groups. Many were shot down trying to flee. Those to the north collected on the hilltop at the end of the ridge. Surrounded on all sides, about one hundred made their "last stand."

White Bull's charge with Crazy Horse had carried him over the battle ridge and down the western slope. There the gullies drained toward a deep ravine that reached from the river to the foot of the hill on which the soldiers had collected. Many Sioux and Cheyennes had worked to the head of the ravine and spread out on the furrowed hillside to fire at the circle of defenders.

Suddenly about forty soldiers spilled off the hilltop and broke for the river. Some rode horseback, but most were on foot. Tall Bull, one of the Cheyennes, "heard a big war whoop that soldiers were coming. Soldiers came on foot and ran right through us into deep gully." As Red Horse put it, "We finished up this party right there in the ravine."[30]

White Bull joined with those who pounced on these soldiers and wiped them out. He spurred toward one to run him down. The soldier fired his pistol at point-blank range. Powder stung White Bull's face, but the bullet missed, and he rode the man down.

Four bullets struck White Bull's horse and killed him. Bear Lice gave him another, a bay army horse. White Bull charged on another soldier, but someone shot him first. Even so, White Bull counted first coup.

Another soldier stood to receive White Bull's attack. The warrior flung himself off his borrowed horse and bore down on his opponent with a pistol in one hand and a whip in the other. White Bull saw the man raise his pistol and aim but not fire. It was either empty or jammed. When White Bull got closer, the soldier threw the pistol at him.

The two wrestled. White Bull got on top and hit him on the head. They struggled and thrashed and rolled around the ground. White Bull yelled to frighten the soldier and also to call for help. "Hey-hey," he shouted twice, "come over and help me!" Crow Boy and Bear Lice rushed to White Bull's aid, but in the confusion they pummeled him instead of his adversary.

The soldier almost succeeded in tearing White Bull's pistol from his left hand. White Bull hit him in the face with the whip and he let go, but then grabbed the pistol with both hands. White Bull hit him again. The soldier smashed White Bull in the jaw and shoulder with his fist, grabbed his hair, and tried to bite his nose.

Finally White Bull prevailed. He hit the soldier on the head several times and knocked him out. "White Bull to strike the enemy first," he shouted in signal of a first coup. Then he shot the man and took his pistol and belt.

Paired with a Cheyenne, White Bull continued to fight against the dwindling band of soldiers trapped in the ravine. Together the two shot down two soldiers simultaneously, then each counted a first coup and a second.

On the hilltop above the head of the ravine, only a few soldiers remained, fighting hand to hand with Indians in their midst. There, said the Miniconjou Lights, the combatants were "near enough to look each other in the eyes."[31]

As Gall noted when he reached the scene: "The men were loading and firing, but they could not hit the warriors in the gully and the ravine [below, on the west]. The dust and smoke was black as evening. Once in a while we could see the soldiers through the dust, and finally we charged through them with our ponies. When we had done this . . . the fight was over."[32]

The proud bearer of no less than seven coups counted in a battle that had lasted hardly more than one hour, White Bull made his way on foot up the hillside to share in the final kill. A spent bullet bounced off his leg. It did not break skin but produced swelling and loss of feeling. White Bull rolled into a ditch and waited for aid.

After the last white had been felled, friends brought a horse and helped White Bull back to the village. They placed him in the lodge of his father, Chief Makes Room, in the Miniconjou camp circle. Sitting Bull came to doctor the leg. After applying a medicinal root, he wrapped it in buffalo fur. "My nephew, you must be careful," he enjoined. "Sometime you may be killed."

As feeling returned to his leg, White Bull mounted and rode back to the battle ridge to look for his saddle and leggings, cast aside at the beginning of the fight. As in the valley after the retreat of the other soldiers, women and children moved among the dead and wounded, stripping and robbing the bodies and mutilating some.

As White Bull surveyed the fallen men scattered around the hilltop where the last had been slain, Bad Soup joined him. A Standing Rock Hunkpapa, he had frequently been among the soldiers. Pointing to a naked corpse, he told White Bull that it was Long Hair. He thought he was the greatest man in the world, Bad Soup remarked, and there he is.[33]

After retrieving his saddle and leggings, White Bull stripped two pairs of pants from dead soldiers as a gift for his father. On the way back to the village, he paused to wash them in the river and water his horse. Another Indian was also watering horses. He was Noisy Walker, Inkpaduta's son. Noting a handsome sorrel, White Bull asked, "Is that a good horse?"

"I know it is a good horse," answered the Dakota, "as it was Long Hair's."

ON A BLUFFTOP four miles south of where Long Hair lay dead, Major Reno's men confronted their own crisis. The sudden departure of the Indians after the battle in the valley had afforded welcome respite. Even more welcome, Captain Benteen rode in with his battalion, and soon afterward the pack train straggled in.

The sound of firing from downriver prompted some of the officers to urge a move in that direction, where Custer must be engaged. But indecision gripped the commanders. A halfhearted move to the north encountered Indians returning from the other battlefield. The units fought a rearguard action back to the original position.

Now numbering about 350, the surviving seven companies of the Seventh Cavalry, ignorant of the disaster that had befallen their commander and comrades, formed a defense perimeter and battled for their own lives.

BECAUSE OF THE packmules and their attendants, White Bull called the clash on the blufftops the "Teamsters Fight." As One Bull noted, the Indians had obtained many fine carbines and plenty of cartridges from the dead soldiers downriver. Now they surrounded the live soldiers and fired at them from all sides.[34]

The soldiers had formed around a saucerlike depression in which they placed their wounded from the valley fight. Until nightfall the Indians kept them busy with heavy firing. Not until darkness could they dig in and arrange the packs as barricades.

Sitting Bull and White Bull both went to the new battlefield that evening. Sitting Bull joined tribesmen firing from a dominating ridge to the northeast of the soldiers' position. White Bull fired from gulches on the south, where a steep-sided ridge projected from the swale behind. Both sides lost men in the fighting.[35]

White Bull spent the night on the battlefield, but Sitting Bull returned to the village. Heralds had announced that the village would not move. Women were raising tipis that had been packed for flight. Others built brush wickiups as temporary shelters to serve until the next move began. People tended their wounded or mourned loudly for their dead. As Kill Eagle recalled, "They kept continually coming in with wounded, thrown over horses, with their heads hanging down and blood running out."[36]

The battle for the bluffs opened at dawn on June 26. White Bull was there, but Sitting Bull remained in the village almost until noon. Then he returned to the heights. Even more than the day before, he believed that these soldiers should not be killed. "Let them go now," he counseled, "so some can go home and spread the news. I just saw some more soldiers coming."[37]

He had not actually seen them himself, but more were in fact coming, and this, rather than a compassionate regard for white soldiers, prompted the Indians to let them go.

White Bull had returned to his lodge to eat a midday meal and take a nap. Someone awoke him with news that more soldiers were coming from the north. With two boys, he rode down the valley and confirmed the reports that scouts had already spread through the six camp circles. When he returned at dusk, he found the village site already vacated. Two tipis remained, burial lodges for slain warriors. Lodge poles, utensils, and other debris littered the valley, but the people had departed.

Without pausing, White Bull continued through the village site and that night caught up with the procession. Strung out on the benchland southwest of the valley, the people were sleeping in the open, each circle in its assigned order, the Cheyennes first, the Hunkpapas last. Not until the next night, once again in the Little Bighorn Valley, did they establish another village.

On the fourth night they staged a victory dance. They celebrated the greatest triumph the Sioux and Cheyennes had ever known or would ever know over any enemy, white or Indian.

Altogether, more than half of Long Hair's regiment lay dead or wounded. The Indians had killed every one of the troopers in his immediate command—210. Of the ones in the valley and on the bluffs, they had killed 53 and wounded 60. The Indians never accurately counted their own losses, but their estimates suggest that White Bull's enumeration of

27 falls short of the true total by no more than about a dozen. Many more, of course, were wounded.[38]

For generations to come, the veterans of the big battle on the Greasy Grass and their children and their children's children would recount the brave deeds witnessed when they destroyed Long Hair.

The victory on the Greasy Grass had fulfilled Sitting Bull's sun-dance vision. Soldiers had fallen right into camp and had all been killed. Yet for Sitting Bull it was an occasion less of joy than of resigned acceptance of the inevitable. "I feel sorry that too many were killed on each side," he said, "but when Indians must fight, they must."[39]

He also felt sad that the people had defied his injunction, as drawn from the sun-dance vision, not to rob the bodies of the soldiers who fell into the village upside down. "He told the people they should not set their hearts on any thing or things the white people had or it would be a curse on them," explained One Bull.

"For failure on your part to obey," Sitting Bull told his people, "henceforth you shall always covet white people's belongings."[40] The specter of dependence on the whites would haunt him to his dying day.

WHILE BRAVE DEEDS and first coups crowded the memory of Indian participants, whites wrestled with other obsessions. They argued, as they would argue for generations to come, over what had happened and why, and above all over who was to blame. Opprobrium fell on Custer, Reno, and Benteen, on Terry, Gibbon, and Crook, and even on President Ulysses S. Grant. That so terrible a disaster to U.S. troops had to have sprung chiefly from someone's blunder came to be an article of faith among the disputants.

And in truth all the accused bore more or less fault for bad judgments, miscalculations, and ethnocentric overconfidence. They could not imagine the cowardly Indians doing anything but running away if they got the chance. That they would stand and fight belied all their assumptions.

In addition to searching for blunders, whites also explained the unthinkable in terms of overwhelming numbers and exemplary Indian generalship. Within days after the battle, the number of warriors had grown in some estimates to ten thousand, in a village of forty thousand people. In all the Lakota tribes, with the Northern Cheyennes thrown in, there were scarcely more than half that many people.

Nor were there any Indian generals, despite reports that Sitting Bull had graduated from West Point Military Academy. Indians did not fight under the command of generals or even chiefs. Accounts of chiefs marshaling their warriors and deploying them with tactical skill to outmaneuver Long Hair did not reflect the way Indians fought. Crazy Horse's martial brilliance owed less to his foresight and command than to personal example that inspired warriors to follow him into the fray. Gall's irresistible assault up the north branch of Medicine Tail to overwhelm the dismounted defenders at the south end of the battle ridge was conducted by warriors who could not even remember seeing Gall there, although he was.

As Robert Higheagle pointed out, "The chief might give orders to fight but he does not direct how to proceed." Each fighting man did that on his own, and if he rode behind a chief such as Crazy Horse or Gall, it was because he wanted to, not because he had been ordered to. That otherwise authoritative Indian accounts implied a command and control by a chief resulted from the assumptions of white interrogators, the shortcomings of interpreters, and the impulse of Indian participants to tell the white man what he wanted to hear.[41]

The Indians did not win the Battle of the Little Bighorn because of generalship or even leadership. They won because they outnumbered the enemy three to one; because they were united, confident, and angry; and above all because the immediate threat to their women and children fired every man with determination to save his family. The Indians won too because their foes allowed themselves to be beaten in fragments and because their leadership broke down. Both in the valley and on the battle ridge, command and control collapsed, discipline evaporated, and men panicked, which left the initiative to the Indians.

If whites ascribed Napoleonic genius to Sitting Bull in 1876, in less than a decade they had produced another interpretation. Abetted by Indians currying favor with the Great Father, white officials then said Sitting Bull did not participate in the battle at all. He remained in his tipi making medicine, or fled to the hills in terror, even abandoning his family, or skulked somewhere else safely out of danger.

In truth, any act that kept him out of the battle would have been more acceptable to his people than the role he played. He was forty-five, a chief several times over whose bravery was questioned by no one. He was far more valuable as an old-man chief, a wise counselor, than as a fighting man. Leave that to the young warriors striving for white feathers. Chiefs were expected to fight only to protect their women and children from harm.

That is what he did. He fought the Reno soldiers when they threatened the women and children at the upper end of the village. After that threat receded, he could have withdrawn with honor. Instead he continued to fire at the soldiers and shout encouragement to the warriors. Later, on the blufftops, he hovered on the edges of the fighting until everyone left to confront Long Hair downstream. Then he went to the northern end of the village where the women and children had collected. Again, his foremost thought lay with them. More than enough young men swarmed on the battle ridge to wipe out Long Hair. That evening and again the next day he climbed the hill where the Reno soldiers held out, his goal apparently not only to give reassurance but to urge an end to the fighting.

The calumny in the effort to recast Sitting Bull's role in the Little Bighorn lay in the allegations of cowardice. Bravery was the first of the cardinal virtues. It was the Hunkpapa man's proudest possession. From the day of Sitting Bull's first coup, thirty-one years before the Little Bighorn, his life's story had been a nearly unbroken record of conspicuous bravery, and he had the white and red feathers to prove it. Nothing he did at the Little Bighorn detracted from that record until some of his people allowed themselves to be enticed into judging behavior according to white norms rather than Indian.

The Cheyenne Wooden Leg delivered an accurate judgment on the issue:

I am not ashamed to tell that I was a follower of Sitting Bull. I have no ears for hearing anybody say he was not a brave man. He had a big brain and a good one, a strong heart and a generous one. In the old times I never heard of any Indian having spoken otherwise of him. If any of them changed their talk in later days, the change must have been brought about by lies of agents and soldier chiefs who schemed to make themselves appear as good men by making him appear as a bad man.[42]

Sitting Bull regretted that he had not killed Frank Grouard when he had had the chance. But it was the Grabber, finally, who voiced a fitting tribute to Sitting Bull's bravery:

No man in the Sioux Nation was braver in battle than Sitting Bull, and he asked none of his warriors to take any chances that he was not willing at all times to share. I could recall a hundred different instances coming under my own observation to prove Sitting Bull's bravery, and in the first great Sun Dance that I ever witnessed after my capture by the Sioux, I heard Sitting Bull recount his "*coups* in action." They numbered sixty-three, most of them being victories over Indian enemies.[43]

Sitting Bull's significance at the Little Bighorn lay not in flaunting bravery, or directing the movements of warriors, or even inspiring them to fight. It lay rather in a leadership so wise and powerful that it drew together and held together a muscular coalition of tribes, one so infused with his defiant cast of mind that it could rout Three Stars and annihilate Long Hair. Never had the Sioux and Cheyennes triumphed so spectacularly, and never would they again. For that, more than any other chief, they could thank Sitting Bull.

13 BEAR COAT

AS SITTING BULL and his fellow chiefs mourned their dead and celebrated their triumph, they failed to understand that in whipping Three Stars and wiping out Long Hair they had decreed their own downfall. A stunned American nation demanded retribution, and Congress and the Grant administration stood ready to back any measure. The generals got the men, the money, and the authority they wanted to end Sioux troubles for all time. Units of "Custer Avengers" flocked to the Sioux country to bolster Crook and Terry and punish the Indians for humiliating the army.

Buffalo, not soldiers, governed the movements of the Indians after the Little Bighorn. When none could be found, they moved rapidly. When herds appeared, they slowed while hunters stockpiled meat. From the upper Little Bighorn, the village crossed to the head of the Rosebud, descended that stream to Greenleaf Creek, then turned east to the Tongue. Part searched up the Tongue for game, while the rest went downstream. August 1 found the two segments reunited on the Powder about twenty miles above its mouth.[1]

After several days there, the chiefs decided on another separation. Provisioning so many people in one village had proved difficult. Although *akicita* soldiered people who wanted to go to the agencies, the bands scattered in search of adequate game. Sitting Bull took most of the Hunkpapas, with some Miniconjous and Sans Arcs, down the Little

Missouri to Killdeer Mountain, site of his fight with General Sully in 1864. Another large contingent followed Crazy Horse up the Little Missouri toward the Black Hills.[2]

Not until after the fugitives scattered did Terry and Crook feel strong enough to move. When they met on the middle Rosebud on August 10, their combined armies numbered more than four thousand soldiers, civilians, and Indian allies. Through rain and mud this unwieldy force followed the Indian trail east to the Tongue and the Powder, growing daily more dispirited and disillusioned. Relations between the two generals deteriorated, and Crook bridled to free himself from Terry.

On August 26, without even telling Terry, Crook simply slipped away with his command and pointed east toward the Little Missouri Badlands. With rations dwindling alarmingly and the march made grueling by rain and mud, he lost his enthusiasm for chasing Indians. Turning sharply south on September 5, he struck out for the Black Hills, where he hoped to find provisions in the mining towns. The rains continued day after day, animals dropped by the score, and the men verged on collapse from hunger and exhaustion. On September 8 Crook dispatched an advance party under Captain Anson Mills to hasten to the Black Hills and buy provisions.

Entirely by accident, Crook's march took him through a formidable gathering of Indians. Dotting the creek valleys at the head of the Moreau River, near a geological formation known as Slim Buttes, stood scattered camps of Oglalas, Miniconjous, Sans Arcs, and Hunkpapas. Crazy Horse was in the neighborhood, as was the Sans Arc Spotted Eagle. With Four Horns, Black Moon, and No Neck, Sitting Bull had come down from Killdeer. He mourned the death of a child, kicked in the head by a horse several days earlier.[3]

One of the camps consisted of thirty-seven lodges of Miniconjous. Mills's command discovered them and attacked just before daybreak on September 9.

People struggled to free themselves from tipis tightly fastened against the rain and rushed into bluffs on the south side of the creek valley. Once the men had placed their families beyond danger, they posted themselves on these bluffs and directed a deadly fire at the soldiers in the village.[4]

By noon couriers had alerted the nearby villages, and warriors rode to the attack. Also, Crook had come up with the main command. For the rest of the day the two sides exchanged fire, the Indians from positions on the bluffs, the soldiers from the village, which they burned.

Sitting Bull fought conspicuously among the Hunkpapas. Wearing a buffalo-horn headdress with a trail of feathers down his back, he fired from the bluffs and shouted encouragement to his men.[5]

The soldiers had no heart for a serious fight. After slogging across more than four hundred miles of plains, they had finally caught up with most of the Indians who had slaughtered Custer. Worn out, hungry, and miserable, the pursuers wanted only to get to the Black Hills. Warriors harassed them the next day as they marched away, but then let them go.

Slim Buttes was touted as a victory for the army, but it was a shabby victory at best and accomplished nothing beyond angering the Indians. The dawn attack had felled women and children, and when the tribesmen crept back into the village after the military withdrawal, they confronted heartrending scenes.[6] Many of the groups in the vicinity of Slim Buttes, including the one struck by Mills, had intended to surrender at an agency. The sight of women and children maimed or slain by army bullets dampened that impulse.

WHILE THE ELECTORATE still mourned the death of Custer and his troopers, the government made haste to resolve another issue. In spite of the official fiction that the Black Hills had nothing to do with the Sioux War, Congress prohibited the expenditure of any funds for rationing the Sioux until they gave up the Black Hills and the unceded territory. In the autumn a commission presented the ultimatum and, ignoring the treaty requirement that three-fourths of adult males agree, lined up the agency chiefs to sign. They did.[7]

Finally, Indian "title" to the Black Hills and the unceded territory had been "extinguished." The mining settlements of the Black Hills, some nearly two years old, were comfortably "legal." The Sitting Bull bands occupied *ceded* territory and were bound by the Treaty of 1868 and the order of December 6, 1875, to settle within the Great Sioux Reservation. And these people, whether at the agencies or in the theater of war, would be received only in accord with a rigid policy of unconditional surrender, yielding their arms, ammunition, and horses, and submitting to military dominion as prisoners of war.

From his Chicago headquarters, General Sheridan plotted "total war" against the hunting bands. First, he would plant permanent forts in the heart of the buffalo ranges and from these bases campaign ceaselessly against the fugitives until they tired and gave up. Second, he would impose military control on the Indian agencies, disarm and dismount the hunting bands as they were driven in, and govern with a no-nonsense firmness that would make future outbreaks impossible. In the aftermath of the Custer disaster, he got everything he asked for.[8]

By late October, with winter approaching, Sheridan made his long-anticipated but still stunning move. General Terry swooped down on Standing Rock and Cheyenne River agencies and confiscated arms, ammunition, and ponies—not just from those who had come in from the hunting bands but from everyone. At the same time, at Red Cloud Agency, General Crook disarmed and dismounted the followers of Red Cloud and Red Leaf, few of whom had fought the soldiers. Crook also "deposed" Red Cloud and appointed Spotted Tail as head chief. Truly now did the army exercise "absolute control" of the agencies.[9]

Against the Sitting Bull bands Sheridan applied the other arm of his strategy—to occupy the buffalo ranges and hound the Indians into unconditional surrender. The forts Congress had approved in the Yellowstone country could not be built until the next summer, when boats could bring up supplies. But during the winter Sheridan expected his troops to keep the Sioux on the move.

AFTER SLIM BUTTES, the ceaseless quest for buffalo again took control of Indian movements. Sitting Bull and the Hunkpapas, with the Miniconjous and Sans Arcs who had accompanied him ever since the breakup of the great village early in August, moved northwest, back toward the Yellowstone.

Since before Slim Buttes, Sitting Bull's lodge had harbored a curious resident. He was a swarthy young mixed blood named John Bruguier who, said White Bull, "spoke Lakota like a Sioux." He had ridden boldly into the Sioux camp one day with large, wing-shaped chaps flapping about his legs—"like a cowboy," according to White Bull. Suspecting him for an army scout, a number of the Hunkpapas wanted to kill him. But Sitting Bull sent White Bull to bring him for questioning. A throng gathered, rolled up the tipi covering from the pegs, and peered in. At any moment one might put an arrow into the stranger. "Well, if you are going to kill this man, kill him," shouted Sitting Bull, "and if you are not, give him a drink of water, something to eat, and a pipe of peace to smoke."[10]

Thus, as he had Frank Grouard, Sitting Bull threw his protection over "Big Leggings" Bruguier. Johnny had been the competent agency interpreter at Standing Rock until the previous December, when he and his brother engaged in a drunken brawl with another agency employee that ended in homicide. With warrants out for his arrest, he kept a step ahead of the law for eight months until he found sanctuary with the Hunkpapas. Sitting Bull took him into his lodge and presented him with a horse, a bay named "Hohe Horse." Bruguier reciprocated with a Winchester rifle.

On the day the Indian cavalcade crossed the Yellowstone, October 10, scouts from the village discovered not only buffalo in great numbers north of the Yellowstone but soldiers too. The northward march of the Indians had intersected the westward march of soldiers. For a month Colonel Nelson A. Miles and his foot soldiers had been throwing up rude huts in which they would winter at the mouth of the Tongue. Because of low water, steamboats could no longer reach the Tongue, and wagon trains protected by infantry escorts hauled freight from a supply dump opposite the mouth of Glendive Creek.

On October 11 Sioux warriors fell on a wagon train as it formed for the day's march. They shot down many of the mules and stampeded others, which so crippled the movement that the train turned back to Glendive.

It appeared again on October 15, eighty-six wagons surrounded by a guard of two hundred soldiers armed with long-range infantry rifles. All day several hundred warriors pressed the train on all sides but were driven back by the deadly rifles. They set fire to the dry prairie grass, but still the train moved forward.

With his usual daring, White Bull and a knot of companions sped to within seventy-five yards of the soldiers, looking for an opening to run them down. A bullet tore into his left arm just above the elbow, shattering the bone. He kept his seat and, aided by friends, rode safely off the battlefield. At the village he almost fell from his horse, but young boys ran out to help him.[11]

Sitting Bull did not participate in this fight. As it resumed sporadically the next morning, the chiefs debated whether they should try to talk peace with the soldier chief. Sitting Bull summoned Big Leggings and had him write a message. Impaled on a stick and thrust into the middle of the road in front of the train, it read:

I want to know what you are doing traveling on this road. You scare all the buffalo away. I want to hunt on the place. I want you to turn back from here. If you don't, I will fight you again. I want you to leave what you have got here, and turn back from here.

I am your friend,

SITTING BULL

> I mean all the rations you have got and some powder. Wish you
> would write as soon as you can.

However clumsily, Big Leggings had succeeded in conveying what
was in Sitting Bull's mind. This was his country. The soldiers were
invaders. They scared the buffalo. They must leave or he would fight.

But the chiefs thought Sitting Bull should talk. Two emissaries sent
from Standing Rock to work for peace, Bear's Face and Long Feather,
thought he should too. They had a written paper given them by the
soldier chief at Standing Rock, and this would serve as the basis for a
parley. Accordingly, waving a white cloth, the two rode to the head of the
soldier column and talked with the officer. They returned with word that
he wanted to confer with Sitting Bull.

He would not shake hands with the officer, Sitting Bull declared. His
comrades remonstrated, but he stood firm. At length he explained that
the shabby clothing that he still wore in mourning for his dead son made
him ashamed to shake hands with anyone. Pressed by all the chiefs,
however, he finally relented.[12]

The delegation met with Lieutenant Colonel Elwell S. Otis. Sitting
Bull seems not to have played a conspicuous role in the conference.
Probably, embarrassed by his clothing and disgruntled at being pressured
into the meeting at all, he let the others do the talking.

The chiefs did not adopt a conciliatory tone but rather reproached Otis
for driving off the buffalo. They said they were hungry, low on ammunition, tired of war, and wanted peace. Otis curtly replied that he could not
give them ammunition, that they had wasted enough shooting at his train
to have lasted a long time. Moreover, he had no authority to treat with
them for peace. Nor would he feed them, he declared, although on this he
relented and had 150 pounds of hard bread and two sides of bacon
deposited on the ground. With that, the train resumed its progress and the
Indians vanished.[13]

After retrieving Otis's gift of rations, they moved up Cedar Creek,
overtaking a big buffalo herd and conducting a surround. Wolves left
behind to watch the soldiers reported more coming down the Yellowstone.
Worried by the delay of the freight train, Colonel Miles had led his entire
regiment, the Fifth Infantry, to the rescue. After confirming Otis's safety,
he turned north on the Indian trail and, on October 20, approached the
village in rough country where Cedar Creek issues to the south from the
divide between the Yellowstone and the Missouri.

The chiefs and many of their warriors gathered on a ridge and saw the soldiers fan out in skirmish formation preparing for battle. Sitting Bull asked Bear's Face and Long Feather to arrange another talk. Under a white flag, the two rode forth. "These troops were on the warpath," remembered Bear's Face. "We ran great risk in going to them, but we went directly to them."[14]

Miles had no interpreter, which led to lengthy confusion in even getting the negotiators together. Finally his adjutant accompanied the two agency Indians into the midst of the chiefs and discovered Big Leggings Bruguier, who was immediately pressed into service as interpreter.

After an hour of the "most painful and excruciating interest and uneasiness on both sides," according to a correspondent with Miles, the two delegations advanced toward each other. From the south, Miles and his staff rode into the open while his companies "fidgeted" in line of battle to the rear, and a cannon "frowned" from a hilltop. From the north Sitting Bull and a dozen chiefs walked toward the soldiers, in "perfect line" and unarmed, followed by a mounted and armed phalanx of warriors.

The day was bright and sunny but very cold. Sitting Bull was attired in buckskin leggings and wrapped in a heavy buffalo robe, but displayed no feathers or other ornament.

The conference brought Sitting Bull face to face with a man who would become his special nemesis. Another "boy general" of Civil War fame, only four months older than Custer, Nelson Miles eagerly welcomed the chance for active service that Sitting Bull presented. No colonel surpassed him in ambition or vanity, nor in energy or ability. He hungered obsessively for distinction and promotion. On the cold day of the conference, he wore a fur cap and a long overcoat trimmed in bear fur and covered by a military cape. The Sioux named him "Man-with-the-Bear Coat," or simply Bear Coat. In the next four years they would learn much about Bear Coat.

Miles and his staff dismounted, and the colonel advanced to shake hands with Sitting Bull. The Indians spread a buffalo robe on the ground and invited Miles to sit. He declined, but finally relented enough to kneel. A pipe ceremony failed to set the proper tone.

The talks, with Bruguier interpreting, lasted all afternoon and featured much rancorous exchange of accusation and reproach. Miles, for example, upbraided Sitting Bull for stealing mules from his freight train on October 11 and demanded their return. Sitting Bull countered by demanding the return of the buffalo that Miles's soldiers had scared off.

Amid all the rhetoric, however, irreconcilable positions emerged.

Miles wanted Sitting Bull to surrender unconditionally and bring his people to the Tongue River post to await the government's decision on their disposition. Sitting Bull wanted Miles to withdraw his soldiers from the Yellowstone altogether, abandon the Tongue River post and Fort Buford too, and leave the Indians free to trade with white traders and follow the buffalo as they had always done.

With the parley leading nowhere, Miles broke it off with the explanation that they should think overnight and meet again the next day. During the night both sides considered attacking the other, and in fact the next morning the Indians observed the soldiers advancing up the creek valley in battle formation. The women and children struck the tipis and prepared for flight while, once again, the chiefs advanced for a talk. On this day a sizable contingent of Miniconjou and Sans Arc chiefs joined the Indian leadership.

This time Miles spread the buffalo robe on the ground, and Sitting Bull refused the invitation to sit, but finally yielded. He was in no better frame of mind than the day before. He repeated much of what he had already said, but also, in deference to the Miniconjous and Sans Arcs, diluted his previous stance somewhat. These chiefs favored a more conciliatory approach, and some thought the time for surrender had come.

At times during the conference, such were the pressures besetting him that Sitting Bull grew almost speechless. As one observer noted, he seemed unable to "talk or express his thoughts," and Pretty Bear, Hunkpapa orator, offered excuses. "We talk," he explained, "but he is our fighting chief."

Finally losing patience, Miles delivered an ultimatum: Refusal to surrender immediately and unconditionally would be regarded as an act of hostility, and he would attack at once. By this time, as White Bull noted, Sitting Bull was angry and Bear Coat was angry, and it was best to end the talks before someone did something foolish. Amid angry recrimination, both parties returned to their lines.

The soldiers advanced to the attack. Warriors gathered on the ridges and in the ravines to cover the withdrawal of their families. The clash, styled in the records the Battle of Cedar Creek, was no more bloody or decisive than the fight with Otis a week earlier, but it afforded Miles the chance to maneuver an entire regiment and laid the groundwork for much self-congratulation. One Indian was hit by a rifle ball and killed, and two soldiers were wounded.

White Bull, his arm in a sling, did not participate. Sitting Bull commanded him to hang back. But Big Leggings, White Bull noted approvingly, "fought for the Indians and was a brave man, riding in a circle toward the soldiers."[15]

The Indians crossed eastward to the head of Bad Route Creek and followed it down to the Yellowstone, Miles in close pursuit. En route, conscious of the split between himself and the Miniconjou and Sans Arc leaders, Sitting Bull turned aside and with thirty lodges headed north, toward the Missouri. White Bull remained with his own people, the Miniconjous.

At the Yellowstone Miles overtook the fugitives. With Sitting Bull no longer present, the chiefs readily surrendered. Rather than burden himself with four hundred lodges, Miles accepted five hostages as a pledge that the people would go to Cheyenne River Agency and surrender. They did not, at least not at once, partly because they did not want to and partly because of *akicita* soldiering.

For Sitting Bull, the confrontation with Bear Coat brought home two painful truths. First, the soldiers had not only invaded his country, they had come to stay, and they seemed determined to have their way. Like Fort Buford, the Tongue River post stood for a lasting military presence in the heart of the buffalo country, with all that meant for the way of life of the hunting bands. Second, his coalition was coming unraveled. The defection of the Sans Arc and Miniconjou chiefs disclosed that not all the hunting bands possessed his stubborn aversion to giving up their freedom and living at the agencies. Even his nephew White Bull had gone with them. Sitting Bull was increasingly isolated.

These stresses probably account for the poor showing Sitting Bull made in the councils. A number of participants noted his apparent melancholy and ineffectiveness, but Miles himself sensed it most clearly. Sitting Bull, he wrote to his wife,

> is a man apparently forty five or fifty years old. He has a large broad head and strong features. He is a man evidently of great influence and a thinking, reasoning being. I should judge his great strength is as a warrior. I think he feels that his strength is somewhat exhausted and he appeared much depressed, suffering from nervous excitement and loss of power. . . . At times he was almost inclined to accept the situation, but I think partly from fear and partly through the belief that he might do better, he did not accept. I think that many of his people were desirous to make peace.[16]

14 WINTER OF DESPAIR

FOR ALL THE hunting bands, the winter of 1876–77 was a winter of despair. Soldiers occupied the hunting grounds and kept the war going even when the snow fell and the temperature plunged. Besides the usual perils of winter—uncertain food and gaunt ponies—the Indians never knew when soldiers might burst into their village, shoot down the people, and destroy their homes and food supplies. The alternative was unconditional surrender, either to the soldiers in the game country or at the agencies. That meant giving up their horses and their guns, a nearly unthinkable notion for people whose culture centered on both.

For Sitting Bull, the despair was especially acute. More than any other Indian leader, he looked on the prospect of exchanging the old free life of the plains for the debilitating and dependent life of the agency as deeply offensive. Even as others gave in and surrendered and the knot tightened around him, he could not bring himself to confront reality.

The councils with Bear Coat Miles marked a turning point. Always before, the soldiers had come, provoked a brief crisis, and then left. After those councils they stayed, and the old life was doomed. The winter of despair brought most of the hunting bands to accept the reality. Sitting Bull and a hard core of holdouts could not. For another four years this paragon of Lakota life and virtue would perform every twist and turn he could conceive of to avoid the cruel certainty that awaited all Indians.

WHILE SITTING BULL parried with Bear Coat north of the Yellowstone, Three Stars Crook gathered his army for another foray into the Powder River country. In mid-November he marched north from Fort Fetterman with a force of more than two thousand men. Ominously foreshadowing the disintegration of Sitting Bull's coalition, Oglala wolves from Red Cloud Agency scouted for the Long Knives. They brought word of a Cheyenne village in a canyon of the Bighorn Mountains.

After pushing through snowdrifts with eleven hundred cavalrymen, in the misty dawn of November 25 Colonel Ranald S. Mackenzie burst into the village of Dull Knife (Morning Star) and Little Wolf, nearly two hundred lodges clustered in a canyon of the Red Fork of Powder River. Driven from their lodges, the men fought back from surrounding slopes but could not regain their village.

It was a crushing blow to the Cheyennes, in logistics more than casualties. They left thirty dead on the battlefield while striking down six soldiers and wounding twenty-six, but they lost everything except what they carried from their sleeping robes when attacked. Tipis, meat, clothing, utensils, ammunition, arts and craft and other finery—all went up in flames; and seven hundred ponies fell captive to the soldiers. Enduring terrible hardship, the victims struggled north in search of succor. Temperatures tumbled to thirty below zero. Eleven babies froze to death in their mothers' arms. After three horrifying weeks, the Cheyennes found relief with Crazy Horse on the upper Tongue.[1]

With Christmas approaching, Crook called off the operation and disbanded his army. His campaign, he explained, had so stirred up the Indians "that it is useless to try to catch them with this command."[2] Instead he turned his energies to enlisting agency Indians in a bid to persuade the hunting bands to surrender. Ultimately this venture bore fruit.

Bear Coat Miles proved more resilient and persistent than Three Stars. He not only maintained his base at the mouth of the Tongue all winter, he did not allow snow and freezing temperatures to confine him to the uncertain comforts of his makeshift shelters. In particular, he wanted to smash Sitting Bull.

In the perception of the white citizenry, Sitting Bull was the man to get, the archdemon of the Sioux holdouts, the architect of Custer's defeat and death, the supreme monarch of all the savage legions arrayed against the forces of civilization. Newspapers vied with one another in profiling this all-powerful ruler, and no story was too silly for their readership.

Equally silly was General Sheridan's effort to deflate Sitting Bull. He had no reason to believe, he declared, that such an individual as Sitting Bull even existed. "I have always understood 'Sitting-bull' to mean *the hostile Indians,* and not a great leader."[3]

The Sitting Bull caricatured by the newspapers, of course, did not exist. But precisely because he was a great leader, Sitting Bull had indeed come to mean, for Indians and whites alike, *the hostile Indians.*

Bear Coat knew Sitting Bull existed, for he had counciled with him on October 20–21. As the first operation out of his Tongue River base, he went after Sitting Bull.

By the end of October, following the split with the Miniconjous and Sans Arcs, Sitting Bull and his paltry thirty lodges had posted themselves on the Big Dry about twenty-five miles south of Fort Peck. With Sitting Bull were Four Horns and Black Moon. They hoped to trade with Yanktonais or Slotas in the neighborhood of the fort.

Another 125 Hunkpapa lodges clustered in the Missouri bottoms immediately below Fort Peck. The core seems to have been Long Dog, but other bands included those of Iron Dog, Crow, and Little Knife. All paid allegiance to Sitting Bull except Iron Dog, who was said to have quarreled with Sitting Bull and would not again follow his lead.

On October 31 most of these Indians, accompanied by their women and children, went to Fort Peck to talk with Agent Thomas J. Mitchell. They said that Sitting Bull remained on the Big Dry awaiting the outcome of the council. "Humbly," according to Mitchell, they described themselves as destitute of food and ammunition and desperate for peace on any terms. Mitchell stated the terms—surrender of arms and government property (animals and booty from the Little Bighorn) pending further instructions from his superiors. After much haggling, they dejectedly agreed. Mitchell distributed rations but, with night approaching, postponed the actual surrender until the next day. Scarcely had the council adjourned than a runner brought word of observing, at Wolf Point, a boat loaded with soldiers steaming up the Missouri toward Fort Peck. By dawn not a single Hunkpapa could be found in the neighborhood.

Colonel William B. Hazen and 140 soldiers from Fort Buford docked at Fort Peck on November 1. They unloaded rations and forage to supply Miles's command when it arrived from Tongue River, left a guard of thirty men, and returned to Fort Buford. Hazen confirmed the impoverished condition of the Hunkpapas. They had no lodges, he said, or anything else except horses "thin as shadows." "I don't think they can stand the winter if kept stirred up."[4]

Bear Coat intended to keep them stirred up. Facing north from Tongue River on November 6, he led his regiment toward Fort Peck. In the teeth of a brutal winter storm, the command struggled across "one of the wildest and least known countries on the continent." "Bundled up to the eyes, on account of the extreme cold," ten days later they reached the Missouri River opposite Fort Peck.[5]

Sitting Bull, his following on the Big Dry swollen to more than a hundred lodges by the stampede from Fort Peck on November 1, kept Bear Coat under close watch. As his soldiers came down the Big Dry, the Hunkpapas shifted east, to the forks of the Red Water, another northward flowing tributary of the Missouri.

There a runner arrived from Crazy Horse asking Sitting Bull to obtain more ammunition and join him on Powder River. When the soldiers left Fort Peck, Sitting Bull intended to go there and trade for ammunition, then head south to unite with Crazy Horse.[6]

Miles erroneously believed Sitting Bull's location to be farther west, toward the Musselshell, and on November 19 he took his regiment up the north bank of the Missouri. Sitting Bull thus benefited from Bear Coat's mistake, and also from the bad luck that brought warm weather and thawed the Missouri, trapping the troops on the north side.[7]

For Sitting Bull, another development proved less beneficial. One who did not flee Fort Peck in the Hunkpapa stampede of November 1 was Big Leggings Johnny Bruguier. Miles found him there on November 17, and the two worked out a bargain. Bruguier would help Miles try to get Sitting Bull to surrender, and Miles would help Bruguier escape the murder charge hanging over him in Dakota. Once again, as with Frank Grouard, Sitting Bull had misplaced his trust in a stranger his people had preferred to kill.[8]

Early in December the river froze again, and Sitting Bull crossed to seek traders who could furnish ammunition. With 250 families crammed into three lodges and ninety-two shelter tents, they camped in the Missouri bottoms below the fort, near the mouth of Milk River. Coincidentally, at the same time Miles detached three companies, 112 men under Lieutenant Frank D. Baldwin, and sent them down the Missouri to Fort Peck.

There, on December 6, Baldwin met Johnny Bruguier. He had left Sitting Bull's camp on December 3, and he informed Baldwin of its exact location. Bruguier had made his final break with Sitting Bull. As agreed two weeks earlier, his name went on the army payroll, and Baldwin sent him with dispatches to Miles. Henceforth he would serve as an army scout, and one day Miles and his officers would be instrumental in freeing him of the murder charge.[9]

Through the bitterly cold night of December 6, Baldwin and his men marched down the Missouri to Milk River. Scattered camps of Yanktonais stood in the timber along the Missouri, and Baldwin gave orders to fire on no Indians for fear of hitting friendlies.

Beyond Milk River, shortly before daybreak of December 7, the soldiers unwittingly marched by Sitting Bull's camp, which since Bruguier's departure had been augmented by ninety lodges. Jumping Bull, Sitting Bull's adopted brother, saw the soldiers, brazenly rode his pony up to the rear guard, and even passed close to Baldwin, who mistook him for one of his own Indian scouts. Jumping Bull then slipped back to camp to give the alarm, and before the soldiers could find their objective the Hunkpapas had hurried across the Missouri on the ice.

After reaching the south bank, the men conducted their families to safety, then took positions in the breaks overlooking the timbered bottom. A company of troops crossed to scout the situation and quickly pulled back when fired on. The officers all agreed that Sitting Bull had six hundred warriors posted to lure the bluecoats into a trap and "make another Custer affair." Followed by Lakota wolves, Baldwin marched down the Missouri and took a defensive position on a hilltop, but the Hunkpapas contented themselves with firing across the river.

That night another norther struck, and the soldiers nearly froze to death before completing a night march back to Fort Peck. With some exaggeration, Baldwin boasted to his wife: "Just think your old man whipping Sitting Bull & driving him across the river when he has set at defiance 2 Brig Genls all summer."[10]

Sitting Bull had succeeded in collecting enough ammunition through trade with the Slotas to form a train of mules loaded with fifty boxes. After the skirmish with Baldwin, with about 120 lodges, he began the journey to rendezvous with Crazy Horse. The procession aimed southeast to the Red Water River, which headed on the divide between the Yellowstone and the Missouri and angled northeast to flow into the Missouri opposite the mouth of Poplar River. On December 17, with two feet of snow on the ground and the weather very cold, his people camped under a range of bluffs on the east side of Ash Creek, a tributary stream near the head of the Red Water.

Embarrassed that he had let Sitting Bull escape a week earlier, Baldwin had loaded his little command into wagons drawn by six-mule teams and pushed out on the frozen plains again. At Fort Peck he had discovered an old howitzer tube and some solid shot. Fastening the tube to the rear axle and wheels of a wagon, he improvised his own artillery. On the morning of December 18, his scouts spotted Sitting Bull's camp.

The Hunkpapas sighted the soldiers, spread out in skirmish formation, advancing up the valley toward their village. The men rushed out to make a stand while their families escaped to the south. Baldwin fired three rounds from his little howitzer, which with each blast jumped from its carriage and had to be remounted. The solid shot did no damage, but the explosions demoralized the warriors and they turned to overtake their fleeing women and children.

Sitting Bull's camp fell into the hands of the soldiers. Lodges, robes, utensils, tons of dried meat, and many horses and mules added up to a loss the Hunkpapas could ill afford in the depths of winter. Burning what they could not use and slaughtering the animals, Baldwin's men crossed the divide and descended to the Yellowstone, where they reunited with Miles and their comrades at the Tongue River post.

Among the booty brought in were several hundred buffalo robes. Some women among the Indians who had already accepted Miles's terms and settled around his station fashioned them into pants, overcoats, and caps. When the troops moved again, Baldwin recalled, "they were wearing warm clothing made from fur captured from Sitting Bull."[11]

Although dealt a severe blow in food and shelter, Sitting Bull had gotten away with the precious ammunition Crazy Horse had asked for. On January 15, 1877, with No Neck and about one hundred Hunkpapa lodges, Sitting Bull arrived in Crazy Horse's village.[12]

The camp lay at the mouth of Prairie Dog Creek, where Tongue River issued from the Bighorn Mountains. Most of the hunting bands were there—Crazy Horse and Little-Big-Man of the Oglalas, Black Shield and Lame Deer of the Miniconjous, Spotted Eagle and Red Bear of the Sans Arcs, Black Moccasin and Ice (White Bull) of the Cheyennes, and now Sitting Bull and No Neck of the Hunkpapas.

Sitting Bull found the bands badly divided on the issue of war or peace. In December the peace faction had nearly prevailed. On the sixteenth five chiefs had gone to the soldier post at the mouth of the Tongue to talk terms with Bear Coat. Much to his chagrin, his own Crow scouts shot them down on the edge of the military reservation.[13]

That shifted dominance to the war faction, and in the first week of January, as Miles and his infantrymen launched an offensive up Tongue

River, Crazy Horse sought to draw them into a trap and win a victory. The village stood at the mouth of Hanging Woman (or Suicide) Creek, and the men took positions amid the buttes and ridges shouldering the valley.

The old decoy trick misfired, as it often did, and on January 8 the two sides clashed. Bundled against the cold in the robes seized from Sitting Bull at the Red Water battle, the soldiers maneuvered energetically and shot up a great amount of ammunition, including artillery rounds that prevented the Indians from massing for an assault. A snowstorm settled on the battlefield and by afternoon turned to a blizzard, which ended the fight without much bloodshed on either side. But once again the Indians had been treated to Bear Coat's readiness to fight through the winter, and the war faction had been discredited.[14]

Buffalo drew the village up the Tongue to the mountains, where Sitting Bull found it a week later. The chiefs still bickered over whether to give up, and *akicita* soldiered people who tried. The Miniconjous and Sans Arcs (except Spotted Eagle) wanted to surrender. The Hunkpapas joined the Oglalas and Cheyennes in arguing for continuing the war. They could never accept the humiliating demand for their guns and ponies, they contended.[15]

As always, big villages strained the game resources, and at the beginning of February 1877 the chiefs decided to split up again. The Oglalas and Cheyennes crossed the Wolf Mountains to the Little Bighorn, where they found buffalo. The Miniconjous and Sans Arcs scattered to the east, some straggling into their agency to call off the war. The Hunkpapas, joined by some of the Miniconjous and Sans Arcs, turned north.

They were going all the way to Canada, the land of the Grandmother, Sitting Bull announced. Some of the Hunkpapa chiefs, including Black Moon, had already gone there. Now Sitting Bull followed, though without a clear resolve actually to cross the border. By the middle of March 1877 he had reached the familiar haunts on the Red Water southeast of Fort Peck. Occasionally some of his men came down to the river and shouted across to the agency interpreter. Once some asked whether soldiers still camped at the fort. Answered yes, they replied, "Damn soldiers everywhere."[16]

That reality bore with increasing weight on all the hunting bands. To the south, Bear Coat's soldiers stubbornly clung to their post at the mouth of the Tongue, a constant reminder of "damn soldiers everywhere." From Red Cloud and Spotted Tail agencies, delegations of kinsmen, sent by Three Stars, made their way north to try to talk the holdouts into giving up. Red Cloud and Spotted Tail themselves joined the movement and lent their great prestige to the effort. Big Leggings Bruguier rode boldly into the Oglala and Cheyenne camps on the Little Bighorn to try to entice those people into Bear Coat's post at the mouth of the Tongue.[17]

Despite the *akicita*, more and more groups broke off to make their way to the agencies. As Red Horse explained at Cheyenne River, "I am tired of being always on the watch for troops. My desire is to get my family where they can sleep without being continually in the expectation of an attack."[18]

Only about fifteen lodges remained with Sitting Bull on the Red Water. The rest that had followed him from the Tongue and Powder, about 150, had continued to Canada. As early as December 1876, Black Moon and fifty-two Hunkpapa lodges had crossed the boundary to Wood Mountain and settled with as many more Sioux of all Lakota tribes—three thousand people in all. In March 1877 Four Horns and another fifty-seven lodges joined the growing gathering.[19]

Beyond unconditional surrender and waging a losing struggle with the bluecoats, Canada did present a third option—fraught with uncertainty but still a means of avoiding the unacceptable or at least gaining some breathing space. That Four Horns, Black Moon, and other respected comrades had grasped this option may have influenced Sitting Bull. The spreading collapse of resistance south of the Yellowstone also had its effect.

In mid-March the Sitting Bull band crossed the Missouri upstream from Fort Peck and camped in the river bottom. On the seventeenth the spring breakup of the ice sent a flood cascading down the valley to destroy nearly everything the people owned. They were fortunate to escape with their lives.

By early April Sitting Bull and others arriving from the south had camped on Beaver Creek, sixty miles northwest of Fort Peck. There, on April 10, they convened a council. Present were Sitting Bull, Pretty Bear, and No Neck of the Hunkpapas, Flying By and Red Thunder of the Miniconjous, Turning Bear and Spotted Eagle of the Sans Arcs, and others of equal prominence. Both Spotted Eagle and Sitting Bull made speeches advocating continuing the war until the whites asked for peace. For himself, Sitting Bull declared, he intended to go to Fort Garry, on Red River in Canada, and wait to see how the hunting people who surrendered were treated. If they were disarmed and dismounted, he would not return to the United States.[20]

By April 16 Sitting Bull had reached a Slota trading camp on the Big Bend of Milk River, clearly headed for the international boundary.[21]

On May 6, 1877, Crazy Horse and 889 people went into Camp Robinson, Nebraska, and surrendered 12,000 ponies and 117 arms. They were the culmination of a steady stream that for weeks had been arriving at all the agencies. Two weeks earlier 300 Sioux had surrendered to Bear Coat at the mouth of the Tongue.

On May 7, 1877, the day after Crazy Horse surrendered, Bear Coat attacked the Miniconjou village of Lame Deer on Muddy Creek, a tributary of the Rosebud. Lame Deer and his head warrior Iron Star died, his people scattered into the hills, and the village went up in flames.

Sometime during this first week of May 1877, Sitting Bull crossed the *chanku wakan*—the sacred road—into Canada.

"They told us this line was considered holy," remembered Robert Higheagle, a boy in the village. "They called that a holy trail. They believe things are different when you cross from one side to another. You are altogether different. On one side you are perfectly free to do as you please. On the other you are in danger."[22]

15 LONG LANCE

WHITE MUD RIVER rose on the eastern edge of the Cypress Hills and troughed a crooked path southeast across the vast Canadian plains to the international boundary. On the Montana side of the line, the stream became Frenchman's Creek for its final thrust south to flow into Milk River about forty miles above its union with the Missouri just below Fort Peck. East of the White Mud the plains stretched toward a horizon relieved by the low, green-dappled mass of Wood Mountain. On the west, the more extensive Cypress Hills, likewise patched with timber, formed a backdrop to the rolling grasslands.

In the first days of May 1877, as the grassy carpet showed the first traces of green after the usual fierce winter, Sitting Bull and 135 Lakota lodges moved slowly up the White Mud. About one thousand people crowded the lodges, some of which were new but most old, ragged, and patched, all that could be salvaged after the Missouri River floodwaters swept through their village in March. Sitting Bull himself, with his extensive family, occupied one of the shabbiest and appeared among the most impoverished—testimony to his continuing dedication to the virtue of generosity. Hungry, destitute, tired, disconsolate over being driven from their homeland, the refugees faced new uncertainty. In the land of the Grandmother, they knew in their minds, they were supposed to be safe; yet in their hearts they could not shake the fear of Long Knives crashing suddenly into their village.

Sitting Bull had occasionally been in this country in the past, following the buffalo or seeking Slotas to trade with. He would later say that he had been reared among the Slotas, who taught him to shoot. They may have, although the relationship doubtless occurred less in the Queen's country than in Dakota and Montana, where the Slotas also ranged much as did the Sioux.

Through the Slotas, and his own experience north of the international boundary, Sitting Bull knew about the Grandmother, who ruled in benevolent and wise contrast to the Great Father in the United States. Probably, however, he now approached his first intimate experience with the Queen's redcoats—the North-West Mounted Police.

The force had been organized only three years previously, as indeed the Dominion of Canada had been organized only ten years previously. In 1867 the eastern Canadian provinces had confederated as a dominion within the British Empire. Not for another two years, however, did the plains and mountains west of Hudson Bay become part of Canada. Before 1869 the Hudson's Bay Company had governed the western lands, and the sprawling firm's mutually beneficial relations with the Indians had sustained an era of peace and profit for both.

With the end of company rule in 1869, strife and lawlessness came to Canada's new western empire. In particular, American whiskey traders working north from Fort Benton spread demoralization and bloodshed among tribes previously held in reasonable amity by the wise if self-interested practices of the Hudson's Bay traders. Most notorious of the whiskey stations was Fort Whoop-up, operated on Belly River by two Fort Benton entrepreneurs, John J. Healy and Alfred B. Hamilton.

These conditions gave birth to the North-West Mounted Police. In 1874 the little force of three hundred marched west to impose the Queen's law on a huge land in which they appeared as tiny red specks. From their first post at Fort Macleod, they suppressed Fort Whoop-up, then flung their little stations to the north and east. In the summer of 1875, the Union Jack rose over Fort Walsh, in the Cypress Hills. From there in 1876–77 the police confronted the dilemma of American Sioux seeking refuge in Canada.

About sixty miles up White Mud Valley from the boundary, Sitting Bull and his following camped near Pinto Horse Butte, a rugged headland thrusting west from the flank of Wood Mountain. There the Sioux had their first introduction to the North-West Mounted Police.

A party of seven horsemen approached the Sioux camp, riding with studied unconcern through Indian pickets dotting every hill. Five wore scarlet tunics, buff riding breeches stuffed into boots, and white helmets. As the Sioux watched with surprise and curiosity, the strangers rode to the very edge of the village, dismounted, and set up their own camp.

A knot of headmen advanced to confront their fearless new neighbors. Spotted Eagle, the handsome young Sans Arc chief whose stature among the hunting bands had come to rival Crazy Horse's, spoke to the redcoats through their interpreter. They had arrived at the village of Sitting Bull, he announced, and never had white men dared approach this close, as if it did not even exist.[1]

The leader of the little party was Major James M. Walsh, inspector in the North-West Mounted Police and commander of Fort Walsh. The Canadian Indians called Walsh "White Forehead," but later the refugee Sioux, noting the lances tipped with red-and-white pennons that the police carried on parade, named him "Long Lance."

In a council lodge that afternoon Walsh and his men sat facing Sitting Bull and his chiefs. After Sitting Bull recited at length the misdeeds inflicted on him by the Americans, the major said what he had come to say—bluntly, without equivocation. The Sioux were now in the land of the Great White Mother. Her laws protected every person of whatever color but also punished any person who violated them. On penalty of swift punishment, the Sioux must obey. In particular, any Indian who returned to the United States to steal or kill forfeited the privilege of asylum in Canada.[2]

The next morning, as the police prepared to leave, Sitting Bull witnessed a telling demonstration of the Queen's justice. White Dog and two other Assiniboines from the Missouri River rode into the village trailing five horses. Walsh's scouts recognized three as stolen property. Under instructions from Walsh, his sergeant and two constables marched up to White Dog and placed him under arrest. Expecting aid from the throng of Sioux warriors watching the drama, the Assiniboine blustered with defiance. When Walsh strode over with the remaining constable dragging a set of leg irons, however, he wilted, mumbled an explanation about finding the horses grazing on the prairie, and surrendered them.

Prudently Walsh chose to accept the explanation and dismissed White Dog. As the Assiniboine turned to leave, he muttered, "I shall see you again." When the words had been translated, Walsh ordered White Dog to repeat them loudly and clearly or head for the lockup at Fort Walsh. Again White Dog backed down, explaining that he had meant no threat. Humiliated, he slunk away from the village.

Sitting Bull and his chiefs and warriors read the lesson clearly. The redcoats laid down the rules unambiguously and then enforced them fearlessly, even at grave risk of their own lives. The Lakota warriors could easily have slain the police for their brazen interference with White Dog, whose offense was no offense at all in the Indian reckoning. But that would have angered the Grandmother and led to their expulsion from her land. Although sorely tempted at times, Sitting Bull never forgot the lesson.

The May council with Sitting Bull was not the first occasion for Walsh's lecture on Canadian law. Shortly before Christmas 1876, he had journeyed across the snow-choked plains from Fort Walsh to Wood Mountain to greet Black Moon, Little Knife, Long Dog, Crawler, and 109 lodges. In March 1877 he had repeated the perilous winter ride to meet with Four Horns and another fifty-seven lodges. All had responded as Sitting Bull now responded. They had fled north to get away from the Great Father's soldiers. They wanted to remain and live in peace. They would obey the Queen's laws and be guided by the advice of her policemen.

A muscular man of medium build with dark hair, mustache, and imperial, Major Walsh had served the North-West Mounted Police since its formation. In ambition, vigor, and flamboyance, he struck some as another Custer. For his icy courage, all the Indians of the Fort Walsh district could vouch. "A man of undoubted pluck," testified one of his constables, "he loved to advertise, and nothing pleased him more than to be alluded to in the American newspapers as 'Sitting Bull's Boss.' "[3]

Inclined like Custer to romanticism, Walsh nonetheless brought to his mission a more informed and sympathetic view of Indians. He looked on Sitting Bull as grievously wronged by the United States government and by corrupt agents, traders, and speculators, in full measure the victim he portrayed himself in the councils with Canadian authorities.

In the first of many meetings, the Lakota chief and the Queen's police officer laid the groundwork for mutual trust and respect and finally true friendship. For the first time in his life, Sitting Bull met a white man he would come to appreciate, a sentiment that would be reciprocated.

Less than a month elapsed before Sitting Bull gained further introduction to the new order. On May 26, 1877, three Americans arrived in the camp near Pinto Horse Butte. One was a Black Robe, but some of the villagers thought they recognized the other two as scouts for Bear Coat Miles. Ordinarily the Sioux would simply have killed the suspected scouts—that they were Americans was sufficient cause—and then pondered what to do about the priest. Instead, mindful of the redcoats'

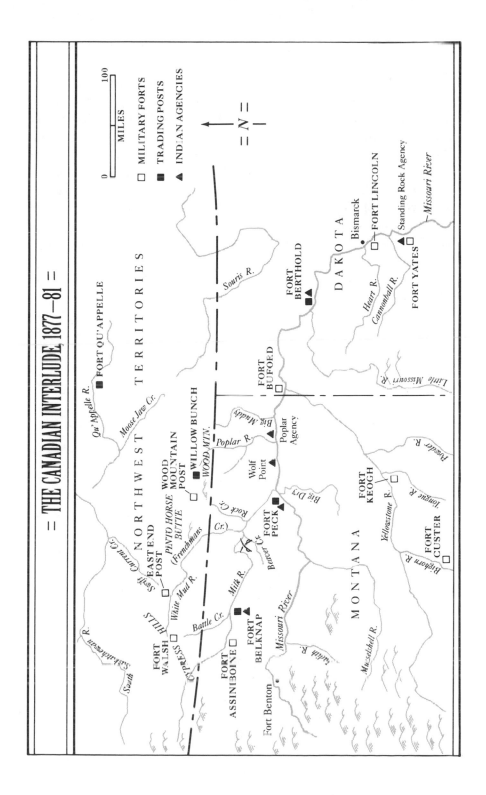

== THE CANADIAN INTERLUDE, 1877–81 ==

MILES

0 — 100

□ MILITARY FORTS
■ TRADING POSTS
▲ INDIAN AGENCIES

== N ==

NORTHWEST   TERRITORIES

■ FORT QU'APPELLE

Qu'Appelle R.

Moose Jaw Cr.

Souris R.

DAKOTA

Bismarck
□ FORT LINCOLN
● Standing Rock Agency ▲ □

Missouri River

▲ ■ FORT BERTHOLD

Heart R.

Cannonball R.

FORT YATES

□ FORT BUFORD

Little Missouri R.

WILLOW BUNCH ▲

■ WOOD MOUNTAIN POST

WOOD MTN.

Poplar R.

Big Muddy

▲ Poplar Agency

▲ Wolf Point

Big Dry

Powder R.

FORT KEOGH □

Tongue R.

Yellowstone R.

FORT CUSTER □

Bighorn R.

PINTO HORSE BUTTE □

Rock Cr.

(Frenchmans Cr.)

EAST END POST □

Swift Current Cr.

White Mud R.

■ ▲ FORT PECK

Beaver Cr.

MONTANA

Missouri River

Milk R.

Battle Cr.

■ ▲ FORT BELKNAP

FORT ASSINIBOINE □

FORT WALSH □

CYPRESS

South Saskatchewan R.

Judith R.

Musselshell R.

Fort Benton ●

warning, Sitting Bull dispatched his nephew and adopted son, One Bull, with five companions to seek counsel at Fort Walsh.

The Black Robe was Abbot Martin Marty, missionary at Standing Rock Agency. The other two were William Halsey, agency interpreter, and John Howard, sometime scout for Colonel Miles. Abbot Martin bore letters from the Commissioner of Indian Affairs and the head of the Bureau of Catholic Indian Missions authorizing him to track down Sitting Bull and see if peace could be arranged. Although hospitably treated and given the freedom of the village, the priest found that Sitting Bull would not meet with him in council until he had heard from his Grandmother.[4]

The three Americans had to wait six days, when once again a handful of redcoats appeared in the village. The contingent included Major Walsh, two captains, and some constables, but it was headed by the assistant commissioner of the force, Lieutenant Colonel Acheson G. Irvine. On the afternoon of June 2, Sitting Bull and his chiefs crowded into a spacious council lodge formed from two large tipis to talk with the officers.

Two councils took place. The first, opened with a solemn pipe ceremony that greatly impressed Colonel Irvine, excluded Father Marty. After speeches by Pretty Bear, Sitting Bull, and Spotted Eagle, Irvine repeated what Walsh had told them a month earlier. They could remain in Canada as long as they obeyed the law.

"The Great White Mother, the Queen, takes care of everyone in her land in every part of the world," he concluded. "In the Queen's land we all live like one family."

In light of these hopeful words, there could be only one answer for the priest, which Sitting Bull bluntly delivered when the second council convened. Already, in fact, the Black Robe had caught the drift of the proceedings and hastened to assure Sitting Bull that perhaps he would be better off on British soil.

> *Sitting Bull* (Turning to Col. Irvine): If I remain here will you protect me?
> *Lieut.-Col. Irvine:* I told you the White Mother would, as long as you behave yourself.
> *Sitting Bull:* What would I return for? To have my horses and arms taken away? What have the Americans to give me? . . . I have come to remain with the Grandmother's children.

It was a significant council, fixing Sitting Bull's unyielding position but also sealing the confidence and admiration that each side felt for the other. Like Walsh, Irvine esteemed Sitting Bull. "He is a man of somewhat short stature," Irvine observed, "but with a pleasant face, a mouth showing great determination, and a fine high forehead. When he smiled, which he often did, his face brightened up wonderfully." His speeches in council, moreover, "showed him to be a man of wonderful capability." "He spoke as a man who knew his subject well, and who had thoroughly weighed it over before speaking."

Late that night, after Irvine had settled into his blankets, Sitting Bull secured the favorable impression by slipping into the officer's tent. "He sat on my bed until an early hour in the morning, telling me in a subdued tone his many grievances against the 'Long Knives.' "[5]

For the first time, Sitting Bull had discovered white officials who seemed trustworthy. After his experiences south of the border, this was a heady experience. In a matter of weeks, the police came to exert extraordinary influence over him and all the chiefs of the refugee Sioux. The explanation lay in a range of qualities that guided the police in their duties: fairness, justice, firmness, courage, tolerance, kindness, honesty, and, of great consequence in light of the record of U.S. officials, a resolve to make good on all promises. Applied to rules that were simple and easily understood, these methods gained the Mounted Police unprecedented sway over a people not noted for bowing to any external authority.

To the Lakota leaders, life in Canada seemed an increasingly appealing prospect. The police calmed their greatest fear: that bluecoats would cross the boundary and attack them. That could not happen, the officers assured them, and if it did the redcoats would protect them. That promise, combined with abundant buffalo between Cypress Hills and Wood Mountain, gave the refugee Sioux a new vision of the future.

For the moment at least, the chiefs sincerely meant to stay in Canada. They may have harbored thoughts of some day going back to fight for their homeland, but for now they were whipped. Bear Coat was everywhere, Sitting Bull conceded. He attacked them in their village, killed the people, and seized provisions needed by the women and children. The exiles had crossed the border tired, hungry, and cold, and they did not want to renew the fight.[6]

Despite the hope offered by the police, Sitting Bull's self-esteem had probably never plunged lower. The defensive policy he and Crazy Horse had raised against white encroachment had failed utterly. For six years Sitting Bull had sought to serve as a shield behind which his people could follow their familiar way of life. Bear Coat and other soldier chiefs had destroyed that aspiration and driven all who refused to give up out of their homeland altogether.

So complete and indisputable was the personal defeat that Sitting Bull could no longer regard himself as a chief. If he did not formally renounce his chieftainships, he repeatedly denied that he held any. "I am nothing," he declared to a reporter several months later, "neither a chief nor a soldier." He told others the same thing, including Father Marty and Major Walsh.[7]

To the sense of failure, Sitting Bull added a bitterness toward all Americans that grew more obsessive as the magnitude of the calamity grew more unmistakable. His distrust and suspicion knew no bounds, and he could credit Americans with any perfidy, no matter how irrational from any point of view but his own. Troublemakers kept him constantly stirred up with stories of soldiers crossing the boundary to attack his village or officials seeking to persuade him to surrender so they could hang him.

Chief or not, Sitting Bull's people accorded him all the respect of old. If his policies had failed, his influence had not. "His power," Walsh observed, "consists in the universal confidence which is given to his judgment, which . . . is worth more than the united voices of the rest of the camp. They listen and they obey."[8]

With buffalo plentiful, all the Sioux needed now was ammunition to hunt. In each of his meetings with the chiefs, Major Walsh had acknowledged the need and granted traders the authority to sell strictly limited quantities of powder and ball. Police exercised close oversight to ensure compliance.

Regular trade afforded another happy outlook. The nearest trading post was at Wood Mountain, where a jovial French-Canadian, Jean Louis Legaré, stocked a variety of merchandise. A veteran trader, he dealt with his customers honestly if profitably, and he entertained a genuine compassion for them. The first expatriates, in December 1876, had begun exchanging buffalo robes for powder, lead, and other goods, and the latecomers took up the practice. For Sitting Bull, Jean Louis became almost as familiar as Long Lance Walsh.[9]

The American Sioux did not instantly turn into model British subjects. As always, the gulf between the policies of the chiefs and the actions of the headstrong young men made trouble. Less ready to give up than their elders, the young men vowed to rebuild their arsenal and their herds and renew the war—boasts that quickly spread south of the boundary and reached, among others, Bear Coat Miles, who regarded Sitting Bull as his unfinished personal business. As his men labored to complete the fine new post at the mouth of the Tongue and another on the Bighorn, named Forts Keogh and Custer, Miles longed to lead an expedition to the very border, and even beyond if his superiors would consent.

For the young Lakotas, because of the warnings of the police and their own chiefs, the boundary exercised a more inhibiting influence than it did for the other tribes and the Slotas who moved back and forth following the buffalo. The chiefs almost never crossed, but the young men sometimes did, when drawn by migrating buffalo. Inevitably, some would steal stock or commit other offenses.

However warmly Walsh and his colleagues greeted the Sioux, they fervently wished the newcomers would go back home. The cadres at Forts Walsh and Macleod had resident Indians to deal with, including Blackfeet, Cree, Piegan, Blood, and Salteaux. These tribes and the Sioux had a tradition of enmity, and if the buffalo grew scarce intertribal warfare could be expected.

Far more troubling to the police, however, was the potential the Sioux presence held for poisoning relations between Canada and the United States. Almost at once, in fact, Sitting Bull set off a diplomatic clash between the two nations, one complicated by the involvement of a third party. In foreign affairs, London acted on behalf of Ottawa, and in Washington the British minister pressed Canada's case.

Throughout the summer of 1877, the two sides danced around the issue. Stripped of diplomacy's elegant verbosity, Canada wanted the United States to drop its demand for unconditional surrender, allow the Sioux to retain their guns and ponies, and persuade them to go to the agencies. For its part, the United States, refusing to treat Sitting Bull any differently from tribesmen who surrendered south of the border, wanted Canada to intern the refugees and guarantee that none would ever cross the border with hostile intent. In effect, that meant creating reservations for the Sioux far north of the boundary and treating them as Canadian Indians, a proposition that Canada stoutly resisted.[10]

United States officials did agree among themselves that, for appearances if for no other reason, an effort should be made to persuade the Sioux to return. On August 14, 1877, the president's cabinet voted to send a commission to Fort Walsh to talk with Sitting Bull.[11]

As the British diplomats and Canadian officials well recognized, the Americans did not long for Sitting Bull's return, and they preferred to regard the problem as one that Canada should solve. With his customary bluntness, General Sherman summed up the U.S. attitude: "The English authorities should *now* elect to adopt these refugee Indians as their own, or force them back to our side of the line before they recuperate their ponies and collect new supplies of ammunition." If the Sioux renewed the war from Canadian refuges, he added, it would be the equivalent of an act of hostility on the part of Canada.[12]

General Terry headed the Sitting Bull Commission, aided by Rhode Islander A. G. Lawrence, a former diplomat without evident qualification, and an army officer as secretary. With a cavalry escort, the commissioners reached the boundary south of Fort Walsh on October 15. On hand to greet them was Lieutenant Colonel James F. Macleod, commissioner of the North-West Mounted Police. After an exchange of salutes and handshakes, the Americans and their host rode across the boundary in front of a line of scarlet-clad horsemen presenting lances tipped with fluttering pennons.

Near dusk the next day, October 16, the colorful procession made its way down a winding road into the grassy valley of Battle Creek. Surrounded by high steep hills mottled with stands of timber, Fort Walsh lay in the middle of a broad meadow, its whitewashed stockade and log buildings bright in the chill, late-autumn sun, the British Union Jack flapping overhead. Log cabins and shanties scattered across the valley north of the fort, together with the tipis of visiting Indians. Tents had been pitched on the east for the American escort.

At the northwest corner of the stockade, comfortably distant from the Americans, a lone tipi stood in solitary isolation. It was a small, unadorned traveling lodge. Several two-wheeled carts such as the Slotas used were parked nearby. Refusing even to enter the fort, Sitting Bull had insisted on camping alone. The entire garrison turned out, however, and staged such an enthusiastic demonstration of welcome that he consented to lodge in the interior room set aside for the Indian guests.[13]

That he had come at all testified to the remarkable influence of Long Lance Walsh. On October 1 a dispatch had arrived from Ottawa suggesting that every effort be made to persuade Sitting Bull to go to Fort Walsh for the conference, rather than forcing the American commissioners to seek out the Sioux village. On the same day Walsh left for Pinto Horse Butte to carry out this directive.

Sitting Bull and his fellow chiefs proved wholly unreceptive. Americans always lied, they declared in council on October 7, and the commissioners could say nothing that the Sioux would believe. Simply meeting them would make their hearts feel bad. They intended to live in the Grandmother's country, and the American officers could not change their minds.

Walsh's arrival coincided with a troubling distraction that doubtless influenced the chiefs' thinking. Eight hundred Nez Perces, fleeing government attempts to force them onto an Idaho reservation, had led the army in a humiliating chase across the Rocky Mountains to the Montana plains, then north to the Canadian sanctuary Sitting Bull had found five months earlier. Marching swiftly from Fort Keogh, on September 30 Bear Coat Miles had cut them off at Bear Paw Mountain, hardly forty miles from Canada.

Runners had kept the Sioux chiefs apprised of the Nez Perces' flight. They knew that a decisive battle had begun a few days earlier not far south of the boundary. Although the Sioux had often fought the Nez Perces, friends and allies of the Crows, the council now debated whether to rush to their aid. As the police had repeatedly pointed out, any armed foray south of the line would bar the refugees forever from Canada. In the end, either from prudence or simply indecision, the chiefs left the Nez Perces to fight their own futile battle.[14]

For Sitting Bull, another distraction argued against a journey to Fort Walsh. Disease had just carried away his nine-year-old son by the long-dead Red Woman, and he was engaged in the customary rites of mourning.[15]

With great reluctance, however, Sitting Bull agreed to accompany Walsh to Fort Walsh. He would do this, he made plain, only because Long Lance and the Grandmother asked it as a favor. The entire village would move slowly to the west, to be closer to Fort Walsh, while Sitting Bull and about twenty chiefs and headmen would go with Walsh to hear what the Americans had to say.

The movement got under way the next day, October 8, but faltered almost at once. Scouts dashed in with word of many people approaching from the south. Sure that Long Knives were coming to attack them, the villagers worked themselves into a pitch of excitement despite Walsh's efforts to calm them. He himself rode to greet the newcomers. They turned out to be Nez Perces. Chief Joseph had surrendered to Miles three days earlier, but White Bird and fifty men, forty women, and their children had escaped. "Many of them were wounded—men, women, and children," observed Walsh. "Some were shot badly through the body, legs and arms."

The pitiable condition of the Nez Perces reopened the question of meeting with the Americans. Once again the chiefs gathered in council. Why, they asked Walsh, did he ask them to talk with men who killed

Indians? "You see these men, women and children, wounded and bleeding, we cannot talk with men who have blood on their hands. They have stained the grass of the Grandmother with it."

All afternoon and again the next morning, Walsh explained, persuaded, and cajoled. Again he prevailed.

Leaving the village to follow slowly, Walsh and about twenty Sioux continued west toward the Cypress Hills. En route, they met Colonel Macleod, hastening to host General Terry after aiding in negotiating the government's Treaty No. 7, with the Blackfeet. In still another council, Sitting Bull and his comrades told the police chief of their fear, intensified by the scenes of Nez Perce suffering, that American soldiers would cross the line and attack them. No, Macleod assured the chiefs, when they crossed that line "there was a wall raised up behind them that their enemies dared not cross," and so long as they behaved they could rest knowing they would be protected by the redcoats. Not entirely convinced, they resumed the journey and reached Fort Walsh two days later. Macleod left at once to meet Terry at the border.[16]

On the night of the commission's arrival at Fort Walsh, the Americans, the police, and the Indians all gathered inside the stockade for an exhibition dance. The night was cold and bright with a full moon, and a bonfire illumined the painted, colorfully bedecked forms of the dancers. Sitting Bull sat in a shadowed corner of the stockade—mourning his dead son, according to the *New York Herald*'s correspondent, and "making medicine."[17]

One dancer in particular impressed a watching policeman. Garbed only in breechcloth, feathered bonnet, and buffalo-horn headgear, he had painted his body black and his ribs white. He brandished a coup stick, a stone-headed club hung with scalps, "and as he recounted his deeds of valour he pointed to these grizzly trophies and told how he had used this stick upon American soldiers at the Custer fight, knocking them from their horses and then dispatching them." The Indian's name, the observer learned, was Rain-in-the-Face. His performance could not have entertained or amused General Terry and his colleagues.[18]

The long-awaited council took place the next afternoon, October 17. The largest room in the post headquarters had been arranged for the talks, with two tables at one end and open floor covered with buffalo robes at the other. Terry and his associates and a stenographer sat behind one table, Macleod and the two journalists, Jerome Stillson of the *New York Herald* and Charles Diehl of the *Chicago Times*, at the other. U.S. and Canadian officers, interpreters, scouts, and other observers stood against the walls.[19]

General Terry was hardly the best choice for the mission, as the Canadian officers remarked among themselves. A gentle, kindly man, a lawyer before the Civil War, he was a more thoughtful, intellectual officer than most of his fellow generals. Those qualities, however, did not endear him to the Sioux. "One Star" (he held the same rank as Three Stars Crook, but the Indians did not understand the U.S. Army's insignia) had been the chief who sent Long Hair Custer to attack their village and then had chased them all over Montana and Dakota. He also had led the soldiers who seized the ponies and guns of the Indians at Standing Rock and Cheyenne River agencies, an act that had stampeded some of the very Indians who now confronted him in Colonel Macleod's office. To send One Star to talk them into giving up was an insult, which the chiefs repaid by bringing a woman into the council and insisting that she too speak.

The chiefs made their entrance at 3:00 P.M. Major Walsh escorted Sitting Bull through the door. He wore a dark shirt with white dots, black leggings with broad red stripes down the sides, a blanket loosely draped over his shoulders, handomely beaded moccasins, a cap of fox fur with badger tail over long unbraided hair, and, Stillson thought, "a quiet, ironical smile."

Seizing Macleod's extended hand, Sitting Bull pumped it warmly and uttered the customary "How, how." Proceeding to the next table, he fixed the Americans with a disdainful look, said "How" very slowly, then took his seat without shaking hands.

When all the chiefs had seated themselves on the buffalo robes, Sitting Bull got to his feet, pointed to the Americans, and said, "I want them to sit here," indicating the floor in front of the tables.

"It is the habit of the whites to sit on chairs," replied One Star.

With the tables intervening, explained Sitting Bull, the Indians could not see the men with whom they were treating.

The Americans then compromised by moving their chairs in front of the table and seating themselves again according to the habit of the whites.

Significantly, a pointed commentary of the Indian view of the event, the council opened without the usual pipe ceremony. Terry simply rose and launched into his address. He had been sent to tell Sitting Bull that the Great Father wanted peace, he said. All the other Indians had surrendered and gone to live at the agencies. Now those who had fled to Canada should follow their example. Sitting Bull and his people would be received kindly and not punished. They would have to give up their ponies and guns, which would be sold and the money spent on livestock with which the Indians could begin a new mode of life.

"It is time for bloodshed to cease," the general concluded. But sternly he added: "You cannot return to your country and your friends unless you accept these propositions. Should you attempt to return with arms in your hands, you must be treated as enemies of the United States."

Throughout the speech, the Indians sat with inscrutable countenances and puffed methodically on their pipes. Once, however, when Terry said the people would be received kindly—clearly another lie—Sitting Bull smiled broadly. Once too Spotted Eagle, a belt filled with Winchester cartridges draped over his shoulder and chest, a huge war club with three knife blades affixed to the head in his lap, turned toward Colonel Macleod and winked mischievously.

When One Star resumed his seat, the Indians sat silently puffing on their pipes. They "continued to smoke, smoke, smoke," Stillson noted. "They smoked. They smoked until the room reeked." None betrayed any emotion as the whites sat waiting.

Finally Sitting Bull rose to his feet and spoke, an interpreter translating. He talked of the long history of bad treatment his people had suffered from the Americans. They had finally hounded him into taking refuge with the British. He intended to remain with them. That was plain to understand, if only the Americans used their eyes and ears. "You come here to tell us lies, but we don't want to hear them." The Grandmother's medicine house was no place for lies.

"Don't you say two more words," he barked at One Star. "Go back home where you came from."

Amid a chorus of "hows," Sitting Bull sat down. Several more Indians, including the woman, gave short speeches, but Sitting Bull had set the tone and said all that needed to be said.

The chiefs rose and turned to the door. Through an interpreter, One Star halted them.

"Shall we say to the President that you refuse the offers he has made to you?"

After a long silence, Sitting Bull replied. "If we told you more, you would have paid no attention. That is all I have to say. This part of the country does not belong to your people. You belong on the other side. This side belongs to us."

"I think we have nothing more to say to them, Colonel," declared Terry.

"Well," replied Macleod, "I suppose you are right."

Led by Sitting Bull, the chiefs all crowded around the redcoats, shaking hands and uttering words of respect and endearment. The Americans stood aside, entirely ignored.

To ensure that the Indians fully understood the implications of their decision, Terry asked Macleod to meet alone with them. Untroubled by the presence of Americans, the chiefs made more eloquent speeches than in the formal council. Sitting Bull, Little Knife, Spotted Eagle, and others all spoke of their experiences south of the line and the new life they looked for north of the line.

As Sitting Bull summed it up: "I could never live over there again. . . . We like you and the Police very much, and it is only for this reason we came to see the United States Commissioners and hear what they had to say."

For the second time, a year after the council with Bear Coat, U.S. officials had personally met the man whose name had become legend throughout the United States. More important for the American people, a real person, with distinctive physical, mental, and emotional characteristics, took shape to connect with the name that had figured so prominently in the public prints. This occurred because two gifted journalists took special care to portray Sitting Bull to the world.

Not only did Stillson and Diehl describe and characterize the Sioux leader in their reports of the Terry Commission, but each succeeded in gaining a personal interview. Major Walsh, ever sensitive to the press, urged Sitting Bull to meet with the journalists. He resisted, but at length, to accommodate his friend, he consented. In separate interviews, with Walsh looking on, he strove to play the willing and informative subject. Although both reporters squandered too much of their time on the Little Bighorn, they etched a portrait of a believable human being, a powerful leader less by rank than wisdom, obsessed with his persecution by Americans, true to his heritage, and possessed of unshakable principles and convictions. The reporting of Stillson and Diehl, repeated by newspapers all over the nation, brought a flesh-and-blood Sitting Bull into American homes for the first time.[20]

Nor was the picture solely verbal. An illustrator of fair ability, Stillson sketched a portrait of Sitting Bull, together with scenes of Fort Walsh. In December they appeared on the cover of *Harpers Weekly*.[21]

Although General Terry had been rudely rebuffed, he had not truly failed in furthering the purposes of the U.S. government. No one expected the Sioux to accept his terms, but they had to be formally offered, both as a show of good faith for the Canadians and as groundwork for further handling of the problem. In truth, the United States did not want Sitting Bull back. Henceforth, the formality of the Terry Commission out of the way, the United States could concentrate on pressing Canada to treat Sitting Bull and his people as Canadian Indians.

For their part, Canadian authorities understood for the first time how serious a problem they confronted. They had acted so fairly and decently toward the refugees that they had made fast friends. No matter how urgently the police pressed the Sioux to return, no matter how plainly they repeated that Canada looked on them as American Indians and would never ration them, grant them a reservation, or treat them as Canadian tribes, the officials could not shake off their worshipful new friends so long as the buffalo supported the traditional pattern of life. And as the police well knew, at any time young men could defy their leaders and slip south of the border to commit depredations, with predictable effect on the already testy relations with the United States.

For Sitting Bull and the Sioux chiefs, the meeting with One Star, however bad it made their hearts feel, allowed them to set forth their position in unmistakable language. In decisively rejecting his terms, they believed they had won a great victory. Untutored in the nuances of international diplomacy, moreover, they fancied that they had dealt One Star such a humiliating defeat that he would have to take his own life.

Such was the message in part of a two-page pictograph prepared in the Miniconjou camp following the Fort Walsh council and dispatched by obscure means to Boston and thence to Cheyenne River Agency. Intended to acquaint kinsmen with events in Canada, it identified various participants in the council and portrayed One Star as about to shoot himself on the edge of a newly dug grave.

At Cheyenne River, the document fell into the hands of a conscientious young army lieutenant, who enlisted the agency interpreter in probing the meaning of the drawings. Forwarded up the chain of command, the pictographs constituted not only a remarkable ethnographic specimen, but the only record from the Indian perspective of a significant council with white officials.

With his usual insight into the minds of his Sioux adversaries, General Sheridan endorsed the papers: "I attach no more interest to these than the drawings on a slate of a boy 12 years old."[22]

16 *PTE*

PTE, the buffalo, had always ordered the pace and direction of Lakota life. In Canada, in the years after the arrival of the Sitting Bull bands, the buffalo governed as never before—not only the Lakotas but all other tribes on both sides of the boundary, not only in their individual fortunes but in their relations with one another and with the Canadians and the Americans. Between 1877 and 1881, the once-limitless herds dwindled to the verge of extinction, sending demographic shock waves from the upper Missouri to the North Saskatchewan. Tribal ranges shifted, intertribal competition intensified, and Canada strove desperately to erect an Indian system that would avert starvation and keep the peace. Sitting Bull and the refugee Sioux exacerbated the crisis but stubbornly refused to believe that *Wakantanka* would ever allow the buffalo to vanish. Neither Canadian nor American could persuade him to face reality. It remained for *Pte* himself to accomplish that feat.

All went well the first year. *Pte* wandered bounteously on the plains between the Cypress Hills and Wood Mountain. The Sioux, scattered across the buffalo range in small camps, laid in ample stores of meat for the winter. They traded their robes to Jean Louis Legaré and other traders drawn to Wood Mountain by the advent of a new market. And they nourished their friendship with the Mounted Police, who in the summer of 1877, to keep watch on their new subjects, established East End Post near Pinto Horse Butte and Wood Mountain Post three miles from Legaré's trading station.

During the winter of 1877–78, Sitting Bull gained new strength—and more mouths for *Pte* to feed. The reinforcements came from the agencies in the United States. As long urged by the generals, Congress had decreed that the Indians of Red Cloud and Spotted Tail agencies must draw their rations at new locations on the Missouri River. Adding to the tensions induced by this unpopular measure, Crazy Horse and his people bridled at agency restraints and kept everyone stirred up. On September 5, 1877, the volatile mix blew up. In a guardhouse scuffle, Crazy Horse received a fatal wound from a soldier's bayonet.

Amid mounting turbulence, the government proceeded with plans to abandon the two agencies. Late in October the move began. All went reluctantly, but none more so than the two thousand "northern Indians" who had once ridden with Crazy Horse and now bore his remains with them. En route, failing to enlist their agency kinsmen in a rebellion, they simply separated from the procession and pointed north.[1]

Some headed at once for Canada, while others lingered on the Powder or Little Missouri. The first sixty lodges reached Sitting Bull's camp near East End Post in late November, and Major Walsh set forth to talk with them. "I have always wanted to go to the land of the Grandmother," the chiefs reported Crazy Horse as saying on his deathbed. "I shall be dead in a few minutes and will then go to the Grandmother's country. I want you all to follow me."[2]

They did. By the spring of 1878, some 240 lodges of the Crazy Horse band, as it came to be called, had found their way to the Canadian sanctuary. Prominent among the leaders were Little Hawk, uncle of Crazy Horse; Low Dog and Black Fox of the Oglalas; the Miniconjous Black Shield and Fools Heart, the latter a son of the slain Lame Deer; and Buffalo Hump of the Sans Arcs. Of high stature too were Red Bear and Big Road (or Broad Trail), both of whom had recently accompanied Red Cloud and Spotted Tail to Washington to confer with the Great Father. Big Road went only because his followers threatened his life if he refused, but in Canada he emerged as the principal chief of the Crazy Horse band.[3]

By the spring of 1878, the Sitting Bull bands consisted of about eight hundred lodges, including the forty-five lodges of White Bird's Nez Perces who had attached themselves to the Sioux. Numbering possibly five thousand people, about fifteen hundred fighting men, this represented a strength half again that of the year-round hunting bands that had occupied the unceded territory in the years before the war of 1876.[4]

The threat posed by so many Indians could scarcely be exaggerated: to the dwindling herds of buffalo, to the Canadian tribes that depended on them for food, to Missouri River travel and commerce and the stockmen edging into the Yellowstone Valley, and to a Canadian government trying to avert a diplomatic crisis with its southern neighbor. Furthermore, as Generals Sherman and Sheridan never tired of pointing out, and as the flight of the Crazy Horse band confirmed, so long as Sitting Bull remained in Canada he would serve as a magnet for every discontented agency Indian on the Great Sioux Reservation.

Pte held the key to all these problems. Throughout the uncommonly mild winter of 1877–78, *Pte* grazed from Cypress Hills to Wood Mountain in numbers sufficient to feed the Sioux. The herds remained through the summer too, but dissolved into scattered bunches as more and more drifted south toward the Missouri. They thus set in motion a trend that would accelerate alarmingly in the next few years. The overland trails and Union Pacific Railroad had already split the buffalo into a northern and a southern herd, and as Montana hide hunters decimated the northern herd, it contracted. Buffalo grew increasingly scarce north of the boundary, and hungry Indians, whether refugees from the United States or natives of Canada, had to ride south to Milk River or beyond to find meat.

Although larger forces than the northward migration of six thousand Sioux ordained the fate of the buffalo, the Canadian tribes held the newcomers at least partly responsible. Blackfeet, Blood, Piegan, Sarsi, Cree, Salteaux, and even Slotas regarded the Sioux as commandeering food that belonged in the mouths of their own hungry children. That they themselves frequently sought the herds as far south as the former Sioux ranges in Montana did not make them any more hospitable toward the invaders.

With the most powerful Canadian group, the Blackfeet, the Sioux had a long tradition of hostility, although the warfare occurred mainly with the southern branch of the tribe in Montana. The Northern Blackfeet range lay northwest of the Cypress Hills, on the plains at the eastern base of the Rocky Mountains, and thus comfortably distant from the Sioux. But in the mild winter of 1877–78 prairie fires swept this country, denying it to the buffalo and forcing the Blackfeet to the edge of the area appropriated by the Sioux. Thereafter, as the herds swiftly declined, few buffalo returned to the Blackfeet homeland.

In September 1877 Canadian officials met with the Blackfeet and neighboring groups to conclude the last of a series of treaties aimed at asserting Canadian authority over the western tribes. Treaty No. 7

defined reservations for each tribe and provided for the yearly distribution of annuity goods, thus laying the groundwork for another kind of life once the buffalo had vanished. For now, however, the Indians ignored their boundaries and searched for the buffalo wherever they ranged. Where the herds could be found, north or south of the boundary, there all the tribes, Canadian and American, including the Sioux, also could be found.

With the Blackfeet in his neighborhood and the redcoats watching him closely, Sitting Bull recognized the need for accommodation. Hostilities would surely lead to his expulsion from the Grandmother's country. In the spring of 1876, pressed by Long Knives, he had sent tobacco to the powerful Blackfeet chief Crow Foot. But the redcoats watched Crow Foot too, and he spurned the invitation to join the war against the Americans. Now, with Crow Foot's men among the buffalo north of the Cypress Hills, Sitting Bull hastened to reach an amicable understanding.

The first of several councils occurred in the summer of 1877, when the two, as Old Bull recalled, "smoked the pipe and declared peace for all time." Each held the pipe stem to the sky, the earth, and the four directions, and each made a speech promising an end to war and horse-stealing. "No need to fear anymore," predicted Sitting Bull. To honor his new friend, he bestowed the name Crow Foot on one of the twins born on the eve of the Little Bighorn.[5]

Sitting Bull and Crow Foot did not entirely do away with mutual fear, but in general the peace held. Years later an old woman remembered her wanderings with a group of ten Blackfeet in search of food, probably in the spring of 1878. Starving, "they'd find old stinking buffalo corpses and cook it." Chancing across a Sioux camp, they feared to enter, "because Sioux are after all our enemies and they may do something harmful." But hunger prevailed, and the little group of Blackfeet found themselves in the Hunkpapa village of Sitting Bull himself. He greeted them warmly and set his wives to cooking kettles of soup and meat. The guests "ate and gorged" until they could hold no more, then received gifts of parfleches stuffed with meat. The Blackfeet remained with their hosts for three days of feasting, then left laden with presents and ample supplies of food.[6]

Beginning in 1878, as *Pte* grew scarce in Canada, the Sitting Bull bands fell into the habit of straddling the line. Sitting Bull and other prominent leaders hesitated to be caught south of the boundary, either by redcoats or bluecoats. Occasionally they did venture into Montana, but not very often and not for long. Instead they spread hunting camps down Frenchman's Creek (the White Mud) and up Milk River while they themselves remained north of the line in villages ranging from a handful of tipis to more than a hundred.[7]

South of the boundary, the Sioux and other Canadian Indians collided with tribes native to the region—Assiniboines, Gros Ventres, and River Crows. In fact, the entire sweep of country from the Missouri River north to the boundary was officially designated Indian reservation, as was a broad belt of territory south of the Missouri assigned to the Yanktonai Sioux.

Fort Peck Agency served Yanktonais and Assiniboines. It was no longer located at Fort Peck; the great flood of March 1877, which wiped out Sitting Bull's village farther up the Missouri, also took out Fort Peck, and by autumn a new and more favorable site had been selected seventy miles downstream at the mouth of Poplar River. There the Fort Peck agent dealt with the Yanktonais while, twenty-five miles up the Missouri at Wolf Point, a subagent took care of the Assiniboines.

Still another agency on this huge reservation was Fort Belknap, far up Milk River to the west. Revived in June 1878 after a four-year hiatus, it ministered to Gros Ventres, River Crows, and another group of Assiniboines, who had gone to Canada after the agency's suspension in 1874.[8]

Besides competing for the buffalo, the refugee Sioux confronted the Missouri River agents with another dilemma. As a result of the peace-making overtures launched at Fort Peck in 1872, many Hunkpapas had drawn rations at the agency ever since. Intermarried with the Yanktonais, they also had relatives with Sitting Bull. The Poplar agency thus attracted hungry Sitting Bull Indians, who mingled with the agency people and sometimes even succeeded in obtaining rations and other government issues. When this proved impossible, they had no trouble calling on the generosity of their relatives. Indeed, caravans laden with food and other goods regularly made their way north from the Yanktonai camps for barter or philanthropy in the Sioux camps of Canada.[9]

The appearance of so many refugee Sioux in Montana led inevitably to raids there. No matter how sincerely Sitting Bull and other chiefs promised the redcoats to allow no depredations south of the boundary, no matter how sternly they lectured their people about the necessity of obeying the Grandmother's laws, young men did what young men had always done.

Once again, as in 1875, the Sitting Bull bands committed the transgressions that had furnished the pretext for the war of 1876. They tormented agency Indians who felt they deserved the protection of the

United States, and they stole stock from white ranchers and took enough white lives to call for countermeasures. Sitting Bull and his fellow leaders had not broken their promises to the redcoats, but plainly, as the American generals had predicted, at least some of the Sitting Bull Indians were using Canada as a secure haven for launching armed incursions into the United States.[10]

On the diplomatic front, the United States continued to press for resolute Canadian action. Ironically, the top three generals concerned with the issue counseled restraint. Generals Sherman, Sheridan, and Terry did not want to get bogged down in another war with Sitting Bull. But Canada resisted the U.S. claim that the Sioux had now become Canadian Indians, and the diplomatic stalemate continued.[11]

In particular, neither Sherman nor Sheridan wanted Nelson A. Miles anywhere near the boundary. Privately, Miles had confided to Sherman (his wife's uncle) his wish, as Sherman put it to Sheridan, "to advance north to the British line, drive back Sitting Bull & Co., and if necessary follow them across the Border." Any such move, Sherman counseled his impetuous nephew-in-law, would "most decidedly" land him in serious trouble. Unless Sitting Bull came down in force, the Missouri River would be the northern limit of Miles's operations.[12]

Aggressions early in 1879 impressed Washington officials as meeting that condition, and Sherman and Sheridan began to relent. Already the army had moved to establish a permanent post on Milk River. Steamboats bearing the garrison up the Missouri in May 1879 angered both the Sitting Bull Sioux and the Yanktonais of Poplar River, but the location of Fort Assiniboine proved too far west to influence the people against whom it was directed.[13]

While his people ranged the Milk River country in search of buffalo, Sitting Bull himself remained close to the boundary, sometimes on one side, sometimes on the other. In midwinter of 1878–79 he set off a minor crisis that in January brought Major Walsh through the deep snows from Wood Mountain Post to his lodge on the White Mud immediately south of the boundary.

White Bird, the Nez Perce chief, was at least partly responsible. Ever since Bear Paw Mountain, he had rivaled Sitting Bull in his implacable hatred of the Americans and his determination not to return to the United States. In the summer of 1877, one of Colonel Miles's officers had escorted a trio of Nez Perces to Canada to try to persuade White Bird and his followers to return. They met with the same brusque refusal that Sitting Bull had hurled at General Terry at Fort Walsh. In White Bird, Sitting

Bull found a spirit more kindred than in most of his Lakota associates, many of whom wanted to give up and go to the agencies.[14]

White Bird's people had a long history of friendship with the Crows, and he planted in Sitting Bull the notion that they would make formidable allies in a new war against the Americans. Although surely with profound distaste, Sitting Bull joined White Bird in sending tobacco to the Crows. The overture not only met a contemptuous rejection but prompted a successful Crow raid that depleted the Sioux horse herds by nearly one hundred head.

Humiliated to fury, Sitting Bull invited all warriors to come to his lodge and plot a war of vengeance. Word also reached Long Lance Walsh, who appeared at the lodge on January 23, 1879.

The chiefs gathered with Sitting Bull to pour out to Walsh their indignation over the effrontery of the Crows. The Grandmother had promised protection, they declared, and now she had allowed the Americans—that is, the Crows—to steal their horses. What did the redcoats intend to do about it?

Dodging that question, Walsh countered. "I believe that you and the Nez Perces are to blame for this raid," he said, addressing Sitting Bull directly. "If you had not tried to plant sedition in the Crow tribe . . . the Crows would never have sent their young men into the Grandmother's country to steal horses from the Sioux."

"I never deny anything I do," Sitting Bull answered defiantly. "I did send messengers to the Crows, asking them to leave their Reservation and join the Sioux camp north of the line." If the Crows joined him, he believed, he would be strong enough to fight the Americans if they tried to attack him again. Now the Americans, through their Crow surrogates, had in fact attacked him, and he intended to fight back.

"I wish you to tell the Grandmother that I will do to the Americans as they have done to me," Sitting Bull announced. "It is not my wish to go to war, but I must. I never told you before that I was a chief; today I tell you I am one."

Aware that he was on United States territory, Walsh forbore the sharp lecture he would have delivered north of the line. Instead he advised Sitting Bull to think well before carrying out his threat, for he might bring great trouble on his people.[15]

The encounter left Walsh deeply pessimistic, but Sitting Bull did in fact reflect well on the advice Long Lance had given him. Within two months his belligerence had cooled, and he appeared at Wood Mountain Post to explain that he had not really meant to wage aggressive war, only to defend himself.

This council took place in Walsh's quarters on March 23, 1879, and included, besides Jumping Bull and One Bull of his immediate family, nearly all the chiefs and headmen of the Hunkpapas and Miniconjous. Possibly apprehensive that his pugnacity in the January meeting had offended the Grandmother, Sitting Bull described his state of mind in terms that left no doubt of his resolve.

"What I wish to say to the Grandmother," he stated, "is that I have but one heart and it is the same today as when I first shook your hand." At that time, in May 1877, he had vowed never again to shake hands with an American. To please Long Lance, he had gone to the Grandmother's fort and listened to the American general, but he would never do this again.

"I am looking to the north for my life," he declared. Those who wished to go south were free to leave. Those who did not could stay and live with him. Perhaps the Grandmother would give them some land to till. "You have for many months been advising us to think of getting our living from the ground. Will you tell me where we will get the ground here?" To this Walsh responded that no country surpassed what they had left; they should settle at their agencies and let the U.S. government help them learn to farm.

For his part, asserted Sitting Bull, he would never farm. "I will remain what I am until I die, a hunter, and when there are no buffalo or other game I will send my children to hunt and live on prairie mice, for where an Indian is shut up in one place his body becomes weak."

Although an unequivocal declaration of intent, the speech contained one concession for which Walsh took credit. Sitting Bull had promised not to interfere with anyone who wanted to surrender. Previously, *akicita* soldiering had inhibited defections. Now, if the promise proved sincere, other chiefs might be persuaded to give up.

The speech also contained an admission of more immediate consequence. Most of his people had moved their camps south of the boundary to hunt buffalo. The ponies were too weak to allow them to make the journey from camps in Canada. "All I am looking for is something for my children to eat," Sitting Bull explained. "But I will not remain south of the line one day longer than I can help."[16]

That would prove too long, for the Indian agents on the Missouri had lost patience with the Sioux. Their complaints afforded the rationale for unleashing Bear Coat Miles. On June 5, 1879, General Terry ordered Miles to drive the "hostile Sioux" back into Canada. In mid-July, with a force numbering nearly 700 infantry, cavalry, and artillery, bolstered by

143 Crow, Cheyenne, and Assiniboine Indian auxiliaries, Miles headed north from ruined Fort Peck.[17]

Sitting Bull, meanwhile, had gone south of the border. Early in June he raised his tipi in one of the Sioux camps on Rock Creek, twelve miles above its confluence with Milk River. There still another American newspaperman found him. Vouched for by Major Walsh and accompanied by a Wood Mountain trader as interpreter, Stanley Huntley of the *Chicago Tribune* sought an interview with the chief.

Certified by Long Lance Walsh, Huntley obtained the coveted interview with Sitting Bull. His black, piercing eyes especially struck Huntley, who thought the heavy lids hung down at the corners "as if the brain had escaped into them." Stocky, muscular, with "awfully dirty" hands, Sitting Bull was garbed in blue leggings, beaded moccasins, a skin shirt, and a blanket loosely drawn around his waist. Long Dog, Pretty Bear, One Bull, Bear's Cap, and Big Road sat in on the interview. Once more for American readers, the man demonized as the slayer of Custer materialized as a real person. Like Walsh's friends Stillson and Diehl two years earlier, Huntley looked into the mind of Sitting Bull.[18]

On the hunt: "I am a hunter, and will hunt as long as there is wild game on the prairie. When the buffalo are gone I will send my children on the prairie to hunt mice." "You must not think that the Great Spirit does not watch me as closely as he watches you. . . . I know that he is watching me, and he will never leave me to starve. When the buffalo are gone he will give me something else."

On Indian agencies in the United States: "I never wanted to go to a gift-house, and I never will. They want my people to farm. I will not farm."

On the loss of his homeland: "Red Cloud and Spotted Tail are rascals. They sold our country without the full consent of our people."

On his faith in the Grandmother and resolve to live in her land: The Sioux had been in Canada two years. Many children had been born during that time. "Are they not the children of the Grandmother? Will she drive her children from the country in which they were born? No; she will let them stay there. . . . She will protect her children born on her soil, and she will protect the fathers and mothers of these children."

And on the Long Knives even then assembling to force the Sioux from the buffalo herds: "We will avoid them if we can. If we cannot, we will fight."

Ever since 1870, that had been Sitting Bull's creed and his practice.

Hardly a month after the Huntley interview, it was once again put to the test.

Buffalo on the Big Bend of Milk River lured Sitting Bull and about six hundred people down Rock Creek to lay in a store of meat. On July 17 the men were hunting up Beaver Creek, a southern tributary of the Milk. By midday they had made a big kill, and the women and children went forward to butcher the carcasses. Most of the band then drew off to the north, leaving about 120 people who had not completed the task. Among them were Sitting Bull, Long Dog, and Jumping Bull.

About an hour later, as the women labored and the men took their ease, the advance elements of Miles's column happened on the scene. The force consisted of two mounted companies screened in front by about eighty Crow and Cheyenne scouts. Lieutenant William P. Clarke commanded.

The scouts, some with red handkerchiefs tied to their weapons to identify them for the soldiers, charged at once. The Sioux, mistaking the handkerchiefs as signals to parley, did not recognize their peril until fired on. When two of their people fell, the men spread out to cover the flight of their women and children. Stubbornly they held off their assailants until the soldiers came up, then began to fall back in successive lines of defense.

One of the Crows, Magpie, a big powerful man of eminence among his people, fought ferociously. He had boasted to the Americans that if only he had the chance, he would rid them of Sitting Bull. As the opposing lines of Indians exchanged fire, a Crow rode forth with a white flag and, to the single Lakota who advanced to meet him, conveyed Magpie's challenge to engage Sitting Bull in personal combat. Sitting Bull accepted. The two spurred their mounts directly at each other. Magpie took aim first, but his rifle misfired. Sitting Bull took aim and blew the top off Magpie's head. Dismounting and obtaining what was left of his enemy's scalp, Sitting Bull mounted Magpie's horse, a prized animal well known among the Indians, and rode slowly back to his own lines.[19]

Word of the fight had sped to the departed portion of the hunting group, and about sixty men raced back to help hold the Long Knives. Thus strengthened, the Sioux turned on their pursuers and pinned them down with heavy fire. At this juncture Miles arrived with the main force, unlimbered his howitzers, and quickly drove off the Sioux with exploding artillery shells.

The vanquished hurried northeast to the villages at the head of Rock Creek, north of the boundary. They had lost five men, whose scalps fell to the Crows, one woman captured, and one thought killed. This was Black Moon's daughter. Wounded, traveling on foot and only at night, she made her painful way home in a journey that covered more than eighty miles in twelve days. Sitting Bull's adopted brother, Jumping Bull, also received a severe wound in the hip.

Counting four hundred enemy warriors instead of seventy-five, Miles trumpeted the "Battle" of Milk River as a great victory. And in fact, since the captive woman disclosed Sitting Bull's presence in the fight, Bear Coat could rightly boast of defeating the great hostile leader himself and running him back across the boundary. This indeed was cause for hearty self-congratulation, for the entire expedition viewed Sitting Bull in the legendary dimensions he had assumed.

Indignant that once again Long Knives had attacked him while peacefully going about his business, Sitting Bull still did not forget his promise to the redcoats or abandon his long-held defensive policy. North of the boundary, at the head of Rock Creek, he united with Big Road, Spotted Eagle, and others. As Miles advanced up Rock Creek, word came from his Cheyenne scouts that if Sitting Bull did not surrender, the boundary would no longer shelter him. The Sioux made ready to fight if the American soldiers crossed into Canada.[20]

When Miles halted at the boundary and went into camp, the crisis passed. On July 23 and again on July 28, Major Walsh, togged in buckskin rather than scarlet, visited Miles and convinced him of the peaceable disposition of the Sioux.

On the second visit, Walsh brought Long Dog with him to reinforce the promise. An accomplished Hunkpapa war chief, he had now become a favorite of the Canadian officers and the newsmen who entered the Sioux camps under their auspices. With bullet-scarred torso and shattered arm, "the hero of a hundred fights," he nonetheless played the role of humorist. In Miles's camp he amused everyone with a running commentary on the artillery in the Milk River fight: "Heap shoot! Bad medicine! God damn."[21]

Bluntly Miles put the question to Long Dog: "whether the Sioux had chosen their country, and on which side of the boundary they intended to remain?" Turning to Long Lance, the Hunkpapa replied, "We intend to remain with him."[22]

The declaration recorded no change in any chief's attitude and policy. From the beginning, they had all vowed to live in Canada, abide by the Grandmother's laws, and refrain from any actions south of the border that would give offense to the Americans. Sioux had always followed the buffalo, and they could hardly be faulted for seeking them out, even on Milk River, if necessary to keep their women and children from starving. And if young men occasionally stole horses or lifted scalps, it was because they did not obey their elders, whose intentions were well understood and whose sincerity could scarcely be doubted.

Whether Miles truly believed that he had won, he chose to declare victory and get out. He found the assurances of Walsh and Long Dog entirely convincing, he said. These Sioux, "the worst Indians in the Northwest," had been driven out of the United States and become "expatriated through their own acts," a result "more important and satisfactory than would have been their unconditional surrender."[23]

All of which was either wishful thinking or a transparent attempt to put the best face on the summer's military operations. The Milk River fight did flash a warning light, instilling caution and serving notice that the Americans were serious about keeping the Sioux north of the border. It may even have prompted chiefs to think more about going to an American "gift-house," although on this issue Sitting Bull himself remained intractable.

Miles's Milk River Expedition focused new attention on Sitting Bull, whose name became even more a household word both in the United States and Canada. John F. Finerty of the *Chicago Times* tried to gain an interview with him, but Walsh failed to bring his usual gusto to the enterprise, probably because Finerty was an Irish patriot who made no secret of his dislike of scarlet tunics. Even so, Finerty described conditions in Sitting Bull's camp, characterized his fellow chiefs, and gave new sanction to the public image of Sitting Bull as all-powerful monarch.

From Miles down to the lowest ranks, at least, this was the expedition's conception of the foe. "I don't care what everybody says about Sitting Bull not being a warrior," Finerty wrote. "If he has not the sword, he has, at least, the magic sway of a Mohammed over the rude war tribes that engirdle him. Everybody talks of Sitting Bull, and, whether he be a figure-head, or an idea, or an incomprehensible mystery, his present influence is undoubted. His very name is potent."[24]

More potent by far in guiding the destiny of the Sioux, however, was *Pte*, which would never again, in numbers sufficient to support the Indian occupants, return to the Canadian plains.

17 FORT BUFORD

IN CLOSENESS TO Sitting Bull, no man surpassed One Bull, his nephew and adopted son. Following the parley and skirmish with Bear Coat in October 1876, his brother White Bull had surrendered with his people and finally settled at Cheyenne River Agency. Of Sitting Bull's inner circle, that left only One Bull and Jumping Bull as completely trustworthy lieutenants.

A stalwart *akicita* leader, One Bull played an especially important role in soldiering would-be defectors. Until March 1879, when Sitting Bull promised Major Walsh not to interfere with any people who wanted to surrender, the Sioux camps had been governed by a strict compact: No family belonged without consent of the council; no family withdrew without consent of the council. Any who tried suffered *akicita* soldiering.[1]

Soldiering incidents sometimes created lasting animosities, as when Gray Eagle, Sitting Bull's brother-in-law, joined with three other men to steal 150 Slota horses. Assembling One Bull and his *akicita*, Sitting Bull summoned the culprits and castigated them for breaking the Grandmother's law and bringing on trouble with the redcoats. He then ordered them to run over a nearby hill while the *akicita* fired over their heads, obtain the stolen animals, and return them to Sitting Bull's lodge. The men did as ordered, suffering public dishonor as the *akicita* fired above them.

After the stolen horses had been retrieved, the *akicita* hauled the thieves before Sitting Bull for sentencing. His two wives, however, cried so loudly for mercy that he relented and exempted their brother from punishment. The other three paid the penalty: Stripped naked and tied to the ground, they endured the assaults of swarms of mosquitoes for a full week before a big feast of reconciliation ended the affair. Although spared this ordeal, Gray Eagle did not forget the shame his brother-in-law had cast on him.[2]

As *akicita* chief and most intimate of all family members, One Bull served throughout the stressful Canadian years as Sitting Bull's closest confidant. Thus there can be no question that the mission he undertook in May 1880 drew sanction from Sitting Bull himself.

Fort Buford had never been a place of welcome for Lakotas, and for one to ride boldly into its precincts called for unusual courage. Yet on May 23, 1880, One Bull presented himself to the commanding officer as an envoy from Sitting Bull. In a council with Colonel William B. Hazen, One Bull recited the usual grievances against the Americans, but said that he had been sent to learn on what terms his uncle might be received. "I want to know what you will do with us if we will surrender," he quoted Sitting Bull as stating. "If it is good, I will come, if not, I won't. I will wait till the young man gets back. He represents my people."

The colonel replied that the terms now were the same as they always had been. Sitting Bull and all his people must come in and give up their ponies and arms. He would be kindly treated, given plenty to eat, and sent to one of the agencies.[3]

One Bull's journey revealed Sitting Bull's deepening despair. Freed from the threat of soldiering, more chiefs had come to see surrender as the only alternative to starvation. The prospect of isolation from the rest of the Sioux leadership loomed as never before. Desperately seeking a way out of an impossible predicament, Sitting Bull waffled in indecision while grasping at every pretext to delay decision.

On June 2, 1880, only a few days after One Bull's return from Fort Buford, the young man set off a crisis with the police. He stole a horse from Wood Mountain trader Jean Louis Legaré, who happened also to be justice of the peace. Legaré deputized two men as special constables and sent them to arrest One Bull. They returned to say that he had refused to be arrested. Legaré reported the matter to Major Walsh, who dispatched two policemen and an interpreter to notify One Bull to go to the post. Sitting Bull intervened to predict that One Bull would be tied up if he complied. Instead he should refuse the summons and allow Sitting Bull to set matters straight with Long Lance. When four more redcoats appeared to take One Bull by force if necessary, he submitted.

By the time the police and their prisoners reached the post, a hundred excited warriors had gathered at the gate with every sign of recapturing their tribesman. Women brought arms and belts of ammunition. Sitting Bull himself, his temper hot, arrived to call on One Bull to resist. Walsh and twelve redcoats suddenly deployed into a skirmish line and leveled their Enfield carbines at the mass of whooping Sioux. Behind them One Bull's escort slipped him through the stockade wicket and slammed the door.

Tensely the two sides faced each other, the Indians looking to Sitting Bull for a signal to pounce. In commanding tones, Walsh shouted that he was the chief here, and the warriors had one minute in which to disperse before his men fired. All supposed that Long Lance meant what he said, and sullenly they turned back to their tipis. Shortly afterward, Legaré arrived, convened court, and dismissed the prisoner.

That night Big Road and Stone Dog of the Oglalas called on Walsh. They had come to the Grandmother's country to obey her laws, they said, and in any trouble like today the Oglalas would help the police, even fighting on their side if necessary.

At the same time, a council of chiefs met in the Hunkpapa village. Sitting Bull conceded that he had just had the closest escape of his life. He was certain he would have been killed if he had raised his hand. But his heart was bad. He had been told he was a rascal and driven away from the post like a dog. Doubtless with a touch of reproach, another chief observed that if they wanted to live in this country they had to obey the Grandmother's law. Long Lance, he said, was like Crazy Horse, not afraid to die in making them do what he told them.[4]

The clash between Sitting Bull and Walsh was symptomatic of a shift in Canada's attitude toward the Sioux refugees. The dictates of humanity and compassion that underlay the early dealings with Sitting Bull gave way as the United States stood firm on unconditional surrender and Canada could find no other acceptable way to ease this irritant to friendly relations. As early as June 1879, the Canadian government resolved to equivocate no more. No encouragement of any kind was to be given the Sioux, and they were to be pressed to return to the United States.[5]

Walsh was hardly the man to carry out a stiffening policy toward Sitting Bull. He liked the Sioux, understood them, and believed them shamefully abused by the United States government. Moreover, both within police circles and before the public at large, he liked to pose as the only official who could control Sitting Bull—a posture not without validity. By 1880 Walsh's personal feelings and ambitions had become so entangled with the future of the Sioux as to compromise his ability to carry out his government's policy.

Walsh's superiors at Fort Walsh and in Ottawa sensed his liabilities, and in the spring of 1880 they moved discreetly to separate him from the Sioux. Due to return east on leave in July, he would not go back to Wood Mountain but instead take command of Fort Qu'Appelle, 140 miles to the northeast.[6]

Before departing on leave, Walsh piled up a mountain of difficulties for his successors, and for Sitting Bull as well. By July Walsh had promised the chiefs to carry east a proposition that he should have known had no chance of acceptance. According to this scheme, if his superiors consented, Walsh would go to Washington and try to persuade the president to grant Big Road, Little Hawk, and the Oglalas a reservation on Tongue River, or failing that, to allow them to live with the Yanktonais at Poplar. Should this mission succeed, Sitting Bull and Spotted Eagle would also surrender. If not, Walsh would ask the Grandmother's chiefs in Ottawa to give the Hunkpapas and Sans Arcs a reservation in Canada.[7]

Walsh told himself that he had done no more than promise to make known the wishes of the Sioux in Ottawa and, if permitted, in Washington. What he had actually done was to plant large expectations in the minds of the Sioux and to appoint himself as the one who would fulfill them. Sitting Bull in particular, despite the recent unpleasantness over One Bull, sank all his remaining faith in Long Lance.

True to his promise, in a September letter from his home in Brockville, Ontario, Walsh outlined the proposal to the Minister of the Interior, Sir John A. Macdonald. He accurately set forth the wishes of the Sioux chiefs and proposed that he be allowed to journey to Washington and negotiate on their behalf.

Offering his own views, however, Walsh opposed granting the Sioux a reservation in Canada, and Sitting Bull was the reason. "He is the shrewdest and most intelligent Indian living," explained Walsh, "has the ambition of Napoleon, and is brave to a fault. He is respected as well as feared by every Indian on the plains. In war he has no equal. In council he is superior to all. Every word said by him carries weight, is quoted and passed from camp to camp." Confronted with a dwindling following but joined by disaffected Indians from the United States, such a man was bound to become a troublesome agitator. "Bull's ambition is I am afraid," concluded Walsh, "too great to let him settle down and be content with an uninteresting life."[8]

As Sir John recognized, Walsh had outlived his usefulness. His vanity and ambition had led him beyond the legitimate role of a subordinate frontier police officer and into paths that ran counter to the direction his government wished to take. He could not be allowed to represent the Sioux or Canada in Washington; that was the function of Her Majesty's minister. He could not even, in fact, be allowed to return to Wood Mountain and report the outcome of his mission to Sitting Bull.

For three years, James M. Walsh represented the Queen in nearly all official relations with Sitting Bull and his compatriots. No white man before or after earned the respect, confidence, and friendship that Sitting Bull accorded the Canadian officer. Even though he was suffused with conceit and romanticism, his genuine compassion, combined with a demeanor of unassailable authority, eased the adjustment of the Sioux to their new circumstances.

Inspector Lief N. F. Crozier replaced Walsh at Wood Mountain Post on July 13, 1880. Three months later a new commissioner, Lieutenant Colonel Acheson G. Irvine, took command of the force from Colonel Macleod at Fort Walsh. Competent, steadfast, lacking Walsh's vision and flamboyance, both set forth to rid Canada of Sitting Bull.

In contrast to Walsh, Crozier ceased to pay court to Sitting Bull. Sensing at once that Sitting Bull would seize on any pretext to avoid surrender, Crozier "concluded to break his influence with the camp; consequently, on subsequent occasions instead of treating him with exceptional deference and addressing myself to him in council, I spoke to the people generally." Picturing the menace of Long Knives south of the boundary, the certainty of starvation north of the boundary, and the full stomachs awaiting them at the agencies, Crozier convinced many of the wisdom of surrender. So effective was the tactic in undermining Sitting Bull's leadership that, alarmed at the defections, he once more unleashed the *akicita*. Secessionists invited soldiering.[9]

The most disheartening defection, and Crozier's greatest triumph, was Spotted Eagle. Within a week after assuming command, Crozier had a long talk with the dynamic young Sans Arc chief, who had stood firmly at Sitting Bull's side for three years. Stressing the futility of remaining in Canada and conveying the wishes of the "Queen's Council House" in Ottawa that the Sioux go back home, the police officer brought Spotted Eagle around. "Now that there is to be no more blood spilt upon the American side," he promised, "I will shake hands with the Americans strong and live in my own country."[10]

South of the boundary, Spotted Eagle and about sixty-five Sans Arc lodges lingered indecisively on the Red Water, between the Missouri and the Yellowstone, until October. Buffalo kept off hunger, and Rain-in-the-Face and his small following of Hunkpapas, likewise indecisive, swelled the camp to about eighty lodges. At last the two chiefs received an officer sent to them from Fort Keogh. On October 31, 1880, they and their people, more than five hundred in all, yielded their ponies and arms to Bear Coat Miles and raised their tipis near the fort.[11]

Ever since 1877, Miles had been playing at Indian agent as well as soldier chief, and in fact he had done at least as well as the civilian agents on the Missouri. The first to settle near Fort Keogh were the 300 Indians who surrendered in the spring of 1877, at the close of the war of 1876. These were about 50 Miniconjous under Chief Hump and 250 Northern Cheyennes of Two Moons. Next, in 1879, came more Cheyennes, followers of Little Wolf and Dull Knife, the pitiable remnant of those who, in a desperate bid to return to their northern homes, had broken free of confinement in the Indian Territory. After terrible hardships and a tragic slaughter at Camp Robinson, 208 had found their way to Fort Keogh. Finally, throughout 1880, groups of Sioux refugees from Canada began to show up at the fort. Spotted Eagle and Rain-in-the-Face were not the only prominent leaders. Big Road of the Oglalas also chose Fort Keogh, thus depriving Sitting Bull of another staunch supporter. By the end of 1880, 1,510 Lakotas had joined the Cheyennes in the Yellowstone bottoms at the mouth of the Tongue.

In contrast to the placid environment at Fort Keogh, near chaos gripped the Poplar River Agency, on the Missouri to the north. Once again the refugee Sioux had crossed the boundary to winter within range of the Milk River buffalo herd. Sitting Bull and 140 lodges camped on Milk River at the mouth of Rock Creek. Another eighty lodges, mostly Hunkpapas, mingled with the Yanktonais on the Red Water and communed with Spotted Eagle before his surrender. From all these villages, people descended on the agency to beg or steal food or talk with the agent about surrendering. Early in October General Terry dispatched Captain Ogden B. Read and two companies of infantry from Fort Custer to guard the agency and keep the "hostiles" at bay.[12]

Buffeted by an invasion from Canada such as had brought Colonel Miles to the boundary in 1879, American policy suddenly shifted to complement Canadian policy. American authorities now joined the Canadians in pressing the Sioux to give up.[13]

An emissary sent by Miles met rebuff, but another dispatched by Major David H. Brotherton, commander of Fort Buford, had greater success. He was Edward H. Allison—"Fish" Allison to the Sioux—

longtime scout and interpreter on the upper Missouri. He spoke the Sioux language fluently, understood Sioux personalities and politics, and advanced a good case for his fitness to undertake a mission to Sitting Bull.

Allison made his first trip early in October. Although he spent two days in the Hunkpapa camp, he failed to win an audience with Sitting Bull. Gall, however, an old friend, proved receptive. Allison returned to Fort Buford with Gall's promise to bring all his followers into Poplar and surrender.

In a second journey late in October, Allison not only connected with Sitting Bull but spent two nights as a guest in his lodge. Sitting Bull conceded the logic of Allison's arguments but said he had promised Major Walsh to make no move until his return from the East, which was expected by November 15.[14]

Late in November, accompanied by the Fort Buford interpreter, Fish Allison embarked on a third trip to Sitting Bull's village. On Poplar River the pair met Gall, en route to the agency with twenty-three lodges. Jumping Bull followed with another fifteen.[15]

By the time Allison found Sitting Bull on November 22, he had moved his village back to the vicinity of Wood Mountain. He had been summoned by the Queen's policeman. Colonel Irvine himself—"Big Bull" to the Sioux—had come over from Fort Walsh to make certain Sitting Bull understood the new firmness of the Canadian government.[16]

The crucial council took place at Wood Mountain on November 23. Backed by Crozier and two other officers, Irvine met with Sitting Bull and about thirty of his headmen.

For Sitting Bull, this was a highly stressful meeting. He could not grasp, despite Big Bull's repeated avowals, that Long Lance would not return to Wood Mountain. Time and again he asked the colonel to send for Walsh, as he could do nothing until he had seen Walsh. Asked why, Sitting Bull replied: "When Walsh was here I told him I did not know what to do. I was like a bird on the fence, not knowing on what side to hop. . . . I was inclined to surrender to the United States. He told me to wait here in Canada until he returned, and he would then advise me what to do."

Pressed further by Irvine, Sitting Bull related that Walsh had said that the government was building houses for him at Fort Qu'Appelle and that if he did not return to Wood Mountain by the time the first snow fell, Sitting Bull was to go to Qu'Appelle to see him.

Still confused and troubled, Sitting Bull asked Irvine to delay his departure four days so he and his chiefs could talk. In a final meeting, he requested Irvine to tell the Americans to wait a little while longer, "a very short time," and he would give his answer. Pressed for specifics, he said about two months or even less. "I still have it in my mind that I may see Supt. Walsh," he explained, "but if not, I will inform you through Supt. Crozier of my plans."

Colonel Irvine left Wood Mountain convinced that Sitting Bull had now faced up to reality and would soon surrender, and also that he would have surrendered at once but for Major Walsh's interference. Conversations with trader Legaré and other Wood Mountain residents disclosed that Walsh had written a number of letters from the East asking that presents and messages be passed on to Sitting Bull, thus reinforcing the expectation of a meeting.

As November 1880 gave way to December, plunging the Canadian plains into deep freeze, Fish Allison remained at Wood Mountain, working on Sitting Bull. At the same time, Major Crozier worked on Low Dog, the most prominent remaining Oglala now that Little Hawk and Big Road had surrendered. When he gave in, Sitting Bull did too. On December 10 Allison started a messenger for Fort Buford with word that Sitting Bull's entire camp, slightly more than one hundred lodges, would begin the trek the next day. However, he cautioned, "Indians are like so many wild cattle—the least thing would excite or stampede them." Above all, "A premature movement of troops would bring about the very catastrophe which we wish to avoid."[17]

At the Poplar agency, meanwhile, the ever-mercurial Gall behaved in a manner calculated to alarm the military and lead to just such a movement of troops. Reaching the agency on November 26, he did not surrender, as he had promised Allison, but raised his tipis in the Missouri bottoms beneath the bench on which the agency stood. Within two weeks his thirty-eight lodges had grown to seventy-three, as more joined from Canada and as some of Spotted Eagle's Sans Arcs slipped away from Fort Keogh. Among them too were Black Moon and Little Knife, whose defection from the Canadian refugees was further evidence of the continuing erosion of the Lakota leadership.

By mid-December Gall had the military so worried that General Terry moved to bolster Captain Read at Poplar. Bear Coat no longer resided at Fort Keogh. His ambition had finally been rewarded with the star of a brigadier general, and he had left for a new station. On Christmas Eve, however, a command from Fort Keogh under Major Guido Ilges camped next to Read's tents at the Poplar agency. A company of cavalry had already arrived from Fort Buford, and the force at Poplar now numbered nearly four hundred.[18]

Traveling with Low Dog, Sitting Bull's people made their way down Rock Creek, crossed east to the Porcupine, and followed down to Milk River. There, sighting big herds of buffalo, they halted to lay in a store of meat. There too, Allison persuaded three men to accompany him to Fort Buford for a talk with Major Brotherton. A favorable report on the officer and his fort, Allison believed, might counter backsliding. One of the three was Crow King, a renowned warrior, a minor chief, and until now an implacable foe of the whites. Leaving the village at the mouth of Milk River about December 19, the delegation reached Fort Buford on Christmas Eve.[19]

Allison had judged correctly: His Hunkpapas liked what they saw at Fort Buford, and on their return to Poplar they said so. On December 31 Major Ilges convened a council of chiefs and headmen to hear Crow King's story. About forty attended, including Gall, Black Moon, and Crow.

Crow King's report led the chiefs to agree to take their people to Fort Buford and give up. When? the impatient Major Ilges wanted to know. "I cannot tell exactly," replied Chief Crow. "We want to hunt on the way to get skins to clothe our women and children."

Still Ilges pressed for a date. "We will go to Buford some day," declared Crow testily. "It is cold and stormy so that we cannot travel. We want to wait for Sitting Bull and go with him."

And still Ilges insisted. January 2, two days hence, he would expect to start the march. "I think I have said enough," concluded Crow, and the council adjourned with everyone in bad humor.[20]

Still smarting from Ilges's words, Crow could not leave well enough alone. The next evening he went to the quarters of the military interpreter and left a message for Ilges. He was tired of talking to the soldier chief. He and his people would move in the spring. If the soldiers wanted to fight, he was ready; they were cowards, cried in the winter, and could not handle a gun. Gall warned friends at the trader's store of impending bloodshed.[21]

Such "impertinence" rankled, and Ilges also may have feared the Indians would decamp. He resolved not to give them a few days after all. The next morning, January 2, he assembled more than three hundred soldiers and moved on the Sioux camps, now considered "hostile." They lay amid willow thickets and underbrush in a bend of the Missouri River beneath the promontory on which stood the agency, trading store, and military camp. Crossing the Missouri on the ice, the troops advanced in two columns from east and west and bottled up the Indians in the river bend.

The Indians put up no resistance, in fact hardly showed themselves. A few who did drew rifle fire, and at least eight were hit, including one woman. When a shouted demand to surrender brought no response, Ilges had his artillery shell the tipis. That produced a fluttering white flag and eventually some men who filed out and laid their arms on the ground in front of the major.

Among them was Gall. As one of the officers remembered, "he came riding out on his pony with his blanket wrapped around him and arms folded and looked around him as like an old Roman as any man I ever saw."[22]

Despite their distress and the brutal weather, Ilges started his destitute prisoners for Fort Buford on January 6 under escort of the cavalry company. They numbered about 75 men with their families, 305 people altogether. The women and children rode in wagons, but many of the men walked. Ilges had given forty of their ponies to the Yanktonais for helping him in the "battle" of January 2. Ignominiously, both Gall and Crow trudged the entire distance to Fort Buford. Enduring four days of hardship, the people arrived at their destination on January 10. Major Brotherton housed them in a vacant warehouse near the steamboat landing.[23]

General Terry had lost patience with diplomacy. Commending the Poplar victors for "extremely valuable service," he instructed Brotherton to recall Allison and alerted Ilges to march up Milk River against Sitting Bull. At the same time, he ordered Colonel Thomas H. Ruger to organize another column at Fort Assiniboine and send it down Milk River to take Sitting Bull in the rear.[24]

The army pincers failed. Fugitives from Ilges's attack had reached Sitting Bull and set off the very stampede Allison had feared. Hurrying in advance of Allison, however, was Crow King, still committed to surrender. In a stormy scene on January 11, he challenged Sitting Bull and spoke so convincingly for surrender that fifty-one lodges fell in behind him and turned south. The other forty lodges pointed north with Sitting Bull. Low Dog and his Oglalas went too. Swiftly they traveled up Porcupine and Rock creeks and on January 24 crossed the boundary into Canada.[25]

Crow King's secession significantly weakened Sitting Bull. Joining Fish Allison, Crow King and his followers made their way slowly and painfully down the Missouri to the Poplar agency and thence on to Fort Buford, arriving on February 5. Numbering 350 people, 80 men, they more than doubled the number of prisoners then held at Buford. Soon another two hundred joined.[26]

The operation at Poplar had been an exercise in military overkill. To be sure, the presence of Gall and other refugees placed Captain Read in a precarious position. Although destitute and hungry, they were independent, ungovernable, and at times threatening. The dispatch of Ilges and his command was justifiable.

Not so justifiable was the decision to force all refugees who wanted to surrender to go to either Fort Keogh or Fort Buford. Had Ilges been authorized to accept surrenders, disarm and dismount the prisoners, and feed them at Poplar, most would have submitted, and his force of nearly four hundred could as readily have controlled them as Miles's force at Fort Keogh or Brotherton's at Fort Buford. But the army did not want them mixed with the Yanktonais at Poplar and preferred them securely under military rule at an established post, from which they could be transferred as soon as possible to their proper agencies.

From the refusal to allow the refugees to be fed at Poplar until they could be shifted down the river flowed Ilges's insistence that they move to Buford in the dead of winter. For hungry and impoverished people, a four-day journey through snow and subzero temperatures was a cruel ordeal, rationalized only by the unwillingness to provide rations at Poplar. General Sherman resisted subjecting the Fort Assiniboine troops to a comparable journey, and they marched in full winter gear. Crow's reluctance to move under such conditions seems eminently sensible.

Crow hardly behaved sensibly, however, in provoking Ilges with inflammatory language. But then Ilges hardly behaved sensibly in bombarding the Sioux village because their chiefs had spoken intemperately. Touted as a great victory, the Battle of Poplar River achieved its objective of forcing the refugees to go at once to Buford, but it was in truth a sorry affair that reflected no credit on the army.

The operations of December and January placed nearly a thousand refugee Sioux under military supervision at Fort Buford. But they also left Sitting Bull exactly where he had been at their onset—ensconced hungrily in his village near Wood Mountain police post.

The wretched exiles who went into camp three miles from Major Crozier's station on January 31, 1881, confronted a bleak future. "They have scarcely any food and are poorly clad," observed Crozier. They returned with many horses and 150 buffalo robes, but within a week nearly all had been bartered to the Wood Mountain traders for food. Even so, Sitting Bull had once more retreated into obstinate denial of his true circumstances.

Early in March 1881, Big Bull Irvine went over from Fort Walsh to lecture the chiefs on the futility of remaining in Canada. The Queen wanted them to go back, he said; they could expect nothing from Canada, neither food nor a reservation. He failed to convince Sitting Bull, but Low Dog once more heeded the appeal. With 20 lodges, 135 people, he trekked south and surrendered at Fort Buford on April 11.[27]

Low Dog's desertion seriously crippled Sitting Bull. Most of the fighting men had gone with him, leaving behind mainly old men, women, and children. Blackfeet and Cree raiders had harried the Sioux all winter, and the exodus of the young men made those who remained acutely vulnerable. Once more Sitting Bull fretted in uncertainty, and on April 3 he sought out Major Crozier for a talk.

"I do not believe everything the Indians who were here the other day said," he began, referring to the four men, including Crow King's own brother, who told of their treatment at Fort Buford. Someone had said the prisoners there were held in chains. He wanted to send his own representatives to learn the truth, and he wanted a policeman to go with them, "for I know what a redcoat says is true." He needed assurances that he would be kindly received, for "I see now that all that the Big Bull said was true." Eagerly Crozier agreed to Sitting Bull's proposition.[28]

Sitting Bull's delegation to Fort Buford, headed by One Bull, left Wood Mountain on April 5. Bone Club and a son of old Four Horns went with him. Escorting them were Crozier's newly assigned second-in-command, Inspector Alexander A. Macdonell, and an interpreter.

As the party made ready to leave, Sitting Bull gave Crozier a message for Brotherton to be included in the letter then being prepared. "Tell the Americans," he said, that "they will see me soon. I have given my word and my body to the Queen, and will do what I am told. I am in earnest. I am going in." From this, the police officers understandably concluded that Sitting Bull had finally made a firm commitment.

The five men reached Fort Buford on April 12, the day after Low Dog's surrender. Amid euphoria over the prospect of Sitting Bull's surrender, Brotherton feasted One Bull and his friends and let them mingle with the prisoners. They now numbered nearly eleven hundred. Some occupied the warehouse near the boat landing, while others lived in tipis and army tents scattered among the trees in the Missouri River bottoms. Brotherton had issued blankets and stoves, and each day the people drew rations that appeased the hunger from which they had suffered so grievously before surrender. They seemed content, at least while the winter weather lasted. His assignment swiftly concluded, One Bull and his companions were back at Wood Mountain by April 17.[29]

But there the scenario did not play out as the police officers had expected. When the chiefs gathered, with Crozier and Macdonell also attending, they heard One Bull report adversely on what he had seen at Buford. As Macdonell recalled, the delegates did not favor surrender, so "they lied about the treatment the Indians were receiving at Buford." Whether One Bull really lied or Macdonell simply thought he did, the report once again scared off Sitting Bull. Pressed by Crozier, he would respond only that he had nothing to say.[30]

If that was not enough to trouble Sitting Bull, an incident on April 18 reminded him of his vulnerability to the aggressions of enemy tribes, now that so many young men had gone to Buford, and also aggravated his relations with the police. In a nocturnal raid, a Cree war party ran off some Sioux horses. Warriors gave pursuit but failed to overtake the culprits, one of whom, however, was spotted during the day in brush near the Wood Mountain police post. As Hunkpapa warriors beat through the brush, the Cree suddenly sprinted into the police compound. At the head of his men, Sitting Bull marched up to the gate, confronted Crozier, and demanded the fugitive. Refused, he and several men moved to enter the compound. The major barred the way and gently shoved the group outside, then had the gate slammed and the garrison turned out under arms.

Enraged by Crozier's rough handling, Sitting Bull and his followers milled menacingly around the post, undecided whether to try to take the Cree by force. At length, seeking to calm the tension, Four Horns proposed smoking the peace pipe. As Crozier reported, "after completing the ceremony, they sat around the fort for some time in a surly manner and then left."

The encounter registered intensifying danger from the resentful Canadian tribes. "They say they will kill Sitting Bull if they have a chance," wrote Crozier. "The Sioux are in terrible fear of the Canadian Indians."[31]

On April 19 the camps near Wood Mountain began to break up and move east. Fear of enemy tribes was one reason. Another was an open rupture with the redcoats. Major Crozier felt betrayed by Sitting Bull, who had explicitly promised to surrender and now apparently had changed his mind again. In council, Crozier had vented his anger and frustration with harsh words and told the chiefs to go elsewhere, that he would have nothing more to do with them.[32]

The Canadian officers believed they had been tricked by Sitting Bull. Doubtless an element of duplicity did enter into the equation, but not nearly so deliberately and significantly as they thought. The Mounted Police, especially Major Walsh, had a somewhat better understanding of Indian character than most of their American counterparts, but culturally they were not much better equipped to understand why the Indians behaved as they did.

The seeming procrastination, the frequent changes of mind were only in part a bid to put off the dreaded day of reckoning, only in negligible measure a calculated manipulation of gullible whites. Rather they reflected the traditional Indian indifference to time, combined with the deeply imbedded need to talk about issues, especially issues that profoundly affected the welfare of the tribe. Indians had to talk until they reached a consensus, no matter how much time it took. Whites forever hurried, had to decide quickly, had to fix agendas and targets, had to resolve problems and get on to the next ones. Indians did not think and behave that way, and if the redcoats could not adjust, that was too bad, for they really were admirable men.

At the same time, Sitting Bull was genuinely undecided. On the one hand, the advices coming from American and Canadian officials and many of his own people guaranteed decent treatment if he gave up. On the other hand, the Americans had never done anything to merit his trust, and self-interested parties constantly fed his paranoia with visions of chains, prison bars, and scaffolds. He could not believe that he would not be hanged for killing Long Hair Custer.

Another cultural current was the attitude toward the food that the Indians lacked and the Grandmother possessed. That a proud race like the Sioux could abase themselves by begging, or resorting to guile to obtain handouts, annoyed the police. The refugees were literally starving, yet they stalled and talked interminably in council when they could end the ordeal at once simply by surrendering. For the Sioux, however, the matter went to the heart of one of their four cardinal virtues: generosity. When someone had food and someone did not, the virtue of generosity ordained sharing. Why would not the redcoats share? They had plenty of food, and they were otherwise kind, just, and truthful men.

With one tactic the police were successful in breaking through the cultural barrier. When the Indian leadership could not reach consensus, divide and conquer worked. Factions that could reach consensus spun off from the undecided and followed their own course. In promoting internal dissension and encouraging hungry people to abandon Sitting Bull and surrender, the redcoats hastened the breakdown of refugee solidarity.

In the end, however, it remained to one man, practicing the virtue of generosity, to precipitate the final collapse.

18 JEAN LOUIS

SITTING BULL'S DESTINATION as he broke camp at Wood Mountain on April 19, 1881, was Willow Bunch, a timbered trough in the plains, thirty-five miles to the east, where an old friend now did business. In three years of trading at Wood Mountain, the Sioux had grown to like and trust Jean Louis Legaré. In the autumn of 1880, possibly fleeing the increasing competition at Wood Mountain, he had moved his trading post to Willow Bunch. Jean Louis had always been generous. Perhaps, now that Major Crozier had grown so miserly, he would give them food.

He did. During a feast at his store on April 25, however, Jean Louis also raised the vexed subject of surrender. With Crozier's deputy Captain Macdonell standing by, Legaré recited all the well-known arguments and pleaded with Sitting Bull and the chiefs to take their people to Buford.

The old suspicions still gripped their minds. They trusted Jean Louis, they replied, but not the Americans. They could not go south until they obtained explicit assurances of good treatment from Major Brotherton. They had already received such assurances, of course, most explicitly in a letter to Sitting Bull brought back by One Bull and read at the Wood Mountain council of April 17. Nevertheless, Jean Louis promised to lead still another delegation to Fort Buford for this purpose. In his own carts, loaded with his own provisions, he would take several families who wanted to surrender and four men who would return with the desired report.[1]

Old Bull was one of the delegates appointed by Sitting Bull to scout the situation at Buford. During a two-day visit in early May, Old Bull was impressed. As soon as Legaré's caravan arrived, the army rolled out the "grub wagon" and issued tents, blankets, and all the pemmican the twenty Hunkpapas could carry. The officers spoke kindly, and all the prisoner chiefs urged the return of the Canadian exiles. The army had brought Running Antelope up from Standing Rock to put the prisoners in a positive frame of mind for their move to the agency. He had already convinced the chiefs, and to his pleas Gall, Crow King, Low Dog, and Fools Heart added their own. Old Bull and his three companions returned to Willow Bunch persuaded to surrender.[2]

Back at Willow Bunch by May 12, Old Bull discovered that on April 28, with thirty-eight lodges, Sitting Bull had struck off to the north, his destination Fort Qu'Appelle. As early as January, Major Walsh had predicted to a Toronto newsman exactly this development. "I know Bull thoroughly and am satisfied he has no intention of returning to U.S. territory until he sees me," Walsh declared. "Bull knows that I am to come back in the course of time, and although my command [Fort Qu'Appelle] is 200 miles distant from his camp, I do not think very many days will elapse before Bull will make his appearance there."[3]

Some sixty lodges remained at Willow Bunch, and Sitting Bull's absence afforded Legaré a favorable climate in which to pursue his campaign. Many of these people liked what they had heard of Fort Buford from Old Bull, but they beseeched Jean Louis to delay another journey until Sitting Bull's return, when all could go together. He refused. Old Bull was one of the thirty-two people loaded into Legaré's well-stocked carts and pointed toward Buford.

Also in one of the carts was Many Horses, eldest daughter of Sitting Bull. A suitor had offered a substantial payment in horses for her hand, only to meet refusal. Ever bound tightly to his children, Sitting Bull could not bear the thought of separating from her. The pair therefore took advantage of his absence at Qu'Appelle to elope, and they accompanied Jean Louis on his second expedition. The loss greatly affected the father.[4]

Reaching Fort Buford simultaneously with another forty-nine prisoners from Poplar, the Wood Mountain party confronted a startling sight. Moored to the Buford landing were three steamboats. The tents and tipis of the prisoners had been struck, and they were filing aboard the vessels with all their meager belongings. The new arrivals scarcely had time to surrender before being hustled onto one of the steamers. Running Antelope pointedly ignored Many Horses until Major Brotherton had shaken her hand. Then the chief shook her hand too, observing that years ago he had told her and her people that they would come to this, and now she could see it was true.[5]

The steamers cast off on May 26 and three days later deposited 1,149 Lakotas at the military post at Standing Rock, now named Fort Yates. Prominent leaders included Black Moon, Gall, Crow King, Low Dog, and Fools Heart. On June 15 another five steamers docked at Fort Yates, bearing 1,700 Sioux who had been held at Fort Keogh, including Spotted Eagle, Big Road, and Rain-in-the-Face. Now Sitting Bull truly was effectively isolated.[6]

Meanwhile, Sitting Bull and his followers, two to four hundred people, mostly old men, women, and children, camped on the shores of Lake Qu'Appelle. Fish and a few ducks eased the chronic hunger, together with flour exchanged for horses with the priest at a nearby Catholic mission. But food still dominated the Indian mind when Indian commissioner Edgar Dewdney arrived on May 24 for a showdown with Sitting Bull.[7]

The next day Sitting Bull and a few of his men crowded into a room of the Mounted Police office for the council. Dewdney began by reproaching Sitting Bull for breaking his promise to Major Crozier.

"It is true I said I would go over the line," conceded Sitting Bull, and he had sent three young men, now present in this room, with Captain Macdonell to investigate conditions at Fort Buford. But "it was afterwards I changed my mind." The police kept making a big issue of it, but it was that simple: He had changed his mind. He had gone across the line, the Americans had fired on his people at Poplar, and he had come back to talk it over with Major Walsh.

Dewdney put forth a proposition conceived in Ottawa. Canada would provide rations for Sitting Bull and his people if they would journey to the United States by way of Pembina and Red River. Dewdney would go with them to ensure that the Americans treated them as well as the Sioux who had already given up.

That would have to be talked over with all the men, Sitting Bull replied. The only food in the village was a few ducks, not enough for a council. Dewdney promised a small quantity of provisions and arranged to meet with all the men at Sitting Bull's village the next day.

The council resumed in the Hunkpapa village on May 26. Sitting Bull introduced each of his headmen. Only Four Horns was absent, he said, not having arrived yet from Willow Bunch. Beside Sitting Bull sat his young son Crow Foot, now five years old and attending his first council.

Sitting Bull took the lead, volubly pouring words on Dewdney, not all of which emerged from the interpreter in an understandable sequence. He spoke of Canada, of the Grandmother, of peace, and of his solution to the present impasse: Gather ten principal men each of the Sioux, the Americans, the Canadians, the Crees, the Slotas, and even the Catholic priests, "so they could talk it over and put everything straight." The proposition, he proposed, should be sent to the Grandmother and an answer awaited.

Most pressing, however, was the matter of food. "Now I beg of you to get some carts to go for some grub," he entreated. "I am wanting now two days some grub, so that the children might be eating and so that we might be finishing this arrangement quick."

Grub would be provided, the commissioner made clear, only when the Indians accepted his plan.

"Now I will go back to my country," Sitting Bull suddenly interjected. "I know it is rich, so send for two hundred carts so that all can eat."

Did that mean he would return to the United States?

"Yes, that is what I said. . . . What our Mother the Queen said to me, I understand, I will go."

And all his people?

"Yes! Hear me. The heavens above hear me. They will all go as one man if I go.

"Now I want to know from you if the grub is going to be brought soon."

Not here, only on the road down, replied Dewdney. Did Sitting Bull really agree to go down?

"I meant that I would go down, if you could get the ten people asked for before to meet at Fort Garry [Winnipeg] and settle what I want."

He could agree to no such proposition, answered Dewdney. There was plenty of grub at Fort Ellice, four days' journey, and the Indians could have it there, on the way to Pembina.

"If there is plenty there, why not send for it?"

No, said Dewdney.

"Then," as the commissioner observed, "he got up and remarked that he was not so poor that he could not live and left the council followed by his Indians."[8]

One after another, the Canadian officials had tried to get Sitting Bull to go back to the United States and surrender. Irvine, Crozier, Macdonell, and now Dewdney—each had pressed the cause with energy and met only frustration and failure. In truth, only one Canadian official had any chance of succeeding, and he had been detained in the East on orders from the Minister of the Interior.

On June 16 the Hunkpapas packed up and started south. Before leaving, Sitting Bull confided to some redcoats that he did not intend to surrender but instead to return to Wood Mountain and await the coming of Major Walsh, the only person in the entire Northwest he could believe.[9]

At Willow Bunch early in July, however, Sitting Bull again changed his mind. With his people once more out of food, he appealed to Jean Louis Legaré for a feast, in return for which he would do whatever the trader advised. All afternoon the people ate. Then Jean Louis announced that in seven days he had to make another trip to Buford, where he obtained much of his merchandise from the post traders. Anyone who wished to go with him should be prepared.

"I am not ready," declared Sitting Bull. "I want to stay here to have a rest."

"I have spent nearly all I have to feed you," said Jean Louis. He could wait no longer.

On July 12, with thirty-seven carts and wagons containing flour and pemmican, Legaré and eleven Slota employees headed out on the road for Buford. At Sitting Bull's camp some of the Indians packed themselves into the carts while the rest, including Sitting Bull, sat in sullen defiance. Finally, leaving seventeen carts for any who wished to follow, the caravan continued. Sitting Bull then ordered his remaining followers into the carts and announced that they would go west to Poplar rather than south to Buford.

That night, however, Sitting Bull's men swarmed into Legaré's camp and pressed their kinsmen to return with them to Willow Bunch. In the early daylight hours, they began to plunder the remaining food stock. Legaré protested. In a fit of petulance, one Indian threw a sack of flour on his feet and fired two bullets into it, whereupon the rest, irate because he would not let them "make free" with his provisions, sat on the ground and for two hours neither moved nor uttered a word. Finally Jean Louis resumed his own journey toward Buford. Morosely the Indians fell into line and accompanied him.

On July 12, before leaving Willow Bunch, Legaré had sent a rider to Buford with notice to Major Brotherton that Sitting Bull had finally agreed to come in and asked that rations be sent to meet his train. On July 15 six wagons headed north from Buford, in charge of a party of soldiers. The next day, about fifty miles out, the two trains met and the Indians fell with relish on an abundance of food.[10]

The next day, during the noon pause, an officer arrived. Responding to word that Sitting Bull might try to divert to Poplar, Captain Walter Clifford with a sergeant and five scouts had ridden twelve hours to make certain that did not happen. An officer of long experience with Indians, noted for his sympathy and fair dealing, Clifford had been placed in charge of the prisoners at Fort Buford and had earned their trust. He went prepared to use any means to ensure that Sitting Bull did not again deflect from the path toward surrender.[11]

Sitting Bull greeted Clifford with "How" but would say nothing more. The next morning, however, he loosened enough to talk about what was on his mind. "What is the reason they put my daughter in irons," he asked, "what has she done? What will they do with me?"

Some mischief-maker, noted Clifford, had written Sitting Bull that his daughter had been placed in irons at Fort Yates. If the Americans would do that, what might they have in mind for him? His anxiety over his daughter, thought Clifford, had decided Sitting Bull to endure whatever fate surrender brought him. "Your daughter was not put in irons," declared the officer. "What am I to gain by lying to you?"

Again Sitting Bull put the question, and again Clifford denied it. Placing a knife in the Indian's hand, Clifford vowed that "If I am lying to you, you may kill me."

"I don't believe it," averred Sitting Bull, and would say no more.

That day he made one last desperate gambit. "We will go to Wolf Point," he announced, "where we will cross the Missouri River and go into the Tongue River mountains. Once there we can hide and find game in abundance."

But they had no food to get there. No longer could he deceive even himself. All but Four Horns and a handful of lesser chiefs had deserted him. A few tribesmen had stayed back at Willow Bunch with No Neck and Black Bull, but the forty families now approaching Fort Buford—44 men, 143 women and children—were all that remained of Sitting Bull's once-vast following. Only from the white man—American, since the Queen would not relent—could they obtain enough food to sustain life. With what tangle of fear, desperation, bewilderment, dejection, suspicion, distrust, uncertainty, helplessness, loathing, and a host of other emotions Sitting Bull rode across the broad flat valley of the Missouri River toward the Fort Buford parade ground can only be imagined. As Captain Clifford concluded, "nothing but nakedness and starvation has driven this man to submission, and that not on his own account but for the sake of his children, of whom he is very fond."

Jean Louis Legaré had played a vital part too. More than Irvine, Crozier, Macdonell, or Allison, Legaré had coaxed and cajoled and prodded and bribed until Sitting Bull and nearly all the remaining refugees reached Fort Buford. His motivation drew on genuine compassion for these suffering people who had been his customers for four years. The police had admitted failure and asked him to use his influence. Major Brotherton had also encouraged his intercession. He had nearly bankrupted himself in feeding the starving refugees, and he also exposed himself to violence and even death by pressing a distraught and troubled people. He clearly was frightened for the entire final trip. Brotherton had led him to hope for reimbursement for his expenses and perhaps some compensation for his trouble. In return for his service, however, the U.S. government put him through years of expensive litigation and disillusionment before finally allowing a niggardly percentage of his total monetary investment.

The procession entered the parade ground at noon on July 19, 1881. Sitting Bull with his chiefs and headmen plodded slowly on their gaunt ponies, of which they retained only fourteen. Except for Four Horns, none of the chiefs were well known: White Dog, High-as-the-Clouds, Bone Tomahawk, and the Miniconjou Scarlet Thunder.

The families followed in Jean Louis's quaint two-wheeled carts. As usual, Sitting Bull boasted one of the largest of the families: his mother and sister, his two wives, and a still-growing retinue of children. They included the twins born on the eve of the Little Bighorn, another pair of twins born in 1880, his adolescent daughter, and his two stepsons by Seen-by-the-Nation, Little Soldier and Blue Mountain. One Bull and his family also formed part of the little assemblage. Absent was Many Horses, now at Standing Rock with her new husband. Absent too were Jumping Bull and Gray Eagle, who had surrendered with an earlier contingent. Throughout the Canadian ordeal, the family to which Sitting Bull was so deeply devoted had endured all the hardships and privations of their head, and now they silently watched as he approached the hardest task of his life.

The caravan moved directly to the appointed camping place, on the flat midway between the fort and the Missouri River. Only there did the men dismount and shake hands with Major Brotherton, yielding their poor ponies and a few second-rate firearms.

Reflecting the poverty that was now real as well as commanded by the virtue of generosity, Sitting Bull wore a threadbare and dirty calico shirt and plain black leggings, with an equally threadbare and dirty blanket draped loosely about his waist. Suffering a severe infection of the eyes, he had tied a calico handkerchief turbanlike around his head and drawn it partly across them.

The people were no less poorly clad. "They are some of them literally naked," observed Brotherton, "and with most of them the clothing is falling off from pure rottenness."[12]

Tired, hungry, and mute with the emotions of the moment, Sitting Bull clung to his fine Winchester rifle and indicated a desire to surrender formally at a later time. Major Brotherton appointed the next day.

At 11:00 A.M. on July 20 the principals crowded into the major's office at post headquarters. Present were Brotherton, Clifford, two other officers, a St. Paul newspaperman, an interpreter, and the redcoated Captain Macdonell, who had ridden in the night before to make sure, on behalf of the Queen, that the long-awaited event really took place. Still dressed in shabby travel attire, Sitting Bull and thirty-two of his men, nearly all the men who remained with him, filed into the room. Sitting Bull sat next to Major Brotherton and placed his rifle on the floor between his feet. Beside him, once again, was young Crow Foot, "a bright little boy."[13]

Major Brotherton opened the council. Sitting Bull and his followers would be sent down to Fort Yates and Standing Rock Agency, he said, where their kinsmen who had surrendered during the winter had already been settled. They would not be harmed by the army so long as they behaved themselves. Their treatment would be the same as all the others who lived there.

The men answered with grunts of approval, but Sitting Bull sat silent and glum. Brotherton invited him to speak. He sat trancelike for fully five minutes, as if, thought the reporter, reviewing his entire life. After a few words to his men that were not interpreted, he gestured to Crow Foot, who picked up his father's rifle and handed it to the soldier chief. Sitting Bull spoke to Brotherton:

> I surrender this rifle to you through my young son, whom I now desire to teach in this manner that he has become a friend of the Americans. I wish him to learn the habits of the whites and to be educated as their sons are educated. I wish it to be remembered that I was the last man of my tribe to surrender my rifle. This boy has given it to you, and he now wants to know how he is going to make a living.[14]

Simple, eloquent, moving, tragic, the last proud utterance of a great leader left no choice but surrender, and contained a pregnant question about the future. He should have stopped there. But he continued to speak, and what he said disclosed a mind either too dazed to allow him to play out the role or still unable to comprehend the full meaning of the occasion.

> I now wish to be allowed to live this side of the line or the other, as I see fit. I wish to continue my old life of hunting, but would like to be allowed to trade on both sides of the line. This is my country, and I don't wish to be compelled to give it up. My heart was very sad at having to leave the Grandmother's country. She has been a friend to me, but I want my children to grow up in our native country, and I also wish to feel that I can visit two of my friends on the other side of the line—Major Walsh and Captain Macdonell, whenever I wish, and would like to trade with Louis Legaré, as he has always been a friend to me.

He wanted to remain at Buford until the people still at Wood Mountain and Willow Bunch could be brought in, together with those still at Poplar. He wanted all his people at Standing Rock to join him on a new reservation on the Little Missouri. And he wanted his daughter sent up from Fort Yates to visit him at Buford.

Sitting Bull could not grasp that he no longer controlled his own destiny. The officials of the U.S. government now held that power, and none of what he asked would they even consider. Indeed, it could not have been a surprise to him that the promise just made by Major Brotherton would be broken.

The reality soon came to him, however, for he composed a song to connect what had been to what would be. It too was simple, eloquent, moving, and tragic.[15]

A warrior / I have been / Now / It is all over / A hard time / I have.

19 PRISONER OF WAR

MUCH HAD HAPPENED on the northern Plains since Sitting Bull's flight to Canada in 1877. On all sides, the Lakotas looked out from the Great Sioux Reservation on growing numbers of white people. That Sitting Bull could think of returning to the Tongue River country, or settling all his people on the Little Missouri, or traveling freely across the international boundary, or even following the old life of the hunt, revealed how little aware he was of the white noose that in his absence had suddenly begun to tighten around his kin.

The "Great Dakota Boom" got underway in earnest in 1878 and lasted for a decade. The Black Hills "agreement" forced on the Sioux in 1877 carved a triangular wedge out of the Great Sioux Reservation and cleared the way for a raucous mining industry in the once-silent haunts of the Indians. To help feed the miners, cattlemen moved their herds onto the grassy foothills falling off to the Cheyenne and Belle Fourche rivers. North of the Black Hills, stockmen filtered westward into the Little Missouri Badlands, where Sitting Bull had fought General Sully in 1864, and into the Yellowstone Valley and its southern tributaries, which Bear Coat Miles had forever denied to Sitting Bull.

East of the Missouri River, a series of wet years endowed the prairies with unexpected agricultural appeal. Long confined to the Yankton area in the extreme southeast corner of the territory, Dakota population fingered up the James, Vermillion, and Big Sioux valleys and spilled onto the open prairies from Minnesota.

The railroads turned a trickle into a rush. As the depression set off by the Panic of 1873 began to subside, railroad promoters once more looked favorably on Dakota, especially as inviting markets sprang up in the Black Hills. In the southern part of the territory, the Chicago and North Western and the Chicago, Milwaukee, and St. Paul built across eastern Dakota, aiming for the Great Sioux Reservation itself and, beyond, the Black Hills. Although the Northern Pacific railhead remained at Bismarck, graders began working west of the Missouri in 1879, and a gold spike driven in the mountains west of Helena in 1883 at last bound St. Paul to Puget Sound.

Commanding huge land grants and extensive promotional apparatus, the railroads triggered a land boom that rivaled the earlier mineral boom in the Black Hills. From the nearby states of the Midwest but also from such distant realms as Norway, Russia, and Wales, the land-seekers came. The buffalo ranges that Sitting Bull had contested with General Sibley in 1863 turned yellow with fields of wheat as the immigrants broke the sod and threw up their rude "soddies." Towns sprouted on the prairie and on paper, to thrive or die according to the vagaries of the railroad builders.

The northern Plains never attracted as many migrants as other parts of the West; but to the Lakotas, whose seven tribes added up to about 20,000 people, the influx seemed as massive as it was sudden. In 1870 all Dakota Territory counted less than 5,000 white citizens. By 1880, the year before Sitting Bull limped into Fort Buford, 17,000 whites dug Black Hills gold and another 117,000 peopled the balance of the territory outside the Great Sioux Reservation. In only five years the number would double.

Sitting Bull returned to a homeland changed and changing. He would never accommodate.

AS SITTING BULL had informed Major Brotherton, he wished to stay at Fort Buford until the last of his people could be brought in from Canada. While waiting, moreover, he wanted his daughter and a delegation of chiefs sent up from Standing Rock to visit him.

When Brotherton refused, Sitting Bull pointed out that he had never received even a handful of corn from the government. He had come in only because his women and children were starving. He thought himself entitled to some consideration by a government that had treated him shabbily. His request still denied, he replied: "All right, it is all of one piece. They have always lied to me."[1]

Resignedly, though not without repeated protest, he waited. But not for long, for he and his little corps of followers found themselves herded aboard the first downriver steamer—named, ironically, the *General Sherman*. After shoving off from Fort Buford early on July 29, the boat nosed into the Bismarck landing on the hot Sunday morning of July 31, 1881.

Several hundred citizens in their Sunday finery crowded the riverbank to gawk at the celebrity. It was a historic moment. For the first time the public looked on the most famous Indian of his epoch, the legendary figure first vilified, then grudgingly lionized as the slayer of the equally legendary Custer. For four years the press had followed the chief's adventures in Canada. Three correspondents had interviewed him and, with a redcoat not averse to interviews himself, filled out a reasonably accurate portrait. But the sensation-mongers showered this image with all manner of fanciful tales and twisted it into a grotesque caricature. For the assembled spectators, Sitting Bull disembarked from the *Sherman* that morning more a circus freak than the once-mighty leader of a proud people.

Nor was the novelty of the occasion confined to the throng of onlookers. For the first time Sitting Bull was about to face sights and sensations never experienced or even dreamed of in his fifty winters. There would be many more in the few winters remaining to him, as also the strange blend of condescension and acclaim to which whites would treat him for the rest of his life. That Sitting Bull handled the culture shock of this day with quiet dignity and relaxed good humor testifies to uncommon self-mastery.

As the Indians shuffled down the gangplank, people noted the contrast in appearance between Sitting Bull and his chiefs. They sported the best finery they could manage in the circumstances, but Sitting Bull affected only blue pantaloons, a dirty white shirt with red stripes painted down the sleeves, and common moccasins sprinkled with a few beads. Red flannel bound the three thick braids of his hair, and red paint streaked his neck, face, and the part of his hair. A large set of smoked goggles, which someone had provided to shield his painful eyes, gave his face a bizarre aspect.

The lack of display, declared a reporter, "is for the purpose of impressing the sentimental white man with his poverty." It was no such thing, but rather the lifelong custom of a man demonstrating his devotion to the virtue of generosity.

At once Sitting Bull confronted a tangible example of an institution he had battled for four years—the Northern Pacific Railway. A spur line had been laid to connect the levee with the depot in Bismarck, and the private coach of the firm's general manager, bearing B. D. Vermilye, his personal secretary, had been run down to the river behind a locomotive. With Fish Allison interpreting, Vermilye invited Sitting Bull to board the plush car and be his guest at a reception in the city. He had never seen a railway train. He approached it with trepidation and asked to see it move. When the engineer demonstrated, Sitting Bull shook his head and declared that he would rather walk. Instead, he rode in an army ambulance, with his sister, Four Horns, and other chiefs crowded in behind him.

Nor had Sitting Bull ever seen a white man's town, and the formal reception in the carpeted and cushioned parlor of the Sheridan House must have struck him as a curious rite indeed. Seated with his Hunkpapa companions in a half circle, he puffed on his pipe, fanned himself with a large hawk's wing, and chatted with Fish Allison.

The affair turned into an autograph session. In Canada a trader, Gus Hedderich, had taught him to write his name. "He writes easily," observed a correspondent, "and held the pencil . . . with true reportorial grace."[2]

A sumptuous dinner at the Merchants Hotel followed. Spectators crowded the doors and windows to watch as the Indians, to the surprise of all, handled their knives and forks with ease. Each guest received a bill of fare describing the succession of courses, and the Indians laughed heartily as Allison identified them by their pretentious labels. Served with great ceremony, "as to the Queen of England," the repast delighted Sitting Bull, who asked many questions. Most startling was dessert—ice cream. Turning to Allison, he observed that he "could not see how such stuff could be frozen in hot weather."

Back at the levee, Sitting Bull held court while the boat prepared to cast off. An old friend relieved Allison as interpreter for a few moments. She was Lulu Harmon, wife of the Fort Lincoln post trader and daughter of Matilda Galpin, Eagle Woman, who had accompanied Father De Smet to Sitting Bull's village in 1868.[3] In Mrs. Harmon's presence, Sitting Bull relaxed noticeably and even grew somewhat voluble. With Four Horns standing next to him, he pointed out and named each member of his family, then thanked the officers of the boat for their kindness.

The exhibition turned commercial when Sitting Bull discovered that his autograph, pipes, and other "trinkets" could earn the white people's money. After a number of such transactions, he boarded the *Sherman* richer in coin and wiser in the strange ways of his captors.

At noon on Monday August 1, the *Sherman* approached its destination, where Sitting Bull expected to live the rest of his life. The nondescript little military camp that had been thrown up in 1875 to guard Standing Rock Agency had grown into an imposing post, complete with barracks, officers' row, warehouses, stables, and corrals, marked by the national colors floating from a tall white flagstaff rising from the neatly tended parade ground. From the "Post at Standing Rock," it had graduated to high military distinction as Fort Yates, named in honor of one of Custer's officers slain at the Little Bighorn. Crowding Fort Yates in unmilitary disorder on the north were the buildings of Standing Rock Agency— offices, residences, council house, shops, storehouses, school, church, and various utility structures. The fort and agency lined the high banks of the Missouri River, overlooking the steamboat landing below. A low hill mass rose to the northwest, lifting some of the agency buildings above the valley, but to the west and south a broad level valley merged into distant foothills.

As the *Sherman* veered from the main channel of the Missouri River toward the Fort Yates dock, Sitting Bull and his chiefs gathered in line at the front of the upper deck. One flung to the breeze a yellow banner bearing the design of a deer, and they began a mournful chant punctuated periodically by sharp shrieks. The song rose in tempo and intensity as the shore drew nearer. Throngs of people, largely the "late hostiles" who had come down from Buford a month earlier, covered the slope above the bank. Only the day before the army had ordered them to move their camp from the river to a new location two miles inland. Now a line of infantry-men with bayonets fixed kept the welcomers at a distance.

Anxiously Sitting Bull scanned the shore for his daughter and for comrades from the Canadian exile. Instead, as official welcomer, the army put forth Running Antelope. He ascended the stairs to the upper deck and emerged directly behind Sitting Bull. Embracing him from the rear, Running Antelope thrust his chin over his old friend's shoulder, pressed his cheek against Sitting Bull's cheek, and murmured, "My son." Sitting Bull stood motionless, showing no sign of recognition.

Next Running Antelope went to the front of the line. Facing each chief in turn, he shook hands and said "How." When he reached Sitting Bull, he found the chief crying while wiping the tears from his face with a large silk handkerchief given him by a Bismarck well-wisher.

Before disembarking, Sitting Bull had to submit to another exhibition of himself. With Four Horns and Running Antelope, his keepers ushered him into the boat's cabin, where the families of the fort and agency had been invited to meet the luminary. As he labored slowly to produce his autograph—free to the ladies, from one to five dollars for the men—the guests expressed their surprise: "Why, he does not look at all as I expected." "He don't look as savage as I thought." "Can that be the instigator of the Custer massacre?"

After half an hour the prisoners filed down the gangway and, surrounded by soldiers, sat in a circle on the ground while their possessions were carried off the boat. Farther up the slope, still held back by the line of bayonets, their kin milled about in silence and gradually dispersed.

There sat "the great chief," observed a reporter, smoking his pipe under the hot noontime sun. "His spirit is broken and he sits on a sandy river bank surrounded by civilization with his last 200 followers calmly awaiting the pleasure of our Uncle Sam."

Although allowed to move back from the sandy riverbank, for a month Sitting Bull and his 190 followers awaited the pleasure of Uncle Sam. Major Brotherton had promised that he would be allowed to live at Standing Rock with the rest of his people, and that had been the assurance repeated over and over again by American and Canadian officials beginning with the Terry Commission of 1877. But now the army high command had second thoughts. Sitting Bull harbored enough potential for mischief, the generals feared, that he should not be quickly relinquished to the Indian Bureau.

While the authorities debated, the people waited. Gall, Crow King, and other of the "late hostiles" invited Sitting Bull to visit their camp on the flats west of the fort and agency, and the military approved. From morning until night he moved from one tipi to another feasting and counciling with his old comrades.

On August 2 the St. Paul newspaperman who had covered the surrender and move to Fort Yates with such thoroughness succeeded in gaining an interview with Sitting Bull, his fourth of any depth. Conducted in Sitting Bull's lodge, it was interpreted by Fish Allison and observed by One Bull, Four Horns, and Bone Tomahawk. A handful of whites also sat in.[4]

Sitting Bull added little to what he had told Charles Diehl and Jerome Stillson at Fort Walsh in 1877. He spoke of his youth, but could not be persuaded to talk much about his life after the age of fourteen. He made a few observations on the Custer Battle and gave his opinion on the recent assassination of President James A. Garfield.

He also disclosed that no longer did the army bar his daughter from his lodge. She "came to see me last night. We both cried. I was happy to see her." Indeed, she seems to have gladdened his heart by abandoning her husband of four months and rejoining her father's household.[5]

Asked about the bravest chiefs of the Hunkpapas, Sitting Bull named the four shirt wearers. Red Horn and Loud-Voiced-Hawk were dead, he said, leaving Four Horns and Running Antelope. After Sitting Bull, Four Horns was the bravest chief. As for Running Antelope, he was a *witko*, a fool. "He made treaties and allowed the white man to come in and occupy our land."

And looking to the future: "When I came in I did not surrender. I want the government to let me occupy the Little Missouri country. There is plenty of game there." Furthermore, "I want to keep my ponies. I can't hunt without ponies." In other words, "I want no restraint. I will keep on the reservation, but want to go where I please. I don't want a white man over me. I don't want an agent."

Even yet, Sitting Bull had not come to understand his true circumstances. For the rest of his life, a white man would be over him, and he would never again be free of restraint.

One of the whites who observed the interview in Sitting Bull's tipi was Orlando S. Goff, a Bismarck photographer. He had brought his camera and equipment down to Fort Yates, and he succeeded in persuading Sitting Bull—for a fee—to sit for his portrait. Although Sitting Bull disliked the result—it made him look like a white man, with a light face—it was the first of many.[6]

Three weeks after the *Sherman* unloaded its human cargo at Fort Yates, the government decided. Sitting Bull and the people who surrendered with him, decreed the Secretary of War, would be taken still farther down the Missouri River, to the military post of Fort Randall. There they would be held as prisoners of war until further notice. Why this broken little band posed more of a threat than those of Gall, Crow King, or Rain-in-the-Face—whom everyone supposed to be the Indian who killed Custer—seems not to have been seriously considered.[7]

When informed of this decision on September 6, Sitting Bull erupted in anger. All night he gave stormy vent to his feelings and in the morning sought a council with the post commander, Colonel Charles C. Gilbert. Refused, Sitting Bull defiantly swore to all that he would never go to Fort Randall, that he would rather die like Crazy Horse than leave his new home at Standing Rock. As the word spread to other groups, they too turned rebellious. In particular, Gall and Crow King with their followers acted as if they might try to join Sitting Bull in an uprising.

At once Colonel Gilbert isolated Sitting Bull by moving him and his people back to the river's edge and surrounding them with troops. When the *Sherman* docked at 11:00 A.M. on September 9, Sitting Bull could plainly see that he must either go or, as he had vowed, die like Crazy Horse. Infantry with bayoneted rifles stood ready to inflict Crazy Horse's fate if provoked. Gradually the blue ring contracted until the Indians had been packed into a tight bunch and herded toward the gangway. Only the hot-tempered One Bull stood firm. A rifle butt between the shoulder blades sent him sprawling, and he too boarded the steamer. With 167 Indians and a company of infantry on board, the *Sherman* cast off at 2:00 P.M. and steamed into the channel.

Once again the Americans had lied to Sitting Bull.[8]

The next twenty months formed the unhappiest and most uneventful period of Sitting Bull's life. He had nothing to do but sit and vegetate. After filing off the *Sherman* on September 17, he and his people raised their thirty-two tipis on the prairie half a mile west of Fort Randall. Thereafter, day in and day out, they devoured army rations, exhibited themselves to occasional curiosity seekers, and ruminated on the iniquity of the white man and even their own kin who had sold out to the white man.

A picket of bluecoats guarded the little cluster of tipis. They were elements of the Twenty-fifth Infantry, a regiment of black enlisted men and white officers. The commander of Fort Randall was Colonel George S. Andrews, an able and sympathetic soldier who could scarcely conceal his feeling that these pitiful people ought to be sent back to Standing Rock and allowed to live with their tribe.

The abrupt removal from Fort Yates and forced exile at Fort Randall wrought an equally abrupt change in Sitting Bull's attitude. For the first time, he seemed to understand the magnitude of his fall. No longer did he talk of a reservation on the Little Missouri, or the old life of the hunt free from a white man over him. He was now at peace with the world and intended to remain so, he informed Colonel Andrews—except, of course, with Crows, Assiniboines, and Piegans.

Two questions troubled his mind, as they would for nearly two years: Why was he sent here, and how long would he have to stay? The colonel could answer neither.[9]

In a little more than a week after his arrival, Sitting Bull took a proposal to his keeper. Conceding the overpowering strength of the Americans, he had come to see that nothing remained for his people but to go to work like other Indians and "raise their living out of the ground." Thus his followers ought to be treated like their relatives on the reservation and supplied with wagons, plows, white-man clothing, horses, and cattle. To arrange such a settlement, he wanted to take Gall and ten or twelve other chiefs to Washington to meet with the Great Father. Failing that, he wanted someone specially commissioned by the president to visit him, and failing that he wanted the president himself to send word in writing just what he intended for Sitting Bull's people and for how long.

Representing a revolutionary change of heart, the words probably drew on sincere conviction. Painful experience, especially in the past two months, proved the necessity for some new course. Even to Sitting Bull, the old life must have seemed irretrievably lost. The mood of the prisoners, Andrews thought, was to submit to anything reasonable. The approaching winter, aggravated by continuing uncertainty, could change the mood, and he urged speedy action.[10]

Instead of speedy action, he got no action. As Sitting Bull could not know, President Chester A. Arthur found little time in his workday to think about his government's treatment of a handful of Indian prisoners on the distant Dakota plains.

Late October of 1881 brought a guest who lightened the monotony for several weeks. Bespectacled Rudolf Cronau, correspondent and artist for a German magazine, arrived to add to a collection of paintings of Indians that he had begun at Standing Rock. There Gall and others had dubbed him Iron Eyes, and at Fort Randall he quickly made friends with Sitting Bull and his entourage. While Sitting Bull sat for his portrait, in breastplate and feathered war bonnet, the two tried to teach each other their respective languages, without success.

With One Bull Cronau formed a close attachment, as the two, with special dispensation from Colonel Andrews, rode the surrounding plains. One Bull too sat for a painting. The artist noted that the young man, "because of his beautifully moulded features, his flashing eyes, and his superb form, was the secretly beloved darling of all feminine members of the officers' families staying at Fort Randall."[11]

Asked by Colonel Andrews to stage an exhibition of his paintings, Cronau fitted up a room at the fort as a gallery and hung a selection of his work from Standing Rock and the Sitting Bull camp. On the second day, after the officers and their ladies had inspected the collection, the Indians were invited. "As they had never before seen any display like this, their interest was intense," recalled Cronau. "With special delight their eyes hung on the portraits of their far away friends and relatives at Standing Rock Agency, the names of whom sounded almost like soft prayers, as they came from their lips."

Iron Eyes's emotional leavetaking left the Indians genuinely sad and once again without diversion from their dreary existence.

In his enforced idleness, Sitting Bull found a meager distraction in autobiography. This began early in December 1881 when the Reverend John P. Williamson, Presbyterian missionary at the nearby Yankton agency, appeared with a sheaf of papers that Sitting Bull instantly recognized as an artifact of his past.

The packet contained pictographs representing significant feats of bravery in his life. They were not originals, but copies executed on blank roster forms of an infantry regiment. Somehow they had come into possession of Dr. James Kimball, post surgeon at Fort Buford in 1870, during the final stages of Sitting Bull's personal war against that Missouri River outpost. From Fort Buford they had found their way into the collections of the surgeon general in Washington. After the Little Bighorn, selections had appeared in the *New York Herald, Harpers Weekly,* and other periodicals and had contributed to the public's fascination with Sitting Bull. Now the army wanted to know what light the author could shed on the drawings, and Colonel Andrews had enlisted the Reverend Williamson, who spoke Sioux, in the effort.[12]

Sitting Bull explained that he had executed the series as a gift for Jumping Bull, whom he thought still owned the originals. In fact, fourteen of the fifty-five drawings depicted feats of Jumping Bull, not Sitting Bull. Two copies had been made by Four Horns, both of which wound up at Fort Buford. Sitting Bull explained two of the drawings, his first coup at age fourteen and an encounter with a Ree, but on the rest he remained "rather reserved." His present situation, Williamson thought, colored his commentary, especially on those depicting fights with soldiers. "If a more full account of his war deeds is desired," the missionary concluded, "a better time to secure it would be at some future date when his status is definitely determined."[13]

Williamson's visit aroused interest in pictographs both in Sitting Bull and in the Fort Randall community. In 1882 he prepared at least three more compilations. Two were for army officers who had given him gifts of food and clothing and performed other acts of kindness, and a third, probably a more commercial transaction, was for the post trader at Fort Randall.

Unlike the earlier drawings, these plainly aimed at a white audience. None dealt with such awkward subjects as the killing of Long Knives. A few reflected some of the techniques he had learned from Iron Eyes Cronau. And now Sitting Bull identified himself with his new white-man autograph rather than, as previously, the glyph depicting a sitting buffalo bull.[14]

Sitting Bull seems to have convinced himself of the need to learn the ways of the white people, but it was an abstract conviction, yet untested by reality. On the Sioux reservation, now that the tribes had been truly conquered, the Indian Bureau and church and reform groups were intensifying the civilization programs. These aimed at transforming the Indians into imitation whites in all but color. Ideally, they would end up on their individually owned farms, dressing, working, worshiping, living, and thinking like white people.

Two of the civilization initiatives, religion and education, reached for the prisoners at Fort Randall. Colonel Andrews turned aside the application of Father Martin Marty, now bishop of Dakota, to place a Catholic missionary among Sitting Bull's people. Episcopal Bishop William H. Hare fared better, largely because his proposal came in the guise of education. Andrews persuaded the parents of three boys and two girls to allow their children to enter Hare's mission school at the Yankton agency. Symptomatic of Sitting Bull's thinking at this time, he consented to the enrollment of his stepson Little Soldier, now thirteen, and with the other parents accompanied the children to Yankton for transfer to Bishop Hare.[15]

Captain Richard H. Pratt's Indian boarding school at Carlisle, Pennsylvania, presented a different prospect. Four years old in 1882, the model for a proliferating system of off-reservation schools, Carlisle recruited industriously on reservations all over the nation. To transform some of the children of Sitting Bull's band from blanket Indians into neatly uniformed and scrubbed Christians, shorn of their braids, seemed like a fine advertisement for Carlisle. In August 1882 Colonel Andrews received instructions from General Sherman himself ordering ten children to Carlisle whether the parents liked it or not.

They did not. Some people, even Sitting Bull, seemed to favor the idea, but they were not the parents who would have to see their treasured children spirited off to a distant place from which they might never return. "If we were on a reservation we would let the children go," Sitting Bull informed the colonel, "but as we are not, we cannot."

Happily, the issue never came to a test, and Carlisle had to wait for Hunkpapas.[16]

An occasional burst of excitement relieved the tedium. Two days after Christmas of 1881, three recruits jumped an Indian woman going for wood, and two raped her. Andrews paraded the entire command, and the woman unhesitatingly pointed to two of the culprits. The other identified himself by deserting. Andrews balked at turning the accused over to civil authorities because frontier jurors rarely showed any respect for Indian rights, even when infringed by blacks. Instead he preferred military charges and timidly suggested the wisdom of avoiding publicity by simply discharging the miscreants.[17]

As the months dragged on, the people grew more and more restive, and quarrels rocked the little camp. Adding to the discontent, visitors came from Standing Rock and other agencies to feast and council and tell of friends and relatives. In November 1882 Jumping Bull and Gray Eagle rode down from Standing Rock to spend ten days with Sitting Bull.[18]

Going home remained the dominant anxiety of all the people. In August 1882 Sitting Bull addressed his own petition to the Commissioner of Indian Affairs. The words were doubtless those of a helpful army officer, but the thought clearly came from the author himself. He had never signed a treaty or benefited from a treaty and so therefore could not be accused of violating a treaty. "Desirous of changing his mode of life," he had voluntarily surrendered on the assurance that he would be fully pardoned for "past offenses" and allowed to live among his people at Standing Rock. Except for the few people with him, all his friends and kin had been transferred from military to civilian control; yet he remained a prisoner of war under military surveillance. These facts led him, "humbly and respectfully," to beg that he and his followers be sent back to Standing Rock. There, he promised, he would conduct himself peaceably and obey the rules of the Indian Service.[19]

The man who finally moved the authorities to give serious thought to the problem was not Sitting Bull but even so, appropriately, an Indian. In December 1882 old Strike-the-Ree, chief of the Yankton Sioux, requested the Reverend Williamson to help him frame a letter to Secretary of War Robert T. Lincoln. "My friend," Strike-the-Ree asked the secretary, "what has Sitting Bull been convicted of doing that you hold him a prisoner for so many long moons?" When was he ever tried and condemned? The imprisoned chief was just across the Missouri River, and "his moaning cry comes to my ear. There is no one else to speak for him so I plead his cause."

Secretary Lincoln agreed. He forwarded Strike-the-Ree's letter to the Secretary of the Interior and expressed the hope that he might obtain appropriations to allow Sitting Bull and his people to be turned over to the Bureau of Indian Affairs at the beginning of the coming fiscal year.[20]

Since the detention of Sitting Bull had been a military decision, Lincoln's endorsement of Strike-the-Ree's letter represented a change in the military attitude. The Secretary of the Interior at once stated a willingness to receive the prisoners at Standing Rock, and the agent there, James McLaughlin, urged that they be sent up early enough in the spring to permit them to put in crops this season. By mid-March of 1883 the paperwork had been completed and the transfer directed.[21]

Not until the end of April did the prisoners, 172 strong, once more board a steamer. Ironically, Grant Marsh captained the *Behan*; in 1876 he had piloted the *Far West* from the Yellowstone to Bismarck with Reno's wounded from the Little Bighorn. The *Behan* paused at Pierre long enough for the citizens to gather at the levee and gape at the celebrity. A correspondent for the local newspaper covered the scene and worded his interview with Sitting Bull, clad in a "biled" white shirt reaching to his knees and with his face resembling "a pot of Chinese vermillion," in the insultingly patronizing terms that would increasingly characterize western reporting on the chief.[22] At this stop, Sitting Bull again held an autograph session and posed for a photographer. The portrait showed him in a wide-brimmed hat with a butterfly pinned to the hatband.

The Sitting Bull who descended the *Behan*'s gangway at Fort Yates on May 10, 1883, probably struggled with a conflict between his mind and his heart. He knew in his mind, as he had openly acknowledged since the beginning of the Fort Randall exile nineteen months earlier, that his people had to make a new life for themselves. No model existed except that of the white man, and anyway the white man had established such firm control that no other choice offered itself. No longer could Sitting Bull indulge the fantasy of roaming freely among the abundant game of the Little Missouri; the animals grazing there now were not buffalo but Texas longhorns.

What logic dictated, however, did not extinguish the deeply imbedded devotion to freedom. The long confinement at Randall had only made it more precious. The ideal that ruled his heart that day as he stepped off the *Behan* found eloquent expression in a virtual manifesto delivered to a newsman at Fort Randall. It summed up his life before the black day when he went into Fort Buford, and it forecast what lay ahead in the years remaining to him:

> White men like to dig in the ground for their food. My people prefer to hunt the buffalo as their fathers did. White men like to stay in one place. My people want to move their tepees here and there to the different hunting grounds. The life of white men is slavery. They are prisoners in towns or farms. The life my people want is a life of freedom. I have seen nothing that a white man has, houses or railways or clothing or food, that is as good as the right to move in the open country, and live in our own fashion.[23]

20 STANDING ROCK

STANDING ROCK AGENCY formed a world entirely alien to anything in Sitting Bull's experience. Except for the Fort Randall interlude, he had never lived on the government dole, never known the enervation of idleness and dependence, never endured curbs on his freedom, never conceived of an environment that could heap scorn on the beliefs and habits and values of a lifetime, above all never submitted to a white overlord.

Sitting Bull stepped ashore at the Fort Yates dock on May 10, 1883, with a conception of his new life wholly at odds with the realities of this world. In his mind, he remained war chief and holy man of the Hunkpapas and, once more prominent in his thinking, supreme chief of the Lakotas. Fresh from a life untainted by significant white influences, he remained the ideal Hunkpapa of old, embodiment of the cardinal virtues, renowned for bravery, generosity, wisdom, and compassion for his people.

He stood ready to compromise. He would yield to hard circumstance, suffer the confinements of a reservation, and learn to take his living from the soil. But he would also guide his people as he had before the debacle of 1876. As head chief at Standing Rock, he could still function as their shield, deflecting the worst effects of white rule even while adapting to new ways of life. He would be to the Hunkpapas what he imagined Red Cloud and Spotted Tail to be to the Oglalas and Brules.

These two chiefs, whom Sitting Bull detested as the main culprits in the Black Hills giveaway, enjoyed considerable influence at their agencies, which in 1879 had been moved to within the Great Sioux Reservation and renamed Pine Ridge and Rosebud. But the agent's instruments of control, chiefly rations, sharply limited the chiefs' power. They achieved their success partly through traditional Indian modes of leadership but also in large part through adroit manipulation of the agent. For Sitting Bull, this was an untested skill, one for which he was temperamentally unsuited.

Standing Rock had a strong-minded agent, effective in imposing his will on his charges. Short and stocky, with a neat imperial and a bowler hat covering thick wavy hair, forty-one in 1883, James McLaughlin had been an Indian agent for twelve years, first at Devils Lake and then, since 1881, at Standing Rock. He owed his political longevity, unusual for an Indian agent, to a demonstrated record of competence and to the powerful support of the Roman Catholic Church, which maintained its own Indian bureau in Washington to lobby for its share of the money allocated to churches for Indian education. As eastern reform groups such as the Indian Rights Association asserted increasing dominion over Indian policy in the 1880s, McLaughlin quickly won their enthusiastic backing too.

Unlike the eastern Indian friends, McLaughlin knew Indians as people rather than as distant abstractions. Even though with paternalistic condescension, he genuinely liked and respected them and devoted his life to their well-being as he saw it. As agent, he labored with them to promote the program of "civilization." A Dakota wife gained him entry and insight into his Indian communities—but also involved him in their factional politics.[1]

Sympathy and friendship, however, never diluted McLaughlin's authoritarian style. He had learned the art of "managing" Indians—of playing one faction against another, one chief against another. He unstintingly employed the powers of his office—control of rations, Indian police, Indian courts, the favor of the agent himself—to impose on Standing Rock his design for Indian progress.

With his own grand design for managing Standing Rock, Sitting Bull descended the steamer *Behan*'s gangway on a collision course with a man fully as dedicated and dogmatic as he—one, moreover, who held all the decisive weapons.

The very next day, May 11, Sitting Bull and his followers trooped into McLaughlin's office. He wanted no ration tickets, Sitting Bull informed the agent; as chief, he would draw all the supplies and distribute them among his people. He did not intend to plant this year but would look around, see how it was done, and perhaps put in a crop next year.

Meanwhile, he had appointed eleven chiefs and thirteen headmen from his band and wished them confirmed.

Finally, the Great Father had written him that at Standing Rock he would be the "big chief of the agency." From the other agencies he might gather in "his people"—that is, all the Lakotas who had followed him in the old days—and give them anything he might desire. A house would be built for him and he and his people provided with wagons, horses, and buggies.

"I heard this inflated nonsense through to the end," reported McLaughlin, "and then gave him some sound advice." The Great Father had written no such letter. (Of course he had not, but someone may have told Sitting Bull he had.) He would not be the "biggest chief" but would be treated the same as every other Indian at Standing Rock. He would receive his own issues individually, like everyone else. He would abide by agency regulations.

And he would plant this year. Within a week McLaughlin had Sitting Bull diligently if awkwardly applying a hoe to a plot of ground.

"Sitting Bull is an Indian of very mediocre ability, rather dull, and much the inferior of Gall and others of his lieutenants in intelligence," pronounced the agent. "He is pompous, vain, and boastful, and considers himself a very important personage." Finding in Sitting Bull an unpliable personality, McLaughlin formed an instant dislike for him.[2]

Sitting Bull did not like McLaughlin either. Wiping out the distinctions of a lifetime, he ignored Sitting Bull's record of stellar achievement, reduced his chieftainships to commonality, and minimized his influence on his people. Nor did Sitting Bull appreciate the agent's imperious manner. As Robert Higheagle commented, "McLaughlin's way of talking in angry tones was enough for Sitting Bull to disrespect him because Sitting Bull considered himself a chief."[3]

In his annual reports and later in his memoirs, McLaughlin created an image of Sitting Bull as an irreconcilable obstructionist, engaged year after year in a struggle with the agent for the hearts and minds of the Hunkpapas. In fact, Sitting Bull sampled most of the innovations he found on the reservation, and he did not mindlessly work to persuade the Indians to reject every measure the agent favored. Loudly condemning tribesmen he thought too ready to surrender the old ways, however, and speaking fearlessly and effectively against government propositions he regarded as harmful to the interests of his people, he came to personify for McLaughlin all the forces that interfered with the swift transformation of the Indians into imitation white Christian farmers.

McLaughlin's devil theory greatly oversimplified Sitting Bull's true role on the reservation. Robert Higheagle's appraisal seems more accurate:

Sitting Bull was considered a disturber which was not true. He tried to use his influence in the right way, but he was rather slow in adopting the policies of the agent. Sitting Bull was a thinker and didn't take anything up until he thought it was good. He was for the Indians and was for protecting their rights. The Indians to this day blame the chiefs who were so willing to sign any treaty that was sent out. [4]

McLaughlin was adept at molding willing chiefs. Even before Sitting Bull returned from Fort Randall, McLaughlin had enlisted Gall and Crow King as lieutenants in the crusade against the old life. They saw "that the day of the Indian was past," McLaughlin later recalled, and "did much to bring the bands under their influence to a realizing sense of the necessity for accommodating themselves to the ways of the whites." [5] Crow King died suddenly in the spring of 1884, with a Black Robe administering the last rites of the Catholic Church, but Gall went on to become the agent's favorite Hunkpapa. [6]

As always a shrewd pragmatist, Gall readily lent himself to McLaughlin's purposes, which included slander and denigration of Sitting Bull and constant attempts to win over his followers. As Robert Higheagle recalled, "The Indians were encouraged to tell falsehoods about Sitting Bull because the agent didn't like him." [7] Among falsehoods suggested by Gall and eagerly embraced by McLaughlin was the canard of Sitting Bull's cowardice at the Little Bighorn. Enjoying the agent's patronage, backed by the formidable array of rewards and penalties at the agent's disposal, Gall expanded his influence among the Hunkpapas and, his great and growing corpulence draped in a business suit, appeared as their spokesman at all official and public events controlled by McLaughlin.

Gradually Gall overshadowed Running Antelope, previously the reigning government chief of the Hunkpapas. Sitting Bull had called him a *witko*, a fool, but Sitting Bull's example seemed to make him long for the old ways and old days, when he was a famous warrior and one of the four shirt wearers of the Hunkpapas. Kind and generous, Running Antelope wanted to please everyone. As "the silver-tongued orator of the Sioux Nation," in a newsman's expression, he often appeared at public functions, but as an admirer of Sitting Bull and a champion of traditional ways, he saw Gall supplant him in the esteem of the agent. [8]

In each of the other tribes at Standing Rock, McLaughlin also cultivated protégés who could influence the people while articulating their
aspirations in terms that furthered his own purposes. For the Yanktonais
they were Mad Bear and Two Bears, for the Blackfeet Charging Bear, or
John Grass. An agency Indian most of his adult life, Grass emerged as
McLaughlin's special favorite, the chief spokesman for all the Standing
Rock Indians. "A good talker," commented White Bull, "not a thinker or
a smart man . . . could always say yes but never no."[9]

In the world of the agency, with the most powerful influences promoting change, Sitting Bull found many sympathizers but few allies willing
to speak out against the agent. Jumping Bull and One Bull remained
constant, as did some of the lesser chiefs who had been at his side to the
last in Canada. But the prestigious stalwarts of old who might have backed
him no longer retained the vigor to lead. Now ancient and tired, Four
Horns and Black Moon finished their long and constructive lives in quiet
idleness. Four Horns died in 1887, Black Moon a year later. Both, according to the agency census, were seventy-three.

In 1884, moreover, Sitting Bull had lost his longest, closest, and
possibly most influential counselor, his revered mother. Ever since the
death of his father, struck down by a knife-wielding Crow twenty-six
years earlier, Her-Holy-Door had lived in Sitting Bull's lodge, enduring
all the vicissitudes of the wars with the Long Knives, the Canadian exile,
and the Fort Randall imprisonment. Throughout, she brought to bear on
her famous son a combination of affection and wisdom that always influenced and often directed his thought. She was an irreplaceable part of
his life.

FOR THE SIOUX as for virtually every other tribe of the American West,
the decade of the 1880s was a time of profound stress and profound
change. They had been truly conquered. As Sitting Bull so painfully
discovered in Canada, no rational choice remained. They had to submit to
the reservation or perish. For the first time, the Great Father had corraled
all Indians on reservations, could keep them there, and could indulge any
social or penal experiment he wished without fear of another major outbreak.

Conquest coincided with the rise of the Indian reform groups in the
East. By the end of the decade, their agenda for the Indian's salvation had
been largely incorporated into federal policy. Their programs, for the most
part, were not new. Some went back to colonial times, others to President

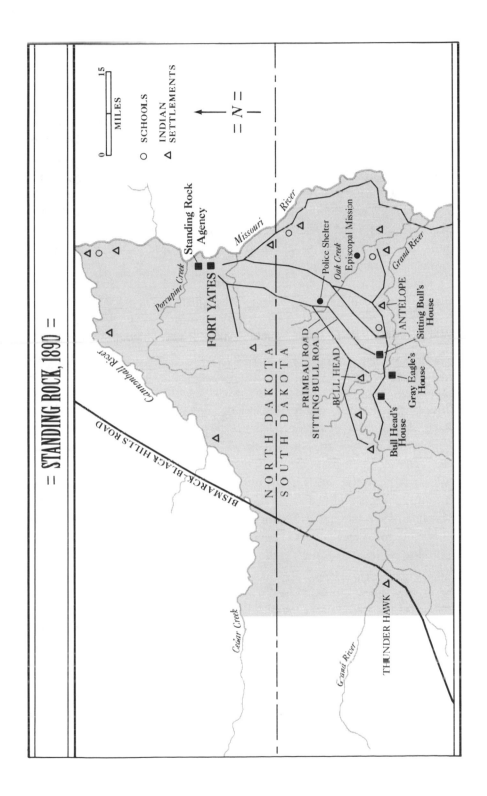

== STANDING ROCK, 1890 ==

Grant's Peace Policy. The new element lay in a conquest so complete that the reservations afforded sealed laboratories in which the experiments could be worked without serious challenge. No unceded territories or independent roamers complicated the process.

"Individualize" the Indian, ran the theory, cut him loose from the authority and society of the tribe. Settle him on an allotment of land and help him learn to support himself and his family by farming. Christianize and "Americanize" him. Teach him to live like his white counterpart on a Midwestern farm, to render patriotic allegiance to flag and country, and ultimately to assume the privileges and obligations of United States citizenship. In short, the reformers wanted to obliterate all that made an Indian an Indian and present him with the most prized gift at their command—their own culture.

James McLaughlin did too, and under his direction Standing Rock provided an ideal laboratory. There in the 1880s the principal institutions of the civilization program took root and flourished. They were farms, intended someday to lead to individual allotments from the commonly held acreage of the reservation; schools, for the education and Americaniz-ation of the Indian youth; mission churches, for the conversion of the people to Christianity; and Indian police and Indian courts, to maintain order but also to root out features of the old life judged "barbarous" or "heathenish" or otherwise inconsistent with civilized refinement.[10]

Spurred by McLaughlin and his farming instructors, the "late hos-tiles" planted their first crops at the Blackfeet Sioux settlement sixteen miles south of the agency. In 1885 McLaughlin marked out twenty farming districts and placed an Indian "boss farmer" in charge of each, with one of the prestigious appointments falling to Gall. In the next two years, the tipi villages near the agency dissolved, and people spread out to build log cabins, fence their gardens, and take up life as aspiring yeomen farmers.

Most of the Hunkpapas headed for Grand River, thirty to forty miles south and southwest of the agency. Running Antelope had already estab-lished a settlement of about sixty families in the picturesque and fertile valley and had even opened a store.[11]

In the spring of 1884, several miles upstream from the Antelope settlement, Sitting Bull took up his final residence.[12] He had intended to settle south of the river, on almost the exact site of his birth fifty-three years earlier, but the river was in flood when he arrived and he halted on the north bank. Gray Eagle, his brother-in-law, provided him with a cabin and a horse and some cattle. In the next few years, under the guidance of the district farmer, Sitting Bull saw his estate grow to twenty horses, forty-five cattle, eighty chickens, and fields of oats, corn, and potatoes. He (or his wives) dug a root cellar, built stock and implement sheds, and piled up two haystacks. "Nonprogressive" he might be, but he had vowed to take his living from the soil, and he did as well at it as any other Indian under McLaughlin's tutelage.[13]

No part of his responsibilities engrossed McLaughlin more than his schools. Among the many obstacles to education, however, was what he termed "the retarding influence of the non-progressive and ignorant leaders." Sitting Bull, of course, ranked as the leading "nonprogressive." When McLaughlin established the Grand River day school at the Sitting Bull settlement in the autumn of 1885, he charged the poor attendance to Sitting Bull's "bad influence." "He has not only withheld his own children but has also been prejudicing others against the schools."[14]

This was simply more of McLaughlin's instinctive negativism. Sitting Bull had often spoken of the need for Indian youth to learn to read and write, and during the Fort Randall imprisonment he had sent his stepson to a boarding school. On Grand River, he placed all five of the children remaining in his household, including Crow Foot, in the Congregational day school, and One Bull and Jumping Bull followed his example with their own children.[15]

The Sioux yielded even less readily to Christianity than to education. Each Sunday Bishop Marty's priests, brothers, and sisters filled their two churches with parishioners even while doubting the depth of their commitment. For Sitting Bull and Gall, the advent of the "White Gowns" of the Episcopal Church offered an alternative to the Black Robes. When an Indian emissary of Episcopal Bishop William H. Hare visited Standing Rock in February 1884, Sitting Bull declared the White Gowns to be the best friends of the Indians, and he wanted them to come to Grand River and teach him and his people. Instead, the Congregationalists preempted the Grand River area while the Episcopalians established themselves on Oak Creek. Gall settled there and joined the church.[16]

At Grand River the Congregationalists stationed Mary C. Collins, an accomplished woman of strong personality and a temperament well suited for Indian work. She won Sitting Bull's respect by ministering to one of his children when gravely ill, and thereafter the two conducted an affable rivalry. "We were always good friends personally," she remembered, "but he hated Christianity and found great satisfaction in taking my converts back into heathendom while of course I felt equal satisfaction in converting his heathen friends."[17]

No Christian dogma made serious inroads into Sitting Bull's body of belief and practice. He remained to his dying day the epitome of Hunkpapa spirituality. But nothing in his faith excluded experimentation with any religion, or part of a religion, that promised the personal and group power at which his own rites and devotions aimed. Nothing was heretical that worked, and any could have coexisted easily with his own scheme. Surely he tested Catholicism and Protestantism as they came his way, only in the end to reject them in favor of the revered creed of his youth.

Indian police and courts afforded McLaughlin the coercive tools to keep order and enforce his will. Reminiscent of the *akicita* and calling on warrior values of the old life, police service attracted good men. Even One Bull, a leading *akicita* in times past, joined the force.

The courts were conceived as a weapon against "demoralizing and barbarous" customs, and the Secretary of the Interior published a list of "Indian offenses" that included feasts and dances, polygamy, "purchase" of wives, medical and religious practices, destruction of property in mourning, and giveaways. Neither agents nor judges seem to have been very zealous in prosecuting such offenses, although their existence afforded a convenient means of penalizing uncooperative people.

More demanding at Standing Rock was the jurisdiction over misdemeanors, as "the conceited and obstinate" Sitting Bull himself discovered in 1887. In the agent's office, he ridiculed Shell King for giving up the old ways so readily. Enraged, Shell King attacked with a knife and Sitting Bull defended with a tomahawk. Hauled before the court, the pair incurred the usual fine for such offenses—Shell King one knife and Sitting Bull one tomahawk. This practice, McLaughlin observed, had greatly reduced the arsenal of weapons at Standing Rock.

Sitting Bull had the last word, however. Within ten days, lightning struck and killed Shell King. "The event had a tremendous effect in restoring the waning prestige of the old medicine chief," recalled McLaughlin, "to whose influence it was credited."[18]

In the estimate of McLaughlin and other theorists, the ration system raised the largest obstacle to the success of the civilization program. It deadened incentive to labor toward self-support at farming, it took people away from their far-flung farms for several days every two weeks for the slaughter and distribution of beef at the agency, and it absorbed appropriations that might better be directed toward school teachers, farming instructors, farm tools and machinery, and decent housing.

Some experts believed that the Indians should raise cattle rather than grow vegetables and grain. Climate and geography favored grazing over farming. In that event, of course, allottees would need more land than for a family farm. McLaughlin strenuously opposed this formula, arguing that the life of the cowboy too vividly recalled the horseback mobility of the old Indian life and would retard progress in civilization. After a series of devastating droughts destroyed the crops of his charges, however, he admitted that Dakota was not farming country and came out in favor of converting the fledgling farmers into fledgling stockmen.[19]

Whether farmers or stockmen, however, the Sioux were judged to have much more land than they would ever need—as much as 11 million "surplus" acres. That realization forged a powerful political combination of Indian reformer and Dakota land boomer, for clearly any land not needed by the Sioux ought to be thrown open to white settlement.

This drive for surplus land, which ultimately fired Sitting Bull's outrage and staunch opposition, underlay his first encounter with Washington officialdom. As yet untutored in reservation ways, lacking the finesse of Gall and John Grass, he bungled it. He emerged embarrassed and humiliated.

In November 1882, while Sitting Bull languished at Fort Randall, a commission touring the Sioux agencies under congressional authorization had visited Standing Rock. Chaired by Newton Edmunds, former Dakota governor and an old hand at bullying Indians, the commission had tried to stampede the Sioux into agreeing to the division of the Great Sioux Reservation into separate tracts, one for each agency. Supposedly that would assure all the Lakota groups of a local tribal ownership uncomplicated by the common ownership of all the Lakotas. What the officials failed to explain clearly was that, besides six separate reservations, there would be a seventh parcel, nearly half the size of all the others together, that would be ceded to the United States and opened to white settlement.

At Standing Rock Edmunds spread confusion, fear, and ultimately panic among the Indians. Convinced of the ultimate benefit of the measure to the Sioux, McLaughlin and Bishop Marty worked for its acceptance, Marty even leaving the impression that failure to sign would displease God. At length John Grass and others rushed to sign. As Grass later explained, "Those men fairly made my head dizzy, and my signing it was an accident."[20]

But the commissioners had overplayed their hand. The Treaty of 1868 required that any cession of land be approved by a vote of three-fourths of the adult Lakota males. This agreement bore the signatures of only a few tribal leaders. The Senate refused to ratify and instead dispatched a select committee to investigate. It was chaired by Senator Henry L. Dawes of

Massachusetts, the special congressional friend of the Indians. The group reached Standing Rock in August 1883, three months after Sitting Bull's return from Fort Randall and before he had mastered the etiquette of agency life.

The senators had come to hear the Indians, but the Standing Rock Indians had gathered to hear the committee. They had not agreed in advance on who should be put forth to speak and what they should say. A few meaningless observations had been coaxed out of Grass, Running Antelope, and Gall when Senator Dawes asked if Sitting Bull had anything to say.

What loomed in Sitting Bull's mind was a need to be assured that the committee understood how important a chief he was. "Do you know who I am?" he asked repeatedly; and finally, in a burst of indignation, "I want to tell you that if the Great Spirit has chosen any one to be the chief of this country it is myself."[21]

When that failed to impress the senators, he scolded them: "You have conducted yourselves like men who have been drinking whisky, and I came here to give you some advice."

And then, as the transcript recorded parenthetically, "Here Sitting Bull waved his hand and at once the Indians left the room in a body."

That wave of the hand ought to have persuaded McLaughlin of the error of his belief that Sitting Bull had lost his power over the Indians. It gave dramatic evidence of his continuing power, but it scarcely gained him the goodwill of white officials who held his destiny in their hands, a thought he recognized as soon as his temper cooled.

Later, after the Yanktonais had assured the committee that Sitting Bull did not speak for them and urged a resumption of the sessions, the embarrassed chief came back and took the floor.

"I am here to apologize to you for my bad conduct," he began. After expressing his sorrow for such behavior, he returned to the matter of his own stature. "I have always been a chief," he said, "and have been made chief of all the land"—that is, of all the Lakotas.

He then launched a rambling discourse suffused with his sense of self-importance and increasingly a self-pitying protest. It was a pathetic performance, lacking the dignity expected of a chief, inappropriate to the setting. Unlike Gall and Grass, Sitting Bull had not learned how to address white officials as self-important as he.

The courtly and patrician Dawes could ignore such behavior, but Senator John A. Logan of Illinois, another member of the committee, could not. Major general in the Civil War, a founder of the Grand Army of the Republic, and one of the most powerful men in the Senate, Logan suffered through Sitting Bull's speech, then declared, "I want to say something to that man before he sits down."

Logan then turned loose with a scathing rebuke. "You were not appointed by the Great Spirit," he asserted. "Appointments are not made that way." Sitting Bull was not even a great chief; "you have no following, no power, no control, and no right to any control." He lived on a reservation at the sufferance of the government, which provided him with food, clothing, and everything else he owned. "If it were not for the Government you would be freezing and starving to-day in the mountains." And if he ever behaved again like he had this day, "you will be put into the guard-house, and be made to work."[22]

Never had a white official talked to Sitting Bull this way. Not even Big Bear Irvine or Major Crozier had presumed to speak so insultingly. Logan had scolded the first chief of the Lakotas in language no Indian would use with anyone, shaming him in front of Blackfeet and Yanktonais as well as his own tribesmen and leaving him to slink away in fury and humiliation.

Sitting Bull's speech and Senator Logan's reprimand exhibited the chief at his worst. For his new life at Standing Rock, the episode was an ominous beginning.

21 THE WORLD BEYOND

SITTING BULL did not storm off to Grand River and spend the rest of his life railing against the agent and indulging the self-pity he exhibited to the Dawes Committee. His brief visit to Bismarck on the way down the Missouri from Fort Buford in 1881 had afforded a glimpse of the spectacles awaiting him in the white man's cities. Talk of an exhibition tour had swirled around him during the final Canadian years and convinced him that, as he had assured the Mounted Police officers, his body was worth a great deal of money. At Bismarck and Fort Randall, he had discovered that people would pay handsomely for his awkwardly contrived autograph. Thus he welcomed excursions to the outside world, both to relieve the tedium of the reservation and to earn money. The Sioux had always striven to acquire riches—ponies instead of gold and greenbacks—not to lavish on themselves and flaunt to their neighbors but to give away to the needy.

During the final six years of his life, Sitting Bull traveled extensively in the white man's world. He marveled at its wonders, admired its achievements, and disdained its failings. He also earned enough money to add impressively to his reputation for generosity.

The first venture occurred early in September 1883, shortly after the fiasco with Senator Logan. After a contentious rivalry with other towns, Bismarck had been voted the new capital of Dakota Territory, and an elaborate ceremony was planned for laying the cornerstone of the capitol building. Always conscious of Sitting Bull's celebrity value, McLaughlin took him to Bismarck as head of an Indian delegation. For the first time, Sitting Bull rode in a railway coach, from Mandan across the river to Bismarck. There, although described as in an "angry, cranky mood," he filled his pockets with cash garnered from selling his autograph for $1.50 and $2.00.

From one supplicant he accepted in return a plug hat, which he wore in the grand parade. He and his comrades rode third in the procession, behind the military band from Fort Yates and in front of the carriages bearing former President Ulysses S. Grant, Territorial Governor Nehemiah G. Ordway, President Henry Villard of the Northern Pacific, former Secretary of the Interior Carl Schurz, and the incumbent secretary, Henry M. Teller. All were en route to Montana to drive the last spike in the Northern Pacific.

Sitting Bull also occupied a prominent place on the speakers' platform and spoke before the other dignitaries. Governor Ordway, alluding to the custom of putting forth the oldest resident first, introduced the chief as probably the oldest pure Dakotaian present. Sitting Bull responded gracefully, expressing pleasure at meeting the governor and his friends and finding inspiration in *Wakantanka* to shake hands with them. The performance helped atone for his uncouth treatment of Senator Dawes and his colleagues not three weeks earlier.[1]

Bismarck only whetted Sitting Bull's appetite. When McLaughlin had to go to St. Paul in March 1884 on agency business, Sitting Bull made "earnest solicitation" to go too. He wanted to see more of the manners and ways of the whites, said McLaughlin, which could be expected to aid in his civilization. The Northern Pacific donated passes for Sitting Bull, one of his wives, and One Bull. Mrs. McLaughlin accompanied as interpreter. The party arrived in St. Paul on March 14.

The visit exposed Sitting Bull to a full array of manners and ways of the whites, which astonished him time and again but failed to shake his composure. Based at the Merchants Hotel, the party embarked on a whirlwind tour of the Minnesota capital and its governmental, financial, industrial, and commercial institutions. He toured the *Pioneer Press*, where the printing machinery and the telegraph prompted awe. He visited a grocery wholesale house, surveyed the immense banks of shelves laden with groceries, and followed coffee beans by the bushel through the process of roasting, grinding, and packing. He toured manufactories for clothing, cigars, and boots and shoes. In the last the foreman took his measurements and within twenty minutes produced a custom-fitted pair of shoes. At the Franklin School, both Sitting Bull and One Bull applauded lustily as the electric fire signal emptied the building in two minutes. A bank, a post office, and the great mills of Minneapolis displayed further mysteries of a world unimagined by Sitting Bull only a week earlier.

The highlight came at the city fire department. The firemen explained the operation of hoses and extension ladders, then staged a dramatic demonstration of responding to a fire call. The alarm clanged, and they slid down the pole from their sleeping quarters, harnessed the horses to the engines, and tore off with such speed and gusto that Sitting Bull insisted on an encore. This time he himself touched the electric signal.

After two dizzying and dazzling weeks, the little group again boarded the Northern Pacific. In St. Paul, to the disgust of the *Bismarck Tribune*, Sitting Bull had been lionized by the city elite and surrounded by curious throngs wherever he went. At each way station on the return, McLaughlin escorted him to the platform to be enveloped by inquisitive townspeople. He enjoyed the attention and reached home immensely impressed with his experience.

"Sitting Bull frequently comes to my house to talk of his visit to St. Paul and civilization," McLaughlin observed a month later. "What influence he has is being turned in the right direction and the recent trip to St. Paul has been largely instrumental in bringing this about."[2]

McLaughlin would later find cause to modify his optimism, but for the time being the acclaim poured on Sitting Bull in St. Paul prompted reflection on the benefits of further travel. Like Major Walsh before him, McLaughlin savored the role of Sitting Bull's keeper and was not blind to the prospect of more tangible gain. The proprietor of the Merchants Hotel in St. Paul, Alvaren Allen, happened also to be a showman, and hardly had his Indian guests checked out than he wrote to a senatorial friend asking his intervention with the Indian Office to obtain Sitting Bull for an exhibition tour.[3]

McLaughlin fell in with the scheme at once. He undertook to persuade "the old fool" to accept Allen's proposition, a delicate task because "he has to be manipulated and managed as you would *eggs*." The agent also enlisted an interpreter and offered Mrs. McLaughlin and his son Harry to accompany the party. "One thing is certain," McLaughlin advised Allen in July 1884, "*we can get him* and no other person can, but he has to be carefully handled to get him started."[4]

Other persons tried—so many, McLaughlin complained, that it had become "considerable of a bore." One was none other than William F.

Cody, proprietor of Buffalo Bill's Wild West, who sent his manager, John M. Burke, to Standing Rock to open negotiations. If Sitting Bull and other Indians were to be allowed to participate in any show, McLaughlin declared at the very time he was organizing them for Allen, he would prefer to have them in Cody's troupe. But no such proposition could be entertained, "when the late hostiles are so well disposed and are just beginning to take hold of an agricultural life."[5]

As finally assembled, the "Sitting Bull Combination" consisted of Sitting Bull, Spotted-Horn-Bull, Gray Eagle, Flying By, Long Dog, Crow Eagle, and several wives. One of McLaughlin's agency protégés, Louis Primeau, went along as interpreter, while Mary and Harry McLaughlin helped with the interpreting and with shepherding the party from depot to hotel to theater. After pausing in St. Paul to outfit, they entrained for New York City, put up at the Grand Central Hotel, and opened on September 15, 1884, at the Eden Musée, a wax museum that aspired to rival Madame Tussaud's in London.

The performance, as pictured by Allen, consisted of "a tipi on the stage and the Indians in full dress smoking and cooking their meal accompanied by a lecture on the inner life of the Indian." Dropping the trappings of poverty for the occasion, Sitting Bull braided his hair with mink and otter and donned leggings, furnished by Allen, plaited with white weasel skins and porcupine quills.

The engrossing "representations of wild life on the plains," noted the *New York Times*, drew a throng of nearly six thousand people during the matinee and evening offerings of the first day. Thereafter the Indians played to a packed house for two weeks before moving on to Philadelphia.[6]

At one of the performances in Philadelphia, a young Lakota named Standing Bear, on leave from the Carlisle Indian School, sat in the audience. Years later he remembered that Sitting Bull made a speech about the end of fighting and the need for the children to be educated. He and his friends, the chief concluded, were on their way to Washington to shake hands with the Great Father and talk about peace.

The white man then rose and "translated" what Sitting Bull had said. It was a lurid rendition of the Little Bighorn, complete with warriors springing from ambush to wipe out all of Custer's soldiers. "He told so many lies that I had to smile," recalled Standing Bear.[7]

Bearing the thespians home in late October, the train stopped in Bismarck. A reporter climbed aboard the coach and interviewed Sitting Bull, who expressed pleasure over his stay in the East. "He said he liked the dancing girls, and he brought down the car by giving an exhibition of the dancing he saw, which led to the belief that Colonel Allen and the other boys must have shown him the town while in New York City."[8] If so, Allen violated repeated assurances to the Interior Department of a church-centered tour entirely insulated from strong drink and lewd influences.

The episode cast McLaughlin in an awkwardly defensive posture, especially after the Commissioner of Indian Affairs sternly demanded to know by what authority Sitting Bull appeared on the New York stage. He had consented, the agent explained to Bishop Marty, solely to head off Father Joseph A. Stephan, his predecessor as agent and now head of the Bureau of Catholic Indian Missions in Washington. Only after he learned that Stephan had obtained Secretary Teller's blessing for a Sitting Bull tour did he aid Allen. "There is money to be made from this if properly managed," McLaughlin observed, "but Fr. Stephan does not have the business qualifications or the tact to succeed and would certainly have spoiled the enterprise for anyone else."[9]

"Disappointed in the results of the recent trip," therefore, McLaughlin turned aside efforts to have Sitting Bull appear in the Dakota exhibits at the forthcoming New Orleans Exposition. Gall went instead.[10]

Whatever McLaughlin's regrets, Sitting Bull had not abandoned the stage. Once more Buffalo Bill renewed the attempt to sign him up for the famous Wild West. General Sherman's endorsement—"Sitting Bull is a humbug but has a popular fame on which he has a natural right to 'bank' "—helped prepare the way at the Indian Office, and on June 6, 1885, the contract was signed. Over a four-month period, Sitting Bull would receive $50 a week, a bonus of $125, and exclusive rights to the sale of his portraits and autographs—a source of handsome revenue.[11]

For Sitting Bull, the travels with Buffalo Bill seem to have been more agreeable and rewarding than the Allen tour of the year before. He got on famously with Cody. A photograph taken in Montreal showed the two clasping hands and was widely displayed on publicity posters with the caption "Foes in '76, Friends in '85."

A special favorite was Annie Oakley, the virtuoso of the rifle. Sitting Bull had seen her perform with another "combination" in St. Paul in 1884 and was so impressed that he had dubbed her "Little Sure Shot" and made her his adopted daughter. During the Buffalo Bill tour, the two became fast friends.[12]

Sitting Bull's role was not taxing. To his credit, Cody presented him to the public simply as Sitting Bull, the famous Hunkpapa chief. He was not sensationalized as the "slayer of Custer" nor used in tableaus or mock battles. Rather he rode in the parades and greeted visitors at his tipi. He enjoyed considerable freedom and lavished his money on street urchins and other hangers-on. The tour played more than a dozen cities, half in Canada, and afforded him a kaleidoscopic and enlightening view of the white man's world.[13]

On June 22, 1885, the circus stormed into Washington, D.C., for a three-day stand. "A Group of Howling Savages Pursue a Defenseless Stage Coach," headlined the *Washington Post* as the ubiquitous Deadwood Stage announced the troupe's arrival. It was Sitting Bull's first visit to the capital. With Cody in attendance, he dropped by the White House to leave a supplicating letter for President Grover Cleveland's consideration, then went next door to army headquarters to meet an old antagonist. Philip Henry Sheridan now commanded the United States Army, but the delegation of fifteen Sioux found the paintings of western scenes adorning his wall more interesting than the man who had orchestrated their conquest. Sitting Bull grunted to his comrades but, fittingly, ignored the corpulent little general who had once denied the very existence of any chief named Sitting Bull.[14]

The season closed in St. Louis on October 3. In the parlor of the Southern Hotel, Sitting Bull reminisced with Colonel Eugene A. Carr, one of Crook's cavalry officers in the campaign of 1876, and told a reporter how much he liked show business. He was tired of the noise and bustle, though, and longed for the fresh air of the prairie.[15]

Throughout the season, Sitting Bull had ridden a light gray horse in the arena appearances and had become very fond of it. After the last show in St. Louis, Cody presented the animal to him and paid the transportation back to Standing Rock. The horse and a big white western hat, also a gift from Cody, remained treasured possessions of Sitting Bull until the day of his death.[16]

Sitting Bull's travels and experiences gave him an enlarged view of the world, and he asserted an independence of McLaughlin that annoyed the agent and fortified his newfound disgust with the whole idea of Indians in shows. "He is inflated with the public attention he received," observed McLaughlin, "and has not profited by what he has seen, but tells the most astounding falsehoods to the Indians."

Among them, according to the agent, was a boast that in his meeting with the Great Father he had been recognized as the greatest Indian living and had been made head chief of all the Sioux. Violating the canons of civilized frugality, moreover, Sitting Bull squandered all his earnings on feasts for his friends—testimony to the dictates of generosity that escaped McLaughlin. "I may be obliged to arrest him and confine him in the Guard-house," he grumped.[17]

Not surprisingly, Buffalo Bill's effort to sign up Sitting Bull for another season met a cool official reception at Standing Rock. "He is such a consummate liar and too vain and obstinate to be benefitted by what he sees, and makes no good use of the money he thus earns," replied McLaughlin. Sitting Bull liked Cody and probably could be persuaded to sign on, "but for the good of the other Indians and the best interests of the Service I am forced to the conclusion that it would be unwise to have him go out this season."[18]

Nor any other season. Sitting Bull's career as a showman had ended.

Now he passed most of his days quietly with his family at the home on Grand River. Illness plagued him often, confining him to his cabin. Now and then he journeyed south to visit Miniconjou friends and relatives enrolled at Cheyenne River Agency. Hump and his people lived on Cherry Creek, a northern affluent of Cheyenne River. Steadfastly "nonprogressive," they tormented their agent much as Sitting Bull tormented his. Farther to the southwest, at the forks of Cheyenne River, lived Spotted Elk and his band. They had once ridden with Sitting Bull and today, like Hump, resisted civilization. Spotted Elk now went by the name Big Foot. At Cheyenne River Agency too were Sitting Bull's brother-in-law, Chief Makes Room, and his nephew White Bull.

In September 1886 Sitting Bull joined in a historic pilgrimage to the Crow Reservation in Montana. A hundred Sioux from both Standing Rock and Cheyenne River agencies petitioned the Indian Office for permission to make this journey. The Crow agent, Henry E. Williamson, protested vigorously but was ignored. For two weeks, within sight of the monument-crowned hilltop where Custer had died a decade earlier, the Sioux delegates and their Crow hosts feasted, reminisced, boasted, and buried the hatchet. Truly the festivities symbolized the dawn of a new day.

Symbolic of a less happy day to come, the Sioux found the Crows in the throes of a government campaign to place them on individual allotments. Special agents had persuaded a majority to enter claims and receive title to their farms.

Suddenly the Crows balked. The surprised officials called a council and included their prime suspect. "Sitting Bull said he did not want his lands allotted yet and had asked the agent to delay," Agent Williamson reported. "During this talk several of the Crow chiefs, who had never uttered a word against allotment, took the same stand as Sitting Bull said he had taken at his agency." Convinced by Sitting Bull, the Crow chiefs stood firm, and the allotment program remained stalled until some months after the Sioux had gone back home.[19]

The issues swirling around land ownership and use disturbed not just the Crows but gathered in ever more menacing and contentious form on the Great Sioux Reservation too. Sitting Bull returned home from his visit to the Crow Reservation to confront them in his own backyard. Coveted by acquisitive whites, the key to a range of innovations judged essential to Indian civilization by benevolent whites, Indian land formed a battle-ground for the clash of Indian and white, Indian and Indian, and white and white. The struggle found Sitting Bull once more interposed as a tough shield between his threatened people and determined white aggressors.

22 LAND

THE SPARK THAT ignited land controversies on every Indian reservation in the West was the General Allotment Act of 1887, sponsored and championed in the Congress by Senator Henry L. Dawes. Allotment of land in severalty had been incorporated into a number of treaties and had been tried among a few tribes. The Dawes Act applied the principle to most of the remaining Indians. Each family head who made application would receive a patent for 160 acres, others for less in varying amounts. The United States would hold the patents in trust for twenty-five years. With the patent went citizenship in the state or territory of residence. When all Indians on a reservation had accepted allotments, or sooner if the president decided, the United States might negotiate with the tribe for its surplus land, which would then be opened to settlement under the homestead laws.[1]

If reformers hailed the Dawes Act as a cure for all the ills afflicting the Indian, Dakota promoters hailed it as the key to unlocking the "surplus" Sioux lands. Within a year they had hurried through Congress a bill applying its provision to the Great Sioux Reservation. This law, however, reversed the procedure laid down in the Dawes Act. It called for negotiations for surplus land before surveys had been run and before allotments had been made to the Indians.

Under the Sioux Act of 1888, six separate reservations would be carved out of the Great Sioux Reservation: Pine Ridge, Rosebud, Cheyenne

River, Standing Rock, Crow Creek, and Lower Brule. Each would contain the amount of land needed for allotments to all its residents. The remaining land, about 9 million acres, would be restored to the public domain and immediately opened to settlers at fifty cents an acre. As provided by the Treaty of 1868, the law could not take effect until accepted by three-fourths of adult males.[2]

Sitting Bull bitterly and vocally opposed allotment in severalty and its handmaiden, cession of surplus lands. Although a farmer himself, he saw individual farms as eroding the social and political cohesion of the tribe and the traditional Sioux way of life. And he denied the existence of any such thing as surplus land. The Lakotas would need all they now owned and more to provide for their children and grandchildren. Sitting Bull had never sanctioned the surrender of a single acre of Sioux domain, and with so little left he could scarcely be expected to begin now.

Sitting Bull's attitude fit Agent McLaughlin's portrait of the mindless obstructionist, devoting all his time and energies to battling the benevolent programs of a generous government. In fact, Sitting Bull dwelled quietly on Grand River, pondering the government's proposals, accepting those that seemed right for his people, rejecting those that did not. That he cultivated grains and vegetables, tended cattle, lived in a log house, and sent his children to the Congregational day school did not prevent McLaughlin from castigating him as the archfoe of progress.

In the spring of 1888, even as the rhetoric continued, McLaughlin privately conceded that for the past few months Sitting Bull's behavior had been "all that could be desired." And such was his agricultural record that the agent appointed him boss farmer of his district. A man with two wives, however, hardly set the proper example for others; when the Indian Office called for a report on polygamy at Standing Rock, McLaughlin made hasty amends by designating another boss farmer.[3]

McLaughlin's fulminations revealed less about Sitting Bull's true state of mind during the late reservation years than a conversation he had with missionary Mary Collins after his travels with the Allen and Cody shows had shown him the seamy underside of the white world. "The farther my people keep away from the whites," he told her, "the better I shall be satisfied. The white people are wicked and I don't want my women to become as the white women I have seen have lived. I want you to teach my people to read and write but they must not become white people in their ways; it is too bad a life, I could not let them do it."

Prophetically he concluded, "I would rather die an Indian than live a white man."[4]

It was a creed McLaughlin and his approving patrons in the East might dimly understand, but never condone.

For the first time, the years on Grand River afforded a life free of danger from Long Knives and Crows and free of the specter of hunger. However bitter over the loss of the old way of life, Sitting Bull now had the leisure to devote to his family. He reveled in his children and grand-children, the children of One Bull and Jumping Bull, indeed in all the children on Grand River. "He always joked any boy who came to his place," recalled Robert Higheagle. "I wasn't afraid of him."[5]

Sitting Bull continued to find deep pleasure in his family. The two adult daughters by Snow-on-Her had married and presented him with grandchildren. The elder, Many Horses, the one who caused so much heartache by eloping on the eve of the surrender at Fort Buford, was married to Thomas Fly. She was twenty-five in 1888. The younger daughter, Walks Looking, had married Andrew Fox and had an infant son when she died suddenly of disease in 1887, at the age of nineteen. Her death set off a paroxysm of grief and mourning on Grand River.[6]

Sitting Bull's immediate household included the two wives he had taken in 1872 and five children approaching adolescence. There were two pairs of twins, all boys, the first pair born just before the Little Bighorn in 1876, the second in Canada in 1880. A daughter born in 1878, Standing Holy, commanded her father's lavish affection.[7]

But the truly special bond ran to Crow Foot, the twin named in honor of the Blackfeet chief in Canada. Crow Foot had sat in on the councils with Canadian officials and in 1881 had handed his father's rifle to Major Brotherton in token of final surrender. Strong and healthy, Crow Foot took his heritage seriously and even in adolescence began to give advice to his father on weighty matters. "Crow Foot was not like the rest of the boys," remembered Robert Higheagle. "He did not get out and mingle with the boys and play their games. He grew old too early."[8]

Evidence of his continuing love of children, Sitting Bull fathered a son in 1887 and a daughter in 1888. At forty-two and forty years of age, respectively, his wives still practiced the Lakota virtue of fecundity.[9]

Besides his immediate and extended family, including One Bull and Jumping Bull, Sitting Bull gathered around him on Grand River many friends and followers from the old days. Generally men with his con-servative dedication to the past, they took their cue from him in most reservation controversies. Among them were Crawler, Black Bird, Strikes-the-Kettle, Catch-the-Bear, and Circling Bear, all comrades since youth.

Another neighbor was brother-in-law Gray Eagle, whose cabin lay across Grand River and slightly upstream. As one of the first of the Canadian exiles to don white-man garb and take up farming, Gray Eagle had earned the praise of McLaughlin and, under his patronage, had steadily gained influence as a leader of the "progressive" factions of the tribe. [10] At the same time, relations with his sisters' husband, strained ever since Sitting Bull had ordered him soldiered for stealing Slota horses in Canada, deteriorated as the two increasingly disagreed over how to cope with the new order.

Except for the hurt caused by changing ways, life on Grand River settled into a placid agrarian routine, interrupted only by the thirty-mile journey to the agency every other Saturday to draw the beef ration. Ration day afforded opportunity to visit with friends and relatives and feast on freshly slaughtered beef.

"Killing day" was a festive occasion, much to the discomfiture of the Indian Office, whose visionaries regarded it as a barbaric reversion to the old wicked life. A north corral and a south corral, one on either side of the agency, penned the cattle cut out of the contract herd for execution. Designated marksmen perched on the fences and shot down the animals with rifles. The women then entered the pen and dressed the carcasses much as they had once done to downed buffalo. As night fell, fires lit the tipis, kettles bubbled with chunks of beef, and the children played while the men smoked, the women gossiped, and all gorged.

A newsman who described the rite in colorful detail in the autumn of 1886 had his attention directed to a solitary figure standing to one side. "He was tall, and had a slight stoop in his shoulders. He wore moccasins, trousers, and a blue checked cotton shirt. On his head he had an old black hat, with the skin and head of a large hawk pinned to its crown. Over all was the blanket, and in his hand was the long stemmed Indian pipe. This man was Sitting Bull."

Reflecting the biases of his hosts, the reporter drew a stark contrast between Standing Rock's two best-known Indians: Sitting Bull, dishonest, cunning, and treacherous; and Gall, "a counselor for peace." [11]

NOT THE "COUNSELOR for peace" nor John Grass nor any of the other progressives liked the Sioux Act of 1888 any better than Sitting Bull did. Nor, for that matter, did McLaughlin, who regarded it as a cession of half the Great Sioux Reservation in exchange for hardly more than already due the Indians under the Treaty of 1868. [12] He could not say so, of course, and he had to play along with the government's attempt to get the required number of signatures on the agreement.

Signing up the Indians was the task not of the agent but of a specially appointed commission. Chairing it was a man more high-minded than Newton Edmunds but no less accomplished at bullying Indians. A captain in the regular army, founder and superintendent of the Carlisle Indian School in Pennsylvania, Richard Henry Pratt was a righteous, dogmatic man utterly convinced of the wisdom of his blueprint for the Indian's salvation. The Sioux knew him as the tall officer with the big nose who had taken some of their children to a far-off place from which not all returned. Backing Pratt were the Reverend William J. Cleveland, missionary to the Lakotas and cousin of the president, and John V. Wright, a Tennessee political crony of the Commissioner of Indian Affairs. Selecting Standing Rock as their first challenge, the commission arrived at the agency on July 23, 1888.

McLaughlin occupied a delicate position. He believed the proposed agreement grossly unfair but was expected to help the commissioners sell it to the Standing Rock people. With the Indians all opposed too, the agent scarcely needed Sitting Bull to complicate his dilemma, and he conceded the appeal of shipping him off for the summer with a circus. As a reporter observed of this chief who had supposedly lost all influence with his people, "He is a dynamite bomb in blankets when harmony is wanted."[13]

But to the mystification of all, Sitting Bull did not even appear as the deliberations got under way. Day after day the commissioners explained, cajoled, and even threatened. Night after night the Indians met in their own private councils to talk over how to respond. They agreed to put forward Grass, Gall, Mad Bear, and Big Head to say that no one would sign. And for a week, as an increasingly exasperated Pratt tried to browbeat the Indians into signing, Sitting Bull kept his distance.[14]

Pratt would not relent. He would not give up and leave as the Indians repeatedly urged, allowing them to return to their homes and their neglected crops and livestock.

Fearful that the people might bend under the pressure, Sitting Bull rode into the great tent camp near the agency on the night of July 30. Within hours, although he himself made no speech, his emissaries had conveyed his wishes, and the council had adopted an oath to *Wakantanka* not to sign. The next day, when the people again formed to listen to the commissioners, Sitting Bull sat his pony outside the circle, alone except

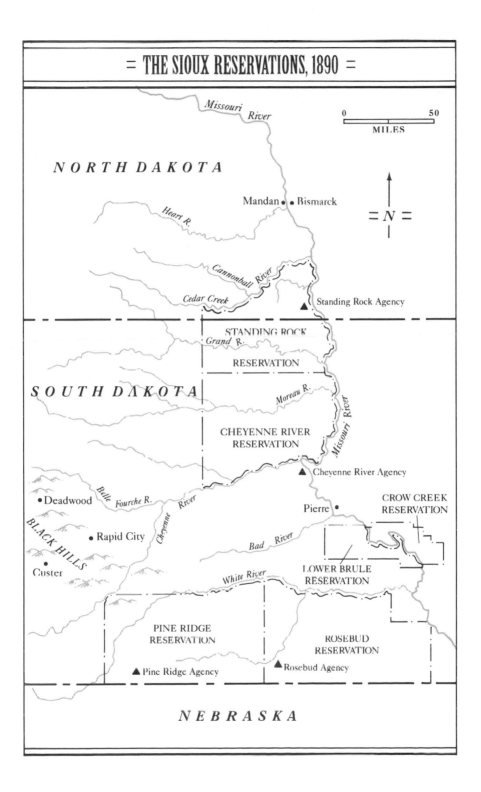

= THE SIOUX RESERVATIONS, 1890 =

Missouri River

0   50
MILES

NORTH DAKOTA

Mandan • • Bismarck

Heart R.

= N =

Cannonball River

Cedar Creek

▲ Standing Rock Agency

STANDING ROCK
Grand R.
RESERVATION

SOUTH DAKOTA

Moreau R.

CHEYENNE RIVER
RESERVATION

▲ Cheyenne River Agency

Belle Fourche R.

• Deadwood

Cheyenne River

CROW CREEK
RESERVATION

Pierre •

Missouri River

BLACK HILLS
• Rapid City

Bad River

LOWER BRULE
RESERVATION

• Custer

White River

PINE RIDGE
RESERVATION

ROSEBUD
RESERVATION

▲ Pine Ridge Agency

▲ Rosebud Agency

NEBRASKA

for Rain-in-the-Face, now so crippled by old wounds that he could walk only with the aid of crutches.[15]

On the night of August 1, during the Indians' council, Sitting Bull rose to speak for the first time. "The speech was moderate and contained none of the expected fire," observed the *Tribune*'s reporter, who regularly gained access to these councils. Sitting Bull urged the people not to give in simply because the commission would not leave, but to push for adjournment so they could get back to their farms.[16]

Although Sitting Bull played a dominant role in the Indians' own deliberations and in stiffening the Indian resolve to stand firm, he left the commissioners to the spokesmen chosen in the first councils. When he finally spoke in a formal commission session, he surprised all with soothing words. An impasse had developed over the insistence that the Indians sign one of two papers, black for acceptance, red for rejection. This seemed a cunning trick—the red paper might turn black before it reached Washington—and they stubbornly refused to sign either. When the debate grew too rancorous, Sitting Bull stepped in to call for moderation. "Speak kindly to each other," he urged. "Talk to each other in a pleasant, quiet manner, and let it rest at that."

But even Sitting Bull lost patience as the people grew more and more restless and the commissioners persisted. "I want to know how many months you expect us to stay here," he demanded, "and by what time you will call it a decision."[17]

On August 4, "killing day" and thus a holiday from Pratt's tedious councils, Sitting Bull paid a courtesy call on the commissioners. The other chiefs were too ignorant to know this was their duty, he explained, but he knew how to act. The visit "revived Pratt's hopes," commented the *Tribune* correspondent, "but Bull was simply giving an exhibition of diplomacy and good training he received on his eastern tour."[18]

As the days slipped by, even Pratt began to see that his mission faced failure. When he and his associates finally left on August 21, they carried only twenty-two signed black ballots from Standing Rock. That doomed the effort to obtain the statutory number elsewhere. Pratt's final report denounced the Sioux, and especially their chiefs, for obstinate refusal to recognize where their best interests lay. It ended by urging that allotments be completed on all the reservations at once and that the land agreement be put into effect without Indian consent.[19]

The Indians had too many politically powerful friends in the East to make that an acceptable course. Better to bring a delegation of chiefs to Washington and see if a compromise could be worked out. Escorted by their agents and interpreters, sixty-one chiefs, representing all the agencies, arrived at the Baltimore and Potomac depot in the capital near midnight on October 12, 1888. Strangely, McLaughlin had included Sitting Bull in the Standing Rock contingent.[20]

Such a large group of Indians caused a stir in the capital. Reporters followed them in visits to the Smithsonian Institution and the National Zoo. At the former the chiefs admiringly inspected George Catlin's famed Indian paintings, and at the latter they critically appraised the various animals while Gray Eagle tried to buy one of the monkeys.

Gathered in the lobby of the Belvedere Hotel, the chiefs discovered the fad sweeping the country—cigarettes. As they puffed furiously on the little white cylinders, however, Sitting Bull smoked a cigar. The secretary to a Texas senator had given it to him, and he savored it "with great relish."

Profiling the more notable Indians, a reporter identified Sitting Bull as the best known of all, the "leading spirit" who "cunningly entrapped and mercilessly slaughtered" Custer and his brave soldiers. Yet now, casting doubt on the McLaughlin caricature, Sitting Bull "has a house, plenty of land to cultivate, and a fine bunch of cattle. He has two wives and five children, all of whom attend the Indian schools on the reservation."

Gall, "a big, stout, bully fellow" weighing fully 250 pounds, also captivated onlookers. In one of history's beguiling ironies, Gall was invited to dinner at an elegant restaurant on Fifteenth Street by Captain Edward S. Godfrey, a troop commander under Reno at the Little Bighorn. Commented an observer: "The big Sioux mogul took to oysters in the shell like a Norfolk oysterman."[21]

The visitors aroused so much curiosity that an amateur bard was moved to pay them tribute in verse:

> Our visitors just now are Sioux
> Who're here to see what they can dioux
> In getting certain measures thrioux,
> To save the remnant of their crioux;
> And we are rather with them tioux,
> Because they've had it rough all thrioux.
> It's true they've killed and scalped a floux,
> But they've joined a church or twioux,
> And latterly they want to dioux
> The decent thing, like yourn and yioux.
> Just give them time, they'll get there tioux,

> Will these same earnest, anxious Sioux;
> And ere you know it, they will scrioux
> The bolts tight down on some poor crioux
> Of others weaker than the Sioux
> As in their cases yourn and yioux
> Have taught them it was right to dioux.[22]

On October 15 the delegations assembled at the Interior Department. Sitting Bull spoke first, but offered nothing substantive. "I hope everything will be done in a quiet manner," he said. Thereafter, as the other chiefs made long speeches exposing the divisions within their ranks, he remained discreetly in the background.

But not in the private councils. As in the proceedings of the Pratt Commission, Sitting Bull took the lead in deciding how to deal with the white officials.

The issue debated now, however, was not whether the Indians opposed a land agreement in any form but on the merits of a new proposal Secretary of the Interior William F. Vilas had laid before them for comment. He had offered to recommend to Congress some liberal changes in the agreement, including a plan to pay one dollar an acre for their land, and he had invited their opinion. By reacting to Vilas's revised scheme at all, of course, the chiefs undermined their previous position and implied a willingness to back an agreement that met their objections.

In long councils at night, the delegates argued. Sitting Bull spoke eloquently against the secretary's formula but, in keeping with most of the others, believed the land was worth more than a dollar an acre. A price of $1.25, payable at once rather than when homesteaders took up claims, seemed to them more fair.

Sitting Bull spoke for two hours urging the $1.25 figure. What prompted so startling and abrupt a change of heart can only be guessed. Inflexibly opposed to the surrender of any land at any price, he now seemed ready to give up 9 million acres if the price was right. Perhaps he recognized the inevitable and held out for the best deal. Perhaps he did not grasp that he was weakening his ability to obstruct further land cessions. Perhaps he simply threw in with the growing consensus. Perhaps he hoped that the government would refuse a higher price and thus kill the issue altogether. Perhaps he was merely anxious to go home.

Whatever his motives, on October 19 Sitting Bull joined with forty-six others in signing a counterproposal, based on their consensus and drafted by the agents. The remaining fourteen adopted a minority report favoring the original offer in the Sioux Act.

If Sitting Bull thought that a demand for $1.25 an acre would end the ordeal and free him to go home, he was right. Secretary Vilas scoffed at the notion, declaring that it could not be entertained for a moment. The chiefs then lined up at the White House to shake hands with President Cleveland and within an hour were packed into railway coaches for the long journey home.[23]

Vilas scoffed too soon, for Indian reformer and Dakota promoter alike wanted the reservation dismembered. In the national elections of 1888, a Republican victory put Benjamin Harrison in the White House. With Dakota solidly in the Republican camp, the incoming administration favored a new Sioux bill. Added impetus came in February 1889 with passage of the Omnibus Bill, which provided for statehood for North and South Dakota together with Washington and Montana. Now, instead of nonvoting territorial delegates, full-fledged senators and congressmen would represent constituents demanding the opening of the Sioux land.

The Sioux Act of 1889 held forth some major concessions. Most important, it raised the price to $1.25 an acre for land homesteaded during the first three years (on the assumption that the best land would be claimed first), 75 cents for the next two years, and 50 cents for all remaining land. If the chiefs had hoped the issue would go away, they were disappointed; their trip to Washington had born fruit after all.[24]

Former Ohio governor Charles Foster chaired the Sioux Commission of 1889. The second member, William Warner, knew as much about Indians as Foster, his qualifications resting on his role as national commander of the Grand Army of the Republic. The third member was the one who was expected to sell the agreement to the Indians—their old adversary Three Stars, now wearing the two stars of a major general. Better than Captain Pratt, George Crook knew how to deal with Indians.

If forty-seven chiefs truly promised in October 1888 to back a more liberal offer, they had changed their minds by June 1889. Like the Pratt Commission, the Crook Commission encountered a solid wall of chiefs counseling their people not to sign the agreement. At each agency the commissioners found that several chiefs had been chosen to do all the talking and to reject the new proposal.[25]

Like Pratt, but more skillfully, the commissioners persisted. They staged great feasts, lifted the ban on dancing, and displayed infinite patience and goodwill. At the same time, they employed the menace that they smilingly denied, although more subtly than Pratt. Often persuasion spilled over into intimidation.

The commissioners left Standing Rock, the hotbed of opposition to the Pratt Commission, until last. Once more, as agreed in private councils, Grass, Gall, Mad Bear, and Big Head spoke for all the Standing Rock Indians, and whatever their true sentiment the previous October, they now stood united in opposition to the agreement. For three days, July 29 to 31, 1889, they explained their objections in daylong exchanges with the commissioners. Again Sitting Bull hung back, his only words a plea to delay the proceedings until more people could arrive.

As he had the previous summer, he labored in the background to keep his people from caving in—a more difficult undertaking this year because of the more liberal law and because now McLaughlin favored it. Sitting Bull recruited boys who had been to school to attend the councils and make notes of what was said.

To his beloved Silent Eaters he made an impassioned plea for unity in resistance. The whites "will try to gain possession of the last piece of ground we possess," he warned. "Let us stand as one family as we did before the white people led us astray."[26]

The unity collapsed because of the adroit maneuvers of the agent and the commissioners and because of the flexible convictions of the four chiefs chosen as spokesmen. One night McLaughlin slipped away from a dinner for the commissioners to meet, secretly and individually, with Grass, Gall, and the others. Patiently he explained the perils of rejecting the agreement and the necessity of modifying their position. By asking for a few additional concessions, he pointed out, they could slide into a new stance without appearing to betray the expectations of the people. In the next council, as McLaughlin recalled, Grass "changed his base with the facility of a statesman."[27]

As the spokesmen switched sides and the people lined up to sign, Sitting Bull's composure dissolved in fury. McLaughlin had seated the commission on a platform at the door to a warehouse and arranged the people to file into and through the building as they signed the paper. As the signing began, Sitting Bull and twenty mounted Silent Eaters charged into the throng of Indians and began to scatter them. McLaughlin had anticipated such a move, however, and Indian police commanded by Lieutenant Bull Head, also called Afraid-of-Bear, swiftly gained control and expelled the troublemakers.

That night, August 3, General Crook summed up the day in his diary: "Met the Indians in council at about three P.M. After a little talking they commenced signing, John Grass taking the lead. Sitting Bull tried to speak after the signing commenced, but I stopped him. Then he tried twice to stampede the Indians away from signing, but his efforts failed, and he flattened out, his wind bag punctured, and several of his followers have deserted him."[28]

At every agency the Indians had overwhelmingly opposed the land agreement. Yet at the six agencies Crook garnered 4,463 signatures out of 5,678 eligible to vote. At Standing Rock the paper bore the names of some of Sitting Bull's staunchest comrades, including Catch-the-Bear, Black Bird, and Rain-in-the-Face, and even worse, a stepson, a son-in-law, and One Bull himself.

That the Sioux could be so united in opposition yet give Crook so clear a victory testified to the general's skill in exploiting factionalism. The technique was to bury the Indians under mountains of words while working behind the scenes to lure individuals away from the influence of the chiefs. If a stampede could be started, even the most determined opponent, afraid of being excluded from the benefits, would rush to sign. With the help of the agents and mixed bloods, who read the newspapers and recognized the truth of Crook's warning, this is what happened. But it left behind a people seething with anger, bitterness, and despair, and a people more than ever turned one against another.

Worse was to come. At every agency spokesmen had expressed fears that, having got their land, the government would cut their treaty rations. The commission's labored reassurances failed to reassure. And hardly two weeks after the commissioners went home, the agents received orders reducing beef issues by several million pounds. That the land agreement had nothing to do with the cut, that Congress had slashed appropriations the previous spring, did not mollify Indians convinced only that the government had tricked them again.

Anxiously the Sioux looked for signs that the government would carry out other promises. To meet a long list of complaints, the commissioners had packed a long list of promises into the record. The law required them to obtain either acceptance or rejection; they could not negotiate changes. Each promise, therefore, as they emphasized over and over, was only a promise to recommend. It remained to the Interior Department and Congress to approve the recommendations. Understandably, the Indians failed to catch the distinction.

To dramatize the importance of following through on these promises, as well as the consequences of the ration cut, the Indian Office again decided to bring a delegation of Sioux chiefs to Washington. This time the

Standing Rock contingent included only "progressives." On Grand River, Mary Collins noted that Sitting Bull and Running Antelope, angry at being left out, "must come and unburden their hearts."[29]

On December 18, 1889, the chiefs trooped into the Interior Department for a council with the new secretary, John W. Noble. They talked him to the verge of exasperation, but he gave them encouraging assurances. He accepted most of the promises that fell within his administrative discretion and pledged to urge on Congress those depending on appropriations. After a brief visit with President Harrison, the chiefs again headed for home.[30]

Gladdened a bit by the meeting with the Great Father, the Sioux nonetheless passed a bad winter. Besides the gnawing anxiety of the land agreement and its train of additional promises, hunger once more visited the Lakotas. With reduced rations and another crop failure, they found it hard to keep the family kettle bubbling. Some may even have confronted starvation. On top of hunger, disease struck. Epidemics of measles, influenza, and whooping cough swept the settlements with fatal effect.[31]

Then came the cruelest blow of all. On February 10, 1890, President Harrison announced acceptance of the land agreement by the required three-fourths majority of adult males and threw open the ceded territory to settlement.[32] The promises had not been carried out. No surveys had been made to determine the precise boundaries of the six new reservations. No provision had been made for Indians living in the ceded land to take allotments there.

The Secretary of the Interior and the Congress, the president noted in proclaiming the agreement, could surely be relied on to keep faith with the Sioux. As the Dakota winter merged into spring, however, the suspicion grew that the Great Council in Washington, having got their land, did not intend to make good the promises of the Crook Commission. And General Crook himself had died suddenly, a bad omen.

"He, at least, had never lied to us," observed Red Cloud.[33]

As an old Indian, veteran of many treaty councils, summed up, "They made us many promises, more than I can remember, but they never kept but one; they promised to take our land and they took it."[34]

23 MESSIAH

FOR THE LAKOTA TRIBES, loss of still more land, the ration cut, and the unfulfilled promises of the Crook Commission climaxed a decade of distress. The reservation had destroyed the very foundations of the Indian way of life. The customs, values, and institutions of war and the hunt—overwhelmingly the central concerns of the people in the old days—withered into nostalgic memory. The government warred on spiritual beliefs and practices, on the office of chief, and on the tribe itself, which provided the political setting and kinship ties that held the people together in meaningful relationship. For the loss, the government offered only unsatisfying substitutes: plows, work oxen, log houses, schools, and Christian churches, together with an alien, repugnant ideal of what people should strive to be. That the Sioux could not help giving up the old, that they could not help sampling or even embracing some of the new, that the ordeal fractured them into "progressive" and "nonprogressive" only deepened the malaise. By 1890 all the Lakota tribes verged perilously on cultural breakdown.

A decade of reservation life left the people ripe for the exciting rumor that reached them in the summer of 1889, even as the Crook Commission went methodically about the task of signing up Indians who had vowed never to sign. Somewhere far to the west, ran the report, a god had come to earth to rescue Indians everywhere from the adversity that had befallen them. The story, rich with spiritual solutions to incurable worldly afflictions, captured the attention of people nearly drained of hope. Leaders at Pine Ridge, Rosebud, and Cheyenne River chose emissaries to seek out the truth.

The Lakota apostles returned in March 1890. The Messiah had indeed come to earth to save his children, they reported. He was a Paiute holy man named Wovoka, and to all who came to his brush lodge in Nevada he delivered an uplifting message. By embracing his faith—a blend of orthodox Indian belief and the new teachings of the Christian missionaries—and by dancing a prescribed "Ghost Dance," Indians could live for eternity in a blissful land. It was a land without white people, a land inhabited by all the generations of Indians that had gone before, a land bounteous in game and all the other riches of the natural world, a land free of sickness and want, a land where all tribes dwelt in peace.

Wovoka's doctrine appealed to the conservative elements at the lower agencies but made little impression on others. It had no effect on Sitting Bull or any of the Indians at Standing Rock. They had heard of the coming millennium but showed scant interest. They had sent no one to Nevada, and no one brought the word from other agencies.

The Indian Office in Washington had learned that something was unsettling the Sioux and early in June 1890 called for reports from the agents. All discounted the danger, but McLaughlin saw a pretext for trying to rid himself of Sitting Bull. The removal of Standing Rock's malcontents, he wrote, "would end all trouble and uneasiness in the future." Sitting Bull, of course, headed the list of these "leaders of disaffection."[1]

Sitting Bull had not led any disaffection since the visit of the Crook Commission in 1889. Rather, quietly tending his farm, he pursued a strange relationship with a Victorian gentlewoman who had become enamored of him. Brooklynite Catherine Weldon represented the National Indian Defense Association, a maverick league that opposed the coercive programs of the mainline reformers. A widow in her early thirties with a fourteen-year-old son, she paid her first visit to Standing Rock in 1888, reappeared in the summer of 1889 to work against the Crook Commission, and in the spring of 1890, resolved to devote her life to the welfare of the Sioux, took up a claim just outside the reservation. Sitting Bull visited her often. She lavished gifts on him and bankrolled his feasts.[2]

The widow wanted to teach an Indian school in the Sitting Bull settlement, a proposition McLaughlin predictably opposed. Sitting Bull, she informed the Commissioner of Indian Affairs, "sees the success of the white people and he knows that the Indians must follow in their footsteps or perish, and he wishes his people to become civilized as soon as possible. He has begged me repeatedly to come and live among them."[3]

Although she may have misunderstood or misrepresented Sitting Bull's true feelings, she did spend weeks among his followers on Grand River. She and her boy, Christie, moved into his cabin and lived as part of his family. "I honor and respect S. Bull as if he was my own father," she had written McLaughlin, "and nothing can ever shake my faith in his good qualities." Quickly the arrangement attracted the attention of newspapers, which labeled her "Sitting Bull's White Squaw." McLaughlin later denied any "criminal" connection between the two, but did not reveal how he knew. Her letters suggest it as a plausible possibility.[4]

At Grand River Weldon instructed the women in domestic skills and, an artist of modest talent, painted Sitting Bull's portrait. She also wrote letters for him, served as his advisor and secretary, and in the autumn threw her formidable powers against a Ghost Dance movement that suddenly burst on the Standing Rock Reservation.

The doctrine drew new life from new afflictions. Once more the bright promise of spring had turned to ashes in midsummer. July winds blasted the greening crops, destroying the grains altogether and leaving little to salvage in the vegetable plots. The scorching gales that withered the cornstalks nourished the Ghost Dance religion. Congress had not yet addressed the promises of the Crook Commission or restored the ration cut. The crop failure combined with reduced rations forecast hunger and even starvation.

With the winds came Kicking Bear, a Miniconjou from Cheyenne River who had gone to Nevada as part of the Lakota investigating team. On the lower reservations he had emerged as the leading apostle of the Ghost Dance religion. The curiosity of the Grand River Hunkpapas at last aroused, Sitting Bull sent a small party of young men to Cheyenne River to invite Kicking Bear for a visit. On October 9, 1890, he and six helpers arrived at the Sitting Bull settlement.

Kicking Bear's sermon, rich in imagery and breathtaking in promise, had an electric effect on the congregation. One Bull, a member of the police force, listened intently and hurried to the agency to repeat it nearly word for word to McLaughlin. While still venerating his uncle and adoptive father, as a policeman and a signer of the land agreement One Bull was increasingly drawn to McLaughlin's principles.

As reported by One Bull, Kicking Bear described his westward journey and his meeting with the prophet. "Take this message to my red children and tell it to them as I say it," Wovoka enjoined, as quoted by Kicking Bear. According to this message, the earth had grown old and tired. The Messiah would cover it with a deep new layer of soil. Sweet grass, running water, and trees would adorn the surface, while herds of ponies, buffalo, and other game would wander in abundance—"that my red children may eat and drink, hunt and rejoice."

This great millennial cataclysm would bury all white people beneath the new thickness of earth. As it advanced, the Messiah would lift on high all Indian believers in the Ghost Dance, all who had danced and sang and prayed and practiced the tenets of the faith. Afterward he would set them down in the utopia, to find all their ancestors, friends, and relatives who had died. Doubters would be confined to undesirable places, to wander unhappily until they saw the light and adopted the "dance of the ghosts."

Meanwhile, "making ready to join the ghosts," everyone should dance. They should have no fear of the whites. A specially contrived "ghost shirt" would render their gunpowder powerless to kill dancers. The powder would not burn when turned on "my children," while the Indians' powder would "burn and kill" when directed at whites. And if any dancer did die at the hands of whites, "his spirit will only go to the end of the earth and there join the ghosts of his fathers and return to his friends next spring."[5]

Next spring. That was the time of the millennium as foreseen by Indians on all the Lakota reservations. They would dance all winter and then enter the promised land.

Disturbed by the spread of this doctrine to his charges, McLaughlin dispatched Captain Crazy Walking and a squad of policemen, including One Bull, to eject Kicking Bear from the reservation. The party arrived at Grand River on October 13, in the midst of a riveting exhortation by Kicking Bear. So powerful were his words that Crazy Walking lost his nerve and contented himself with merely ordering Kicking Bear and his acolytes to leave. While scolding the policemen, Sitting Bull promised that Kicking Bear would depart the next day.

Shaken by the failure of his police captain, who returned to the agency "dazed" and awed by Kicking Bear's medicine, McLaughlin promptly sent Lieutenant Chatka and another policeman to make certain Kicking Bear had truly left. They arrived at Grand River on October 15 to find that he had not. Of firmer mettle than Crazy Walking, Chatka and his aide not only delivered the agent's command but escorted the interlopers to the reservation boundary.[6]

But the evangelist had done his work well. Under Sitting Bull's oversight, the dances began. People abandoned their cabins and pitched tipis on the flat north of Sitting Bull's cluster of cabins. Attendance at the new government day school four miles down the river shrank from ninety to three as parents withdrew their children so they could go to "church."[7] Near the base of the foothills, duplicating the sun-dance circle of old, the faithful fashioned a ring of brush arbors and raised a prayer tree. A row of wickiups for the *inipi*, the sweat bath, stood nearby. Early each morning dancers purified themselves in the sweat lodge before launching the daylong dances.

Whether Sitting Bull was a true believer is impossible to know. He never danced himself, and he never directed the dances, leaving that to Bull Ghost, the dance director. To Mary Collins and others, he hinted at skepticism.

On the other hand, from a tipi next to the dance circle he presided over the community of believers and officiated as the chief apostle of the religion at Standing Rock. He encouraged his people to dance and interpreted the revelations of those who had "died" and visited the spirit land. And doggedly, at considerable personal risk, he defied all efforts, by government officials, by missionaries and schoolteachers, and by unbelieving fellow tribesmen, to persuade or compel him to cast off the religion and send the people home.

As one of the greatest Hunkpapa holy men of his era, who had always devoted his sacred powers to the benefit of his people, Sitting Bull would have felt a commanding obligation to himself and them to test the new faith even while harboring doubts. So great was the promise that it justified persevering through the winter until spring either brought the prophesied millennium or did not. On a more pragmatic level, the Ghost Dance afforded an opportunity to revive his own authority and influence, which had steadily slipped away ever since Senator Logan scathingly denied his chieftainship in 1883. Finally, once kindled, the passions of the Ghost Dance were not easily cooled, and more than once Sitting Bull implied that they flamed too fiercely even for him to extinguish. And so he led, reluctant but resolute, uncertain but committed.

On October 17 McLaughlin sat at his desk to scrawl a long and truly remarkable letter to the Commissioner of Indian Affairs. In paragraph after paragraph he excoriated Sitting Bull with nearly every epithet his dictionary could suggest: vain, pompous, untruthful, and cunning; abject coward, disaffected intriguer, polygamist, libertine, habitual liar, active obstructionist, and chief mischief-maker; and, in stunning contradiction to the litany of abuse, "an Indian unworthy of notice."

As "high priest and leading apostle of this latest Indian absurdity," however, Sitting Bull was making a lot of trouble, and the agent declared that he and like-minded reactionaries had to be neutralized. McLaughlin urged, therefore, that some time during the winter Sitting Bull and the others named in his letter of June 18 be seized and transported to a military prison distant from the Sioux country. "With these individuals removed, the advancement of the Sioux will be more rapid and the interests of the Government greatly subserved thereby."

Reluctant to face the political implications of such a move, Washington officials took refuge in an evasive delaying tactic. On October 29 orders went out to Standing Rock for McLaughlin to inform Sitting Bull and his cohorts that the "honorable Secretary of the Interior" was "greatly displeased with their conduct" and would hold Sitting Bull "to a strict personal responsibility" for any trouble resulting from "his bad advice and evil councils." To demonstrate his submission to government authority, he must at once bring his influence to bear against "the medicine men who are seeking to divert the Indians from the ways of civilization."[8]

McLaughlin must have shrugged grimly at the almost laughable irrelevance of these instructions to the volatile situation on Grand River. He did not rush off to repeat the secretary's inanities to Sitting Bull.

Newspapers pictured Catherine Weldon as a convert. "She furnishes the grub pile for the dance," charged the *Bismarck Tribune*. In fact, she battled valiantly against Kicking Bear, "this false prophet & cheat," during his stay at Grand River, and later ridiculed his teachings. "I have turned my former Uncpapa friends into enemies," she lamented, "& Some feel very bitter towards me. Even Sitting Bull's faith in me is shaken, & he imagines that I seek his destruction."

Giving up, she announced her departure. On October 22 Sitting Bull drove her to Cannonball, where she took passage on a downriver steamer. Before boarding, her boy, Christie, stepped on a rusty nail; he died of lockjaw on the boat. Devastated by the loss and by the rupture with Sitting Bull, Catherine Weldon withdrew altogether from the Indian country.[9]

On his return to Grand River, Sitting Bull paused at the agency long enough to pick up his rations on October 25. Even though One Bull had brought a message a week earlier summoning him to a meeting with McLaughlin, Sitting Bull did not call at the agency office before leaving for home. This was his last visit to Standing Rock Agency. Spies there had already reported rumors of an impending attempt to arrest him, and henceforth he would send family members to get his rations.

Without much doubt, McLaughlin could have contained the Ghost Dance on the Standing Rock Reservation without imprisoning anyone. The movement had not spread beyond the Sitting Bull settlement, and with his long experience and accumulated power over his charges, the agent could surely have kept it confined, to run its course through the winter. More plausibly, McLaughlin shrewdly seized on the Ghost Dance as a means of ridding himself of his longtime nemesis, even though incarceration in a military prison seems an outrageously arbitrary solution.

But McLaughlin did not control events on the other Lakota reservations, where no agent remotely rivaled his ability. At Cheyenne River, Rosebud, and Pine Ridge, the dances assumed an increasingly militant and alarming aspect. At Pine Ridge in particular, a new and woefully inept agent watched his reservation verge on anarchy. Hysteria swept the white communities of Nebraska and North and South Dakota as citizens warned of an Indian uprising and appealed for government arms and military intervention.

The Pine Ridge agent, Daniel F. Royer, finally precipitated the move that positioned the army for active intervention. Bombarding the Indian Office with emotional appeals for help, he also fed the anxieties of neighboring whites in Nebraska. "The police force are overpowered and disheartened," he telegraphed on November 12, "we have no protection, are at the mercy of these crazy dancers." That sent a signal that could no longer be ignored in Washington. The next day Secretary of the Interior Noble conferred with President Harrison, who directed the Secretary of War "to assume responsibility for any threatened outbreak."[10]

The crisis had erupted at Pine Ridge, not Standing Rock, but McLaughlin got caught in the fallout. Together with all the other Sioux agents, he received the telegram of November 14 that assigned the army "responsibility for any threatened outbreak," whatever that meant.

Two days later McLaughlin decided to visit Grand River. Late on the afternoon of November 17, with his interpreter, Louis Primeau, he steered his buggy down the steep slopes to the Sitting Bull settlement. The dance circle vibrated with a Ghost Dance in full swing. A hundred people watched as another hundred danced. "The dancers held each other's hands, and were all jumping madly, whirling to the left about the pole, keeping time to a mournful crooning song, that sometimes rose to a shriek as the women gave way to the stress of their feelings."

A woman swooned and rolled on the ground. Dance officers carried her to a nearby tipi with open flaps. There sat "my old friend, Sitting Bull." Next to him stood the dance director, Bull Ghost, "fantastically dressed."

The woman was laid on the ground in front of Sitting Bull. Bull Ghost announced that she had gone to the spirit land, and the dancing ceased as all watched. Sitting Bull leaned forward and placed his ear next to her mouth. As he spoke in low tones, Bull Ghost repeated in a commanding voice the woman's account of her visit with dead relatives in the promised land. "The excitement was very intense," observed the agent, "the people being brought to a pitch of high nervousness."[11]

Wisely withdrawing from the scene, McLaughlin drove across the river and upstream three miles to spend the night with Lieutenant Bull Head, the local police commander and director of an espionage network that kept the agent informed of affairs on Grand River. Able, courageous, and fiercely loyal to McLaughlin, Bull Head had no love for Sitting Bull or for one of his most devoted adherents, Catch-the-Bear, the last a "big man" and a "trouble maker," as Robert Higheagle remembered. The three had clashed over some trivial incident, and bad blood had bubbled ever since.[12]

Accompanied by Bull Head, McLaughlin and Primeau returned at daybreak the next morning, accosting Sitting Bull as he emerged from a sweat bath. "He was naked, but for a breech-cloth and moccasins, and he looked very thin and more subdued than I had ever seen him."

"How," said the agent, and as the two shook hands McLaughlin steered him to the shelter of a nearby wagon, away from the curious throng that had begun to gather. A family member handed him a blanket.

With great earnestness, McLaughlin launched into a discourse aimed at persuading Sitting Bull of the error of his ways and the danger his course posed for his people. He recalled their association reaching back to the September day in 1881 when McLaughlin, the newly appointed Standing Rock agent, stepped off the boat on which Sitting Bull and his little band were being loaded for the journey to Fort Randall. He portrayed himself, with considerable exaggeration, as a friend who had done many favors for Sitting Bull, including securing his liberation from Fort Randall and his escape from punishment for insulting Senator Logan. He ended, as he recalled, "by reproaching him for leading the people astray and setting them back for years, besides making it certain that they would all be punished."

Sitting Bull responded calmly. He believed in the new religion. It would bring only good to his people.

McLaughlin interrupted to say that it would bring nothing but trouble, and Sitting Bull knew it to be rubbish.

"Father," Sitting Bull answered, "I will make you a proposition which will settle this question. You go with me to the agencies to the West, and let me seek for the men who saw the Messiah; and when we find them, I will demand that they show him to us, and if they cannot do so I will return and tell my people it is a lie."

That, McLaughlin declared, would be like trying to catch the wind that blew last year. Instead, Sitting Bull should come to the agency and give McLaughlin an entire night to show him the absurdity of the doctrine he preached.

"My heart inclines to do what you request, but I must consult with my people," replied the chief. "I will talk to the men tonight, and if they think it advisable I will go to the agency next Saturday."

Apprehensive, the agent and his interpreter mounted their buggy and drove away, "the crowd threatening and sneering, but held in check by the upraised arm of the old medicine man, standing almost naked in the bright but chilly morning sunlight."

The following Saturday, November 22, was ration day. Strikes-the-Kettle rode into the agency to inform the agent that one of Sitting Bull's children was ill, and he could not come as promised.

Some twenty other Grand River men did not come either, sending their wives to draw rations. McLaughlin refused to issue to them. Henceforth, family heads must come in or go hungry.[13]

There was another good reason for Sitting Bull to stay away from the agency. Two days earlier, November 20, troops had moved suddenly to occupy the Pine Ridge and Rosebud agencies. A further strident appeal from Agent Royer on November 15 had ended the debate over military aid. Issuing the marching orders from his Chicago headquarters was a soldier chief well known to the Sioux, Bear Coat: Major General Nelson A. Miles.

SEVEN YEARS OF reservation confinement had not diminished the powers of prophecy for which Sitting Bull had long enjoyed renown. In the spring of 1890, he had predicted the hot summer winds that destroyed the crops. Now he forecast a mild winter. No snow or bitter cold would curb the dances. "Yes, my people," he announced, "you can dance all the winter this year, the sun will shine warmly and the weather will be fair."[14]

Another prophecy, framed not long after he settled at Standing Rock, still hung over Sitting Bull like a dark and foreboding cloud.

He had been released from Fort Randall but had not found the agency what he expected. His chieftainship had been ridiculed and denied.

McLaughlin demeaned him constantly. Senator Logan had mortified him. Lesser men had been lifted to false chieftainships and enjoyed official favor.

At daybreak one morning, borne down by this somber mood, he walked three miles out on the prairie to where he had hobbled some horses. As he mounted a hilltop, he suddenly heard a voice from nearby. Halting, he strained his ears until, on a low knoll ahead of him, he spied a meadowlark. From his earliest years, he had enjoyed a special relationship with birds. None were more closely his friends than meadowlarks, whom he regarded as full of wise counsel if only his people would heed them.

Now this meadowlark spoke, in Sioux: "Lakotas will kill you."

The warning of the friendly little bird greatly grieved Sitting Bull. He tried to forget it but could not.

"From that time on," recalled One Bull, "he seemed to feel—really—he was to be killed by his own people."[15]

24 DEATH

MARY COLLINS, Congregational missionary at the Antelope settlement, battled the Ghost Dance even more dauntlessly than had Catherine Weldon. On a Sunday early in December she invaded the very heart of Sitting Bull's domain. While drums, songs, wails, and shrieks sounded from the dance circle, she directed her assistant to set up a small portable organ in front of Sitting Bull's cabin and summon her own faithful for Congregational services.

Three came, and their rendition of "Nearer My God to Thee" scarcely soothed troubled Christian souls. "Our converts sang the song in a wild rough way," she remembered, "and the music, screams, and shouting of the awful dance were mingled with our voices until you could scarcely hear anything."

Dismissing her little congregation, Miss Collins marched resolutely up to the dance circle and the tipi of "Brother Sitting Bull." Twice he refused her demand to come out and talk. Upon the third request, he told her to enter. Standing with his back to her, Sitting Bull directed that she pass to the left and avoid stepping in certain places. After this "trifling tomfoolery," he invited her to speak.

"Brother," she scolded, "you are ruining your people. You are deceiving them and you well know it. You must stop it at once and send them away."

"Sister, I cannot do it," he replied calmly. "I have gone too far."

"You must do it. The people are neglecting their homes and their property. There will be great suffering. They are likely to commit violence. The soldiers will come, and you will be to blame for it."

But Sitting Bull would talk no more. Turning, Collins ducked out of the tipi and stalked to the edge of the dance circle. A man lay on the ground, supposedly in a trance.

"Louis," she commanded, "get up, you are not unconscious, you are not ill; get up and help me to send these people home."

Louis rose and looked around sheepishly. The spell of the dance broken, people drifted from the circle, and some even loaded into their wagons and headed home.[1]

But the dances did not stop.

Gray Eagle tried to bring his influence to bear. "Brother-in-law," he beseeched, "we have settled on the reservation now and we are under the jurisdiction of the government, and we must do as they say. We must cut out the roaming around and live as they say, and must cut out this dancing."

"Yes, you are right," answered Sitting Bull, "but I could not give up my race as it is seated in us. You go ahead and follow what the white man says, but for my part leave me alone."[2]

McLaughlin sent one of his best policemen, Lone Man, a Hunkpapa who farmed on Grand River about thirty miles east of the Sitting Bull settlement. The dance leaders packed themselves into Sitting Bull's cabin to listen. "They did not treat me with much courtesy," Lone Man observed.

"I suppose you have come on the same errand as the rest," said Sitting Bull.

"I said that I had come to advise him to drop the Ghost Dance as it would come to nothing and might deceive the people who were looking to him as a chief." Besides, many were old and could not stand the strain, and many were Lone Man's friends.

"In the hostile days we young men followed you," the policeman reminded his old chief.

"Yes," replied Sitting Bull, "I depended on you then, but now you have turned with the whites against me. I have nothing to say to you. . . . So far as I am concerned you may go home."[3]

As Sitting Bull sought to convince all these meddlers, his religion was nobody's business but his. The Ghost Dance threatened no one. The dancers meant violence to no one. The whites had their religion, the Indians had theirs, and neither should interfere with the other.

Jack Carignan, who taught the Grand River day school, foresaw no danger. "The Indians seem to be very peaceably inclined," he informed McLaughlin on November 27. Although rumors that soldiers might come to break up the dance had frightened them, "I am positive that no trouble need be apprehended from Sitting Bull and his followers, unless they are forced to defend themselves." He thought it advisable to keep strangers away, however, "as Sitting Bull has lost all confidence in the whites since Mrs. Weldon left him."[4]

Sitting Bull and the dancers could be pardoned for fearing that soldiers might march on them. They kept in touch with events on the southern reservations, where soldiers had indeed appeared on November 20. Frightened, the dance elements of both Pine Ridge and Rosebud took refuge on an elevated tableland, well watered and protected by steep cliffs and bluffs, that quickly became known as the Stronghold. There they continued to dance while military authorities tried to decide how to get them down without provoking a fight. A large contingent of "war correspondents" descended on the agencies and with breathless dispatches kept the nation in daily suspense.

McLaughlin wanted no such scenes at Standing Rock. He knew that the moment a blue column marched out of Fort Yates for any purpose, the Grand River Ghost Dancers would stampede, either to unite with their kin in the Stronghold or flee to their own Stronghold. He therefore intended that his Indian police, not soldiers, should arrest Sitting Bull— but not until winter set in and chilled the dancers' fervor. Week after week, however, as Sitting Bull had prophesied, pleasant weather persisted.

The Fort Yates commander, Lieutenant Colonel William F. Drum, shared McLaughlin's convictions, as did his superior in St. Paul, Brigadier General Thomas H. Ruger. Above Drum and Ruger, however, General Miles felt no such dedication to interagency harmony. He too believed that Sitting Bull should be removed, but that timing might be a delicate matter, that McLaughlin might have his own strategy, or even that McLaughlin retained any authority at Standing Rock probably never occurred to him. Often an imperious potentate with his subordinates, he now cavalierly ignored not only McLaughlin but Ruger and Drum as well.

On November 28 a curious entourage appeared at Fort Yates. Heading it was Buffalo Bill Cody, fresh from a European tour, and a few of his lieutenants, including Robert H. Haslam (Pony Bob) and Frank Powell (White Beaver). "Colonel" Cody produced orders, dated November 24 and signed by General Miles, directing him to "secure the person of

Sitting Bull and deliver him to the nearest com'g officer of U.S. troops." The circus prince also handed Colonel Drum one of Miles's calling cards on the back of which the general had scribbled in pencil an order for military officers to provide such transportation and protection as Cody might request.

Drum and McLaughlin were chagrined. Bill Cody and Sitting Bull had been friends for a season's tour, but to turn the one loose on the other in the present situation might lead to unpredictable consequences.

Fortunately for McLaughlin, Cody could not get underway that day. As Drum later explained delicately, he "was somewhat intoxicated. Dr. Powell thought the Colonel would be all right after a few hours rest, and we were to meet later in the day and decide on measures to be taken but the Colonel continued to drink and was in no condition to attend to business that afternoon and evening."[5]

What Drum discreetly failed to mention was that the Fort Yates officers conspired to ensure that "the Colonel continued to drink." At the officers' club they worked in relays while Drum and McLaughlin frantically sought to head off what they feared would become a trip to disaster. At once McLaughlin telegraphed a protest to Washington. Cody's mission would set off a fight, he warned the Indian Office, and should be canceled at once.

Early the next morning, November 29, as Drum had to concede, "Col. Cody appeared quite straight and announced that he and Dr. Powell would start for Sitting Bull's camp." Drum had no choice but to provide a wagon and team for the journey.

McLaughlin, however, had still not lost the game. En route, Cody's party met Louis Primeau, the agency interpreter. He stated that Sitting Bull would not be found at his home, that even then he was headed for the agency on the other road. Whether this was Primeau's quick thinking or, as some would have it, a clever contrivance of McLaughlin, made no difference. With McLaughlin's telegram in hand, Secretary Noble had hurried to see the president, who overruled Miles and rescinded Cody's authority. As McLaughlin later congratulated himself, "My telegram saved to the world that day a royal good fellow and most excellent showman."[6]

It probably did no such thing. Although conceived impulsively and in ignorance of true conditions at Standing Rock, Miles's scheme is not likely to have cost Buffalo Bill his life, or anyone else either. Sitting Bull would surely have received his old friend with his usual hospitality and listened politely to his arguments. As with McLaughlin two weeks earlier, Sitting

Bull would have promised to give careful thought to the summons, talk it over with his advisors, and possibly go to the agency at some future date. Cody would have been foolish indeed to try to enforce his request with coercion. The dancers would not have permitted it, and bloodshed or worse would have been the outcome. Even with a full measure of bottled stimulation, Buffalo Bill is hard to picture in such a stance.

As the Cody fiasco should have made clear, the initiative had passed to the army. Although McLaughlin had not fully grasped the reality, he did dread that at any moment Miles might emit another decree. A moderate snowfall on December 5 afforded a pretext for trying to head off the army. The next day would be ration day, when all but the most dedicated dancers would be at the agency.

"Weather cold and snowing," he telegraphed the Indian Office. "Am I authorized to arrest Sitting Bull and other fomenters of mischief when I think best?"

The reply came promptly: "Make no arrests whatever except under orders of the military or upon an order from the Secretary of the Interior."[7]

That ceded entire control of the issue to General Miles. Angry over the Cody affair, he moved at once. On December 10 General Ruger received explicit orders from Miles's Chicago headquarters: "You will now direct the Commanding Officer Fort Yates to consider it his especial duty to secure the person of Sitting Bull using any practical means. The agent at that post is under his direction and orders for any purpose of this kind."[8]

Reaching Fort Yates on December 12, this directive dropped responsibility for Sitting Bull's arrest squarely on Colonel Drum. At the risk of further provoking his division commander, Drum turned to McLaughlin, and together they plotted to carry out the original plan. The arrest would be made on the next ration day, December 20, and it would be made by police backed as needed by soldiers.

For a month McLaughlin had been unobtrusively strengthening the police, whose performance in ejecting Kicking Bear had momentarily discomfited him. Gradually he shifted reinforcements to Lieutenant Bull Head's Grand River district, ostensibly to gather logs for the construction of a shelter for travelers at the Oak Creek crossing of the Sitting Bull Road. Augmenting the regulars were twenty special policemen, whom Washington authorized to be sworn in for three months' service.[9]

One Bull was no longer a *ceska maza*—a metal breast. Either he dropped out of the force because he foresaw an impossible personal conflict, or he was discharged. As he remembered it years later, "Bull Head reported to McLaughlin that I had been converted into this new belief and hence I was fired from my police job."[10]

Even before Drum received the arrest order, Sitting Bull had unwittingly altered the timetable. The dance leaders of Pine Ridge and Rosebud had invited him to visit the dance camp in the Stronghold, and he and his counselors had decided that he ought to go. On the night of December 11, therefore, he sat in his tipi at the dance circle with Bull Ghost, Spotted-Horn-Bull, and Black Bird to compose a letter to McLaughlin. To commit it to paper, they summoned Andrew Fox, Sitting Bull's young son-in-law, widower of the daughter who had died in 1887.

Andrew had only a smattering of schooling, and what he wrote in English as Sitting Bull dictated emerged almost incoherent in translation. Most of the missive dealt with the right of all people to pray as they saw fit, but it ended with the revelation that "I got to go to Pine Ridge agency, and to know this pray"—to learn what the apostles there were teaching.[11]

Bull Ghost served as courier and presented the letter to McLaughlin on the evening of December 12, the day the order to arrest Sitting Bull clicked into the Fort Yates telegraph office. From Bull Ghost McLaughlin extracted clarification of the letter. Sitting Bull wanted a pass to visit the southern agencies, Bull Ghost explained, and if denied he intended to go anyway.[12]

McLaughlin answered the next day with a letter of his own, carried back by Bull Ghost. Packed with the usual hollow professions of friendship and more pleas to send the dancers back to their homes, it addressed the pressing question of the journey to Pine Ridge. "Therefore, my friend, listen to this advice," the agent wrote, "do not attempt to visit any other agency at present."[13]

Meanwhile, on December 12 interpreter Louis Primeau, filling in as police chief for Crazy Walking, had sent a courier to alert Bull Head. Referring to the letter brought in by Bull Ghost, Primeau warned that Sitting Bull might try to leave the reservation and should therefore be watched closely. "If he should you must stop him and if he does not listen to you do as you see fit." The police force should now be concentrated on the pretext of beginning construction of the road shelter on Oak Creek. Sergeant Shave Head would report to him with additional men and further instructions.[14]

The very next day, Saturday, even as Bull Head received this order, two of his spies slipped into the Sitting Bull settlement and eavesdropped on still another council. Sitting Bull and his followers planned to leave on

Monday morning, they learned, and would shoot any police who tried to stop them.[15] Bull Head hurried down the river to report this finding to Jack Carignan at the Grand River school. At 12:30 A.M. on December 14, Carignan put it into English, and one of the special policemen, Hawk Man, carried it to the agency, arriving at 4:00 P.M.:

> Bull Head wishes to report what occurred at Sitting Bull's camp at a council held yesterday [December 13]. It seems that Sitting Bull has received a letter from the Pine Ridge outfit asking him to come over there as God was to appear to them. Sitting Bull's people want him to go, but he has sent a letter to you asking your permission, and if you do not give it he is going to go anyway; he has been fitting up his horses to stand a long ride and will go on horseback in case he is pursued. Bull Head would like to arrest him at once before he has the chance of giving them the slip, as he thinks that if he gets the start it will be impossible to catch him. . . .[16]

Did Sitting Bull really intend to go to Pine Ridge? Andrew Fox, One Bull, and others declared emphatically that he did not, assertions contradicted by Fox's letter, Bull Ghost's statements to Primeau and McLaughlin, and Bull Head's findings. Bull Head, of course, may have misunderstood or misrepresented happenings in the dance camp, and McLaughlin, seeking to justify his course, may have exaggerated.

Even so, the Fox letter leaves little doubt that Sitting Bull intended to leave for Pine Ridge. There, in the Stronghold, were the high priests of the Ghost Dance, Kicking Bear and Short Bull. Also there were the most zealous of the Lakota faithful. In the Stronghold Sitting Bull might learn more about the religion from those most qualified to teach while also restoring his former luster as chief of all the Lakotas.

Whatever the intent, McLaughlin can hardly be faulted for believing Sitting Bull on the verge of leaving. And even had McLaughlin been disposed to move more deliberately, Colonel Drum could not be expected to acquiesce. His career, not McLaughlin's, was on the block, and if Sitting Bull escaped, General Miles's reaction was predictable.

Drum had seen Hawk Man gallop into the agency and, suspecting important news, hurried to McLaughlin's office. The arrest could not now be delayed until ration day, the two agreed; it had to be made the next morning. All the regular and special police in the Grand River area were to be concentrated at once, and Bull Head was to lead them into the Sitting Bull settlement before daybreak the next day and take the chief into custody. Two troops of cavalry from Fort Yates under Captain Edmond G. Fechet would make a night march and position themselves to help the police if needed.

Scarcely half an hour had passed after Hawk Man's arrival before McLaughlin and Drum had written three documents: orders to Bull Head in English and Sioux and a letter to Carignan. For the latter McLaughlin added a postscript: "Be sure to see that they have a light wagon ready to bring Bull in, so that there will be no delay by such oversight." McLaughlin had already impressed this measure on both Bull Head and Shave Head, but he wanted Carignan alerted too. If Bull Head did not have a wagon, Carignan should lend his.[17]

The letter to Bull Head also added a postscript: "You must not let him escape under any circumstances."

McLaughlin entrusted the documents to Sergeant Red Tomahawk, a mixed Yanktonai-Hunkpapa who lived on the Cannonball north of the agency and was unfamiliar with the people or the country to the south. He got lost, but even so managed to find Bull Head's home by 10:00 P.M. There he discovered that Bull Head had already assembled twenty-eight of his men. The balance, eight sent to Oak Creek to begin work on the shelter (whom Red Tomahawk had missed in his confusion), and others from down Grand River, were still en route.[18]

In his cramped little cabin, Bull Head, backed by First Sergeant Shave Head, gathered the men. The regulars wore their blue uniforms and badges. The specials had tied white handkerchiefs around their necks as identification.

A somber mood lay on the group. Some, including Bull Head, had followed Sitting Bull's lead and fought with him at the Rosebud and Little Bighorn. Some had starved with him in Canada. Not lost on them was the coincidence that Bull Head's home stood on almost the exact site on the south bank of Grand River where Sitting Bull had been born fifty-nine winters before. "We all felt sad," said Lone Man.[19]

After the mixed-blood interpreter had read McLaughlin's instructions, Bull Head outlined his plan. The police would ride down the river on the south bank, then cross to enter the Sitting Bull settlement from the south. The residents would not be looking for trouble from that direction, for Fort Yates and the agency lay to the north. The privates would surround Sitting Bull's cabin while the officers went inside to make the arrest.

Red Tomahawk had also brought the letter McLaughlin had written to Jack Carignan. Bull Head assigned Lone Man to carry it seven miles down the river to the school. There Carignan quickly hitched his team to his buggy and, escorted by Lone Man and three special policemen who had come to the school, hurried through the dark to Bull Head's place. Long after midnight they crept cautiously along the edge of the Sitting Bull settlement, setting off a noisy chorus of dogs but eliciting only one sleepy challenge from a resident. The little cavalcade reached Bull Head's as the force began to saddle for departure.[20]

After a briefing on the plan for the arrest, Carignan asked Bull Head: "How about the spring buggy you are going to use to take Sitting Bull to the agency? You can't take it over that rough trail on the south side of the river."

He would obtain a wagon in the Sitting Bull settlement, Bull Head answered. Now he wanted his wife and children driven to the agency in Carignan's buggy.[21]

Already Bull Head had decided against the wagon. According to Lone Man, as part of his arrest plan Bull Head had assigned Red Bear and White Bird to hurry to Sitting Bull's corral, where he stabled the gray circus horse presented him by Buffalo Bill, and saddle it in readiness for a quick getaway.[22]

At 4:00 A.M., with an icy drizzle filling the air, the police gathered in front of the cabin. Bull Head led them in a Christian prayer. After mounting, they formed a column of twos. "Hopo," commanded the lieutenant, and they trotted into the cold black night.

Two miles downstream stood Gray Eagle's cabin. The column paused there at 4:30, as Sergeant Eagle Man's detachment from Oak Creek finally caught up. The force now numbered one officer, four sergeants, fourteen privates of the regular force, and twenty special policemen.[23]

At Gray Eagle's he and four more joined as volunteers. They made forty-four. The men guided their horses through the wet bottoms of Grand River and, hooves rattling and slipping on the ice, crossed to the north bank. Owls hooted and coyotes howled. Even they gave warning, growled someone, "so beware."[24]

Sitting Bull slept on his pallet with the elder of his two wives and one of his two small children. Also in the room were two old men, guests invited after the night's dance ended; Crow Foot, the serious-minded favorite son, now fourteen; and Red Whirlwind, One Bull's wife. In her husband's absence, hauling freight to the agency from Mandan, she had moved in with Sitting Bull's family. The rest of Sitting Bull's family occupied the other, smaller cabin to the north, across the wagon road.[25]

Shortly before 6:00 A.M., the clatter of galloping hooves and the barking of dogs broke the predawn stillness. The sleeping people stirred as someone pounded and kicked on the door and shouted Sitting Bull's name. The door burst open, and the room filled suddenly with dark forms. A match flared and went out. Another caught a candle wick and cast a flickering light across the room.[26]

"Brother, we came after you," barked Sergeant Shave Head as he seized Sitting Bull.

"How, all right" was the reply.

As more police crowded into the room, the two old men slipped out, as did One Bull's wife, who ran to the chicken coop and watched. Remaining inside were Crow Foot and Sitting Bull's wife, with the child clinging to her back. She began to wail, partly in lamentation and partly in reproach of the police and her husband's acquiscence.

Nervous over confronting the mighty Sitting Bull, some of the police manhandled the prisoner and shoved one another. One and then another of the officers wrestled Sitting Bull, naked, toward the door.

"This is a great way to do things," he exclaimed, "not to give me a chance to put on my clothes in winter time."

His wife went to the other cabin and retrieved the clothes he wanted to wear. When she returned, policemen hurried him through the process of dressing, then thrust him again toward the door. He braced his hands and feet against the door frame.

"Let me go," he cried, "I'll go without any assistance."

They emerged from the door and paused. Bull Head and Shave Head flanked Sitting Bull, the former grasping his right arm, the latter his left. Sergeant Red Tomahawk stood in the rear, pistol in hand.

The gray circus horse was there, saddled and ready, but barking dogs, the shrieks of Sitting Bull's wife, and the general commotion had alerted the entire settlement. In the faint light of daybreak, people converged from all directions, pressing against the cordon of nervous police and shouting taunts and insults.

Catch-the-Bear shouldered his way through the throng to confront his mortal enemy Bull Head, whose hand gripped Sitting Bull's arm.

"Now, here are the *ceska maza*," he spat out scornfully, so all could hear, "just as we had expected all the time. You think you are going to take him. You shall not do it."

Turning to the crowd behind him, he yelled, "Come on now, let us protect our chief."

As men began to work through the police line and press closely on the cabin, Crow Foot, the youth who had grown up too fast, came to the doorway.

"Well," he chided his father, "you always called yourself a brave chief. Now you are allowing yourself to be taken by the *ceska maza*."

For several moments Sitting Bull lost himself in thought. "Then I shall not go," he declared.

"Come now," implored Bull Head, "do not listen to anyone."

Bull Head turned to Jumping Bull, who had come unarmed on the scene, and asked his aid.

"Brother," said Jumping Bull, "you ought to go with the police and not cause any trouble."

"Uncle," Lone Man added, "nobody is going to hurt you. The agent wants to see you and then you are to come back—so please do not let others lead you into any trouble."

Sitting Bull hung back. Bull Head and Shave Head tightened their grip and pulled. Red Tomahawk pushed from behind. They moved toward the waiting horse.

The crowd went wild. People shook their fists, cursed the police, and shouted, "You shall not take our chief."

"The police tried to keep order," recalled Lone Man, but "it was like trying to extinguish a treacherous prairie fire."

Suddenly Catch-the-Bear shouldered his Winchester, took aim, and squeezed the trigger. The bullet tore into Bull Head's right side and sent him sprawling. As he fell, he turned his revolver up and shot Sitting Bull full in the chest. Red Tomahawk fired another bullet into the back of his head. An instant later Strikes-the-Kettle fired, the bullet punching into Shave Head's stomach. All three fell together in one heap.

As the three men crumpled to the ground, Lone Man sprang at the smoking muzzle of the weapon that had gunned down his relative and superior. Catch-the-Bear swung it toward Lone Man and pulled the trigger, but it misfired. Lone Man tore the rifle from his grasp, clubbed him with the butt, and shot him dead.

Infuriated, Sitting Bull's men swarmed over the metal breasts with knives, clubs, and guns. It was a vicious battle at close quarters. Bullets laced the little battleground, fired at pointblank range.

Police fire killed five more of Sitting Bull's followers, including Black Bird, Spotted-Horn Bull, and Brave Thunder. Jumping Bull, who had counseled submission and who was not even armed with a knife, also died, with his son, Chase-Them-Wounded. Three more, Bull Ghost, Strikes-the-Kettle, and another Brave Thunder, dropped with wounds that did not prove fatal.

Three more bullets plowed into the wounded Bull Head. Four more policemen took fatal rounds: Sergeant Little Eagle and Privates Afraid-of-Soldier, Strong Arm, and Hawk Man No. 2 (the same who had carried Carignan's letter to McLaughlin the day before). Private Middle sustained a painful wound that cost him a foot.[27]

In only a few minutes, the bloody fight ended as abruptly as it had begun. The dancers broke away and raced to a grove of trees along the river behind Sitting Bull's cabin.

As the ranking sergeant still on his feet, Red Tomahawk took command and ordered the wounded Bull Head, Shave Head, and Middle dragged into the cabin and made as comfortable as possible on the bedding. The rest took defensive positions in the barn and corral.

Inside the cabin, one of the men spied a slight movement in a pile of blankets. Lone Man pulled them aside and uncovered Crow Foot.

"My uncles," the boy cried, "do not kill me. I do not wish to die."

The police asked Bull Head what to do with the youth. Four bullets in him, the lieutenant looked up from his pallet.

"Do what you like with him," he answered bitterly. "He is one of them that has caused this trouble."

Lone Man smashed Crow Foot across the forehead with a rifle butt, which sent him reeling across the room and out the door. There Lone Man and two others, tears streaming down their cheeks, pumped bullets into him.[28]

Red Tomahawk summoned Hawk Man No. 1—No. 2 lay dead on the ground outside—and ordered him to mount the circus horse and ride swiftly toward Oak Creek to alert the soldiers. As he galloped from the battleground, Sitting Bull's people opened fire from the timber. Bullets zipped around Hawk Man and tugged at his clothing. The police took cover in the sheds and corrals behind the cabin and returned the fire. For more than an hour, the two sides exchanged fire.

Daylight, made hazy by a thin fog, had spread over the Grand River Valley by the time Captain Fechet's cavalry squadron galloped to the bluffs overlooking the battlefield. Distracted by the spattering fire from the timber, the police failed to see the white flag fluttering from the crest. Not until artillery began to explode in the valley did Lone Man tear a white curtain from a window and rush outside waving it. Artillery drove the dancers from the timber and from a knoll to the west on which others had gathered.

Some of the dancers driven out of the timber met One Bull. He had reached his home shortly before daybreak, exhausted by an all-night drive from the agency, and had promptly taken to his robes. "All at once in my

Among Sitting Bull's allied chiefs in the war of 1876 (and during the Canadian exile) were Spotted Eagle of the Sans Arcs, above, and Spotted Elk of the Miniconjous, right. They were photographed at Fort Keogh shortly after their surrender in October 1880. Spotted Elk, also known as Big Foot, died at Wounded Knee ten years later.

MONTANA HISTORICAL

SOCIETY

Sitting Bull as prisoner of war, Fort Randall, 1882, left, with Seen-by-the-Nation, the elder of his two wives. He appears, right, with both wives, the twins Crow Foot and Run-Away-From (the one left in the tipi when the cavalry attacked at the Little Bighorn), and Standing Holy.

Sitting Bull's final surrender at Fort Buford on July 19, 1881, left, as depicted by Harpers Weekly. *The formal surrender took place the next day, when Sitting Bull handed his Winchester rifle (still preserved at the Smithsonian Institution) to his five-year-old son Crow Foot, who in turn handed it to Major David H. Brotherton.*
SMITHSONIAN
INSTITUTION

On their return from imprisonment at Fort Randall in May 1883, Sitting Bull and his band pitched their tipis south of Fort Yates and Standing Rock Agency where they planted their first crops. A year later they moved to Grand River and began to erect log cabins. DENVER PUBLIC LIBRARY WESTERN HISTORY DEPARTMENT

Sitting Bull with his mother, Her-Holy-Door, and his eldest daughter, Many Horses, and her son, about 1883. His mother died in 1884. SMITHSONIAN INSTITUTION

*S*tanding Rock Agency, above,
looking southeast, toward the
Missouri River. Fort Yates
adjoins agency at extreme right of
photograph. James McLaughlin,
right, Standing Rock's efficient
and authoritarian agent, battled
with Sitting Bull for seven years
and during the Ghost Dance
troubles issued the arrest order
that led to the chief's death.
NORTH DAKOTA
HISTORICAL SOCIETY

Gray Eagle, brother of Sitting Bull's final two wives, endured a humiliating "soldiering" ordered by his brother-in-law in Canada. On the reservation Gray Eagle embraced government programs and drifted away from Sitting Bull.
LIBRARY OF CONGRESS

Sitting Bull's associates pictured below at Standing Rock Agency shortly after their arrival from Forts Buford and Keogh in the summer of 1881. Left to right: Gall, Crawler, Crow King, Running Antelope, and Rain-in-the-Face. Crawler, a longtime friend and ally of Sitting Bull, had played a key role in liberating the captive white woman Fanny Kelly in 1864. Crow King's decision to surrender in December 1880 fatally split Sitting Bull's following in Canada. A noted orator, Running Antelope was one of the four Hunkpapa shirt wearers and one of the earliest agency chiefs. Rain-in-the-Face, credited by legend as the slayer of Custer, displays a photographic portrait probably of himself. HAYNES FOUNDATION COLLECTION, MONTANA HISTORICAL SOCIETY

*Gall, before and after. When
he surrendered at Fort Buford
in 1881, above, Gall was the
physical embodiment of the
ideal Hunkpapa. In 1888,
right, after seven years under
the influence of Agent
McLaughlin, he won praise
as an ideal agency chief.*
NORTH DAKOTA HISTORICAL
SOCIETY; SMITHSONIAN
INSTITUTION

White Bull, right, and One Bull, below, nephews of Sitting Bull, were the sons of Miniconjou chief Mukes Room and Sitting Bull's sister Good Feather. Sitting Bull adopted One Bull and reared him as his own son. Both died in 1947.

Sitting Bull sat for this likeness in 1883, when the steamer bearing him from imprisonment at Fort Randall to Standing Rock Agency paused at the town of Pierre. Note butterfly pinned to hatband.
SMITHSONIAN INSTITU-
TION

Standing Rock Agency took its name from a rock formation resembling an Indian woman with a child on her back. Because it possessed great meaning for the Sioux, Agent McLaughlin had it moved from its original site to a new site at the agency. He poses with Sitting Bull during dedication ceremonies in 1886.
SMITHSONIAN INSTITUTION

"Foes in '76, Friends in '85." Buffalo Bill Cody and Sitting Bull joined in a publicity photo in Montreal in 1885.
SMITHSONIAN INSTITUTION

Sitting Bull's favorite children: Crow Foot, above, and Standing Holy, right. Crow Foot died at the age of fourteen with his father in the Grand River shootout in 1890. Standing Holy, born in Canada in 1878, married and lived at Pine Ridge. NORTH DAKOTA HISTORICAL SOCIETY

Crow Foot.
(Sitting Bull's Son.)

Visit of the Sioux chiefs to Washington, D.C., October 1888. Though they could not work out an acceptable land agreement with government officials, they gathered on the steps on the Interior Department for a photograph. Characteristically, Sitting Bull stands somewhat apart, left. The Standing Rock delegation included John Grass and Gall (39 and 40) and was escorted by Agent James McLaughlin (42). The Sioux commissioners stand in front: Richard H. Pratt, William J. Cleveland, and John V. Wright (1-3), next to Commissioner of Indian Affairs John H. Oberly (4). SMITHSONIAN INSITUTION

At daybreak on December 15, 1890, the Standing Rock ceska maza, *or Indian police, above, entered Sitting Bull's cabin on Grand River with orders to arrest him for removal from the reservation during the Ghost Dance troubles. When his followers intervened, a fight broke out and Sitting Bull fell with fatal rounds fired by Lieutenant Bull Head, right, and Sergeant Red Tomahawk, far right.* NORTH DAKOTA HISTORICAL SOCIETY; SMITHSONIAN INSTITUTION

Teacher Jack Carignan escorted Associated Press reporter Sam Clover to the Ghost Dance at Sitting Bull's settlement. With a small Kodak hidden under his overcoat, Clover surreptitiously snapped this picture of a dance in progress. Note prayer tree in center and Sitting Bull's "command tipi" at right.
MINNESOTA HISTORICAL SOCIETY

The Indian policemen killed in the attempt to arrest Sitting Bull were buried in the Catholic cemetery at Standing Rock Agency on December 17, 1890.
MINNESOTA HISTORICAL SOCIETY

Widows and daughters stand near the doorway where Sitting Bull was killed. Left to right: Many Horses, Four Robes, Seen-by-the-Nation, and Standing Holy.
SMITHSONIAN INSTITUTION

sleep," he remembered, "I heard the report of guns." Hurrying toward Sitting Bull's cabin, he learned of his uncle's death from the people fleeing the advancing soldiers.

At the cabin, police pointed their rifles at him. "Son-in-law, do not come any further," urged Sergeant Eagle Man. "Stop right where you are."

One Bull halted while Cross Bear, a police private, came to him and explained what had happened. One Bull asked about the women and was assured that they were all safe. His own wife, Cross Bear said, pointing to the chicken coop, had taken refuge in that building.

"Go and get her back and then go to your home and stay there," ordered the *ceska maza* to his former comrade on the force.

One Bull obeyed. "Such a sadness we had experienced," he later recalled.[29]

A blue skirmish line descended the slopes and advanced rapidly across the flats to the settlement. Mounting, Red Tomahawk took the white flag from Lone Man and rode to meet the soldiers. As the skirmishers drew into the settlement, Sergeant Eagle Man aligned the police in military formation and advanced smartly to salute the young lieutenant in charge.

Dismounting in front of Sitting Bull's cabin, Captain Fechet surveyed the grisly scene. "I saw evidence of a most desperate encounter," he later wrote. "In front of the house, and within a radius of 50 yards, were the bodies of 8 dead Indians, including that of Sitting Bull, and 2 dead horses. In the house were 4 dead policemen and 3 wounded, 2 mortally. To add to the horror of the scene the squaws of Sitting Bull, who were in a small house nearby, kept up a great wailing."[30]

Some of Policeman Strong Arm's relatives, who lived nearby, came to where the troops had gathered. They saw the body of their kinsman and added their own fearful wails to those of Sitting Bull's widows. Strong Arm's brother, Holy Medicine, picked up a neck yoke, walked over to Sitting Bull's corpse, and with a savage blow smashed in the face.

"What the hell did you do that for?" asked a cavalryman. "The man is dead. Leave him alone."[31]

Fearing that the spreading pool of Sitting Bull's blood would freeze the body to the ground, a sergeant detailed a soldier to move it and stand guard against further mutilation.

Lieutenant Matthew F. Steele led a squad to Sitting Bull's second cabin, where he found the two wives and several other women and children. The wives sat firmly on a low bed covered with a thick straw tick. Suspicious, Steele had them moved and the bedding stripped off. Pressed against the floor, fearful of Crow Foot's fate, lay two young men, Sitting Bull's deaf-mute stepson and another son of Jumping Bull.[32]

On the wall of this cabin, framed in ornate gilt, hung the portrait of Sitting Bull painted by Catherine Weldon. Steele had forbidden the soldiers to touch anything, but a tearful policeman, mourning the death of a brother in the shootout, dashed into the room, tore down the painting, smashed the frame with his rifle butt, and ripped a gash in the canvas with the barrel. Steele grabbed the mutilated picture before it could be destroyed. Taking it back to Fort Yates, he later, through McLaughlin, bought it from Sitting Bull's widows for two dollars.[33]

Nearly all the dancers had fled across Grand River and hidden in the hills south of the valley. One of the most devout of the believers, however, was not ready to give up so easily. Clad in his red bulletproof ghost shirt, mounted on a splendid black horse, and brandishing a long staff, Crow Woman burst from the timber eighty yards from the settlement and charged up the valley.

As he galloped, he sang: "Father, I thought you said / We were all going to live."

Police opened fire with their Winchesters, and Crow Woman reined into the timber. Once more he charged into the open, and once more police bullets turned him back to the timber. A third time he dashed into the valley, this time passing between two cavalrymen sent out as pickets. Both fired at close range, but missed. Crow Woman rode triumphantly up the valley and out of sight, a living demonstration of the protective powers of the ghost shirt.[34]

The mission of the police and soldiers had been to bring in Sitting Bull, nothing more. Captain Fechet had some of the women move up and down the valley spreading word that he was returning to the fort and would not give chase. Sergeant Red Tomahawk, intent on carrying out Bull Head's instructions to the letter, meant to deliver Sitting Bull's corpse to the agent. Tenderly the wounded Bull Head, Shave Head, and Middle were hoisted into Fechet's ambulance, while the dead police were loaded into an old farm wagon appropriated from the settlement and hitched to Indian ponies.

When Red Tomahawk ordered Sitting Bull thrown into the wagon too, the police balked. Sitting Bull had caused the death of their comrades, and to haul him in the same wagon was to dishonor them. Red Tomahawk insisted, and at last they obeyed, but only if Sitting Bull was on the bottom and the dead policemen on top.[35]

Shortly after noon on December 15, 1890, the little cavalcade crawled up the trail to the plains and pointed north on the road to Standing Rock. On the floor of the wagon, jostled by the bodies of Sergeant Little Eagle, Privates Afraid-of-Soldier and Strong Arm, and Special Policeman Hawk Man, bounced the mangled corpse of Sitting Bull.

"NO SCHOOL FOR us this afternoon!" shouted the children of the post school at Fort Yates at noon on December 16. "No school, and we can see them bring in Sitting Bull."

Seven-year-old Frank Fiske, whose father was a soldier, remembered the scene vividly. He ran to the post trader's store and found a back window affording a view of the procession as it dropped off the brown, snow-spotted foothills to the southwest and crawled across the flat valley floor. He watched the head of the caravan draw slowly along the road marking the east edge of the fort, on the high bank overlooking the river.

The first part of the parade consisted of several worn farm wagons drawn by tired Indian ponies, together with an army ambulance with a red cross painted on each side panel. A solitary old man on a pony rode in advance, moaning a mournful death song. Indian women in the wagons keened in accompaniment. A contingent of police rode escort.

As the wagons and horsemen passed, Frank spied the second unit of the parade, following a mile in the rear. Officers to the front, guidons snapping overhead, two troops of cavalry trotted up the road, angled left into the post, and drew up at the stables. An infantry column brought up the rear.[36]

After the police dead were placed in the agency meeting hall, the wagon returned to Fort Yates to unload Sitting Bull in the dead house behind the post hospital. That night some of the garrison's old-timers, veterans of the years of warfare with Sitting Bull's Sioux, went to view the body.

In the hospital, surrounded by weeping attendants and officials, Shave Head lay in the agony of an abdominal wound. He knew he would die.

"Did I do well," he asked the agent. James McLaughlin could only nod.

"Then I will die in the faith of the white man and to which my five children already belong, and be with them. Send for my wife, that we may be married by the Black Gown before I die."

Shave Head's wife lived eighteen miles from the agency. She arrived fifteen minutes after he had died in the arms of a Catholic priest. It was

7:00 A.M. on December 17. Crumpled in the doorway to the hospital, she sang the death song.[37]

Bull Head struggled into the next day as the agency prepared to pay homage to the heroes. In the afternoon, Indians and whites crowded into the little frame church of the Congregational mission south of the agency, where Catholic and Protestant divines conducted joint services. Then the people walked to the cemetery next to the Catholic mission church at the agency. A company of infantry snapped to attention and fired three volleys over the graves. As the coffins sank into the ground, the notes of "taps" mingled with the mourning wails of the Sioux.

In the hospital Bull Head thrashed in a coma and reopened his four wounds. On December 18 at 4:00 P.M. he died without regaining consciousness. The following afternoon he was honored at another military funeral.[38] Sergeant Little Eagle was returned to his Grand River home to be buried. The nearby Antelope settlement took the name Little Eagle.

Of the wounded, only Private Middle survived. Surgeons amputated a foot, and he recovered.

As the ceremonies concluded on December 17, McLaughlin opened the cemetery gate and walked slowly to Fort Yates. At the post cemetery he joined three army officers who stood beside another open grave. On the bottom rested a rough wooden box that contained the canvas-wrapped remains of Sitting Bull. As a "pagan," he did not qualify for burial in the Catholic cemetery, and besides, the Indian police objected. A detail of four soldiers—prisoners from the guard house—shoveled dirt into the hole.[39]

THE RESERVATION EQUIVALENT of a pauper's grave, combined with the grief and honor showered on the slain policemen, afforded a final touch of the irony and the poignancy that had dogged Sitting Bull's last years.

One of the few people equipped to appreciate this truth had once worn the scarlet tunic of the North-West Mounted Police. After reading the Winnipeg newspaper on December 16, James M. Walsh sat at his desk in the Dominion Coal, Coke & Transportation Company and scrawled his musings on a sheet of company stationery:

> I am glad to learn that Bull is relieved of his miseries even if it took
> the bullet to do it. A man who wields such power as Bull once did,
> that of a King, over a wild spirited people cannot endure abject

poverty slavery and beggery without suffering great mental pain and death is a relief. . . . Bull's confidence and belief in the Great Spirit was stronger than I ever saw in any other man. He trusted to him implicitly. . . . History does not tell us that a greater Indian than Bull ever lived, he was the Mohommat of his people the law and king maker of the Sioux.[40]

EPILOGUE

ALERTED BY A courier from Grand River, Colonel Drum led two companies of infantry out of Fort Yates early in the afternoon of December 15, 1890. Infantry and cavalry joined late that night on Oak Creek. Bearing the dead and wounded—and two "prisoners," Sitting Bull's stepson and Jumping Bull's son—they marched back to Fort Yates on December 16.

No sooner had Fechet's column disappeared on the road to Fort Yates than the dancers returned to their homes, collected their families and ponies, and fled up Grand River Valley. But the women had passed on Fechet's conciliatory message, and even before the troops reached Fort Yates on December 16 refugees had begun to attach themselves to the column. Prompted by couriers dispatched by McLaughlin, still more sought the security of the agency.[1]

The other survivors of the Grand River shootout traveled rapidly south, into the Cheyenne River Reservation. There they intruded into another theater of the "threatened hostilities" that General Miles sought to avert.

The drama in this theater ended tragically two weeks later. Big Foot, called Spotted Elk when he rode with Sitting Bull in the wars against the Long Knives, had earned himself a place on the list of troublemakers the government thought should be removed. On December 29, as the Seventh Cavalry, Long Hair's old outfit, attempted to disarm Big Foot and his band, tensions rose to the flashpoint and exploded in the bloody maelstrom of Wounded Knee. The slaughter not only dashed Miles's diplomatic offensive but poisoned relations between the Sioux and whites for generations to come.

Wounded Knee gave promise of still another Indian war. Miles averted it brilliantly. Combining diplomacy with a shrewd show of force, he gradually nudged the dancers, little by little, toward Pine Ridge Agency. On January 15, 1891, Kicking Bear laid his rifle at Bear Coat's feet, and the Ghost Dance "war" ended.

On New Year's Day of 1891, a detail of soldiers marched to the field of Wounded Knee. They gathered the mangled bodies of the Miniconjou victims, frozen in grotesque shapes by a winter storm, and buried them in a mass grave. Nearly two hundred people had been cut down.

The next day, on Grand River, a similar rite was enacted on a lesser scale. Congregational missionary Thomas L. Riggs led a Hunkpapa burial party into the Sitting Bull settlement. The cluster of cabins and, beyond, scattered tents and tipis of the Ghost Dancers stood as silent sentinels over the valley, deserted except for a gabble of chickens, a litter of puppies, and a dead horse. Fifteen white willow stakes thrust into the ground marked where each man, police and dancer, had fallen. A clump of three rose from a single spot ten feet in front of the doorway to Sitting Bull's cabin. In a log shed, properly attired for the spirit world, lay the bodies of the seven men killed with Sitting Bull.

Solemnly the group dug a long trench, placed the bodies in it side by side, then stood as Riggs prayed to the Christian God. After spreading a sheet of tenting over the bodies, the men shoveled dirt in the grave. The seven had received more care and homage than their chief had two weeks earlier.[2]

ALTHOUGH THE WAR had ended, the controversies had just begun— over how the war got started, over how it was prosecuted by military and civil authorities, over responsibility for the terrible bloodletting at Wounded Knee, and of course over how Sitting Bull came to be killed.

He had been murdered, charged a few eastern friends of the Indians. McLaughlin and Drum had quietly instructed the police to bring in a corpse, and the soldiers had stood by to make certain they did not fail in their duty.

McLaughlin could not have been more astonished at the furor that burst over his head, nor more angry at the wild stories hurled back and forth by the press. Instead of protesting the outcome, he felt, the public ought to be pouring out its gratitude to the men who had laid down their lives in the cause of progress.[3]

James McLaughlin weathered the storm and went on to become a highly regarded Indian inspector for the Interior Department. Laboring long past the retirement age, he died in office in 1923, at the age of seventy-four.

Despite McLaughlin's bright reputation, the historic record is peppered with enough allegations of assassination or murder to require a retrospective look at the question. It is twofold. Did McLaughlin order, or otherwise convey his wish, that Sitting Bull not be brought in alive? And even if he did not, did the police seize on the occasion to even old scores or remove a troublesome irritant from the Standing Rock community? As the fate of Bear's Rib, Bull Bear, Spotted Tail, and others demonstrated, assassination of divisive chiefs ran deep in Lakota tradition.

If McLaughlin used the police as a murder squad, either explicitly or implicitly, no compelling evidence survives to convict him. He cannot have been too sorry over the death of Sitting Bull, but he certainly was not prepared to risk the lives of his policemen for it. Confinement of Sitting Bull in some distant prison suited McLaughlin's purposes fully as well as death, and without much doubt that is what he intended.

The most persuasive refutation of the charge against the police lies in their own actions. However badly they handled the arrest, they clearly made every possible effort to get their prisoner out of the Sitting Bull settlement alive. Only when fired on and when the two senior officers were cut down did Bull Head and Red Tomahawk ensure, as the agent had ordered, that under no circumstances was Sitting Bull to be allowed to escape. As Captain Fechet pointed out in his official report, "If it had been the intention of the police to assassinate Sitting Bull, they could easily have done so before his friends arrived."[4]

Despite scattered dissent, the historic record convincingly acquits the police of a premeditated attempt to kill Sitting Bull. Rather than see him escape, they would kill him, as they did. But they did not plot that outcome.

The record also acquits the police of the related charge of drunkenness. A few members of both the agency and Grand River communities averred that the police imbibed heavily on the night of December 14 and that some, including Bull Head, were drunk when the arrest was attempted. Again the actions and testimony of the police are the best rejoinder. They denied they had been drinking, they did not behave as if intoxicated, and those who brought the charge could not be regarded as credible witnesses.

A more serious question for history is whether Sitting Bull's arrest and removal were justified. To answer no requires a total recasting of the attitudes and perceptions of the civil and military establishment. From their standpoint, it was completely warranted. The militant features of the Ghost Dance—bulletproof shirts, the millennial interment of the entire white race, the bellicose rhetoric of the dance leaders—decreed that any potential troublemaker not already in the Stronghold be removed from the theater of war.

In historical hindsight, by contrast, the only thing likely to have triggered violence was military aggression. Left to their own devices in the Stronghold, the dancers would probably have danced until the movement collapsed, either when the Messiah failed to appear in the spring or, more likely, when cold and hunger dampened their fervor.

Patience and diplomacy, combined with avoidance of provocation, offered the army better solutions than saber-rattling or an assault on the Stronghold. The slaughter at Wounded Knee, infuriating the dancers, furnished the provocation. In the end, however, Miles triumphed through patience and diplomacy, albeit backed by the threat of force.

Sitting Bull was not going to Pine Ridge to make trouble but "to know this pray"—to investigate the Ghost Dance at its source among the Sioux. The high priests of the Ghost Dance were in the Stronghold, and that is probably where Sitting Bull would have headed.

He would not have gotten there. His departure from Standing Rock, however pacific in intent, would certainly have set off the same military scramble that Big Foot's actions did, with consequences possibly similar to Wounded Knee.

To Indians practicing the very principle of religious freedom that the white people celebrated, the government's reasoning made no sense. If whites could choose among all the mutations of Protestantism and Catholicism, so the Indians should have the same right to choose between them or, if they wanted, a Ghost Dance religion that drew on Christian principles. If whites could be suffered to predict a second coming or any other kind of millennium, including apocalypse, why should not the Indians be indulged a similar anticipation? And if white people could travel for spiritual purposes, why should not Sitting Bull enjoy the same privilege?

In retrospect, neither Big Foot nor Sitting Bull, if allowed to proceed unhindered to his destination, was likely to have provoked violence— certainly not on the scale of Wounded Knee. The decision makers, however, dealt in prospect, not retrospect, and in that contemporary climate they harbored no doubts about the wisdom of their decision to arrest Sitting Bull.

SITTING BULL HAD rested in his grave less than two months when North Dakota's Senator Lyman R. Casey urged the Indian Office to move swiftly to acquire as many of the chief's personal effects as possible.[5] The process of acquiring Sitting Bull's effects got underway at once and has been in progress ever since.

What North Dakota really wanted, and got, was Sitting Bull's cabin, to form part of the state's exhibition at the Chicago World's Fair of 1892. With Interior Department blessing, state agents entered into negotiations with Sitting Bull's widows and by the end of 1891 had removed the structure log by log for reconstruction in Chicago. McLaughlin certified it as the residence in which Sitting Bull had lived from the spring of 1884 until his death and where he had been killed on December 15, 1890. The agent preferred that it be presented not as Sitting Bull's home, but as the place where Indian police "made such a gallant and determined stand in up-holding the Government against their own race and kindred." The public saw it, of course, as the home of the celebrated chief who had wiped out Custer and his troopers.[6]

Another coveted possession of Sitting Bull's was the gray circus horse. Buffalo Bill himself bought the animal from the widows. When the Wild West opened at the Chicago World's Fair, the horse led the grand proces-sion bearing a man carrying the American flag.[7]

But the Sitting Bull "effects" destined to fuel the liveliest interest, as well as bitter contention, were his own bones. Almost at once the press raised a cry that the coffin had not contained Sitting Bull's body. McLaughlin easily refuted the charge with the testimony of the Fort Yates post surgeon and other military officers who had witnessed the disposal of the body.[8]

But Sitting Bull was not forever to rest in peace. Hunkpapas who remembered him admiringly agitated to have his body moved from the military cemetery to Grand River and suitably memorialized. Agents and their Indian allies stoutly resisted.

One who would not let the matter drop was Clarence Gray Eagle, son of Sitting Bull's brother-in-law, who as a boy had watched from a clump of brush as his father helped the policemen seize and then kill Sitting Bull.

Acting with and on behalf of Sitting Bull's grandchildren, Gray Eagle pushed the proposal doggedly but unsuccessfully.

The issue acquired new urgency after World War II, when construction of the Missouri River dams got underway. Initial plans called for the Fort Yates flats to be inundated, and Gray Eagle again sought Sitting Bull's removal to Grand River. However, North Dakota, which had spruced up the grave and was now reluctant to lose a celebrity, refused to grant an exhumation permit. In April 1953, therefore, Gray Eagle led an expedition that swooped down on the gravesite in the dark of night and carried off the object of all the controversy. Sitting Bull was reburied on a scenic site overlooking the Missouri a short distance below where the mouth of Grand River lay beneath a great reservoir. Twenty tons of steel rails and concrete ensured that he would stay there, and a bust sculpted by Korczak Ziolkowski provided the memorialization.[9]

But is he truly there? Subsequent research by North Dakota historians established a reasonable doubt that Gray Eagle's grave robbers had got Sitting Bull, or at least all of his bones. The North Dakota site, which was not flooded after all, bears a marker hedging the question: "He was buried here but his grave has been vandalized many times."[10]

There are thus three, even four, possibilities. Sitting Bull's grave is in the old post cemetery of Fort Yates, where he was interred on December 17, 1890. He is buried on the Missouri Valley heights opposite the city of Mobridge, South Dakota, where Gray Eagle and his friends sank him beneath concrete in 1953. He is in both places, part of him in North Dakota, part in South Dakota. Or he is in neither place; the record is replete with hints that the grave was opened more than once between 1890 and 1953. It is conceivable that some grave robber preceded Gray Eagle and that Sitting Bull's bones no longer exist or, if they do, now lie in an unmarked and unknown grave.

MORE THAN HIS bones, Sitting Bull's memory endures, the more so since the onset of the "red power" movement of the 1960s. The polemics of that time gained the Indian new attention and new respect beyond his own world. They also, laying a heavy burden of guilt on whites for the conduct of their ancestors toward Indians, created a romanticized caricature of the real Indians of horse-and-buffalo times.

In this distortion of history, Sitting Bull has not escaped canonization. His name evokes images of all the appealing characteristics that people like to assign to the Plains Indians, whether grounded in the historic record or not. In this rendering, as misshapen as the portrait etched by General Sheridan or Agent McLaughlin, Sitting Bull emerges as a paragon of virtues he would not have recognized.

The reality is more compelling. He was a real Indian, and a real person, completely faithful to his culture. He earned greatness as a Hunkpapa patriot, steadfastly true to the values and principles and institutions that guided his tribe. In this guise, not as some generic ideal Indian of the popular imagination, his memory achieves contemporary significance.

ACKNOWLEDGMENTS

HEADING THE LIST of those deserving my gratitude is anthropologist Raymond J. DeMallie of Indiana University. A leading authority on Lakota language and culture, Ray read all the chapters and offered extensive comment. He saved me from many embarrassing errors and offered insights into Lakota ways and thought that had eluded me. In addition to his personal comment, his distinguished publications, cited in the notes and sources, proved indispensible. He cannot be held responsible for my mistakes, but he contributed more to my book than even he understands.

Others who critically read the entire manuscript and decisively influenced its final shape were my agent, Carl Brandt, my editor at Holt, Jack Macrae, and, as always my severest critic, my wife, Melody Webb. To all three I am deeply indebted for urging revisions that greatly improved the book.

Among library and archival staffs deserving special notice and thanks are these: at the University of Oklahoma Library, Brad Koplowitz and Brad E. Gernand; at the South Dakota Historical Society, Ann B. Jenks and Nancy Tystad Koupal; at the North Dakota Historical Society, James E. Sperry, Gerald G. Newborg, and Norman Paulson; at the Glenbow Institute in Calgary, Alberta, Hugh A. Dempsey and Douglas E. Cass; at the Beinecke Library at Yale University, George A. Miles; at the National Archives and Records Administration in Washington, D.C., Michael Musick; at the Nebraska State Historical Society, Eli Paul; at the Harold B. Lee Library at Brigham Young University, David J. Whittaker; at the National Archives of Canada, Roderick McFall; at the Provincial Archives of Manitoba, Barry Hyman; at the Assumption Abbey Archives in Richardton, North Dakota, Fr. Odo Muggli; at the Southwest Museum in Los

Angeles, Michael Wagner; at the Academy of Natural Sciences of Philadelphia, Karen D. Stevens; at the Newberry Library in Chicago, Frederick E. Hoxie and Fr. Peter Powell; at the Jesuit Missouri Province Archives, Nancy Merz; and at the Montana Historical Society, Lory Morrow.

For comment, advice, and source material I am indebted to the following: Harry H. Anderson of the Milwaukee County Historical Society; S. George Ellsworth of Utah State University; Brian W. Dippie of the University of Victoria, British Columbia; Paul Feese of the Buffalo Bill Museum in Cody, Wyoming; Stephen Feraca, formerly of the Bureau of Indian Affairs; the late A. M. Gibson of the University of Oklahoma; Jerome A. Greene, Paul L. Hedren, and Jock F. Whitworth of the National Park Service; Charles E. Hanson of the Museum of the Fur Trade in Chadron, Nebraska; Richard G. Hardorff of DeKalb, Illinois; Brian Hubner of Parks Canada; James S. Hutchins of the Smithsonian Institution; Paul A. Hutton of the University of New Mexico; William L. Lang of Hood River, Oregon; John D. McDermott of Sheridan, Wyoming; James Mundie and Cornelius J. O'Sullivan of Houston, Texas; Joseph C. Porter of the Joslyn Art Museum in Omaha; Erwin N. Thompson of Golden, Colorado; James Wengert of the Veterans Administration in Omaha; Robin W. Winks of Yale University; and Stephen D. Youngkin of Salt Lake City.

Special thanks are due Lee and David Blumberg of Coral Gables, Florida, who first introduced me to their collection of Henry Raschen paintings nearly thirty years ago and who generously provided the color transparency and permission to reproduce the portrait of Sitting Bull that appears on the frontispiece of this book. (Raschen family tradition holds that this portrait was painted from life, though Raschen's visit to Standing Rock has not been documented.)

Ron Tyler of the Texas State Historical Association and University of Texas, whose scholarly achievements range far from Sitting Bull, nevertheless played a critical role in this book, which was written during my years in Texas. Ron arranged for me to be anointed a visiting scholar at the University of Texas in Austin, which enabled me to draw heavily on the excellent resources and splendidly helpful staff of the university library, to whom I express my heartfelt appreciation.

Finally, I must acknowledge the aid of George Kush of Monarch, Alberta. He not only introduced me to the North-West Mounted Police and the scenes of their early achievements in Alberta and Saskatchewan but also took me into his home during my exploration of Sitting Bull's Canadian haunts. George's encyclopedic knowledge of the Mounted Police and his irrespressible enthusiasm for their history provided both information and inspiration.

SOURCES

THE MOST IMPORTANT body of source material for this book is the Walter S. Campbell Collection at the University of Oklahoma Library in Norman. Campbell, whose pen name was Stanley Vestal, pursued his research for a biography of Sitting Bull during the late 1920s and early 1930s, while many of Sitting Bull's associates still lived on the reservations in North and South Dakota. Boxes 100 to 116 are devoted mainly to Sitting Bull. Most valuable are Vestal's interviews with White Bull, One Bull, Old Bull, and other old Indians who knew Sitting Bull intimately. These are recorded on fifty-nine pencil tablets filed in boxes 105 and 106.

Second in importance are the official records of the United States and Canadian governments. The annual reports of the U.S. Secretary of War and Commissioner of Indian Affairs are printed in the U.S. Serial Set, while the annual reports of the Canadian North-West Mounted Police and the Minister of the Interior are printed in the House of Commons Sessional Papers. The U.S. Serials also include many documents, some voluminous, dealing with special subjects on which the Congress had requested to be informed.

Far more extensive are the unpublished records of both governments, most of which are available on microfilm. The following microfilm publications of the U.S. National Archives and Records Administration were consulted for this book:

Record Group 75, Records of the Bureau of Indian Affairs, microfilm publication M234, letters received from the following entities: Dakota Superintendency 1861–80; Cheyenne River Agency 1871–80; Grand River Agency 1871–75; Montana Superintendency 1871–80; Red Cloud Agency 1871–80; Spotted Tail Agency 1875–80; Standing Rock Agency 1875–80; Upper Missouri Agency

1852–69; Upper Platte Agency 1846–70. RG 75, Records of the Dakota Superintendency, 1861–78, M1016. RG 75, Special Case 188, relating to the Ghost Dance. RG 75, Indian Census Rolls, Standing Rock Agency 1885–93, M595.

RG 393, Records of U.S. Army Continental Commands, Special Files of the Military Division of the Missouri 1863–85, M1495. Also consulted in this record group, not published on microfilm, were letters received by the Department of the Northwest and the Department of Dakota, and letters sent and received by Forts Buford, Stevenson, Yates, Randall, Keogh, and the post at Poplar River.

RG 94, Letters received by the Office of the Adjutant General, M666, arranged in the following special files: 2019 AGO 1871 (Sioux attacks on Gallatin Valley and Milk River); 3323 AGO 1872 (Battle of Arrow Creek); 3512 AGO 1872 (Stanley Expedition of 1872); 3159 AGO 1873 (Stanley Expedition of 1873); 1224 AGO 1874 (Arrest of Rain-in-the-Face); 3517 AGO 1875 (Sioux aggression against Crow Agency); 6160 AGO 1875 (Operations against the Sioux, November 1875–July 1876); 2440 AGO 1876 (Battle of Powder River); 3570 AGO 1876 (Battle of the Rosebud); 3770 AGO 1876 (Battle of the Little Bighorn); 4163 AGO 1876 ("Sioux War Papers," 1876–96).

Pertinent Canadian records are also available on microfilm: RG 7, Records of the Governor General's Office (T-1385, T-1386, and T-1387, containing files 2001 parts 3a and 3d, and files 2001–9); RG 10, Records of the Indian Affairs Branch (C-10114, file 8589, parts 1 and 2); and RG 18, Records of the Royal Canadian Mounted Police (T-6268 and T-6269). A warehouse fire destroyed most of the early Mounted Police records, but copies of the more important documents are found in the Indian Affairs and Governor General records.

Additional manuscript collections consulted include: James McLaughlin Papers, Assumption Abbey Archives, Richardton, N.D. (microfilm). James M. Walsh Papers, Provincial Archives of Manitoba, Winnipeg (microfilm). Walter M. Camp Collection, Harold B. Lee Library, Brigham Young University, Provo, Utah. Another extensive Camp Collection is in the Lily Library, Indiana University. Copies of many of these papers are in the Kenneth Hammer Collection at Brigham Young. Eli S. Ricker Collection, Nebraska State Historical Society, Lincoln. George B. Grinnell Collection, Southwest Museum, Los Angeles. Sherman Miles Compilation of Nelson A. Miles's letters to his wife, U.S. Military Academy Library, West Point. At the Huntington Library, San Marino, California: papers of Thomas L. Sweeny and Frank D. Baldwin. At the North Dakota Historical Society, Bismarck: papers of Orrin G. Libby, Lewis F. Crawford, and E. D. Mossman. At the Beinecke Library, Yale University, New Haven, Connecticut: papers of Alfred Sully, Samuel R. Curtis, Charles A. R. Dimon, and George Bent. At the South Dakota Historical Society, Pierre: papers of Mary C. Collins and Doane Robinson. At the Glenbow Institute, Calgary, Alberta: papers of Richard Nevitt, Lucien Hanks, Edgar Dewdney, and William Morris Graham. At the Library of Congress: papers of William T. Sherman and the Sherman-Sheridan letters. At the National Anthropological Archives of the Smithsonian Institution, the Sitting Bull autobiographical pictographs and other data pertaining to Sitting Bull and his associates.

Of newspapers, the *Bismark Tribune* was especially useful. Other newspapers consulted: *Army and Navy Journal, Army and Navy Register, Chicago Times, Chicago Tribune, Fort Benton Record, Harpers Weekly, Helena Herald, National Republican, Manitoba Free Press, New York Herald, New York Times, New York World, Saskatchewan Herald, St. Paul Pioneer Press, Washington Post.*

PUBLISHED MATERIAL

Allison, Edwin H. "Sitting Bull's Birthplace." *South Dakota Historical Collections* 6 (1912): 270–72.

―――――. "Surrender of Sitting Bull." Ed. Doane Robinson. *South Dakota Historical Collections* 6 (1910–12): 231–70.

Anderson, Gary C. "Early Dakota Migration and Intertribal War: A Revision." *Western Historical Quarterly* 11 (January 1980): 17–36.

Anderson, Harry H. "The Controversial Sioux Amendment to the Fort Laramie Treaty of 1851." *Nebraska History* 37 (September 1956): 201–20.

―――――. "Indian Peace Talkers and the Conclusion of the Sioux War of 1876." *Nebraska History* 44 (December 1963): 233–54.

―――――. "A Sioux Pictorial Account of General Terry's Council at Fort Walsh, October 17, 1877." *North Dakota History* 27 (July 1955): 93–116.

Athearn, Robert G. "The Fort Buford 'Massacre.' " *Mississippi Valley Historical Review* 41 (March 1955): 675–84.

Athearn, Robert G., ed. "A Winter Campaign against the Sioux." *Mississippi Valley Historical Review* 35 (September 1948): 272–85.

Atkins, C. J., ed. "Log of Steamer Robert Campbell, Jr., from St. Louis to Fort Benton, Montana Territory." *North Dakota Historical Society Collections* 2 (1908): 267–84.

Bailey, Paul. *Wovoka, The Indian Messiah*. Los Angeles: Westernlore Press, 1957.

Barry, David F. *Indian Notes on the Custer Battle*. Baltimore: privately printed, 1937.

Barsness, John, and William Dickinson. "The Sully Expedition of 1864." *Montana the Magazine of Western History* 16 (July 1966): 23–29.

Bean, Geraldine. "General Alfred Sully and the Northwest Indian Expedition." *North Dakota History* 33 (Summer 1966): 240–59.

Bland, Thomas A. *A Brief History of the Late Military Invasion of the Home of the Sioux*. Washington, D.C.: National Indian Defense Association, 1891.

Blish, Helen H. *A Pictographic History of the Oglala Sioux*. Lincoln: University of Nebraska Press, 1967.

Board of Commissioners. *Minnesota in the Civil and Indian Wars, 1861–1865.* St. Paul: Pioneer Press Co., 1890.

Boyes, W. *Custer's Black White Man.* Washington, D.C.: privately printed, 1972.

Braden, Charles. "The Yellowstone Expedition of 1873." *Journal of the United States Cavalry Association* 16 (October 1905): 218–41.

Bradley, James H. "Account of the Attempts to Build a Town at the Mouth of the Mussellshell River." *Montana Historical Society Contributions* 2 (1896): 302–13.

————. "Adventures of Three Wolfers." *Montana Historical Society Contributions* 8 (1917): 137–39.

————. "Affairs at Fort Benton from 1831 to 1869. From Lieut. Bradley's Journal." *Montana Historical Society Contributions* 3 (1900): 201–87.

————. "Capture of Two Mackinaws by Indians on the Missouri River and the Massacre of Their Crews." *Montana Historical Society Contributions* 8 (1917): 142–44.

————. "Journal of James H. Bradley, The Sioux Campaign of 1876 under Command of General John Gibbon." *Montana Historical Society Contributions* 2 (1896): 140–228. Also published as *The March of the Montana Column: A Prelude to the Custer Disaster.* Norman: University of Oklahoma Press, 1991.

————. "Yellowstone Expedition of 1874." *Montana Historical Society Contributions* 8 (1917): 105–26.

Brown, D. Alexander. *The Galvanized Yankees.* Urbana: University of Illinois Press, 1963.

Brown, Joseph Epes, ed. *The Sacred Pipe: Black Elk's Account of the Seven Rites of the Oglala Sioux.* Norman: University of Oklahoma Press, 1953.

Burdick, Usher L. *The Last Days of Sitting Bull, Sioux Medicine Chief.* Baltimore: Wirth Bros., 1941.

Carroll, John M., ed. *The Arrest and Killing of Sitting Bull.* Glendale, Calif.: Arthur H. Clark Co., 1986.

Cleveland, William J. "Rev. William J. Cleveland's Investigation of the Causes of the Sioux Trouble." Indian Rights Association, *Ninth Annual Report,* 1891.

Clow, Richmond L. "Mad Bear: William S. Harney and the Sioux Expedition of 1855–56." *Nebraska History* 61 (Summer 1980): 133–51.

————, ed. "The Autobiography of Mary C. Collins." *South Dakota Historical Collections* 41 (1982): 1–66.

Collins, Dabney Otis. "The Fight for Sitting Bull's Bones." *American West* 3 (Winter 1966): 72–78.

Collins, Ethel A. "Pioneer Experiences of Horatio H. Larned." *North Dakota Historical Collections* 7 (1925): 1–58.

Coyer, Richard J., ed. "This 'Wild Region of the Far West': Lieutenant Sweeny's Letters from Fort Pierre, 1855–56." *Nebraska History* 63 (Summer 1982): 232–54.

Creelman, James. *On the Great Highway: The Wanderings and Adventures of a Special Correspondent.* Boston: Lothrop Publishing Co., 1901.

Cronau, Rudolph. "My Visit among the Hostile Dakota Indians and How They Became My Friends." *South Dakota Historical Collections* 22 (1946): 410–25.

Crook, George. *General George Crook: His Autobiography.* Ed. Martin F. Schmitt. Norman: University of Oklahoma Press, 1946.

Culbertson, Thaddeus A. "Journal of an Expedition to the Mauvaises Terres and the Upper Missouri in 1850." Fifth Annual Report Board of Regents of the Smithsonian Institution, 1850, in Senate Miscellaneous Documents, 34th Congress, special session, no. 1.

DeBarthe, Joe. *Life and Adventures of Frank Grouard.* Ed. Edgar I. Stewart. Norman: University of Oklahoma Press, 1957.

De Girardin, M. E. "A Trip to the Bad Lands in 1849." *South Dakota Historical Review* 1 (January 1936): 56–58.

DeLoria, Ella. *Speaking of Indians.* New York: Friendship Press, 1944.

DeLoria, Vine V., Sr. "The Standing Rock Reservation: A Personal Reminiscence." *South Dakota Review* 9 (Summer 1971): 169–95.

DeMallie, Raymond J. "The Sioux in Dakota and Montana Territories: Cultural and Historical Background of the Ogden B. Read Collection," in *Vestiges of a Proud Nation: The Ogden B. Read Northern Plains Indian Collection.* Burlington, Vt.: Robert Hall Fleming Museum, 1986.

————, ed. *The Sixth Grandfather: Black Elk's Teachings Given to John G. Neihardt.* Lincoln: University of Nebraska Press, 1984.

————, and Douglas H. Parks, eds. *Sioux Indian Religion.* Norman: University of Oklahoma Press, 1987.

Dempsey, Hugh A. *Crowfoot: Chief of the Blackfeet.* Norman: University of Oklahoma Press, 1972.

Denig, Edwin Thomas. *Five Indian Tribes of the Upper Missouri.* Ed. John C. Ewers. Norman: University of Oklahoma Press, 1961.

Denny, Sir Cecil. *The Law Marches West.* Toronto: J. M. Dent and Sons, 1939.

Densmore, Frances. *Teton Sioux Music.* Bureau of American Ethnology Bulletin 61. Washington, D.C.: Government Printing Office, 1918.

De Smet, Fr. Pierre-Jean. *Life, Letters, and Travels of Father Pierre-Jean De Smet, S.J., 1801–1873* . . . Ed. H. M. Chittenden and A. T. Richardson. 4 vols. New York: Francis P. Harper, 1905.

Dorsey, James O. "The Social Organization of the Siouan Tribes. *Journal of American Folk-Lore* 4 (1891): 257–63.

————. "A Study of Siouan Cults." Bureau of American Ethnology Eleventh Annual Report, 1889–90. Washington, D.C.: Government Printing Office, 1894.

Dykshorn, Jan, ed. "Sitting Bull Collection." *South Dakota History* 5 (Summer 1975): 245–65.

Eastman, Elaine Goodale. "The Ghost Dance War and Wounded Knee Massacre of 1890–91." *Nebraska History* 26 (January–March 1945): 26–42.

English, Abner N. "Dakota's First Soldiers: History of the First Dakota Cavalry, 1862–1865." *South Dakota Historical Collections* 9 (1918): 241–307.

Ewers, John C. "Intertribal Warfare As the Precursor of Indian-White Warfare on the Northern Great Plains." *Western Historical Quarterly* 6 (October 1975): 397–410.

————, ed. *Indian Life on the Upper Missouri*. Norman: University of Oklahoma Press, 1968.

Fechet, Edmond G. "The Capture of Sitting Bull." *South Dakota Historical Collections* 4 (1908): 185–93.

————. "The True Story of the Death of Sitting Bull." *Proceedings and Collections of the Nebraska State Historical Society*, 2d series 2 (1898): 179–89.

Finerty, John F. *War-Path and Bivouac: or, The Conquest of the Sioux*. Norman: University of Oklahoma Press, 1961.

[Fisk, James L.] "Expeditions of Capt. Jas. L. Fisk to the Gold Mines of Idaho and Montana, 1864–1966." *North Dakota Historical Collections* 2 (1908): 421–61.

Fiske, Frank Bennett. *Life and Death of Sitting Bull*. Fort Yates, N.D.: Pioneer-Arrow, 1933.

Fitzgerald, Sister Mary Clement. "Bishop Marty and His Sioux Missions, 1876–1896." *South Dakota Historical Collections* 20 (1940): 523–58.

Friswold, Carroll. *The Killing of Chief Crazy Horse*. Glendale, Calif.: Arthur H. Clark Co., 1976.

Frost, Lawrence A. *Custer's 7th Cav and the Campaign of 1873*. El Segundo, Calif.: Upton & Sons, 1986.

Gibbon, John. "Hunting Sitting Bull." *American Catholic Quarterly Review* 2 (October 1877): 665–94.

————. "Last Summer's Expedition against the Sioux and Its Great Catastrophe." *American Catholic Quarterly Review* 2 (April 1877): 271–304.

Goodwin, Carol G. "The Letters of Private Milton Spencer, 1862–1865: A Soldier's View of Military Life on the Northern Plains." *North Dakota History* 37 (Fall 1970): 233–69.

Graham, W. A. *The Custer Myth: A Source Book of Custeriana*. Harrisburg, Pa.: Stackpole Co., 1953.

Gray, John S. "Arikara Scouts with Custer." *North Dakota History* 35 (Spring 1968): 443–78.

————. "Bloody Knife, Ree Scout for Custer." *Westerners Brand Book* (Chicago) 17 (February 1961): 89–96.

————. "Captain Clifford's Newspaper Dispatches." *Westerners Brand Book* (Chicago) 27 (January 1971): 81–82, 88.

————. "Captain Clifford's Story of the Sioux War of 1876." *Westerners Brand Book* (Chicago) 26 (December 1969): 73–78; (January 1970): 81–83, 86–88; 29 (August 1972): 41–43, 48.

————. *Centennial Campaign: The Sioux War of 1876*. Norman: University of Oklahoma Press, 1988.

————. *Custer's Last Campaign: Mitch Boyer and the Little Bighorn Reconstructed.* Lincoln: University of Nebraska Press, 1991.

————. "Custer Throws a Boomerang." *Montana the Magazine of Western History* 11 (April 1961): 2–12.

————. "Frank Grouard: Kanaka Scout or Mulatto Renegade?" *Westerners Brand Book* (Chicago) 16 (October 1959): 57–59, 60–64.

————. "Peace-Talkers from Standing Rock Agency." *Westerners Brand Book* (Chicago) 23 (May 1966): 17–29.

————. "Sitting Bull Strikes the Glendive Supply Trains." *Westerners Brand Book* (Chicago) 28 (June 1971): 25–27, 31–32.

————. "The Story of Mrs. Picotte-Galpin, a Sioux Heroine." *Montana the Magazine of Western History* 36 (Spring 1986): 2–21; (Summer 1986): 2–21.

————. "What Made Johnny [Bruguier] Run?" *Montana the Magazine of Western History* 14 (April 1964): 34–49.

Greene, Jerome A. *Evidence and the Custer Enigma: A Reconstruction of Indian-Military History.* Kansas City, Kans.: Kansas City Posse of Westerners, 1973.

————. *Slim Buttes: An Episode of the Great Sioux War.* Norman: University of Oklahoma Press, 1982.

————. *Yellowstone Command: Colonel Nelson A. Miles and the Great Sioux War.* Lincoln: University of Nebraska Press, 1991.

Grinnell, George B. "Account of the Northern Cheyenne Concerning the Messiah Superstition." *Journal of American Folk-Lore* 4 (January–March 1891): 65–66.

————. *The Fighting Cheyennes.* Norman: University of Oklahoma Press, 1956.

Guthrie, Chester L., and Leo L. Gerald. "Upper Missouri Agency: An Account of the Indian Administration on the Frontier." *Pacific Historical Review* 10 (March 1941): 47–56.

Hafen, LeRoy R., and Ann W., eds. *Powder River Campaigns and Sawyer's Expedition of 1865: A Documentary Account Comprising Official Reports, Diaries, Contemporary Newspaper Accounts, and Personal Narratives.* Glendale, Calif.: Arthur H. Clark Co., 1961.

Haines, Francis, ed. "Letters of an Army Captain on the Sioux Campaign of 1879–80." *Pacific Northwest Quarterly* 39 (January 1948): 39–64.

Hammer, Kenneth. "Sitting Bull's Bones." English Westerners Society *Brand Book* 23 (Winter 1984): 1–8.

————, ed. *Custer in '76: Walter Camp's Notes on the Custer Fight.* Provo, Utah: Brigham Young University Press, 1976.

Hampton, H. D. "The Powder River Indian Expedition of 1865." *Montana the Magazine of Western History* 14 (Autumn 1964): 2–15.

Hardorff, Richard G. *Hokahey! A Good Day to Die! The Indian Casualties of the Custer Fight.* Spokane, Wash.: Arthur H. Clark Co., 1992.

————. *Lakota Recollections of the Custer Fight: New Sources of Indian-Military History.* Spokane, Wash.: Arthur H. Clark Co., 1991.

————. *Markers, Artifacts and Indian Testimony: Preliminary Findings on the Custer Battle*. Short Hills, N.J.: W. Donald Horn, 1985.

————. *The Oglala Lakota Crazy Horse: A Preliminary Genealogical Study and An Annotated Listing of Primary Sources*. Mattituck, N.Y.: J.M. Carroll & Co., 1985.

Hassrick, Royal B. *The Sioux: Life and Customs of a Warrior Society*. Norman: University of Oklahoma Press, 1964.

Hayden, F. V. "Contributions to the Ethnography and Philology of the Indian Tribes of the Missouri Valley." *Transactions of the American Philosophical Society*, n.s. 12, pt. 2 (Philadelphia: American Philosophical Society, 1862): 232–377.

Hewett, J. N. B., ed. *Journal of Rudolph Frederick Kurz*. Lincoln: University of Nebraska Press, 1970.

Higginbotham, N. A. "The Wind-Roan Bear Winter Count." *Plains Anthropologist* 26 (February 1981): 1–42.

Hilger, M. Inez. "The Narrative of Oscar One Bull." *Mid-America* 28 (July 1946): 149–72.

Hilger, Nicholas. "General Alfred Sully's Expedition of 1864." *Montana Historical Society Contributions* 2 (1896): 314–28.

Hinmann, Eleanor H. "Oglala Sources on the Life of Crazy Horse." *Nebraska History* 57 (Spring 1976): 1–51.

Holley, Frances C. *Once Their Home: or, Our Legacy from the Dahkotahs*. Chicago: Donohue & Henneberry, 1892.

Hoover, Herbert T. "Sitting Bull." In *American Indian Leaders: Studies in Diversity*, ed. R. David Edmunds. Lincoln: University of Nebraska Press, 1980.

Hosmer, J. Allen. "A Trip to the States [1856]." *South Dakota Historical Review* 1 (July 1936): 177–224.

Howard, James H. *Dakota Winter Counts as a Source of Plains History*. Bureau of American Ethnology Bulletin 173, no. 61 (1960): 335–416.

————. "Two Dakota Winter Count Texts." *Plains Anthropologist* 5 (December 1955): 13–30.

————. "Two Teton Dakota Winter Count Texts." *North Dakota History* 27 (1960): 66–79.

————. *The Warrior Who Killed Custer: The Personal Narrative of Chief Joseph White Bull*. Lincoln: University of Nebraska Press, 1968.

Howe, George F., ed. "Expedition to the Yellowstone River in 1873: Letters of a Young Cavalry Officer." *Mississippi Valley Historical Review* 39 (December 1952): 519–34.

Hutchins, James S. "Poison in the Pemmican: The Yellowstone Wagon Road Prospecting Expedition of 1874." *Montana the Magazine of Western History* 8 (July 1958): 8–25.

Hutton, Paul A. *Phil Sheridan and His Army*. Lincoln: University of Nebraska Press, 1985.

Hutton, Paul A., ed. *The Custer Reader*. Lincoln: University of Nebraska Press, 1992.

Jackson, Donald. *Custer's Gold: The United States Cavalry Expedition of 1874*. New Haven, Conn.: Yale University Press, 1966.

Joyner, Christopher C. "The Hegira of Sitting Bull To Canada: Diplomatic Realpolitik, 1876–1881." *Journal of the West* 13 (April 1974): 6–18.

Kappler, Charles J., comp. *Indian Affairs: Laws and Treaties*. 2 vols. Washington, D.C.: Government Printing Office, 1904.

Kasper, Shirl. *Annie Oakley*. Norman: University of Oklahoma Press, 1992.

Kelly, Fanny. *My Captivity among the Sioux Indians*. New York: Corinth Books, 1962.

Kimball, James P. "Fort Buford." *North Dakota Historical Quarterly* 4 (January 1930): 73–77.

Kingsbury, David L. "Sully's Expedition against the Sioux in 1864." *Minnesota Historical Society Collections* 8 (1898): 449–62.

Kingsbury, George M. *History of Dakota Territory*. 5 vols: Chicago: S. J. Clarke Publishing Co., 1915.

Koch, Peter. "Life at Musselshell in 1869 and 1870." *Montana Historical Society Contributions* 2 (1896): 292–303.

Kraus, Herbert, and Gary D. Olson. *Prelude to Glory: A Newspaper Accounting of Custer's 1874 Expedition to the Black Hills*. Sioux Falls, S.D.: Brevet Press, 1974.

Larpenteur, Charles. *Forty Years a Fur Trader on the Upper Missouri, 1833–1872*. Ed. Milo M. Quaife. Chicago: Lakeside Classics/R. R. Donnelley & Sons, 1933.

Lass, William E. *A History of Steamboating on the Upper Missouri River*. Lincoln: University of Nebraska Press, 1962.

Lingk, Ray W. "The Northwestern Indian Expedition: The Sully Trail (1864) from the Little Missouri River to the Yellowstone River." *North Dakota History* 24 (October 1957): 181–200.

Lounsberry, Clement A. *Early History of North Dakota*. Washington, D.C.: Liberty Press, 1919.

Lowe, Percival G. *Five Years a Dragoon and Other Adventures on the Great Plains*. Ed. Don Russell. Norman: University of Oklahoma Press, 1965.

McDonnell, Anne, ed. "The Fort Benton Journal, 1854–56, and the Fort Sarpy Journal, 1855–56." *Montana Historical Society Contributions* 10 (1940): 100 87.

MacEwan, John W. G. *Sitting Bull: The Years in Canada*. Edmonton, Alta.: Hurtig Publishers, 1973.

McGinnis, Anthony. *Counting Coups and Cutting Horses: Intertribal Warfare on the Northern Plains, 1738–1889*. Evergreen, Colo.: Cordillera Press, 1990.

McLaughlin, James. *An Account of the Death of Sitting Bull and of the Circumstances Attending It*. Philadelphia: Indian Rights Association, 1891.

McLaughlin, James. *My Friend the Indian*. Lincoln: University of Nebraska Press, 1989.

Mallery, Garrick. "A Calendar of the Dakota Nation." *United States Geological Survey Bulletin* 3, no. 1 (April 1877).

_____. *Pictographs of North American Indians*. Bureau of American Ethnology Fourth Annual Report, 1882–83. Washington, D.C.: Government Printing Office, 1886. Pp. 89–146.

_____. *Picture Writing of the American Indians*. Bureau of American Ethnology Tenth Annual Report, 1888–89. Washington, D.C.: Government Printing Office, 1893. Pp. 266–328.

Mangum, Neil C. *Battle of the Rosebud: Prelude to the Little Bighorn*. El Segundo, Calif.: Upton & Sons, 1987.

Manzione, Joseph. *"I Am Looking to the North for My Life": Sitting Bull, 1876–1881*. Salt Lake City: University of Utah Press, 1991.

Mark, Constant R. "Letellier's Autobiography." *South Dakota Historical Collections* 4 (1908): 215–53.

Marquis, Thomas B. *Memoirs of a White Crow Indian*. Lincoln: University of Nebraska Press, 1974.

_____. *A Warrior Who Fought Custer*. Minneapolis: Midwest Company, 1931.

Marsh, Elias J. "Journal of Elias J. Marsh." *South Dakota Historical Review* 1 (January 1936): 79–125.

Marty, Martin. "Abbot Martin Visits Sitting Bull." *Annals of the Catholic Indian Missions of America* 2 (January 1878): 7–10.

Mattison, Ray H., ed. "The Fisk Expedition of 1864: The Diary of William L. Larned." *North Dakota History* 36 (Summer 1969): 227–38.

Meyer, Roy W. *History of the Santee Sioux*. Lincoln: University of Nebraska Press, 1967.

Meyers, Augustus. "Dakota in the Fifties." *South Dakota Historical Collections* 10 (1920): 130–94.

Mirsky, Jeannette. "The Dakota." In Margaret Mead, ed., *Cooperation and Competition among Primitive Peoples*. New York: McGraw-Hill Book Co., 1937.

Mooney, James. *The Ghost-Dance Religion and the Sioux Outbreak of 1890*. Fourteenth Annual Report of the Bureau of American Ethnology, 1892–93, pt. 2. Washington, D.C.: Government Printing Office, 1896; Lincoln: University of Nebraska Press, 1991.

Morton, Desmond. "Cavalry or Police: Keeping the Peace on Two Adjacent Frontiers, 1870–1900." *Journal of Canadian Studies* 12 (Spring 1977): 27–37.

Myers, Frank. *Soldiering in Dakota among the Indians in 1863–4–5*. Huron, D.T.: Huron Printing Co., 1888.

Neihardt, John G. *Black Elk Speaks*. New York: William Morrow & Co., 1932.

Newcomb, W. W., Jr. "A Re-examination of the Causes of Plains Warfare." *American Anthropologist* 52 (July–September 1950): 317–30.

Oliver, Symmes C. *Ecology and Cultural Continuity as Contributing Factors in the Social Organization of the Plains Indians*. Berkeley: University of California Press, 1962.

Olsen, Louise P. "Mary Clementine Collins, Dacotah Missionary." *North Dakota History* 18 (October 1951): 59–81.

Olson, James C. *Red Cloud and the Sioux Problem*. Lincoln: University of Nebraska Press, 1965.

Papers Relating to Talks and Councils Held with the Indians in Dakota and Montana Territories in the Years 1866–1869. Washington, D.C.: Government Printing Office, 1910.

Parker, Watson. *Gold in the Black Hills*. Lincoln: University of Nebraska Press, 1982.

Pattee, John. "Dakota Campaigns." *South Dakota Historical Collections* 5 (1910): 306–11.

———. "Reminiscences of John Pattee." *South Dakota Historical Collections* 5 (1910): 273–350.

Pennanen, Gary. "Sitting Bull: Indian Without a Country." *Canadian Historical Review* 51 (June 1970): 123–40.

Pfaller, Louis L. *Father De Smet in Dakota*. Richardton, N.D.: Assumption Abbey Press, 1962.

———. "'Foes in '76, Friends in '85—Sitting Bull and Buffalo Bill." *Prologue: The Journal of the National Archives* 1 (Fall 1969): 16–31.

———. "The Forging of an Indian Agent." *North Dakota History* 34 (Winter 1967): 62–76.

———. *James McLaughlin: The Man with an Indian Heart*. New York: Vantage Press, 1978.

———. "Sully's Expedition of 1864: Featuring the Killdeer Mountain and Badlands Battles." *North Dakota History* 31 (January 1964): 25–77.

———, ed. "The Galpin Journal: Dramatic Record of an Odyssey of Peace." *Montana the Magazine of Western History* 18 (April 1968): 2–23.

Phillips, George H. "The Indian Ring in Dakota Territory, 1870–1890." *South Dakota History* 2 (1972): 344–76.

Phister, N. P. "The Indian Messiah." *American Anthropologist* o.s. 4 (April 1891): 105–8.

Powell, Peter J. *People of the Sacred Mountain: A History of the Northern Cheyenne Chiefs and Warrior Societies, 1830–1879*. 2 vols. New York: Harper & Row, 1981.

Powers, William K. *Oglala Religion*. Lincoln: University of Nebraska Press, 1977.

Praus, Alexis A. *A New Pictographic Autobiography of Sitting Bull*. Smithsonian Miscellaneous Collections, vol. 123, no. 6. Washington, D.C.: Smithsonian Institution, 1955.

———. *The Sioux, 1798–1922: A Dakota Winter Count*. Cranbrook Institute of Science Bulletin 44. Bloomfield Hills, Mich., 1962.

Prucha, Francis Paul. *American Indian Policy in Crisis: Christian Reformers and the Indian, 1865–1890*. Norman: University of Oklahoma Press, 1977.

_____. *The Great Father: The United States Government and the American Indians*. 2 vols. Lincoln: University of Nebraska Press, 1984.

Quivey, Addison M. "The Yellowstone Expedition of 1874." *Montana Historical Society Contributions* 1 (1876): 268–84.

Raynolds, W. F. "Report of Brevet Colonel W. F. Raynolds, U.S.A., Corps of Topographical Engineers on the Exploration of the Yellowstone and Missouri Rivers, in 1859–'60." Senate Executive Documents, 40th Congress, 2d session, no. 77, 1868.

Riggs, Stephen R. *Mary and I: Forty Years with the Sioux*. Minneapolis: Ross and Haines, 1969.

Riggs, Thomas L., as told to Mary K. Howard. "Sunset to Sunset: A Lifetime with My Brothers the Sioux." *South Dakota Historical Collections* 24 (1958): 258–69.

Robertson, Francis B. " 'We Are Going to Have a Big Sioux War': Colonel David S. Stanley's Yellowstone Expedition, 1872." *Montana the Magazine of Western History* 34 (Autumn 1984): 2–15.

Robinson, Doane. *A History of the Dakota or Sioux Indians*. Minneapolis: Ross and Haines, Inc., 1956.

_____. "The Rescue of Frances Kelly." *South Dakota Historical Collections* 4 (1908): 109–17.

_____. "Some Sidelights on the Character of Sitting Bull." *Collections of the Nebraska State Historical Society* 16 (1911): 187–92.

Rolston, Alan. "The Yellowstone Expedition of 1873." *Montana the Magazine of Western History* 20 (Spring 1970): 20–29.

Russell, Don. *The Lives and Legends of Buffalo Bill*. Norman: University of Oklahoma Press, 1960.

Sandoz, Mari. *Crazy Horse: Strange Man of the Oglalas*. New York: Hastings House, 1942.

Saum, Lewis O. "Stanley Huntley Interviews Sitting Bull: Event, Pseudo-Event, or Fabrication?" *Montana the Magazine of Western History* 32 (Spring 1982): 2–15.

Schell, Herbert S. *History of South Dakota*. Lincoln: University of Nebraska Press, 1961.

Silliman, Lee. "The Carroll Trail: Utopian Enterprise." *Montana the Magazine of Western History* 24 (Spring 1974): 2–17.

The Sisseton and Wahpeton Bands of Dakota or Sioux Indians v. the United States. U. S. Court of Claims, no. 22524 (1901).

Spence, Clark C. "A Celtic Nimrod in the Old West [Sir George Gore on Upper Missouri]." *Montana the Magazine of Western History* 9 (April 1959): 56–66.

Stacy, C. P. "The Military Aspect of Canada's Winning of the West, 1870–1885." *Canadian Historical Review* 21 (March 1940): 1–24.

Standing Bear, Luther. *My People the Sioux*. Lincoln: University of Nebraska Press, 1975.

Steele, Mathew F. "Buffalo Bill's Bluff." *South Dakota Historical Society Collections* 9 (1918): 475–85.

Stewart, Edgar I. "Major Brisbin's Relief of Fort Pease: A Prelude to the Bloody Little Big Horn Massacre." *Montana the Magazine of Western History* 16 (Spring 1966): 23–27.

Stirling, Matthew W. *Three Pictographic Autobiographies of Sitting Bull*. Smithsonian Miscellaneous Collections, vol. 97, no. 5. Washington, D.C.: Smithsonian Institution, 1938.

Sunder, John E. *The Fur Trade on the Upper Missouri, 1840–1865*. Norman: University of Oklahoma Press, 1965.

Sunder, John E., ed. "Up the Missouri to the Montana Mines: John O'Fallon Delany's Pocket Diary for 1862." *Missouri Historical Society Bulletin* 19 (October 1962): 3–22.

Sword, George. "The Story of the Ghost Dance." Trans. Emma Sickels. *Folk-Lorist* 1 (1891–92): 28–31.

Taylor, Joseph Henry. *Kaleidoscopic Lives: A Companion Book to Frontier and Indian Life*. 2d ed. Washburn, N.D.: privately published, 1902.

————. *Sketches of Frontier and Indian Life on the Upper Missouri and Great Plains*. Pottstown, Pa.: privately published, 1897.

Traub, Peter E. "The First Act of the Last Sioux Campaign." *Journal of the United States Cavalry Association* 15 (April 1905): 872–79.

Trennert, Robert A. "The Fur Trader as Indian Administrator: Conflict of Interest or Wise Policy?" *South Dakota History* 5 (Winter 1974): 1–19.

Trobriand, Phillipe Régis de. *Military Life in Dakota: The Journal of Phillipe Régis de Trobriand*. Trans. and ed. Lucile M. Kane. St. Paul, Minn.: Alvord Memorial Commission, 1951.

Turner, C. Frank. *Across the Medicine Line*. Toronto: McClelland and Stewart, 1973.

Turner, John P. *The North-West Mounted Police, 1873–1893*. 2 vols. Ottawa: Kings Printer and Controller of Stationery, 1950.

Utley, Robert M. *Cavalier in Buckskin: George Armstrong Custer and the Western Military Frontier*. Norman: University of Oklahoma Press, 1988.

————. *Frontier Regulars: The United States Army and the Indian, 1866–1890*. Lincoln: University of Nebraska Press, 1984.

————. *Frontiersmen in Blue: The United States Army and the Indian, 1848–1865*. Lincoln: University of Nebraska Press, 1981.

————. *The Indian Frontier of the American West, 1846–1890*. Albuquerque: University of New Mexico Press, 1984.

————. *The Last Days of the Sioux Nation*. New Haven, Conn.: Yale University Press, 1963.

Van Osdel, A. L. "The Sibley Expedition." *Monthly South Dakotan* 2 (May 1899):

54–57; (September 1899): 95–100; (November 1899): 115–19; (April 1900): 30–34; 3 (May 1900): 30–34; (June 1900): 60–63.

Vaughn, J. W. *Indian Fights: New Facts on Seven Encounters.* Norman: University of Oklahoma Press, 1966.

————. *The Reynolds Campaign on Powder River.* Norman: University of Oklahoma Press, 1961.

————. *With Crook at the Rosebud.* Harrisburg, Pa.: Stackpole Co., 1956.

Vestal, Stanley. "The Man Who Killed Custer." *American Heritage* 8 (February 1957): 4–9, 90–91.

————. *New Sources of Indian History, 1850–1891.* Norman: University of Oklahoma Press, 1934.

————. *Sitting Bull, Champion of the Sioux.* 2d ed. Norman: University of Oklahoma Press, 1957. 3d ed., with introduction by Raymond J. DeMallie, 1989.

————. *Warpath: The True Story of the Fighting Sioux Told in a Biography of Chief White Bull.* Ed. Raymond J. DeMallie. Lincoln: University of Nebraska Press, 1984.

————. "White Bull and One Bull—An Appreciation." *Westerners Brand Book* (Chicago) 4 (October 1947): 46–48.

————. "The Works of Sitting Bull, Real and Imaginary." *Southwest Review* 19 (April 1934): 265–78.

Wade, F. C. "Surrender of Sitting Bull." *Canadian Magazine* 24 (February 1905): 335–44.

Walker, James R. *Lakota Belief and Ritual.* Ed. Raymond J. DeMallie and Elaine A. Jahner. Lincoln: University of Nebraska Press, 1980.

————. *Lakota Society.* Ed. Raymond J. DeMallie. Lincoln: University of Nebraska Press, 1982.

————. "The Sun Dance and Other Ceremonies of the Oglala Division of the Teton Dakota." American Museum of Natural History *Anthropological Papers* 16, pt. 2 (1917).

Walker, Judson E. *The Campaigns of General Custer in the Northwest and the Final Surender of Sitting Bull.* 1881; facsimilie rpt, as *The Final Surrender of Sitting Bull.* New York: Argonaut Press, 1966.

Warren, G. K. "Explorations in the Dahcota Country in the Year 1855." Senate Executive Documents, 34th Congress, 1st session, no. 76, 1856, serial 822.

————. *Explorations in Nebraska and the Dakotas in 1855–56–57.* Washington, D.C.: Government Printing Office, 1875.

Watson, Elmo Scott. "Orlando Scott Goff, Pioneer Dakota Photographer." *North Dakota History* 29 (January–April 1962): 210–15.

————. "The Photographs of Sitting Bull." *Westerners Brand Book* (Chicago) 6 (August 1949): 43, 47–48.

White, Richard. "The Winning of the West: The Expansion of the Western Sioux in the Eighteenth and Nineteenth Centuries." *Journal of American History* 65 (1978): 319–43.

Wilson, Frederick T. "Fort Pierre and Its Neighbors" (with notes by Charles E. DeLand). *South Dakota Historical Collections* 1 (1902): 263–79.

————. "Official Correspondence Relating to Fort Pierre." *South Dakota Historical Collections* 1 (1902): 381–440.

Wishart, Bruce. "Grandmother's Land: Sitting Bull in Canada." *True West* 37 (May 1990): 14–20; (June 1990): 26–32; (July 1990): 20–27; (August 1990): 28–32.

Wissler, Clark. "Societies and Ceremonial Associations in the Oglala Division of the Teton-Dakota." American Museum of Natural History *Anthropological Papers* 11 (1912): 1–99.

NOTES

ABBREVIATIONS

AAAG	Acting Assistant Adjutant General
AAG	Assistant Adjutant General
AGO	Adjutant General's Office
AGUSA	Adjutant General, U. S. Army
BIA	Bureau of Indian Affairs
CIA	Commissioner of Indian Affairs
CO	Commanding Officer
CRA	Cheyenne River Agency
DOI	Department of the Interior
GRA	Grand River Agency
LB	Letter Book
LR	Letters Received
LS	Letters Sent
MRA	Milk River Agency
NAC	National Archives of Canada
NARA	National Archives and Records Administration

NDHS   North Dakota State Historical Society

NHS   Nebraska State Historical Society

NWMP   North-West Mounted Police

NWT   Northwest Territories

OR   Official Records of Union and Confederate Armies

PRA   Pine Ridge Agency

RCA   Red Cloud Agency

RCMP   Royal Canadian Mounted Police

RG   Record Group

SDHS   South Dakota State Historical Society

SI   Secretary of the Interior

SIA   Superintendent of Indian Affairs

SRA   Standing Rock Agency

SW   Secretary of War

USIA   U.S. Indian Agent

USMA   U.S. Military Academy

PROLOGUE

1. Quoted in Elaine A. Jahner, "Lakota Genesis: The Oral Tradition," in *Sioux Indian Religion: Tradition and Innovation*, ed. Raymond J. DeMallie and Douglas R. Parks (Norman: University of Oklahoma Press, 1987), 52. There are variations of the myth, of course, and numerous scholarly analyses. Most originate with the researches of James R. Walker among the Pine Ridge Oglalas in the years at the turn of the century. Walker's work first appeared as *The Sun Dance and Other Ceremonies of the Oglala Division of the Teton-Dakota*, Anthropological Papers of the American Museum of Natural History, vol. 16, pt. 2 (New York: American Museum of Natural History, 1917). See also, however, James R. Walker, *Lakota Belief and Rituals*, eds. Raymond J. DeMallie and Elaine A. Jahner (Lincoln: University of Nebraska Press, 1980); William K. Powers, *Oglala Religion* (Lincoln: University of Nebraska Press, 1975); Raymond J. DeMallie and Douglas R. Parks, eds., *Sioux Indian Religion: Tradition and Innovation* (Norman: University of Oklahoma Press, 1987); Raymond J. DeMallie, ed., *The Sixth Grandfather: Black Elk's Teachings Given to John G. Neihardt* (Lincoln: University of Nebraska Press,

1984); and Royal B. Hassrick, *The Sioux: Life and Customs of a Warrior Society* (Norman: University of Oklahoma Press, 1964).

CHAPTER 1

Youth

1. *New York Herald*, November 16, 1877.
2. Stanley Vestal, Sitting Bull's most thorough biographer, fixes the date as 1831 and the place as Many Caches. *Sitting Bull, Champion of the Sioux* (2d ed., Norman: University of Oklahoma Press, 1957), 3. Vestal does not cite sources, although White Bull and One Bull were his principal informants. An interview with One Bull, box 104, folder 11, W. S. Campbell (Stanley Vestal) Collection, Western History Collections, University of Oklahoma Library, states that Sitting Bull was born on Grand River near his (later) home in March of "the Year When Yellow Eyes Played in the Snow" (1831). In a letter of June 21, 1932, to Lawrence K. Fox, Vestal named several of Sitting Bull's family, including One Bull and White Bull, as authorities for his birthplace at Many Caches; box 1, folder 11, Lawrence K. Fox Papers, SDHS.

Sitting Bull told James McLaughlin, his first and only agent, that he was born on Grand River in 1834. James McLaughlin, *My Friend the Indian* (Lincoln: University of Nebraska Press, 1989), 141; and McLaughlin to J. M. Stevenson, May 13, 1884, roll 20, frame 210, James McLaughlin Papers, Assumption Abbey Archives, Richardton, N.D.

In 1880, before his surrender, Sitting Bull told army scout E. H. Allison that he was born on Willow Creek near old Fort Pierre, a statement Allison later confirmed by asking Sitting Bull's wife and his uncle, Chief Four Horns. A year later Sitting Bull gave the same information to a newspaper interviewer, adding that he was forty-four, which would have made his birth year 1837. E. H. Allison, "Sitting Bull's Birthplace," *South Dakota Historical Collections 6 (1912): 270-72*. *St. Paul Pioneer Press*, August 4, 1881.

The annual censuses of Standing Rock Agency, beginning in 1885, do not resolve the issue. The 1885 census gives Sitting Bull's age as fifty-one, which indicates a birth year of 1834. For each year thereafter through 1889, the census agent simply added a year to his age. In 1890, however, the year in which Sitting Bull was killed, the census records his age as fifty-eight, which yields a birth year of 1832. The Standing Rock rolls for the relevant period are RG 75, Indian Census Rolls 1885–1940, NARA (M595, rolls 547 and 548).

In this book I shall base all calculations involving Sitting Bull's age on an assumed birth year of 1831.
3. These distinctions are made with special clarity in Raymond J. DeMaille, "The Sioux in Dakota and Montana Territories: Cultural and Historical Background of the Ogden B. Read Collection," in *Vestiges of a Proud Nation: The Ogden*

B. *Read Northern Plains Indian Collection* (Burlington, Vt.: Robert Hall Fleming Museum, 1986), 20–21.

4. White Bull, box 105, notebooks 8 and 24; and notes of conference with White Bull, One Bull, and relatives regarding family of Sitting Bull, Rapid City, S.D., 1937, box 106, notebook 48, Campbell Collection. One Bull and White Bull, interview by Walter M. Camp, Standing Rock Agency, 1912, box 3, folder 6, Kenneth Hammer Collection, Harold B. Lee Library, Brigham Young University, Provo, Utah. James McLaughlin to J. M. Stevenson, May 13, 1884, roll 20, frame 210, McLaughlin Papers, gives his youthful name as Standing Holy, although when McLaughlin wrote *My Friend the Indian*, 141, he gave it as Jumping Badger. See also One Bull, "How Sitting Bull Got His Name," and White Bull, "Sitting Bull's Skill with Bow and Arrow," MSS, in box 104, folder 20, Campbell Collection.

5. *St. Paul Pioneer Press*, August 4, 1881. White Bull, box 105, notebooks 8 and 24; and notes of conference with White Bull, One Bull, and relatives regarding family of Sitting Bull, Rapid City, S.D., 1937, box 106, notebook 48, Campbell Collection. (Hereafter Vestal material will be cited simply by name of informant and location in the Campbell Collection.) James McLaughlin to J. M. Stevenson, May 13, 1884, roll 20, frame 210, McLaughlin Papers.

6. Robert P. Higheagle, in Frances Desmore, *Teton Sioux Music*, Bureau of American Ethnology Bulletin 61 (Washington, D.C.: Government Printing Office, 1918), 70.

7. Ella Deloria, *Speaking of Indians* (New York: Friendship Press, 1944), 39.

8. James R. Walker, *Lakota Society*, ed. Raymond J. DeMallie (Lincoln: University of Nebraska Press, 1982), 57.

9. White Bull, box 105, notebook 24, p. 21, Campbell Collection.

10. Deloria, *Speaking of Indians*, 25. This work has an excellent description of the importance of kinship.

11. White Bull, box 106, notebook 53, Campbell Collection.

12. Statements of Little Soldier and Young Eagle, as given to Frank Zahn. Zahn to W. S. Campbell, Fort Yates, N.D., August 6, 1933, box 107, Zahn folder, Campbell Collection. See also Little Soldier, c. 1932, box 104, folder 6, Campbell Collection.

13. One Bull, "Sitting Bull's Skill with Bow and Arrow," box 104, folder 20, Campbell Collection. One Bull named the offending youth as Black Bird and the one who proposed that Slow receive the award as Red Feather. These boys were in fact close friends of Sitting Bull in later years, but they were eight and thirteen years younger, respectively. Thus, unless One Bull was citing other boys of the same name, they are not likely to have engaged in this contest with Sitting Bull. I have kept the story but omitted the names.

14. *St. Paul Pioneer Press*, August 4, 1881.

15. This discussion is drawn primarily from Royal B. Hassrick, *The Sioux: Life and Customs of a Warrior Society* (Norman: University of Oklahoma Press, 1964), chap. 2.

16. Quoted in Jeannette Mirsky, "The Dakota," in Margaret Mead, ed., *Cooperation and Competition among Primitive Peoples* (New York: McGraw-Hill Book Co., 1937), 385.

17. The literature is extensive but see especially James R. Walker, *Lakota Belief and Ritual*, ed. Raymond J. DeMallie and Elaine A. Jahner (Lincoln: University of Nebraska Press, 1980); and William K. Powers, *Oglala Religion* (Lincoln: University of Nebraska Press, 1977).

CHAPTER 2

Warrior

1. One Bull, "Why Sitting Bull Wears a White Eagle Feather as a Head Ornament," MS, box 104, folder 20, Campbell Collection. White Bull, box 106, notebook 53, ibid. Robert P. Higheagle Manuscript, box 104, folder 21, p. 46, ibid. The Higheagle Manuscript is a random compilation of material gathered for Vestal by one of the most astute Hunkpapa historians, who earlier assisted ethnologists of the Bureau of American Ethnology. Standing Bear, interview by Walter M. Camp, Camp Notes, MS, p. 818, Robert S. Ellison Collection, Indiana University. James McLaughlin, *My Friend the Indian* (Lincoln: University of Nebraska Press, 1989), 141. McLaughlin to J. M. Stevenson, May 13, 1884, roll 20, frame 210, McLaughlin Papers.

2. The origin and description of the shield are drawn from Robert Higheagle Manuscript, box 104, folder 21, pp. 17–18; One Bull, box 104, MS 125, One Bull folder, no. 11, Campbell Collection; and "Note on Sitting Bull's Shield," in Stanley Vestal, *New Sources of Indian History, 1850–1891* (Norman: University of Oklahoma Press, 1934), 152–56. M. W. Stirling, *Three Pictographic Autobiographies of Sitting Bull*, Smithsonian Miscellaneous Collections, vol. 97, no. 5 (Washington, D.C.: Smithsonian Institution, 1938).

3. One Bull, "Why Sitting Bull Wears a Red Feather as a Head Ornament," MS, box 104, folder 20, Campbell Collection.

4. Richard White, "The Winning of the West: The Expansion of the Western Sioux in the Eighteenth and Nineteenth Centuries," *Journal of American History* 65 (September 1978): 319–43. John C. Ewers, "Intertribal Warfare as the Precursor of Indian-White Warfare on the Northern Great Plains," *Western Historical Quarterly* 6 (October 1975): 397–410.

5. Royal B. Hassrick, *The Sioux: Life and Customs of a Warrior Society* (Norman: University of Oklahoma Press, 1964), chap. 4. Frances Densmore, *Teton Sioux Music*, Bureau of American Ethnology Bulletin 61 (Washington, D.C.: Government Printing Office, 1918), 332–87. Clark Wissler, "Societies and Ceremonial Associations in the Oglala Division of the Teton Dakota," American Museum of Natural History *Anthropological Papers* 11 (1912): 52 ff.

6. Stirling, *Three Pictographic Autobiographies of Sitting Bull*. Alexis A. Praus, *A*

New Pictographic Autobiography of Sitting Bull, Smithsonian Miscellaneous Collections, vol. 123, no. 6 (Washington, D.C.: Smithsonian Institution, 1955).

7. I infer this from Densmore, *Teton Sioux Music*, 313 and 320. Informants at Standing Rock Agency told her the Strong Hearts were founded by Sitting Bull, Gall, and Crow King. They also hinted of another society, "Strong Heart at Night," which she thought had no connection with the Strong Hearts. Since the Strong Hearts appear to have predated Sitting Bull's membership, and Vestal's informants made Sitting Bull the prime organizer of the Midnight Strong Hearts, it seems likely that Densmore's sources either confused the two or confused her.

8. Little Soldier, c. 1932, box 104, folder 6, Campbell Collection.

9. White Bull, box 106, notebook 53, Campbell Collection.

10. Little Soldier, c. 1932, box 104, folder 6, Campbell Collection.

11. White Bull, box 105, notebook 8, Campbell Collection.

12. White Bull, box 105, notebook 4, p. 11, Campbell Collection.

13. Black Prairie Dog, box 104, folder 6; and White Bull, box 105, notebook 4, p. 10, Campbell Collection.

14. One Bull, box 104, MS 127, folder 11; and Aaron M. Beede to W. S. Campbell, Fort Yates, N.D., December 23, 1929 (repeating contents of his diary entry of 1925 recording recollections of Sitting Bull by a group of old men), box 107, A. M. Beede folder, Campbell Collection.

15. White Bull, box 105, notebook 8, Campbell Collection. "Note on Sitting Bull's Shield," Vestal, *New Sources of Indian History*, 153.

16. Hassrick, *The Sioux*, chap. 6.

17. White Bull, box 105, notebook 5, Campbell Collection.

18. Sitting Bull, as told to One Bull, "A Crow Indian Spied in a Buffalo Horn Spoon," MS, box 104, folder 20, Campbell Collection. Since Sitting Bull told this story, or One Bull assured Vestal he did, I have included it. However, variations feature other people and places, and it may be largely myth. One Bull may have confused Pretty Door with Sitting Bull's mother, for in another source Pretty Door is given as an alternate name for Her-Holy-Door. In no other source does Pretty Door appear as the name of one of Sitting Bull's wives. White Bull (box 105, notebook 24, pp. 18–21, Campbell Collection) is authority for the name Light Hair.

19. Pictograph no. 6 in Stirling, *Three Pictographic Autobiographies*, graphically portrays this episode. See also Circling Hawk (who was there), box 105, notebook 13; One Bull, "Information in Sioux and English with Regard to Sitting Bull," MS, box 104, folder 11; Little Soldier, c. 1932, box 104, folder 6; One Bull, MS 127, box 104, One Bull folder, no. 11, Campbell Collection.

20. Old Bull, box 105, notebook 12, Campbell Collection.

21. White Bull, box 105, notebook 28, Campbell Collection. The Standing Rock censuses of 1885 and 1886 assign Four Horns an age that places his birth year at 1814.

22. Old Bull, box 105, notebook 12, Campbell Collection.

23. Robert Higheagle Manuscript, box 4, folder 21, pp. 17–18, Campbell Collection.

24. Ibid.

25. One Bull, "Information in Sioux and English with regards to Sitting Bull," MS, box 104, folder 11, Campbell Collection.

26. See especially Stanley Vestal, "White Bull and One Bull—An Appreciation," *Westerners Brand Book* (Chicago) 4 (October 1947): 46–48.

27. There are several versions of the fight in which Sitting Bull acquired an adopted brother. I have relied mainly on the account of Circling Hawk, who was there, box 105, notebook 13, Campbell Collection. See also White Bull, box 106, notebook 53; One Bull in box 104, One Bull folder, no. 11; and (an entirely different version) One Bull, "Sitting Bull Adopts an Assiniboine Lad," MS, box 104, folder 20, all in ibid. Sitting Bull portrays the episode in pictograph no. 8 of the Kimball record and no. 13 of the Smith record, in Stirling, *Three Pictographic Autobiographies*.

28. Old Bull, box 105, notebook 11; White Bull, box 105, notebook 8; One Bull, box 104, One Bull folder, no. 11; Circling Hawk, box 105, notebook 13, all in Campbell Collection. Old Bull and Circling Hawk were there. White Bull was not but got the story soon after from participants. In nos. 2 and 9 of the Kimball record, Sitting Bull portrayed the Rainy Buttes fight, himself lancing the Crow who killed his father, and the women captives. No. 10 of the Smith record is probably Rainy Buttes too. Stirling, *Three Pictographic Autobiographies*.

CHAPTER 3

Wichasha Wakan

1. White Bull, box 105, notebook 6, Campbell Collection.

2. Royal B. Hassrick, *The Sioux: Life and Customs of a Warrior Society* (Norman: University of Oklahoma Press, 1964), 39.

3. White Bull makes the point specifically that Sitting Bull was both war chief and sacred man at the same time: box 105, notebook 4, Campbell Collection.

4. For a clear and succinct analysis, see Raymond J. DeMallie, "Lakota Belief and Ritual in the Nineteenth Century," in DeMallie and Douglas R. Parks, eds., *Sioux Indian Religion* (Norman: University of Oklahoma Press, 1987), 25–44.

5. Robert P. Higheagle Manuscript, box 4, folder 21, p. 17, Campbell Collection.

6. Jerome Stillson in *New York Herald*, November 16, 1877.

7. White Bull, box 105, notebook 4, Campbell Collection.

8. Robert P. Higheagle Manuscript, p. 14.

9. Ibid., pp. 3–4, 17. Frances Densmore, *Teton Sioux Music*, Bureau of American Ethnology Bulletin 61 (Washington, D.C.: Government Printing Office, 1918), 285–93. Clark Wissler, "Societies and Ceremonial Associations in the Oglala

Division of the Teton Dakota," American Museum of Natural History *Anthropological Papers* 11 (1912): 91–92.

10. Densmore, *Teton Sioux Music*, 157–72. Wissler, "Oglala Societies," 82–85.

11. Robert P. Higheagle Manuscript, p. 19.

12. Ibid., p. 133. Robert P. Higheagle, "Twenty-five Songs Made by Sitting Bull," MS, box 104, folder 17, Campbell Collection.

13. A sampling, obtained from One Bull, White Bull, No Flesh, and other old comrades, appears in ibid.

14. Robert P. Higheagle Manuscript, p. 17.

15. Two Bulls, "Sitting Bull's Kindness to Birds," MS, box 104, folder 20, Campbell Collection.

16. Higheagle, "Twenty-five Songs."

17. One Bull, in ibid.

18. Walker, *Lakota Belief and Ritual*, 83.

19. Ibid., 96.

20. The basic authority remains James R. Walker, "The Sun Dance and Other Ceremonies of the Oglala Division of the Teton Dakota," American Museum of Natural History *Anthropological Papers* 16, part 2 (1917). See also Hassrick, *The Sioux*, 239–48; and Densmore, *Teton Sioux Music*, 87–151.

21. One Bull is the source, but in two interviews he contradicts himself on the date, giving it variously as 1856, 1859, and 1865. He seems to be talking about the same dance, as the site and circumstances are similar. Box 104, folder 6; and box 105, notebook 19, box 106, folder 6, in Campbell Collection.

22. White Bull, box 105, notebook 8, Campbell Collection.

23. Robert P. Higheagle Manuscript, p. 20.

24. White Bull, box 105, notebook 24; and One Bull, box 104, folder 11, both in Campbell Collection.

25. White Bull, box 105, notebook 4, p. 12, Campbell Collection.

26. White Bull, "Sitting Bull's Act of Kindness," MS, box 104, folder 20, Campbell Collection.

27. Stanley Vestal, notes on One Bull, box 106, notebook 57, Campbell Collection.

28. One Bull, "Sitting Bull Finds a Lost Pony for His Nephew," MS, box 104, folder 20, Campbell Collection.

29. Bear Soldier, "Sitting Bull Donates Two Buffaloes He had Killed," MS, box 104, folder 20, Campbell Collection.

30. Much of this characterization is drawn from the statements of a group of old men who gathered in the office of Fort Yates attorney Aaron M. Beede in 1925, as recorded in Beede's diary. Beede to W. S. Campbell, Fort Yates, N.D., December 23, 1929, Campbell Collection. See also Robert P. Higheagle Manuscript, pp. 9, 37, ibid.; and Black Prairie Dog (re tipi), box 104, folder 6, ibid.

31. Robert P. Higheagle Manuscript, p. 18.

CHAPTER 4

Wasichus

1. Little Soldier, box 104, folder 6, Campbell Collection.

2. An excellent history of the Chouteau company is John E. Sunder, *The Fur Trade on the Upper Missouri, 1840–1865* (Norman: University of Oklahoma Press, 1965).

3. I have dealt with these matters at greater length in *The Indian Frontier of the American West, 1846–1890* (Albuquerque: University of New Mexico Press, 1984), chap. 2.

4. Sunder, *Fur Trade on the Upper Missouri*, 26–31.

5. Stanley Vestal included in *New Sources of Indian History* (Norman: University of Oklahoma Press, 1934), 185–207, a lengthy account of Four Horns leading a Hunkpapa delegation to the Fort Laramie council and Sitting Bull accompanying him. Sitting Bull's activities, impressions, and even conversation are detailed. No basis for this has been found in the Campbell Collection nor in any other source I have consulted. If an official transcript of the council was made, apparently it has not survived. The principal source is a series of letters written by A. B. Chambers, editor of the *Daily Missouri Republican* of St. Louis, or his correspondent B. Gratz Brown, both of whom were present, which appeared in the newspaper October 29, November 9, and November 30, 1851. In addition, much colorful detail appears in Percival G. Lowe, *Five Years a Dragoon and Other Adventures on the Great Plains*, ed. Don Russell (Norman: University of Oklahoma Press, 1965), 60–73.

Although no upper Missouri Lakotas signed the treaty, at least two may be inferred to have been present. Jesuit missionary Pierre-Jean De Smet, who was there, named One Horn (Lone Horn) and Goose as among the Sioux "deputies" who accompanied him east after the Fort Laramie council. The former was a Miniconjou, the latter a Blackfeet Sioux. Hiram M. Chittenden and Alfred T. Richardson, eds., *Life, Letters, and Travels of Father Pierre-Jean De Smet, S.J., 1801–1873*, 4 vols. (New York: Francis P. Harper, 1905), vol. 2, 688.

6. Charles J. Kappler, comp., *Indian Affairs: Laws and Treaties*, 2 vols. (Washington, D.C.: Government Printing Office, 1904), vol. 2, 594–96.

7. The legalisms of the treaty and the amendment on which ratification was conditioned, which escaped the understanding of the Indians, are ably treated in Harry H. Anderson, "The Controversial Sioux Amendment to the Fort Laramie Treaty of 1851," *Nebraska History* 37 (September 1956): 201–20.

8. I have dealt with this incident in my *Frontiersmen in Blue: The United States Army and the Indian, 1848–1865* (New York: Macmillan Publishing Co., 1967; Lincoln: University of Nebraska Press, 1981), 113–15.

9. Vaughan to Cumming, Fort Pierre, February 15, 1856, RG 75, LR Upper

Missouri Agency 1852–64, NARA (M234, roll 885, frame 131). For the Harney expedition, see Richmond L. Clow, "Mad Bear: William S. Harney and the Sioux Expedition of 1855–1856," *Nebraska History* 61 (Summer 1980): 132–49; and Utley, *Frontiersmen in Blue*, 115–20. An account of the government's purchase of Fort Pierre, together with associated official correspondence, is in Frederick T. Wilson, "Fort Pierre and Its Neighbors," *South Dakota Historical Collections* 1 (1902): 263–440. An intimate view of events at Fort Pierre through the winter of 1855–56 is contained in a series of letters from Lt. Thomas Sweeny to his wife, box 8, SW 850, Sweeny Papers, Huntington Library, San Marino, Calif. Sweeny is the authority for the Indians' name of Mad Bear for Harney.

10. The transcript is in House Executive Documents, 34th Congress, 1st session, no. 130, serial 859, p. 36.

11. USIA Bernard S. Schoonover (who was there) to SIA A. M. Robinson, Fort Union, August 23, 1860; P. Chouteau and Company to Robinson, St. Louis, January 2, 1861. RG 75, LR Upper Missouri Agency 1852–64, NARA (M234, roll 885, frames 411 and 414).

12. Little Soldier, box 104, folder 6, Campbell Collection.

13. Interview with reporter during tour with Buffalo Bill's Wild West, *St. Louis Critic*, October 3, 1885.

14. Little Soldier, folder 6, box 104, Campbell Collection.

15. Samuel Latta to CIA William P. Dole, Yankton, D.T., August 27, 1862, CIA, *Annual Report, 1862*, 192–93.

16. Charles Primeau to P. Chouteau & Co., Fort Pierre, June 20, 1862, in CIA, *Annual Report, 1862*, 373–75. See also Charles E. DeLand, interview with Basil Claymore (who was standing next to Bear's Rib), September 10, 1899, folder 29, DeLand Papers, SDHS. This and other firsthand material is quoted in a note on Bear's Rib by Doane Robinson, *South Dakota Historical Collections* 1 (1902): 366–68.

17. Hunkpapa chiefs (Feather-Tied-to-His-Hair, Bald Eagle, Red Hair, One-That-Shouts, Little Bear, Crow-That-Looks, Bear Heart, Little Knife, White-At-Both-Ends) to Agent, Fort Berthold, July 25, 1862, CIA, *Annual Report, 1862*, 372–73.

CHAPTER 5

Long Knives

1. Hunkpapa chiefs to Indian Agent, Fort Berthold, July 25, 1862, CIA, *Annual Report, 1862*, 373.

2. As estimated by Indian Agents Henry Reed and Samuel Latta: Reed and LaBarge, Harkness & Co. to CIA W. P. Dole, Washington, D.C., January 14, 1863; Latta to Dole, Washington, D.C., March 7, 1863. Both in RG 75, LR Upper Missouri Agency 1852–64, NARA (M234, roll 885, frames 488 and 495).

3. Latta to Dole, Washington D.C., March 7, 1863, RG 75, LR Upper Missouri Agency 1852–64, NARA (M234, roll 885, frame 495). Lt. Col. H. C. Nutt to Governor Samuel Kirkwood, Council Bluffs, Ia., September 15, 1862, *War of the Rebellion: Official Records of the Union and Confederate Armies*, series 1, vol. 13, pp. 638–40. (Hereafter cited as *O.R.*) Governor William Jayne to Dole, Yankton, D.T., October 8, 1862, CIA, *Annual Report, 1862*, 177.

4. According to Acting Dakota Governor John M. Hutchinson to Dole, Yankton, D.T., September 23, 1863, RG 75, LS Dakota Superintendency 1861–70, NARA (M1016, roll 11, frame 199).

5. I have dealt with the Sibley-Sully campaigns from the military standpoint in my *Frontiersmen in Blue: The United States Army and the Indian, 1848–1865* (New York: Macmillan Publishing Co., 1967; Lincoln: University of Nebraska Press, 1981), chap. 13.

6. Note by Arthur Daniels in Eugene M. Wilson, "Narrative of the First Regiment of Mounted Rangers," *Minnesota in the Civil and Indian Wars, 1861–1865* (St. Paul, Minn.: Pioneer Press Co., 1980), vol. 1, pp. 523–24. M. W. Sterling, *Three Pictographic Autobiographies of Sitting Bull*, Smithsonian Miscellaneous Collections, vol. 97, no. 5, pictograph no. 24. This pictograph is identified as occurring in a subsequent skirmish on Apple Creek, near the Missouri. However, no incident is known to have occurred there that resembles the scene depicted.

7. This is clear from the report of General Sully, September 11, 1863, in *O.R.*, series 1, vol. 22, part 1, p. 558, in identifying the Indians facing him at the Battle of Whitestone Hill. Sully drew this information from his Indian scouts and from prisoners taken at the battle.

8. Most of what is known of the movement and activities of the Indians after they crossed the Missouri came from prisoners Sully took at the Battle of Whitestone Hill and was set forth in his official report and reports of his subordinates, in *O.R.*, series 1, vol. 22, part 1, pp. 555–68. See also J. R. King, "A Synopsis of the Organization and Movements of the Sully Indian Expedition . . . in the Summer of 1863," MS, encl. to King to O. G. Libby, October 14, 1914, A85, box 33, folder 1, Orin G. Libby Collection, NDHS. In some ways this document, written by Sully's adjutant general, is more informative than Sully's official report.

9. White Bull, box 105, notebook 45; and box 105, notebook 24, Campbell Collection. White Bull said this took place at harvest time when he was thirteen—1863.

10. A. M. English, "Dakota's First Soldiers: History of the First Dakota Cavalry, 1862–1865," *South Dakota Historical Collections* 9 (1918): 278.

11. The customary military estimate of Sioux strength was sixteen hundred lodges and six thousand warriors. I have used the smaller figure of fourteen hundred lodges, because that was the number given by the officer who destroyed the village after the battle. Report of Col. R. N. McLaren, July 29, 1864, *O.R.*, series 1, vol. 41, part 1, pp. 172–73. Moreover, the army invariably overestimated the number of fighting men in battle, and five per lodge is excessive.

12. Most accounts have the Sioux camped there for a long time waiting to give battle. However, I think they were there only a day or two before the Battle of Killdeer Mountain. White Bull, the principal Indian informant, said the move occurred a day before the battle. White Bull, box 105, notebook 24, pp. 1–6, Campbell Collection. Fanny Kelly's captivity narrative can be read to support this construction. While confusion of time and place makes this source difficult to use, Kelly described a move that took the village away from a fight the warriors had with the troops, inferentially Killdeer Mountain, then deals at length with a battle that came so close as to threaten the village, inferentially the Battle of the Badlands. I believe she confused the two, since her account of the Badlands closely conforms to what is known of Killdeer. The first action could have been the skirmish between a Sioux scouting party of thirty warriors and Sully's Winnebago Indian auxiliaries two days before Killdeer. Fanny Kelly, *My Captivity among the Sioux Indians* (New York: Corinth Books, 1962), chap. 9. The original edition was published in 1872.

13. White Bull's extended account, cited above, is the only detailed Indian testimony. White sources, however, contain many clues to what happened on the Indian side. The Sioux and Sully's Winnebago scouts, both on this field and later, in the Badlands, shouted across the lines, taunting each other but also exchanging information. Principal white sources: official reports of Sully and his subordinates in *O.R.*, series 1, vol. 41, part 1, pp. 131–73; regimental histories in *Minnesota in the Civil and Indian Wars*, vol. 1, pp. 387–91, 544–47, 581–82, 672–74, 752–53; John Pattee, "Dakota Campaigns," *South Dakota Historical Collections* 5 (1910): 306–11; A. M. English, "Dakota's First Soldiers: History of the First Dakota Cavalry, 1862–1865," ibid. 9 (1918): 281–85; David L. Kingsbury, "Sully's Expedition against the Sioux in 1864," *Minnesota Historical Society Collections* 8 (1898): 453–56; and Frank Myers, *Soldiering in Dakota among the Indians in 1863– 4–5* (Huron, D.T.: Huron Printing Co., 1888), 14–23. A good synthesis, chiefly from the military perspective, is the Rev. Louis Pfaller, "Sully's Expedition of 1864 Featuring the Killdeer Mountain and Badlands Battles," *North Dakota History* 31 (January 1964): 25–77. In addition, the Alfred Sully Papers, box 2, folder 54, Beinicke Library, Yale University, contain four affidavits by officers of Sully's command, executed on September 23, 1865, describing aspects of the battle. These were prepared for Sully's use in a controversy with one of his subordinates.

14. Lt. Col. John Pattee tells the story from the military viewpoint: "Dakota Campaigns," 308. As the Indian gesticulated, according to Pattee, an aide from Sully rode up and said, "The general sends his compliments and wishes you to kill that Indian for God's sake." Pattee summoned three sharpshooters, who took careful aim and fired, sending the Indian behind the hill. Sully later contended that the Indian fell from his horse, although Pattee did not see this.

15. All the sources touch on this action, but it is most graphically described in Isaac Botsford, "Narrative of Brackett's Battalion of Cavalry," *Minnesota in the Civil and Indian Wars*, vol. 1, p. 581. White Bull also tells of it, identifying the Indians

as Yanktonais and Dakotas, whom he regarded as strangers to the Lakotas, and conceding thirty killed.

16. White Bull, box 105, notebook 24, pp. 6–10, Campbell Collection. White sources on the Badlands battle are as cited in note 13, above. See also Nicholas Hilger, "General Alfred Sully's Expedition of 1864 . . . from the Diary of Judge Nicholas Hilger," *Montana Historical Society Contributions* 2 (1896): 314–28.

17. Hilger, "General Alfred Sully's Expedition," 319.

18. White Bull, box 105, notebook 8, Campbell Collection. In this interview White Bull tells the story as if it occurred at the Battle of Killdeer Mountain. In his extended account of Killdeer (box 105, notebook 24), however, he emphatically declares that Killdeer occurred before Sitting Bull was shot in the hip. Other sources support the conclusion that Sitting Bull was not wounded at Killdeer Mountain. The only hand-to-hand fighting known to have taken place after Killdeer was the initial attack on the Fisk wagon train, and I have therefore fitted this incident into that encounter. Vestal (*Sitting Bull, Champion of the Sioux*, 62–63) places it a little later, when a relief column came out to rescue the emigrants, but the official report of this expedition clearly reveals that no fight with Indians occurred. (Report of Col. Daniel J. Dill, October 4, 1864, *O.R.*, series 1, vol. 41, part 1, pp. 795–96.) Moreover, Vestal's version of Sitting Bull's wound follows the somewhat different account of Circling Hawk. Although Circling Hawk was there, White Bull was closer to the event, and I have relied on his memory.

For white sources bearing on the adventures of the Fisk wagon train, see "Expeditions of Capt. Jas. L. Fisk to the Gold Mines of Idaho and Montana, 1864–1866," *North Dakota Historical Collections* 2 (1908): 421–61; Ray H. Mattison, ed., "The Fisk Expedition of 1864: The Diary of William L. Larned," *North Dakota History* 36 (Summer 1969): 227–38; Journal of William D. Dibbs, "Overland Expedition from St. Anthony Falls towards Big Horn River," A85/33/12, Orin G. Libby Collection, NDHS; H. H. Larned (one of the emigrants) to Orin G. Libby, February 11 and March 10, 1923, box 22, folder 15, ibid.; H. H. Larned, interview by Lewis F. Crawford, June 25, 1921, box 1, A58, Lewis F. Crawford Papers, NDHS; and Ethel A. Collins, "Pioneer Experiences of Horatio H. Larned," *North Dakota Historical Collections* 7 (1925): 1–58.

19. The text of the messages is printed in Kelly's book, *My Captivity among the Sioux*, 274–78. Her narrative contains helpful details, but also many misstatements and obscurities.

20. Pell to Sully, Fort Sully, October 26, 1864, RG 393, Records of U.S. Army Continental Commands, LR Department of the Northwest, entry 3446, box 2, 1864, NARA.

21. This is White Bull's version, box 106, notebook 53, and also box 105, notebook 8, Campbell Collection. There are several other versions, including Fanny Kelly's in *My Captivity among the Sioux*, with differing details. The main Indian sources, however, agree in assigning Sitting Bull a significant role in effecting her release. For other Indian accounts, see Doane Robinson, "The

Rescue of Frances Kelly," *South Dakota Historical Collections* 4 (1908): 109–17; Old Bull, box 105, notebook 12, Campbell Collection; Robert P. Higheagle Manuscript, box 14, folder 21, pp. 24–25, ibid; and Mary Crawler, interview by Lewis F. Crawford, March 12, 1925, box 1, notebook 28, Lewis F. Crawford Papers, NDHS. Additional details from Mrs. Kelly are in Hugh S. Walsh to SI O. H. Browning, Wamego, Kansas, October 24, 1866, RG 75, LR Upper Missouri Agency 1865–66, NARA (M234, roll 886, frame 738).

22. White Bull, box 106, notebook 53, Campbell Collection. Documents relating to Kelly's release are appended to her book, *My Captivity among the Sioux*. For a firsthand view of her arrival at Fort Sully, see Myers, *Soldiering among the Indians in Dakota*, 32–40.

CHAPTER 6

Lance

1. In his meeting with Father De Smet in 1868, to be treated subsequently, Sitting Bull said that he had waged war on the whites because his people "pushed me forward." Although perhaps a shade disingenuous, I think it likely the Hunkpapa militant faction did press him into an offensive leadership role, but I doubt that he was unwilling. "Statement by the Rev. P. J. De Smet, S.J., of his Reception by and Council with the Hostile Uncpapa Indians," *Papers Relating to Talks and Councils Held with the Indians in Dakota and Montana Territories in the Years 1866–1869* (Washington, D.C.: Government Printing Office, 1910), 111.

2. Events at Fort Rice during the winter of 1864–65, as well as an excellent commentary on the activities of the Sioux obtained from fairly reliable intelligence sources, may be followed in Dimon's official reports and private correspondence. Although some of the official material appears in *O.R.*, series 1, vol. 48, parts 1 and 2, the most complete run of both is contained in the Charles A. R. Dimon Papers, Yale Collection of Western Americana, Beinecke Library, Yale University. Another rich source, through the summer and autumn of 1865, is the *Frontier Scout*, a newspaper published by the soldiers themselves. The Yale Collection of Western Americana contains a complete run.

3. Sully to Pope, Fort Rice, July 17 and 20, 1865, *O.R.*, series 1, vol. 48, part 1, pp. 1090–1, 1109–10.

4. Sully to AAG Department of the Northwest, Fort Berthold, August 8, 1865, *O.R.*, series 1, vol. 48, part 1, pp. 1172–74. One Bull confirmed this report but denied that Sitting Bull had cut himself with a knife. One Bull, box 104, One Bull folder, MS 127, no. 11, Campbell Collection.

5. The most authoritative and detailed account of the Battle of Fort Rice was penned by several military participants and printed in *Frontier Scout*, August 3, 1865. See also D. Alexander Brown, *The Galvanized Yankees* (Urbana: University of Illinois Press, 1963), chap. 4.

6. *Frontier Scout*, October 12, 1865.

7. Sully to AAG Department of the Missouri, Fort Berthold, August 13, 1865, *O.R.*, series 1, vol. 48, part 1, pp. 1181–82. Sully sent a scout to trail the village. Described as half Hunkpapa and half Arikara, he was Bloody Knife, later to gain fame as General Custer's favorite Indian scout.

8. The official reports of Cole and Walker appear in LeRoy R. and Ann W. Hafen, eds., *Powder River Campaigns and Sawyers Expedition of 1865: A Documentary Account, Comprising Official Reports, Diaries, Contemporary Newspaper Accounts, and Personal Narratives* (Glendale, Calif.: Arthur H. Clark Co., 1961), 60–63. White Bull, box 105, notebook 24, pp. 15–18, Campbell Collection. George Bent, half-blood son of William Bent, was with the Cheyennes and Oglalas during this period. His letters to George Hyde (Yale Western Americana Collection, Beinecke Library, Yale University) are rich in detail about the activities of these tribes but touch only lightly on the Missouri River Lakotas. Consult also Fr. Peter J. Powell, *People of the Sacred Mountain: A History of the Northern Cheyenne Chiefs and Warrior Societies 1830–1879*, 2 vols. (New York: Harper & Row, 1981), vol. 1, pp. 381–87.

9. White Bull, box 105, notebook 24, Campbell Collection. Pictographs 27, 28, 31, and 37 of the Kimball record in M. W. Stirling, *Three Pictographic Autobiographies of Sitting Bull*, Smithsonian Institution Miscellaneous Collections, vol. 97, no. 5 (Washington, D.C.: Smithsonian Institution, 1938).

10. The domestic upheaval of 1865 and the mother's urgings are from White Bull, box 105, notebook 24, pp. 18–21, Campbell Collection. White Bull said that this occurred when he was fifteen—1865.

11. The treaties, which were ratified in March 1866, are printed in Charles J. Kappler, comp., *Indian Affairs: Laws and Treaties*, 2 vols. (Washington, D.C.: Government Printing Office, 1904), vol. 2, pp. 883–87, 896–908. By error of the editor of this compilation, the Hunkpapa signatories were appended to the Yanktonai treaty and the Yanktonai signatories to the Hunkpapa treaty. They are correct in the originals. The treaty commissioners, in addition to General Sully, were Dakota Governor Newton Edmunds, Indian Superintendent Edward B. Taylor, Generals Samuel R. Curtis and Henry H. Sibley, Henry W. Reed, and Orrin Guernsey. The commission's official report, October 28, 1865, is in CIA, *Annual Report, 1865*, 537–42. See also Edmunds to CIA D. N. Cooley, October 14, 1865, in ibid., 183–89. The commission's activities are well documented in official correspondence in RG 75, BIA LS Dakota Superintendency 1861–70, NARA (M1016, roll 11); and BIA LR Upper Missouri Agency 1865–66, NARA (M234, roll 886). Finally, much colorful detail appears in private and official letters of General Curtis contained in the Samuel R. Curtis Papers, Yale Collection of Western Americana, Beinecke Library, Yale University.

12. For White Bull's account, see box 104, folder 12, Campbell Collection; and White Bull, interview by Walter M. Camp, July 17, 1912, Walter M. Camp Papers, Lilly Library, Indiana University, copy in box 3, folder 6, Hammer

Papers, Harold B. Lee Library, Brigham Young University. See also Stanley
Vestal, *Warpath: The True Story of the Fighting Sioux Told in a Biography of Chief White
Bull*, ed. Raymond J. De Mallie (Lincoln: University of Nebraska Press, 1984),
chap. 6.

13. For details of depredations in August and September, see Rankin to AAAG
Fort Rice, Fort Buford, September 14, 1866, RG 393, Department of Dakota
LR, box 5, NARA. See also USIA Mahlon Wilkinson to Gov. A. J. Faulk, Fort
Berthold, September 17, 1866, RG 75, BIA LR Dakota Superintendency 1861–
70, NARA (M1016, roll 3, frame 794). The commanding officer said his assailants
were Dakotas, but the more knowledgeable Wilkinson reported that they had
identified themselves as Hunkpapas and numbered about two hundred.

The December action is described in detail in Capt. William G. Rankin to
AGUSA, Fort Buford, December 31, 1866. This is a long report covering construction and other activities since the garrison's arrival in June 1866. I have used a
copy in the Ben Innis Collection at Fort Union Trading Post National Historic
Site, North Dakota. The event is also covered in the Fort Buford Post Returns for
December 1866 in the same source. See also USIA Mahlon Wilkinson to Gov.
A. J. Faulk, Fort Union, January 1, 1867, RG 75, BIA LR Dakota Superintendency 1861–70, NARA (M1016, roll 4, frame 522). Sitting Bull and the saw is
recounted by pioneer Joseph Henry Taylor, *Sketches of Frontier and Indian Life on
the Upper Missouri and Great Plains* (Pottstown, Pa., privately published, 1897),
77, and variations on the story appear in other accounts.

14. Affidavit of Charles B. Hoffman, December 2, 1902, James B. Hubbell
Papers, AH876, Minnesota Historical Society. I am indebted to Paul Hedren,
superintendent of Fort Union Trading Post National Historic Site, for calling my
attention to this document.

15. James P. Kimball, "Fort Buford," *North Dakota Historical Quarterly* 4 (October
1929): 77–78. This is the same Kimball who subsequently came into possession
of the most authoritative of the Sitting Bull pictographic autobiographies. For
subsequent depredations around Fort Buford and Sitting Bull's part in them, see
USIA Mahlon Wilkinson to Gov. A. J. Faulk, Fort Sully, May 21, 1867, RG 75,
BIA LR Dakota Superintendency 1861–70, NARA (M1016, roll 4, frame 537);
USIA John W. Wells to CIA N. G. Taylor, 60 miles west of Fort Union, October
22, 1867, RG 75, BIA LR Montana Superintendency, NARA (M234, roll 488,
frame 858); and Rankin to AAAG Middle District, Fort Buford, November 7,
1867, RG 393, Department of Dakota LR, box 4, NARA. The last, reporting an
attack on a wood wagon involving two casualties and four stolen mules, is supported by Sitting Bull's pictograph no. 29 in the Kimball record, in which "Sitting
Bull captures a fine brown Army mule with a black spot on the withers, off side.
He gave the mule to his sister."

16. Charles Larpenteur, *Forty Years a Fur Trader on the Upper Missouri, 1833–
1872*, ed. Milo M. Quaife (Chicago: Lakeside Classics/R. R. Donnelley & Sons
Co., 1933), 358–60.

17. Events connected with Forts Stevenson and Totten are documented in a series of reports contained in RG 393, Department of Dakota LR, box 3, NARA. The record of his tour at Fort Stevenson kept by the commanding officer has become a minor classic of western literature: *Military Life in Dakota: The Journal of Philippe Régis de Trobriand*, trans. and ed. Lucile M. Kane (St. Paul, Minn.: Alvord Memorial Commission, 1951).

18. H. H. Larned, interview by Lewis F. Crawford, June 1921, box 1, Lewis F. Crawford Papers, NDHS.

19. Frederick F. Gerard, interview by Walter M. Camp, c. April 1909, box 6, folder 3, Walter M. Camp Papers, Harold B. Lee Library, Brigham Young University.

20. There are many versions of this story. Bloody Knife told this version to Joseph Henry Taylor, who retold it in *Kaleidoscopic Lives: A Companion Book to Frontier and Indian Life*, 2d ed. (Washburn, N.D., privately published, 1902), 143–59. Another version is that of Horatio Larned, who was at Fort Berthold as a trader: interview by Lewis F. Crawford, April 29, 1925, box 1, Lewis F. Crawford Papers, NDHS. Larned implies a date of early 1868. I have followed the analysis and conclusions of John S. Gray, "Bloody Knife, Ree Scout for Custer," *Westerners Brand Book* (Chicago) 17 (February 1961): 89–96. When Father De Smet visited Sitting Bull's village in 1868, as recounted in chapter 7, Gall showed him the scars of his wounds and gave still another version.

CHAPTER 7

Head Chief

1. Lt. Cornelius Cusick to Post Adjutant Fort Buford, May 14, 1868, RG 393, Fort Buford LR (but mislabeled Fort Sumner, N.M., box 1), NARA.

2. Col. Philippe Régis de Trobriand to Gen. A. H. Terry, Fort Stevenson, May 30, 1868, RG 393, Department of Dakota LR, box 4, NARA. See also Capt. George W. Hill to AAG Department of Dakota, Fort Totten, May 23, 1868, ibid., box 3.

3. Three sources document the De Smet mission, a journal kept by Galpin and two accounts De Smet wrote based on the Galpin journal: Rev. Louis Pfaller, ed., "The Galpin Journal: Dramatic Record of an Odyssey of Peace," *Montana the Magazine of Western History* 18 (April 1968): 2–23; Hiram M. Chittenden and Alfred T. Richardson, eds., *Life, Letters, and Travels of Father Pierre-Jean De Smet, S.J., 1801–1873*, 4 vols. (New York: Francis P. Harper, 1905), vol. 3, pp. 899–922; and "Statement of the Rev. P. J. De Smet, S.J., of his Reception by and Council with the Hostile Uncpapa Indians," *Papers Relating to Talks and Councils Held with the Indians in Dakota and Montana Territories in the Years 1866–1869* (Washington, D.C.: Government Printing Office, 1910), 108–13. The Rev. Pfaller, who worked out De Smet's route both in the documents and on the ground, identified the probable location of the village as on Powder River about a dozen miles above its mouth. However, De Smet wrote that the eighteen Hunkpapas who returned

with his scouts said that the village was on the Yellowstone above the Powder. Later he places his first meeting with a large welcoming delegation on the Powder about eight miles above its mouth. This delegation then escorted him to the village about twelve miles distant. The sources do not indicate whether this was exclusively a Hunkpapa village or included other Lakota tribes as well. The implication is Hunkpapa, since no other chiefs are named. If so, the five to six thousand people De Smet estimated as living there is excessive.

Late in life, Matilda Galpin gave her account of the mission to Frances C. Holley, a Bismarck resident. She portrayed the Indians as planning to kill De Smet's party and represented their intent as a threat throughout the entire stay in the village. If so, no hint of the danger creeps into the contemporary accounts of either De Smet or Charles Galpin. Frances C. Holley, *Once Their Home; or, Our Legacy from the Dahkotahs* (Chicago: Donohue & Henneberry, 1892), 303–11.

An excellent biographical sketch of Matilda Galpin, also known as Eagle Woman, is John S. Gray, "The Story of Mrs. Picotte-Galpin, a Sioux Heroine," *Montana the Magazine of Western History* 36 (Spring 1986): 2–21; (Summer 1986): 2–21.

4. Chittenden and Richardson, *Life, Letters, and Travels of Father Pierre-Jean De Smet*, vol. 3, p. 912.

5. *Papers Relating to Talks and Councils*, 111.

6. "Council of the Indian Peace Commission with the Various Bands of Sioux Indians at Fort Rice, Dakt. T., July 2, 1868," *Papers Relating to Talks and Councils*, 95.

7. The text of the treaty is in Charles J. Kappler, comp., *Indian Affairs: Laws and Treaties*, 2 vols. (Washington, D.C.: Government Printing Office, 1904), vol. 2, pp. 998–1007.

8. Capt. C. D. Dickey to AAAG Middle District, Fort Buford, August 21, 1868, RG 393, Department of Dakota LR, box 4, NARA. Details of unsuccessful attempts to recover the cattle appear in subsequent correspondence in the same source. For a lengthy analysis of the military situation on the upper Missouri at this time, see Col. Philippe Régis de Trobriand to AAG Department of Dakota, Fort Stevenson, September 6, 1868, ibid. Same to same, September 22, 1868, ibid., links Sitting Bull to the Fort Buford raid through a rifle he had taken from one of the mail carriers the previous May, which was seized in association with some of the cattle run off from Fort Buford.

9. Old Bull, box 105, notebook 11, Campbell Collection.

10. Scarcely any event in Sitting Bull's life has bred more confusion in the sources than his designation as supreme chief. The year, the place, the dynamics of the selection, and its meaning are all muddled in the surviving evidence. I have balanced the sources against one another and against a test of plausibility and emerged with my own interpretation of what happened. It is based mainly on the following: Robert P. Higheagle Manuscript, box 104, folder 21, pp. 2, 4, 43; Higheagle, "Twenty-five Songs Made by Sitting Bull," box 104, folder 17; One

Bull, box 104, One Bull folder, no. 11, MS 127; White Bull, "Life of Sitting Bull," box 105, notebook 4; White Bull, box 105, notebook 4, p. 9; White Bull, notebook 8; White Bull, box 106, notebook 53; Old Bull, box 105, notebook 11; all in Campbell Collection.

11. For Crazy Horse, see Encouraging Bear or Chips (Crazy Horse's holy man), interview by Eli S. Ricker, February 14, 1907, Ricker Collection, tablet 18, microfilm roll 3, NHS; and He Dog and other Oglalas, interviews by Eleanor H. Hinman, in Hinman, "Oglala Sources on the Life of Crazy Horse," *Nebraska History* 57 (Spring 1976): 1–51. The standard biography is Mari Sandoz, *Crazy Horse, The Strange Man of the Oglalas* (New York: Hastings House, 1942). It is better literature than history.

12. Other locations mentioned are Rainy Buttes at the head of the Cannonball and the lower Powder. The Rosebud, as an increasingly favored Lakota rendezvous, is my preference. Although 1867 is often given as the year, I do not believe it occurred until after the conclusion of the Treaty of 1868, when the tribal divisions began to grow acute. The Galpin–De Smet record of the council with the Hunkpapas in June 1868 makes clear that Sitting Bull appeared in the role of Hunkpapa war chief, while Four Horns and Black Moon were the political functionaries who acted as chief negotiators.

13. One Bull, box 104, One Bull Folder, no. 11, Campbell Collection.

14. Robert P. Higheagle, "Twenty-five Songs Made by Sitting Bull," box 104, folder 17, Campbell Collection. White Bull, who was present at the ceremony, sang this song for Higheagle.

15. Thomas B. Marquis, *A Warrior Who Fought Custer* (Minneapolis, Minn.: Midwest Company, 1931), 205.

16. This pattern emerges clearly in James C. Olson, *Red Cloud and the Sioux Problem* (Lincoln: University of Nebraska Press, 1965).

CHAPTER 8

Shield

1. Unidentified newspaper clipping, c. October 27, 1870, enclosure to SIA J. A. Viall to CIA E. S. Parker, Helena, November 9, 1870, RG 75, BIA LR Montana Superintendency, NARA (M234, roll 490, frame 766). Joseph Henry Taylor, *Sketches of Frontier and Indian Life on the Upper Missouri and Great Plains* (Pottstown, Pa., privately published, n.d.), 78–80. Taylor was a member of the wood party. He names the victim Teck Aldrich rather than Charles Teck, as reported in the newspaper.

2. White Bull, box 105, notebook 8; and Robert P. Higheagle Manuscript, box 104, folder 21, p. 3, Campbell Collection.

3. CIA, *Annual Report, 1872*, 8.

4. These developments are described in detail in a series of documents ap-

pended to Acting SI B. R. Cowen to SW, Washington, June 8, 1871, RG 94, AGO LR 1871–80, file 2019 AGO 1871, NARA (M666, roll 16, frames 506ff.). Lt. William Quinton to Post Adjutant, Fort Shaw, May 19, 1871, RG 75, BIA LR Montana Superintendency, NARA (M234, roll 491, frame 1106). Quinton was in charge of a wagon train escort at the agency when the Indians came in. Viall to CIA, Helena, August 21, 1871, ibid. (frame 871).

5. Report of Commissioners to Visit the Teton Sioux, Washington, D.C., October 15, 1872, CIA, *Annual Report, 1872*, 457. See also *Chicago Tribune*, August 4, 1876, which told of a "Kannacka" among the Sioux who was "a dangerous customer. He speaks English well and was formerly employed as a mail carrier on the Missouri river routes. This man is an excellent scout, and from his acquaintance with English can prove, and no doubt has proved, himself very efficient in learning the intentions of the white men and aided in frustrating their designs." The reference to the head soldier is in the Quinton document cited in note 4.

6. Frank Grouard's parentage and early life are no longer mysterious, thanks to documentation in the Addison Pratt Papers. I am grateful to S. George Ellsworth, editor of the Pratt Papers, for bringing this to my attention and furnishing me a copy of a long autobiographical letter from Grouard to his adoptive mother, written from the Belle Fourche River in the Black Hills while a scout for General George Crook, December 16, 1876. Additional biographical details are contained in John W. Christian to W. M. Camp, Beaver, Utah, February 7, 1918, and Mrs. Thomas Willis to W. M. Camp, Idaho Falls, Idaho, February 25, 1918, box 2, folder 3, Walter M. Camp Papers, Harold B. Lee Library, Brigham Young University, Provo, Utah. Frank was originally named Ephriam, while an older brother bore the name Frank. After leaving the Pratts, however, Ephriam, for reasons unknown, adopted his brother's name.

   In the 1890s, Grouard told his story to a journalist who added much of his own imaginative embroidery but left more or less of his subject's reminiscences intact: Joe DeBarthe, *Life and Adventures of Frank Grouard*, ed. Edgar I. Stewart (Norman: University of Oklahoma Press, 1957). It should be read in conjunction with a fine exercise in historical sleuthing: John S. Gray, "Frank Grouard: Kanaka Scout or Mulatto Renegade?" *Westerners Brand Book* (Chicago) 16 (October 1959): 57–59, 60–64. I have used the DeBarthe book sparingly, where the words are Grouard's and seem plausible when fitted into the context of other evidence.

7. The sister was clearly Good Feather, mother of White Bull and One Bull, although Grouard called her White Cow, which could have been an alternate name.

8. Simmons to Viall, Fort Browning, December 5, 1871, House Executive Documents, 43d Congress, 3d session, no. 96, pp. 11–15.

9. Durfee and Peck to CIA F. A. Walker, Leavenworth, Kansas, January 5, 1872, RG 75, BIA LR Montana Superintendency, NARA (M234, roll 492, frame 158). Simmons to Walker, Fort Benton, May 18, 1872, ibid. (frame 562). Same to same, Fort Peck, June 9, 1872, ibid. (frame 565). Viall to Walker, Helena, June 13, 1872, ibid. (roll 493, frame 96). Same to same, Helena, June 20, 1872, ibid.

(frame 940). Simmons to Viall, Milk River Agency, June 1, 1872, ibid. (M833, roll 2, frame 402). Simmons to Viall, Milk River Agency, September 1, 1872, ibid. (frame 411). USIA Theodore M. Koues to Walker, CRA, January 20, 1872, RG 75, BIA LR CRA, NARA (M234, roll 127, frame 339). USIA J. C. Connor to Walker, GRA, June 17, 1872, ibid. (roll 305, frame 440).

10. Walker to SI Columbus Delano, January 23, 1872, and Delano to Speaker of the House, January 24, House Executive Documents, 43d Congress, 3d session, No. 96, pp. 8–10. 17 Stat. 165–91 (May 29, 1872).

11. The commission's report is printed in CIA, *Annual Report, 1872*, 456–63.

12. Simmons to Cowen, Fort Peck, December 8, 1872, RG 75, BIA LR Montana Superintendency, NARA (M234, roll 495, frame 760). Simmons to N. J. Turney, Fort Peck, December 15, 1872, ibid. (frame 753). M. C. Thum (Durfee and Peck agent) to C. K. Peck, Helena, January 17, 1873, ibid. (frame 550). Thum to N. J. Turney, Helena, January 16, 1873, ibid. (roll 496, frame 165). Simmons to Walker, January 11, 1873, ibid., RG 75, BIA LR Montana Superintendency, NARA (M833, roll 2, frame 440). *Helena Herald*, January 16, 1873.

13. SI Columbus Delano to CIA, December 11, 1872, RG 75, BIA LR Montana Superintendency, NARA (M234, roll 492, frame 461). Simmons to CIA, Fort Peck, May 8, 1873, ibid. (roll 695, frame 816). For additional history see Inspector J. E. Bevier to CIA E. P. Smith, Fort Belknap, August 3, 1874, ibid. (roll 498, frame 512).

14. White Bull, box 105, notebooks 8 and 24; Old Bull, box 106, notebook 50; Circling Hawk, box 105, notebook 13, Campbell Collection. Frank Grouard gave his version of the fight in Joe DeBarthe, *Life and Adventures of Frank Grouard*, ed. Edgar I. Stewart (Norman: University of Oklahoma Press, 1958), 46–48. Col. David S. Stanley got the story from a Miniconjou, Little-White-Swan, and passed it on to higher headquarters: Stanley to AAG Department of Dakota, Fort Sully, February 12, 1870, RG 75, BIA LR Montana Superintendency, NARA (M833, roll 2, frame 669). The site is now known as Crow Rock and is near the community of Crow Rock, Montana.

15. White Bull, box 105, notebooks 4 and 24; Circling Hawk, box 105, notebook 13, Campbell Collection. James H. Howard, trans. and ed., *The Warrior Who Killed Custer: The Personal Narrative of Chief Joseph White Bull* (Lincoln: University of Nebraska Press, 1968), 41–47.

16. Gray Eagle, box 106, notebook 54; White Bull, box 105, notebook 24, pp. 18–21, 48; Little Soldier, box 104, folder 6; genealogical chart compiled at conference with White Bull, One Bull, and families, 1937, box 106, notebook 48, Campbell Collection.

17. Robert P. Higheagle Manuscript, pp. 2, 10; White Bull, box 105, notebook 8; One Bull, box 105, notebook 19, Campbell Collection. Clark Wissler, "Societies and Ceremonial Associations in the Oglala Division of the Teton-Dakota," American Museum of Natural History *Anthropological Papers* 11 (1912): 75. James R. Walker, *Lakota Belief and Ritual*, ed. Raymond J. DeMallie and Elaine A. Jahner

(Lincoln: University of Nebraska Press, 1980), 101. Stanley Vestal, *New Sources of Indian History, 1850–1891* (Norman: University of Oklahoma Press, 1934), 231–33.
18. Frances Densmore, *Teton Sioux Music*, Bureau of American Ethnology Bulletin 61 (Washington, D.C.: Government Printing Office, 1918), 330. See also One Bull, box 104, One Bull folder, no. 11; and Old Bull, box 105, notebook 11, Campbell Collection. Vestal, *New Sources of Indian History*, 183.
19. All the categories of official records cited in these pages, both civil and military, heavily document the arms trade by all these parties. Undoubtedly some arms passed through the licensed traders, but fewer, I believe, than the military charged. Unlicensed traders, licensed traders operating without oversight by Indian agents or army officers, and the Slotas, together with weapons taken in raids, account for the improved arms that found their way to the hunting bands in the 1870s.
20. DeBarthe, *Life and Adventures of Frank Grouard*, 48–49. White Bull, box 105, notebook 8, Campbell Collection. Grouard says the camp contained two to three hundred lodges. If his dating of winter 1872–73 is accurate, the camp had to have been the small group of diehards who refused to go to Fort Peck and remained with Sitting Bull.
21. This account relies on Old Bull, box 105, notebook 12; and White Bull, box 105, notebook 24, pp. 39–43, Campbell Collection. See also Howard, *Warrior Who Killed Custer*, 65–66.

CHAPTER 9

Wasichus *on Elk River*

1. SW, *Annual Report, 1871*, 24–31. Capt. Edward Ball to Post Adjutant, Fort Ellis, December 10, 1871, RG 94, AGO LR 1871–80, file 3512 AGO 1872, NARA (M666, roll 81, frame 470). Special USIA Theodore M. Koues to CIA F. A. Walker, CRA, March 30, 1872, RG 75, BIA LR CRA, NARA (M234, roll 127, frame 383).
2. Stanley to CIA F. A. Walker, Fort Sully, April 7, 1872, RG 75, BIA LR CRA, NARA (M234, roll 127, frame 475). This was a copy of a letter he sent to Gen. Winfield S. Hancock, his department commander.
3. Indian sources for the Arrow Creek fight are White Bull, box 105, notebook 24, and box 104, White Bull folder, no. 12; Old Bull, box 105, notebooks 1, 2, and 9; and box 106, notebook 51, Campbell Collection. White sources include Maj. E. M. Baker to AAG Department of Dakota, Fort Ellis, October 18, 1872, RG 94, AGO LR 1871–80, file 3323 AGO 1872, NARA (M666, roll 80, frame 132ff); Maj. J. M. Barlow to AAG Division of the Missouri, Chicago, October 16, 1872, ibid. (frame 132ff); *Helena Herald*, August 22, 1872. Major Baker was so drunk he could not direct the fight and was superseded by a subordinate. He later faced court-martial charges. Major Barlow was General Sheridan's chief

engineer, who accompanied the expedition and wrote a detailed report. The surveyors, of course, were under the direction of their own engineer, J. A. Hayden.

4. Capt. Carlile Boyd to AAG Department of Dakota, U.S. Military Station CRA, September 6, 1872, RG 94, AGO LR 1871–80, NARA (M666, roll 80, frame 132).

5. Capt. S. C. Kellogg to AAG Division of the Missouri, Chicago, September 13, 1872; and Col. D. S. Stanley to AAG Department of Dakota, Fort Sully, October 28, 1872, RG 94, AGO LR 1871–80, file 3512 AGO 1872, NARA (M666, roll 81, frames 338–50 and 383–420). An excellent account, based on these sources as well as private letters of one of the officers and a journal kept by the Northern Pacific engineers, is Francis B. Robertson, "We Are Going to Have a Big Sioux War: Colonel David S. Stanley's Yellowstone Expedition, 1872," *Montana the Magazine of Western History* 34 (Autumn 1984): 2–15. The Indian source is Old Bull, box 106, notebook 51, Campbell Collection.

6. Stanley's report, October 28, 1872, as cited in note 5. Capt. Clarence Bennett to his wife, August 26, 1872, quoted in Robertson, "We Are Going to Have a Big Sioux War," 12.

7. Old Bull, box 106, notebook 51, Campbell Collection.

8. Congressional Globe, 42d Congress, 3d session, p. 2096 (March 3, 1873).

9. Much original documentation is set forth in Lawrence A. Frost, *Custer's 7th Cav and the Campaign of 1873* (El Segundo, Calif.: Upton & Sons, 1986). Military reports of Stanley and Custer are in RG 393, Division of the Missouri Special Files, NARA (M1495, roll 1). I have treated the subject from the military viewpoint in *Cavalier in Buckskin: George Armstrong Custer and the Western Military Frontier* (Norman: University of Oklahoma Press, 1988), chap. 5.

10. Joe DeBarthe, *Life and Adventures of Frank Grouard*, ed. Edgar I. Stewart (Norman: University of Oklahoma Press, 1958), 52–53.

11. Custer to AAAG Yellowstone Expedition, Pompey's Pillar, August 15, 1873, RG 393, Division of the Missouri Special Files, NARA (M1495, roll 1, frame 719ff). George A. Custer, "Battling with the Sioux on the Yellowstone," *Galaxy* 22 (July 1876): 91–102, in Paul A. Hutton, ed., *The Custer Reader* (Lincoln: University of Nebraska Press, 1992), 201–20.

12. White Bull, box 105, notebook 24, Campbell Collection.

13. Sanding Elk in Raymond J. DeMallie, ed., *The Sixth Grandfather: Black Elk's Teachings Given to John G. Neihardt* (Lincoln: University of Nebraska Press, 1984), 163–64. As historical sources, Neihardt's original interview transcripts are more valuable than his poetic rendition in *Black Elk Speaks* (New York: William Morrow and Co., 1932) and will be used instead in this work. DeMallie's annotations are extremely helpful.

14. For the Black Hills Expedition, see my own *Cavalier in Buckskin*, chap. 6; and Donald Jackson, *Custer's Gold: The United States Cavalry Expedition of 1874* (New Haven, Conn.: Yale University Press, 1966).

15. USIA H. W. Bingham to CIA E. P. Smith, CRA, August 17, 1874, RG 75, BIA LR CRA, NARA (M234, roll 128, frame 236).

16. USIA James Wright to CIA E. P. Smith, Crow Agency, July 14, 1874, RG 75, BIA LR Montana Superintendency, NARA (M234, roll 500, frame 1005).

17. USIA Dexter E. Clapp to CIA E. P. Smith, Crow Agency, September 10, 1875, CIA, *Annual Report, 1875*, 301–4. Clapp to Smith, Crow Agency, July 5, 1875, RG 75 BIA LR Montana Superintendency, NARA (M234, roll 501, frame 503). W. Y. Smith to Charles Rich, New Crow Agency, July 2, 1875, RG 94, AGO LR 1871–80, file 3517 AGO 1875, NARA (M666, roll 221, frame 142). Clapp to Capt. D. W. Benham, New Crow Agency, July 5, 1875, ibid. (frame 148). Benham to AAAG District of Montana, Fort Ellis, July 7, 1875, ibid. (frame 151).

18. Potts to CIA E. P. Smith, Virginia City, August 24, 1874, RG 75, BIA LR Montana Superintendency, NARA (M234, roll 500, frame 179). Potts to SI Columbus Delano, Helena, July 8, 1875, RG 94, AGO LR 1871–80, file 3517 AGO 1875, NARA (M666, roll 221, frame 178).

19. This account is drawn from Addison M. Quivey, "The Yellowstone Expedition of 1874," *Montana Historical Society Contributions* 1 (1876): 268–84; James H. Bradley, "Yellowstone Expedition of 1874," ibid. 8 (1917): 105–26; J. E. Cook to W. M. Camp, Belle Fourche, S.D., March 16, 1919, box 2, folder 4, Camp Papers, Harold B. Lee Library, Brigham Young University; and a series of interviews conducted by Walter M. Camp, Camp Papers, Lilly Library, Indiana University, copies in Hammer Collection, Harold B. Lee Library, Brigham Young University: William C. Barkley, box 3, folder 4; Red Hawk and No Flesh, box 3, folder 6; and White Bull, box 6, folder 9. An excellent synthesis is James S. Hutchins, "Poison in the Pemmican: The Yellowstone Wagon-Road and Prospecting Expedition of 1874," *Montana the Magazine of Western History* 8 (Summer 1958): 8–15.

20. Capt. D. W. Benham to AAAG District of Montana, Fort Ellis, June 23 and 29, 1875, RG 94, AGO LR 1871–80, file 3517 AGO 1875, NARA (M666, roll 221, frames 75, 123). Capt. George L. Tyler to Post Adjutant, Fort Ellis, June 28, 1875, ibid. (frame 127). USIA Dexter E. Clapp to CIA E. P. Smith, Crow Agency, July 5, 1875, RG 75, BIA LR Montana Superintendency, NARA (M234, roll 501, frame 503). Capt. George L. Browning to AAG District of Montana, Camp Lewis, July 30, 1875, NARA, ibid. (frame 593). *Bismark Tribune*, August 11, 1875.

21. Affidavit of Paul McCormick and Benjamin Dexter, Bozeman, February 18, 1976, RG 75, BIA LR Montana Superintendency, NARA (M234, roll 505, frame 726). Maj. James Brisbin to USIA Dexter E. Clapp, Fort Ellis, February 20, 1876, ibid. (frame 323). James H. Bradley, "Adventures of Three Wolfers," *Montana Historical Society Contributions* 8 (1917): 139–39. Paul McCormick, interview by Walter M. Camp, Camp Papers, Lilly Library, Indiana University, copy in box 3, folder 6, Hammer Collection, Harold B. Lee Library, Brigham Young University. George Herendeen, interview by Walter M. Camp, box 6, folder 4, Camp Papers, Brigham Young University.

CHAPTER 10

War

1. Thomas B. Marquis, *A Warrior Who Fought Custer* (Minneapolis, Minn.: Midwest Company, 1931), 177.

2. Peter J. Powell, *People of the Sacred Mountain: A History of the Northern Cheyenne Chiefs and Warrior Societies*, 1830–1879, 2 vols. (New York: Harper & Row, 1981), vol. 2, pp. 928–29.

3. George B. Grinnell, account of Sitting Bull's sun dance in the summer of 1875 as given in letter of White Bull (Ice) to Grinnell, September 22, 1906, Grinnell notebook 345 and also envelope 497, George B. Grinnell Papers, Southwest Museum, Los Angeles.

4. Like my previous references to Grouard, this is drawn from Joe DeBarthe, *Life and Adventures of Frank Grouard*, ed. Edgar I. Stewart (Norman: University of Oklahoma Press, 1957), chaps. 15, 17, and 28; as modified by John S. Gray, "Frank Grouard: Kanaka Scout or Mulatto Renegade?" *Westerners Brand Book* (Chicago) 16 (October 1959): 57 59, 60 61. Grouard's background and mission to the northern Indians is also touched on in the *New York Herald*, September 22, 1875.

5. DeBarthe, *Life and Adventures of Frank Grouard*, chap. 28. USIA J. J. Saville to CIA E. P. Smith, RCA, August 16, 1875, RG 75, BIA LR RCA 1871–75, NARA (M234, roll 719, frame 1012) reports the return of the delegation, which portrayed the Indians as more divided than Grouard recalled and indicated that many were coming in for the council. William Garnett, interview by Eli S. Ricker, January 15, 1907, tablet no. 2, p. 121, Ricker Collection, NHS, states that the delegation persuaded only a few Indians to come to Red Cloud. Garnett was on the payroll at Red Cloud at the time.

6. Enumerating people from elsewhere who had come for the council and needed rations, the Red Cloud agent counted four hundred "northern Indians not belonging to any agency." USIA J. J. Saville to CIA E. P. Smith, RCA, September 23, 1875, RG 75, BIA LR, RCA 1871–75, NARA (M234, roll 719, frame 1096). Details of the council appear in dispatches filed from the scene appearing in the *New York Herald*, September 22 and 27, October 1, 6, and 7, 1875. The best secondary account, with sound interpretations, is James C. Olson, *Red Cloud and the Sioux Problem* (Lincoln: University of Nebraska Press, 1965), chap. 11. Little-Big-Man's threats were remembered by Sioux participants and set down in the Robert P. Higheagle Manuscript, box 104, folder 21, p. 34, Campbell Collection. Valentine T. McGillycuddy, later Oglala agent, also recorded Little-Big-Man's role and remarked, "I met the senator [Allison] in Washington the following Winter and the mere mention of 'Little Big Man' brought on a chill." McGillycuddy to Doane Robinson, November 26, 1923, box 8, folder 126, Doane Robinson Papers, SDHS. The official record is "Report of the Commis-

sion Appointed to Treat with the Sioux Indians for the Relinquishment of the Black Hills," Washington, D.C., n.d., c. October 1875, CIA, *Annual Report, 1875*, 184–205.

7. Iron Hawk, a Hunkpapa, in Raymond J. DeMallie, ed., *The Sixth Grandfather: Black Elk's Teachings Given to John G. Neihardt* (Lincoln: University of Nebraska Press, 1984), 171–72.

8. This and other documents tracing the unfolding policy are printed in House Executive Documents, 44th Congress, 1st session, no. 184, Serial 1691. For an excellent analysis of what really happened and why, see John S. Gray, *Centennial Campaign: The Sioux War of 1876* (Norman: University of Oklahoma Press, 1988), chaps. 2 and 3. See also Paul A. Hutton, *Phil Sheridan and His Army* (Lincoln: University of Nebraska Press, 1985), 297–301.

9. USIA Dexter E. Clapp to CIA, Crow Agency, February 29, 1876 (enclosing two letters from Brisbin), RG 75, BIA LR Montana Superintendency, NARA (M234, roll 504, frame 318). Brisbin to AAG Department of Dakota, Fort Ellis, March 21, 1876, ibid. (roll 505, frame 1010). Edgar I. Stewart, "Major Brisbin's Relief of Fort Pease: A Prelude to the Bloody Little Big Horn Massacre," *Montana the Magazine of Western History* 6 (Summer 1956): 23–27.

10. The numbers and movements of the hunting bands are brilliantly reconstructed in Gray, *Centennial Campaign*, chaps. 26 and 27. I have examined all of his sources and agree with his analysis.

11. USIA H. W. Bingham to CIA, CRA, February 12, 1876, RG 75, BIA LR CRA, NARA (M234, roll 129, frame 52).

12. *Bismarck Tribune*, March 11, 1876, reporting dispatch from Fort Buford, February 27. Acting USIA William Courtenay to Lt. Col. Daniel Huston, Fort Berthold, March 27, 1876, RG 393, Division of the Missouri Special Files, NARA (M1495, roll 2, frame 718).

13. Gray, *Centennial Campaign*, 55, 322–23. Powell, *People of the Sacred Mountain*, vol. 2, pp. 937–46.

14. Lt. George Ruhlen to AAG Department of Dakota, CRA, April 19, 1876, RG 393, Division of the Missouri Special Files, NARA (M1495, roll 2, frame 739).

15. White Bull, box 105, notebooks 4 and 8, Campbell Collection.

CHAPTER 11

Soldiers Upside Down

1. The literature of the Great Sioux War is voluminous and need not be cited here. I find the best history to be John S. Gray, *Centennial Campaign: The Sioux War of 1876* (Norman: University of Oklahoma Press, 1988), which should be used in conjunction with his more detailed study of the Little Bighorn campaign, *Custer's*

Last Campaign: Mitch Boyer and the Little Bighorn Reconstructed (Lincoln: University of Nebraska Press, 1991).

2. I am following Gray's reconstruction in *Centennial Campaign*, chap. 27, entitled "The Gathering of the Winter Roamers."

3. Thomas B. Marquis, *A Warrior Who Fought Custer* (Minneapolis, Minn.: Midwest Company, 1931), 171–72.

4. Two Moons, interview by Richard Throssel, 1909, in Richard G. Hardorff, ed., *Lakota Recollections of the Custer Fight: New Sources of Indian-Military History* (Spokane, Wash.: Arthur H. Clark Co., 1991), 133.

5. Marquis, *Warrior Who Fought Custer*, 178–79.

6. The clearest and most detailed account of the progress of the village is Wooden Leg's in Marquis, *Warrior Who Fought Custer*, chap. 6. But consult for this and other sources Gray, *Centennial Campaign*, chap. 27. See also Peter J. Powell, *People of the Sacred Mountain: A History of the Northern Cheyenne Chiefs and Warrior Societies, 1830–1879*, 2 vols. (New York: Harper & Row, 1981), vol. 2, pp. 947–53.

7. White Bull, box 105, notebook 24, pp. 70–71, Campbell Collection. Marquis, *Warrior Who Fought Custer*, 185.

8. Lt. James H. Bradley, *The March of the Montana Column: A Prelude to the Custer Disaster* (Norman: University of Oklahoma Press, 1991), 87.

9. The hunting party included Wooden Leg, for which see Marquis, *Warrior Who Fought Custer*, 193–98. For Little Hawk, see George B. Grinnell, *The Fighting Cheyennes* (Norman: University of Oklahoma Press, 1956), 328–29.

10. One Bull, box 110, "Prophecy of Sitting Bull," Campbell Collection.

11. One Bull, box 105, notebook 24, Campbell Collection.

12. Wooden Leg locates the dance site and is the authority for its character as exclusively Hunkpapa. Marquis, *Warrior Who Fought Custer*, 191–92. John G. Neihardt, *Black Elk Speaks* (New York: William Morrow & Co., 1932), 95–99, has Black Elk, a boy whose people had just arrived from Red Cloud Agency, describe four days of ceremony. Neihardt's informant, however, was Standing Elk, not Black Elk, and he did not describe the ceremony. Neihardt himself derived the description of the sun dance attributed to Black Elk from conventional published sources. Raymond J. DeMallie, ed., *The Sixth Grandfather: Black Elk's Teachings Given to John G. Neihardt* (Lincoln: University of Nebraska Press, 1984), 173–74.

13. White Bull, box 105, notebook 24, and Old Bull, box 106, notebook 57, Campbell Collection.

14. White Bull, box 105, notebook 8; One Bull, box 104, folder 10, and box 105, notebook 19, Campbell Collection.

15. This seems the most reasonable reading of Little Hawk's account in George Bird Grinnell, *The Fighting Cheyennes* (Norman: University of Oklahoma Press, 1955), 330–32. It is somewhat confusing in implying that there was only one expedition, the one that resulted in the skirmish of June 9. Chronology and topography dictate two.

16. Little Hawk places his arrival at dawn, but chronology does not permit this. Wooden Leg got it right, in Marquis, *Warrior Who Fought Custer*, 198. Wooden Leg also said the Cheyennes told the Sioux of Little Hawk's find, but conceded that they may have had the report from their own scouts.

17. Wooden Leg in Marquis, *Warrior Who Fought Custer*, 198.

18. Ibid., 199.

19. Old Bull, box 105, notebook 7; White Bull, box 104, notebook 54 and box 105, notebooks 4, 23, and 24, Campbell Collection.

20. Marquis, *Warrior Who Fought Custer*, 202.

21. James H. Howard, *The Warrior Who Killed Custer: The Personal Narrative of Chief Joseph White Bull* (Lincoln: University of Nebraska Press, 1968), 49–50. White Bull, box 106, notebook 54, Campbell Collection. Hamlin Garland, "General Custer's Last Fight as Seen by Two Moon," *McClure's Magazine* (September 1898), in W. A. Graham, *The Custer Myth: A Source Book of Custeriana* (Harrisburg, Pa.: Stackpole Co., 1953), 102.

22. Crook's first official dispatch, June 19, 1876, is in RG 94, AGO LR 1871–80, file 3570 AGO 1876, NARA (M666, roll 271, frame 160). His full report, June 20, with annexed reports of subordinates, is in ibid. (frame 207). See also Neil C. Mangum, *Battle of the Rosebud: Prelude to the Little Bighorn* (El Segundo, Calif.: Upton & Sons, 1987); J. W. Vaughn, *With Crook at the Rosebud* (Harrisburg, Pa.: Stackpole Co., 1956); and Vaughn, *Indian Fights: New Facts on Seven Encounters* (Norman: University of Oklahoma Press, 1966), chap. 4.

23. Again, I am following the reconstruction of Gray, *Centennial Campaign*, chaps. 28 and 29, entitled "The Summer Migrations" and "The Strength of the Little Big Horn Village." The clearest exposition of the moves is Wooden Leg in Marquis, *Warrior Who Fought Custer*, 204–12.

24. White Bull, box 105, notebook 24, p. 48, Campbell Collection. One Bull, box 104, folder 6, said he lived in the tipi with Sitting Bull, but White Bull seems the more explicit and reliable.

25. One Bull, as recounted to Robert Higheagle, in Higheagle, "Twenty-five Songs Made by Sitting Bull," box 104, folder 17, Campbell Collection. One Bull was explicit in identifying the site of this ceremony as the hill where Custer fell the next day. However, Lt. Charles A. Varnum, testifying at the Reno Court of Inquiry, noted incidentally that on climbing another hill on June 28 he had observed "lots of little piles of stone, and Indian medicine-bags on top of it." This hill, three miles south of Custer Hill, later took the name Weir Point. Opposite the Hunkpapa circle, it would have been a more convenient elevation for Sitting Bull to choose, and it is possible that Varnum had unknowingly stumbled on to Sitting Bull's offerings. *The Reno Court of Inquiry: The Chicago Times Account* (Fort Collins, Colo.: Old Army Press, 1972), 161.

CHAPTER 12

Long Hair

1. John S. Gray, "Bloody Knife: Ree Scout for Custer," *Westerners Brand Book* (Chicago) 17 (February 1961): 89–96. Custer's scout contingent consisted of thirty-seven Rees, four Sioux, and four mixed bloods. They are all identified in John S. Gray, "Arikara Scouts with Custer," *North Dakota History* 35 (Spring 1968): 443–78.

2. An excellent analysis of Indian testimony, most of which I have examined, is Richard G. Hardorff, "Custer's Trail to Wolf Mountains: A Reevaluation of Evidence," in John M. Carroll and Jay Smith, eds., *Custer and His Times Book Two* (Fort Worth, Tex.: Little Big Horn Associates, 1984), 85–122. See also Hardorff's *Hokahey! A Good Day to Die! The Indian Casualties of the Custer Fight* (Spokane, Wash.: Arthur H. Clark Co., 1992); and Black Bear, interview by Walter M. Camp, July 18, 1911, in Kenneth Hammer, ed., *Custer in '76: Walter Camp's Notes on the Custer Fight* (Provo, Utah: Brigham Young University Press, 1976), 203.

3. Black Elk, Standing Elk, and Iron Hawk, in Raymond J. DeMallie, ed., *The Sixth Grandfather: Black Elk's Teachings Given to John G. Neihardt* (Lincoln: University of Nebraska Press, 1984), 181, 184, 190. Curiously, virtually every Indian account places the onset of battle in the morning, which can only be explained by the typical Indian unconcern for time. The timing of Custer's progress, as established by mountains of corroborative documentation, places the opening of the fight at midafternoon. Some students have attempted to account for time discrepancies by assuming watches were set by Chicago time, which they were not, but that still would not close the time gap between white and Indian sources. A minute-by-minute reconstruction of the progress of all the military units has been charted, with accompanying time-motion tables, by John S. Gray, *Custer's Last Campaign: Mitch Boyer and the Little Bighorn Reconstructed* (Lincoln: University of Nebraska Press, 1991), passim.

4. Moving-Robe-Woman (Mary Crawler), interview by Frank B. Zahn, 1931, in Richard G. Hardorff, *Lakota Recollections of the Custer Fight* (Spokane, Wash.: Arthur H. Clark Co., 1991), 93.

5. One Bull, box 105, notebook 19, Campbell Collection. One Bull, interview by Mary C. Collins, box 2, folder 16, Collins Papers, SDHS. In the latter One Bull tells of getting their mothers to safety. In the former he says they entrusted that to old men and stayed to fight.

6. E. H. Allison to E. S. Ricker, March 7, 1906, Ricker Collection, NHS. Allison was married to a Hunkpapa woman and figures in this story later, when he tried to persuade Sitting Bull to come back from Canada and surrender.

7. One Bull, box 104, folder 6, and box 105, notebook 19, Campbell Collection.

8. White Bull, box 105, notebook 24, Campbell Collection. There are two detailed interviews by White Bull, the other in notebook 23. Hardorff, *Lakota Recollections of the Custer Fight*, 107–26, has expertly fashioned the latter into a coherent narrative, faithful to the substance of the original notes, with footnotes drawing from the former.

9. From 1886 interview at Custer Battlefield, in W. A. Graham, *The Custer Myth: A Source Book of Custeriana* (Harrisburg, Pa.: Stackpole Co., 1953), 90. The *Bismarck Tribune* extra of July 7, 1876, told of ten women killed here by the Ree scouts.

10. Iron Hawk, interview by E. S. Ricker, May 12, 1907, roll 3, notebook 25, Ricker Collection, NHS.

11. White Bull, box 105, notebook 24, Campbell Collection.

12. White Bull, box 105, notebook 23, Campbell Collection. See Hardorff, *Lakota Recollections of the Custer Fight*, 111.

13. The complicated sequence of movements in Reno's valley fight is ably reconstructed by J. W. Vaughn, *Indian Fights: New Facts on Seven Encounters* (Norman: University of Oklahoma Press, 1966), chap. 5.

14. The description of Crazy Horse's arrival is from Black Elk in DeMallie, *Sixth Grandfather*, 182. Indian accounts agree on Crazy Horse's dramatic arrival, but just when it occurred is vague. They seem to suggest that the charge in which he bore a conspicuous part was aimed at the timber, and no other took place after Reno was routed from his second position. The fighting in the open lasted no more than fifteen minutes before the line reformed on the old riverbank. Since Crazy Horse is said to have taken so long to prepare for battle that his warriors grew impatient, and they had to ride nearly two miles from the Oglala circle, the arrival cannot have been prompt. My interpretation seems as reasonable as any. See for other Indian references to Crazy Horse Standing Bear in ibid., 188; Nicholas Ruleau, Iron Hawk, and Red Feather in Hardorff, *Lakota Recollections of the Custer Fight*, 40, 64–65, 82–84; Standing Bear in Hammer, *Custer in '76*, 214–15; Iron Hawk and Ruleau in notebooks 25 and 29, Ricker Collection, NHS.

15. One Bull, box 105, notebook 19, Campbell Collection. One Bull, interview by Mary C. Collins, box 2, folder 34, Collins Papers, SDHS. In the Collins interview, One Bull seems to say that this occurred during the mounted charge on Reno's second position. In the Campbell interview, he clearly indicates that the bullet came from soldiers who were getting back on their horses, which occurred at the end of the timber fight. White Bull said Good-Bear-Boy got hit in the timber. White Bull, box 105, notebook 24, Campbell Collection.

16. Hamlin Garland, "General Custer's Fight as Seen by Two Moon," *McClure's Magazine* (September 1898), in Graham, *Custer Myth*, 102.

17. Wooden Leg in Thomas B. Marquis, *A Warrior Who Fought Custer* (Minneapolis, Minn.: Midwest Co., 1931), 223. One Bull, box 105, notebook 19, Campbell Collection. Mrs. Spotted-Horn-Bull in Graham, *Custer Myth*, 84.

18. George Bird Grinnell, *The Fighting Cheyennes* (Norman: University of Oklahoma Press, 1956), 355. See also Gray, "Bloody Knife," 96.

19. Bear's Ghost as told to Frank Zahn, box 104, folder 4, Campbell Collection.

20. Eagle Elk, interview by John G. Neihardt, November 27, 1944, in Hardorff, *Lakota Recollections of the Custer Fight*, 101–02. For a short biography, see W. Boyes, *Custer's Black White Man* (Washington, D.C., privately published, 1972).

21. One Bull, box 105, notebook 19, Campbell Collection. One Bull, interview by Mary C. Collins, box 2, folder 34, Collins Papers, SDHS.

22. In Graham, *Custer Myth*, 60.

23. One Bull, box 105, notebooks 19 and 41; Gray Whirlwind, box 105, notebook 14, Campbell Collection.

24. Motives, of course, are speculative. What happened is less so. Indian testimony, archeological evidence, the observations of the men who buried the dead, and the other recollections of people close to and far from the event permit analysis and conclusions. The best are three: John S. Gray, *Custer's Last Campaign: Mitch Boyer and the Little Bighorn Reconstructed* (Lincoln: University of Nebraska Press, 1991); Richard G. Hardorff, *Markers, Artifacts and Indian Testimony: Preliminary Findings on the Custer Battle* (Short Hills, N.J.: W. Donald Horn, 1985); and Jerome A. Greene, *Evidence and the Custer Enigma: A Reconstruction of Indian-Military History* (Kansas City, Kans.: Kansas City Posse of Westerners, 1973).

25. White Bull's two extended interviews on the Custer Battle are box 105, notebooks 23 and 24, Campbell Collection. The essence of both is most easily followed in the printed version in Hardorff, *Lakota Recollections of the Custer Fight*, 107–26.

26. Gall in Graham, *Custer Myth*, 92.

27. Julia Face, interview by Sewell B. Weston, June 1909, in Hardorff, *Lakota Recollections of the Custer Fight*, 189.

28. Red Feather, interview by Gen. Hugh L. Scott, August 19, 1920, in ibid., 87–88. Several Indians mention Crazy Horse's brave deed. See especially He Dog in ibid., 75. This action destroyed Company I, Captain Myles W. Keogh. In one interview, White Bull alleged that Crazy Horse backed out at the last moment. In the other, he said Crazy Horse made the ride, which other Indian accounts conclusively show that he did.

29. He Dog, interview by Walter M. Camp, June 13, 1910, in Hammer, *Custer in '76*, 207. This occurred at the Keogh position, he said.

30. Tall Bull, interview by Walter M. Camp, July 22, 1910, in Hammer, *Custer in '76*, 213. Red Horse in Graham, *Custer Myth*, 60.

31. Lights, interview by Sewell B. Weston, 1909, in Hardorff, *Lakota Recollections of the Custer Fight*, 169.

32. David F. Barry, *Indian Notes on the Custer Battle* (Baltimore, Md.: privately published, 1937), 27.

33. In the revised edition of *Sitting Bull, Champion of the Sioux*, published after

White Bull's death, Stanley Vestal had White Bull say at this point, "Well, if that is Long Hair, I am the one who killed him." No such statement appears in Vestal's notes of White Bull's account of this incident. Vestal identifies the soldier who tried to bite White Bull's nose as Custer and describes that struggle in vivid detail. A close reading of White Bull's accounts, however, places this encounter at the foot of the last-stand hill or in the deep ravine and also makes clear that White Bull did not view the last-stand group on the hilltop until after he had been taken to his father's lodge and treated for his wounded leg.

Neither in the first edition of *Sitting Bull*, published in 1932, nor in his biography of White Bull (*Warpath: The True Story of the Fighting Sioux Told in a Biography of Chief White Bull*), published in 1934, did Vestal claim this distinction for White Bull. He later explained that he feared some hothead might harm the old man. After White Bull's death in 1947, Vestal thought the truth should be revealed.

There is an inference in the White Bull interviews that at the fiftieth-anniversary observance at the Little Bighorn Battlefield in 1926, someone planted in his mind the notion that he was Custer's slayer, and he may well have thought so. If he told Vestal he was, it did not find its way into Vestal's notes. Nowhere in White Bull's accounts of the Little Bighorn does he claim responsibility for the deed. No serious student of the Little Bighorn today believes he was responsible.

White Bull's story as recorded by James H. Howard, *The Warrior Who Killed Custer: The Personal Narrative of Chief Joseph White Bull* (Lincoln: University of Nebraska Press, 1968), reinforces Vestal's claim in the title but not in the contents. Howard simply took Vestal's word that White Bull's victim was Custer.

The issue is well treated by Raymond J. DeMallie in the introductions to the current editions of both *Sitting Bull* (Norman: University of Oklahoma Press, 1989) and *Warpath* (Lincoln: University of Nebraska Press, 1984).

Vestal first told the story in "The Man Who Killed Custer," *American Heritage* 8 (February 1957): 4–9, 90–91.

34. White Bull, box 105, notebook 24; One Bull, box 105, notebook 11, Campbell Collection.

35. White Bull, box 105, notebook 24, Campbell Collection.

36. In Graham, *Custer Myth*, 53.

37. One Bull, box 105, notebook 11, Campbell Collection.

38. See Richard Hardorff's analysis in *Hokahey!*

39. White Bull, box 105, notebook 24, Campbell Collection.

40. One Bull, box 110; see also White-Hair-on-Face, box 105, notebook 41, Campbell Collection.

41. Higheagle Manuscript, p. 44, box 104, folder 21, Campbell Collection. Readers of some of my earlier works will note that I have not been wholly free of these tendencies myself. Close study of a mass of Indian evidence for this book has reshaped some of my previous ideas about what happened and why.

42. Marquis, *Warrior Who Fought Custer*, 383.

43. Joe DeBarthe, *Life and Adventures of Frank Grouard*, ed. Edgar I. Stewart (Norman: University of Oklahoma Press, 1958), 48.

CHAPTER 13

Bear Coat

1. The movements of the Indians can be followed readily in reports from the agencies, both civil and military, that recorded what Indians arriving from the hostile camps had to say. This evidence is analyzed and authoritatively set forth in John S. Gray, *Centennial Campaign: The Sioux War of 1876* (Norman: University of Oklahoma Press, 1988), chap. 28. In addition, after Sitting Bull's surrender in 1881, officers at Fort Randall worked with him to prepare a map tracing his movements from the Little Bighorn to his entry into Canada in May 1877. The route shown on this map, filed in RG 94, NARA, conforms closely to the documentary evidence.

2. USIA C. W. Darling to Lt. Col. Daniel Huston, Fort Berthold, August 22, 1876; and Huston to AAG Department of Dakota, Fort Stevenson, August 22, 1876, RG 393, Division of the Missouri Special Files, NARA (M1495, roll 3, frames 1275 and 1271). *Bismarck Tribune*, August 30, 1876. The breakup of the village was related by prisoners Crook's command took at the Battle of Slim Buttes. Crook to Sheridan, September 15, 1876, RG 94, AGO LR 1871–80, file 3570 AGO 1876, NARA (M666, roll 271, frame 369).

3. The tribes and chiefs were identified by Indian runners who came into Cheyenne River Agency on September 8 and 9. Lt. Col. George P. Buell to AAG for Terry in the field, CRA, September 9, 1876, RG 393, Division of the Missouri Special Files, NARA (M1495, roll 4, frame 296). For the death of Sitting Bull's son: White Bull, box 104, notebook 53, Campbell Collection. This death is also mentioned in other sources, but I cannot identify the child. I believe the son by Red Woman was more likely to have been the child who died in Canada a year later, for which see chapter 15.

4. The standard history is Jerome A. Greene, *Slim Buttes: An Episode of the Great Sioux War* (Norman: University of Oklahoma Press, 1982). Greene reprints all the official reports of the officers.

5. Old Bull, box 105, notebook 11, Campbell Collection.

6. Old Bull, ibid., describes them in detail.

7. 19 Stat. 254–64 (February 28, 1877). The agreement was signed at Spotted Tail on September 23, at Red Cloud on September 26, at Standing Rock on October 11, and at Cheyenne River on October 16.

8. Sheridan to Sherman, July 18 and August 10, 1876, RG 94, LR AGO 1871–80, file 4163 AGO 1876, NARA (M666, roll 277, frame 12; and roll 278, frame

133). For an excellent history of Sheridan's thinking and his role, see Paul A. Hutton, *Phil Sheridan and His Army* (Lincoln: University of Nebraska Press, 1984), chap. 15.

9. Telegram, Terry to Sheridan, SRA, October 25, 1876, RG 393, Division of the Missouri Special Files, NARA (M1495, roll 4, frame 412). Telegram, Crook to Sheridan, Camp Robinson, October 23, 1876, ibid. (frame 404).

10. As related by Bruguier to his nephew, quoted in John S. Gray, "What Made Johnny Run?" *Montana the Magazine of Western History* 14 (April 1964): 42–43. This is the most authoritative source on Bruguier's life. See also White Bull, box 105, notebooks 23 and 24, Campbell Collection.

11. White Bull, box 105, notebook 24, Campbell Collection.

12. This according to the Miniconjou Spotted Elk (later Big Foot), who was there: Col. W. H. Wood to AAG Department of Dakota, CRA, March 1, 1877, RG 393, Division of the Missouri Special Files, NARA (M1495, roll 4, frame 739). Spotted Elk asserted that Sitting Bull did not go and was abused by the other chiefs for refusing. However, other sources make clear that he was one of the chiefs who went forward to confer. See John S. Gray, "Peace-talkers from Standing Rock Agency," *Westerners Brand Book* (Chicago) 23 (May 1966): 17–29; and Gray, "Sitting Bull Strikes the Glendive Supply Trains," ibid. 28 (June 1971): 25–27, 31–32. The first reproduces with annotations Lt. Col. W. P. Carlin to AAG Department of Dakota, SRA, November 6, 1876, forwarding the account of their mission as given by Bear's Face and Long Feather. The second reprints two contemporary accounts, with annotations. See also *Army and Navy Journal*, February 10, 1877.

13. Otis to AAG Department of Dakota, Glendive, October 27, 1876, in SW, *Annual Report, 1876*, 515–18. On the back of the dispatch signed by Colonel Carlin at Standing Rock and carried by Bear's Face, Otis entered an endorsement: "This scout reported to me on the morning of the 15th [sic, 16th] of October and brought in Sitting Bull to council." Gray, "Peace-talkers," 18.

14. Gray, "Peace-talkers," 18. This source gives a good account of the two meetings that followed. Accounts are conflicting but generally agree on substance. Among Indian accounts, White Bull's is the most detailed but also suspect: White Bull, box 105, notebook 24, pp. 93ff., Campbell Collection. Also in the Campbell Collection, box 106, notebook 54, is an interview with Gray Eagle, Sitting Bull's brother-in-law, who was there too. Another White Bull source is interview by Walter M. Camp, box 6, folder 9, Camp Papers, Harold B. Lee Library, Brigham Young University. Spotted Elk also provides a good account in Col. W. H. Wood to AAG Department of Dakota, CRA, March 1, 1877, RG 393, Division of the Missouri Special Files, NARA (M1495, roll 4, frame 739). White sources include Miles to AAG Department of Dakota, Camp opposite Cabin Creek on Yellowstone River, October 25, 1876, RG 94, AGO LR 1871–80, file 4163 AGO 1876, NARA (M666, roll 279, frame 431); *Army and Navy Journal*, November 11, 1876, and February 10, 1877; H. C. Thompson (a sergeant under

Miles), interview by Stanley Vestal, box 106, notebook 51, Campbell Collection. An authoritative account appears in Jerome A. Greene, *Yellowstone Command: Colonel Nelson A. Miles and the Great Sioux War* (Lincoln: University of Nebraska Press, 1991), chap. 5.

15. White Bull, box 104, folder 12, Campbell Collection.

16. Miles to Mary Miles, Yellowstone River 20 miles above Glendive, October 25, 1876, Sherman Miles Compilation, USMA Library.

CHAPTER 14

Winter of Despair

1. For official reports, see telegram, Crook to Sheridan, Camp on Crazy Woman Fork, November 26, 1876, and same to same, November 30 (forwarding Mackenzie's report, November 26), RG 393, Division of the Missouri Special Files, NARA (M1495, roll 4, frames 496, 498, 579). For the Indian perspective, see George B. Grinnell, *The Fighting Cheyennes* (Norman: University of Oklahoma Press, 1956), chap. 27; and Fr. Peter J. Powell, *People of the Sacred Mountain: A History of the Northern Cheyenne Chiefs and Warrior Societies*, 2 vols. (San Francisco: Harper & Row, 1981), vol. 2, pp. 1056–71. See also John G. Bourke, "Mackenzie's Last Fight with the Cheyennes: A Winter Campaign in Wyoming and Montana," *Journal of the Military Service Institution of the United States* 11 (1890)—reprint, Bellevue, Neb.: Old Army Press, 1970; and Lessing H. Nohl, Jr., "Mackenzie against Dull Knife: Breaking the Northern Cheyennes in 1876," in K. Ross Toole, ed., *Probing the American West: Papers from the Santa Fe Conference* (Santa Fe: Museum of New Mexico Press, 1962), 86–92.

2. Telegram, Crook to Sheridan, Camp on Belle Fourche River, December 21, 1876, RG 393, Division of the Missouri Special Files, NARA (M1495, roll 4, frame 541).

3. Endorsement of September 7, 1876, on Carlin to AAG Department of Dakota, SRA, August 28, 1876, RG 94, AGO LR 1871–80, file 4163 AGO 1876, NARA (M666, roll 278, frame 572). By December Sheridan had conceded that Sitting Bull was a person, but no "more than an insignificant warrior with a few thieving followers." *Army and Navy Journal*, December 23, 1876.

4. Hazen to AAG Department of Dakota, Fort Peck, November 2, 1876; and Hazen to Miles, same date and place, SW, *Annual Report, 1876*, 481–82. Hazen to AGUSA, Fort Buford, January 1, 1877, RG 94, AGO LR 1871–80, file 4163 AGO 1876, NARA (M666, roll 279, frame 756). Mitchell to CIA, Fort Peck, November 11 and 13, 1876, RG 75, BIA LR Montana Superintendency, NARA (M234, roll 505, frames 598, 602, and 639). *Bismarck Tribune*, November 8 and 22, 1876.

5. Miles to Mary Miles, Forks of Big Dry, November 13, 1876, Sherman Miles Compilation, USMA Library. Pocket diary of Lt. Frank D. Baldwin, November 16 and 17, 1876, Baldwin Papers, Huntington Library, San Marino, California;

and Baldwin to wife, Fort Peck, November 17, 1876, box 11, Baldwin Papers. A thorough and authoritative account is Jerome A. Greene, *Yellowstone Command: Colonel Nelson A. Miles and the Great Sioux War* (Lincoln: University of Nebraska Press, 1991), chap. 6.

6. Lt. R. H. Day to Col. W. B. Hazen, Fort Peck, November 25, 1876, RG 393, Division of the Missouri Special Files, NARA (M1495, roll 4, frame 517). Day, left in charge of the guard for the supply stockpile at Peck, interrogated the runner, a Sans Arc, who had arrived in the Yanktonai camp.

7. Miles's annual report, Fort Keogh, December 27, 1876, SW, *Annual Report, 1877*, 523–30, details these and later operations. See also Miles to Mary Miles, Missouri River opposite Musselshell, November 30, 1876, Sherman Miles Compilation, USMA Library. Pocket diary of Lt. Frank D. Baldwin, November 19–30, 1876, Baldwin Papers, Huntington Library. Baldwin to wife, November 30, 1876, box 11, ibid.

8. Pocket diary of Lt. Frank D. Baldwin, November 17, 1876, Baldwin Papers, Huntington Library.

9. Mitchell to CIA, Wolf Point, December 9, 1876, RG 75, BIA LR Montana Superintendency, NARA (M234, roll 505, frame 693). *Bismarck Tribune*, December 20, 1876. Agent Mitchell learned of Sitting Bull's move from Yanktonais. A long entry in Baldwin's pocket diary, December 6, 1876, Baldwin Papers, Huntington Library, is the principal source for what follows, but see also Baldwin, interview by Walter M. Camp, June 16, 1919, box 6, folder 1, Camp Papers, Harold B. Lee Library, Brigham Young University.

10. Baldwin to wife, Fort Peck, December 8, 1876, box 11, Baldwin Papers, Huntington Library.

11. Baldwin, interview by Walter M. Camp, June 16, 1919, box 6, folder 1, Camp Papers, Harold B. Lee Library, Brigham Young University. This and an interview with Baldwin's scout, Joe Culbertson, box 2, folder 4, are the most detailed sources for the Red Water incident. Because of primitive living conditions and severe weather, the contemporary documents are sparse, but see Baldwin's pocket diary, December 12–21, 1876, Baldwin Papers, Huntington Library; telegram, Miles to AAG Department of Dakota, Tongue River Cantonment, December 20, 1876, RG 393, Division of the Missouri Special Files, NARA (M1495, roll 4, frame 573); and same to same, December 24, 1876, SW, *Annual Report, 1877*, 493–94. Greene, *Yellowstone Command*, 140–44.

12. The date of Sitting Bull's arrival, together with the composition and location of the camp, are drawn from reports made by Indians arriving at Cheyenne River Agency, some of whom were sent out as peace emissaries and some of whom were "hostiles" coming in to surrender. In particular, see Fool Bear and Important Man in Col. W. H. Wood to AAG Department of Dakota, CRA, January 24, 1877; Eagle Shield in same to same, February 16 and 19, 1877; and Swelled Face in same to same, February 24, 1877, RG 393, Division of the Missouri Special Files, NARA (M1495, roll 4, frames 606, 667, 684, and 673).

13. Miles to AAG Department of Dakota, Tongue River Cantonment, December 17, 1876, RG 393, Division of the Missouri Special Files, NARA (M1495, roll 4, frame 593).

14. Miles to AAG Department of Dakota, Tongue River Cantonment, January 23, 1877, RG 94, AGO LR 1871–80, file 4163 AGO 1876, NARA (M666, roll 280, frame 88). Greene, *Yellowstone Command*, chap. 7. Don Rickey, Jr., "The Battle of Wolf Mountain," *Montana the Magazine of Western History* 13 (Spring 1963): 44–54. Eagle Shield's account is in Col. W. H. Wood to AAG Department of Dakota, CRA, February 19, 1877, RG 393, Division of the Missouri Special files, NARA (M1495, roll 4, frame 684).

15. See sources cited in note 12. These and other sources, all of which I have examined, are the basis for an excellent synthesis of the surrender process: Harry H. Anderson, "Indian Peace-talkers and the Conclusion of the Sioux War of 1876," *Nebraska History* 44 (December 1963): 233–54. My treatment closely follows this account.

16. Col. W. H. Wood to AAG Department of Dakota, CRA, February 24, 1877, RG 393, Division of the Missouri Special Files, NARA (M1495, roll 4, frame 673). See also Lt. W. P. Clark to Lt. John G. Bourke, Camp Robinson, March 3, 1877, ibid. (frame 727). *Bismarck Tribune*, April 11, 1877, repeating dispatch from Fort Buford, March 28.

17. The process is detailed in Anderson, "Peace-Talkers."

18. Col. W. H. Wood to AAG Department of Dakota, CRA, February 27, 1877, RG 393, Division of the Missouri Special Files, NARA (M1495, roll 4, frame 714).

19. Draft report, Inspector J. M. Walsh, North-West Mounted Police, to Lt. Col. J. F. Macleod, Fort Walsh, NWT, December 30, 1876; and untitled summary of crossings, both in J. M. Walsh Papers, Provincial Archives of Manitoba, Winnipeg.

20. The Yanktonai Black Tiger described the council to the detachment commander at Fort Peck. Lt. R. H. Day to Post Adjutant Fort Buford, Fort Peck, April 14, 1877, RG 393, Division of the Missouri Special Files, NARA (M1495, roll 4, frame 964).

21. Day to Post Adjutant Fort Buford, Fort Peck, May 2, 1877, RG 393, Division of the Missouri Special Files, NARA (M1495, roll 4, frame 1016).

22. Robert P. Higheagle Manuscript, p. 41, box 104, folder 21, Campbell Collection.

CHAPTER 15

Long Lance

1. James M. Walsh to My Dear Cora, May 21, 1890, James M. Walsh Papers, Provincial Archives of Manitoba, Winnipeg. This document is a long, rambling, frequently illegible or incoherent account of police service penned by Walsh for

his daughter. Despite its flaws, including exaggeration and even fabrication, it contains much valuable information. If Walsh wrote an official report of his first meeting with Sitting Bull, it seems not to have survived. Although most of the early police records were destroyed in a warehouse fire in 1897, copies of key documents found their way into the official civil records and are thus available to researchers. For the first meeting with Sitting Bull, however, Walsh's reminiscence is the major source. Walsh's superior reported on this meeting from Fort Benton, Montana: Lt. Col. A. G. Irvine to Secretary of State R. W. Scott, May 23, 1877, in NWMP, *Annual Report, 1877*, 33. See also John Peter Turner, *The North-West Mounted Police, 1873–1893*, 2 vols. (Ottawa: Kings Printer and Controller of Stationery, 1950), vol. 2, pp. 318–23. This is a detailed and authoritative history of the force in its formative years.

2. In dealing with the Indians, the police used the term "Great White Mother," or a variant. The Sioux preferred "Grandmother," a term connoting much greater respect. I have used the latter term, even when the translation in the source is Great White Mother, for that is what the speaker almost certainly said in the native language. Only when the police used Great White Mother themselves have I retained it in my text.

3. MS, George Gurnsey, "My Memories of Fort Walsh," n.d., Fort Macleod Historical Society, Alberta, copy furnished by George Kush, Monarch, Alberta.

4. Marty got an accurate translation. "Grandmother" is what he reported Sitting Bull as saying.

5. Father Marty left three accounts of his mission: "Abbot Martin Visits Sitting Bull," *Annals of the Catholic Indian Missions of America* 2 (January 1878): 7–10; newspaper interview in *Bismarck Tribune*, June 15 and 18, 1877; and interview in *St. Louis Globe-Democrat* reprinted in *Army and Navy Journal*, December 15, 1877. The police record, including a transcript of the council, is in NWMP, *Annual Report, 1877*, 35–41. See also another account by Irvine quoted in Turner, *North-West Mounted Police*, vol. 1, pp. 326–30. Irvine is authority for One Bull's presence in the party that went to Fort Walsh, although he identifies him simply as Sitting Bull's nephew. As White Bull had gone to the agency, One Bull was the only nephew now with his uncle. For biographies of Marty, see Robert F. Karolevitz, *Bishop Martin Marty: "The Black Robe Lean Chief"* (Yankton, S.D.: Sacred Heart Convent, 1980) and Sister Mary Clement Fitzgerald, "Bishop Marty and His Sioux Missions, 1876–1896," *South Dakota Historical Collections* 20 (1940): 525–58.

In his accounts, Father Marty portrayed his reception in Sitting Bull's village as one of "gladness and welcome." The police account suggests that it met only the minimum requirements of civility. As the police surgeon, Dr. Richard Nevitt, put it in a letter to his wife, Sitting Bull sent word that he had three Americans and wanted to know what to do with them, "saying that if he was on the American side he would know very well—which meant that their scalps would adorn some lodge pole." Nevitt to My dear Lizzie, Fort Macleod, NWT, June 11, 1877, box 2, folder 8, Nevitt Papers, Glenbow Institute, Calgary, Alberta.

6. Reported by a Canadian recently in Sitting Bull's camp, in *Bismarck Tribune*, June 22, 1877.

7. *New York Herald*, November 16, 1877.

8. Ibid.

9. Legaré told his story in a long letter to Walter M. Camp, Willow Bunch, Saskatchewan, October 27, 1910, box 1, folder 14, Walter M. Camp Papers, Harold B. Lee Library, Brigham Young University. Much of value is also found in the voluminous depositions of *Legare v. United States*, Records of the U.S. Court of Claims, General Jurisdiction, no. 15713, RG 123, NARA. Biographical material appears in the Rev. Clovis Rondeau, as revised by the Rev. Alexis, *History of Southern Saskatchewan*, chapter entitled "La Montagne de Bois" (Wood Mountain), typed translation furnished by Brian Hubner of Parks Canada at Fort Walsh National Historic Park.

10. The diplomatic story may be followed in RG 7, Records of the Governor General's Office, G21, vol. 318, file 2001, pt. 3a; and in a publication entitled *Papers Relating to the Sioux Indians of the United States Who Have Taken Refuge in Canadian Territory*, printed confidentially for the use of the Ministers of the Crown, in ibid., pt. 3d, National Archives of Canada, Ottawa. The diplomacy of the Sitting Bull issue has been well treated by several scholars using Canadian and British sources: Gary Pennanen, "Sitting Bull: Indian without a Country," *Canadian Historical Review* 51 (June 1970): 123–40; Christopher C. Joyner, "The Hegira of Sitting Bull to Canada: Diplomatic Realpolitik, 1876–1881," *Journal of the West* 13 (April 1974): 6–18; and Joseph Manzione, *"I Am Looking to the North for My Life": Sitting Bull, 1876–1881* (Salt Lake City: University of Utah Press, 1991). In additional to Manzione, two monographic studies of Sitting Bull's Canadian years are Grant MacEwan, *Sitting Bull: The Years in Canada* (Edmonton, Alta.: Hurtig Publishers, 1973); and C. Frank Turner, *Across the Medicine Line: The Epic Confrontation between Sitting Bull and the North-West Mounted Police* (Toronto: McClelland and Stewart, 1973). A detailed and authoritative account in four parts is Bruce Wishart, "Grandmother's Land: Sitting Bull in Canada," *True West* 37 (May 1990): 14–20; (June 1990): 26–32; (July 1990): 20–27; and (August 1990): 28–32.

11. *New York Herald*, August 14, 1877. *National Republican* (Washington, D.C.), August 15, 1877.

12. Sherman to SW George W. McCrary, Cantonment on Tongue River, July 16, 1877, RG 94, AGO LR 1871–80, file 4163 AGO 1876, NARA (M666, roll 282, frame 184). Generals Sherman and Terry were inspecting Colonel Miles's new fort on the Yellowstone, soon to become Fort Keogh, when this letter was drafted.

13. *New York Herald*, October 22, 1877. *Chicago Times*, October 22, 1877. Macleod to Mills, Fort Macleod, October 27, 1877, NWMP, *Annual Report, 1877*, 45.

14. Walsh's report of his mission to Pinto Horse Butte was written at Fort Walsh on October 14 and a copy provided the *New York Herald*'s correspondent with the Terry Commission, who included it in his dispatch printed in the *Herald*, October 22, 1877. I have found no official copy in other sources. The telegram that

prompted the mission was dispatched from Ottawa on September 13, but had to be carried by mail courier from Fort Benton, so it could not have arrived much before October 1, the date Walsh said he received it. Although marred by some typographical errors in dates, the newspaper rendering of the report clearly indicates that Walsh left Fort Walsh for Sitting Bull's camp on October 1 and arrived on October 7, when the council took place. The report contains no hint that the Sioux debated going to the aid of Nez Perces. However, in his reminiscences for "My dear Cora," May 21, 1890, Walsh Papers, Provincial Archives of Manitoba, Walsh described in graphic and animated detail Sioux preparations to help the Nez Perces, with himself playing the critical role in restraining them. As the Nez Perces camped on Snake Creek on September 29, and the battle and siege lasted from September 30 to October 5, there is an obvious conflict in timing, especially since Walsh claimed in his Cora letter that he had been in Sitting Bull's camp continuously for three weeks. It is possible that other police influenced the Sioux during the crucial week of September 30 to October 5. It is also possible, though not officially reported, that the issue was addressed in the council with Walsh on October 7, for the Sioux did not yet know the battle had ended. If so, of course, Walsh drastically embellished it in his Cora letter. My own view is that the Sioux, especially the young men, gave serious consideration to helping the Nez Perces, but that the consequences of doing so, with regard to their intent to live in Canada, were so plain that the chiefs prevailed.

15. The death and mourning were reported by both Jerome Stillson and Charles Diehl, the reporters accompanying General Terry to Fort Walsh. *New York Herald*, October 22, 1877; and *Chicago Times*, October 22, 1877.

16. In addition to Walsh's report of October 14 and his Cora letter, cited above, see Macleod to Minister of the Interior David Mills, Fort Macleod, October 27, 1877, NWMP, *Annual Report, 1877*, 45–47; and *New York World*, October 21, 1877, which contains a dispatch from Fort Walsh via Winnipeg, October 14. The identity of the *World*'s "special correspondent" at Fort Walsh is not known. He sent no dispatches concerning the conference itself, which was thoroughly reported by the three journalists who accompanied Terry, but he sent periodic reports after their departure. The *World* correspondent was either Walsh himself or someone close to him; the writer of the October 14 dispatch almost certainly was present during Walsh's journey to Pinto Horse Butte and back. Walsh loved to see his name in the newspapers and did all he could to make sure it appeared often.

17. *New York Herald*, October 22, 1877.

18. Sir Cecil E. Denny, *The Law Marches West* (Toronto: J. M. Dent and Sons, 1939), 125.

19. In fact, a third journalist attended—John J. Healy of the *Fort Benton Record*. A leading Fort Benton merchant, politico, and journalist, Healy had been one of the two American whiskey peddlers whose Fort Whoop-up had created such chaos in the former territory of the Hudson's Bay Company as to prompt the formation of

the North-West Mounted Police. His dispatches to the *Record* lacked the wealth of detail that characterized the reports of the New York and Chicago journalists. Healy later made a name for himself on Alaska's Yukon River.

The Stillson and Diehl dispatches are voluminous and richly detailed: *New York Herald*, October 22 and 23, 1877; *Chicago Times*, October 22 and 23, 1877. The official Canadian report, with a transcript of the council, is in NWMP, *Annual Report, 1877*, 45–52. The U.S. report, with less detailed record of the council, is in SI, *Annual Report, 1877*, House Executive Documents, 45th Congress, 2d session, no. 1, serial 1800, pp. 719–28.

20. Stillson in *New York Herald*, November 16, 1877. Diehl in *Chicago Times*, November 15, 1877.

21. *Harpers Weekly*, December 8, 1877. Whether this first likeness of Sitting Bull ever to reach a mass audience came from Stillson's pen is questionable. Dr. Nevitt, the police surgeon who recorded the Irvine meeting with Sitting Bull in June, was also at Fort Walsh. He too depicted Sitting Bull and on October 18 wrote to his wife: "Mr. Stillson for the N.Y. Herald was also an amateur artist and took several sketches but liked mine better so I loaned my sketches and I gave them to him—They will probably appear in Harper's Weekly." Nevitt to My dear Lizzie, Fort Walsh, October 18, 1877, box 2, folder 9, Nevitt Papers, Glenbow Institute, Calgary, Alberta.

22. Lt. R. M. Hoyt to Post Adjutant, CRA, November 20, 1877, with endorsement of Sheridan, RG 74, BIA LR CRA, NARA (M234, roll 130, frame 418). Hoyt's interpretation is analyzed and modified in Harry H. Anderson, "A Sioux Pictorial Account of General Terry's Council at Fort Walsh, October 17, 1877," *North Dakota History* 27 (July 1955): 93–116.

CHAPTER 16

Pte

1. James C. Olson, *Red Cloud and the Sioux Problem* (Lincoln: University of Nebraska Press, 1965), 239–55.

2. Fort Walsh dispatch, November 29, 1877, in *Bismarck Tribune*, December 20, 1877.

3. For the progress and arrival of these people after leaving White River, see the following sources: Capt. Joseph Lawson to AAG Department of Dakota, New RCA, December 4, 1877, RG 94, AGO LR 1871–80, file 4163 AGO 1876, NARA (M666, roll 283, frame 354); Telegram, Miles to AAG Department of Dakota, Fort Keogh, January 6, 1878, ibid. (roll 284, frame 71); same to same, n.d. but c. same date, ibid. (frame 103); Lt. Col. Daniel Huston to same, Fort Buford, January 17, 1878, ibid. (frame 148); *Bismarck Tribune*, March 5, 1878; *Manitoba Free Press* (Winnipeg), May 29, 1878; Telegram, Assistant Commissioner A. G. Irvine to Secretary of State R. W. Scott, Fort Benton, April 2, 1878,

RG 7, Records of the Governor General's Office, G21, vol. 318, file 2001, pt. 3d: *Papers Relating to the Sioux Indians of the United States Who Have Taken Refuge in Canadian Territory*, p. 115, NAC. For Big Road's reluctant breakaway from his agency, as related by Skunk Horse, a defector from Sitting Bull's camp, see USIA V. T. McGillycuddy to CIA, PRA, October 7, 1879, RG 94, AGO LR 1871–80, file 4163 AGO 1876 (M666, roll 287, frame 120).

4. Many estimates of the Sioux in Canada were impossibly high, in some instances amounting to more than half the entire Lakota population. The most consistent figures, including police estimates, average eight hundred lodges, eight to ten thousand people, two thousand to twenty-five hundred warriors. This is still too many people in relation to total Lakota population (about twenty thousand), to the number of lodges, and to the number whose surrender was officially recorded (as distinguished from those who slipped unnoticed into the agencies). Lodges were easier to count than people, and eight hundred seems about right, but I have arbitrarily trimmed the refugee population as reflected in the above paragraph.

5. Old Bull, box 105, notebook 11, Campbell Collection. Hugh A. Dempsey, *Crowfoot, Chief of the Blackfeet* (Norman: University of Oklahoma Press, 1972), chap. 8. See also *Fort Benton Record* (Montana), September 12, 1879; and John P. Turner, *The North-West Mounted Police, 1873–1893*, 2 vols. (Ottawa: King's Printer and Controller of Stationery, 1950), vol. 1, p. 400.

6. Lucien Hanks, Field Notes Relating to Blackfoot Indians, c. 1939, interview with Mrs. Take-Gun-Himself, folder 11, pp. 105 ff, Hanks Papers, Glenbow Institute, Calgary, Alberta.

7. The Mounted Police kept close watch on the refugee Sioux and reported their location regularly. In fact, the police had a "confidential scout" who maintained almost a running inventory of chiefs, lodges, and locations. This pattern is drawn from analysis of these reports, both in official police records and in newspaper dispatches from Fort Walsh and Wood Mountain.

8. CIA, *Annual Report, 1877*, 137; *1878*, 89–90; *1879*, 98.

9. Bird to CIA, Fort Peck Agency, Poplar River, April 7, 1879, RG 75, BIA LR Montana Superintendency, NARA (M234, roll 513, frame 316). Lt. Fred Kislingbury to Gen. A. H. Terry, Bismarck, May 6, 1879, RG 94, AGO LR 1871–80, file 4163 AGO 1876, NARA (M666, roll 286, frame 29).

10. Colonel Miles described some of this activity in his annual report for 1879: SW, *Annual Report, 1879*, 68–71. See also for examples USIA W. L. Lincoln to CIA, Fort Belknap, March 10 and 21, 1879, RG 75, BIA LR Montana Superintendency, NARA (M234, roll 514, frames 428 and 453); telegram, Maj. James Brisbin to AAG Department of Dakota, Fort Ellis, April 23, 1879, ibid. (roll 515, frame 670); USIA Wellington Bird to CIA, Fort Peck Agency, Poplar River, May 5, 1879, ibid. (roll 513, frame 339); Miles to CO Fort Buford, Fort Keogh, June 10, 1879, and Bird to Lt. Col. Daniel Huston, Poplar, June 11, 1879, ibid. (roll 515, frames 731 and 732); Lt. Fred F. Kislingbury to Gen. A. H. Terry, Bismarck,

May 6, 1879, RG 94 AGO LR 1871–80, file 4163 AGO 1876, NARA (M666, roll 286, frame 29); *Bismarck Tribune*, April 19, 1879.

11. Sir Edward Thornton to Foreign Secretary the Marquis of Salisbury, March 28 and 31, 1879, RG 7, Records of the Governor General's Office, G21, vol. 320, file 2001, pt. 4b, NAC (roll T-1386, frames 68 and 80); Thornton to Governor General of Canada the Marquis of Lorne, May 8, 1879; and Secretary of State William M. Evarts to Thornton, May 27, 1879, ibid., vol. 318, file 2001, pt. 3b (roll T-1386, frames 113 and 165). The British tried unsuccessfully to link the Sitting Bull problem with U.S. tolerance of Irish Fenians using American territory as a base for aggressions against Canada.

12. Sherman to Sheridan, February 9, 1878, RG94, AGO LR 1871–80, file 4163 AGO 1876, NARA (M666, roll 284, frame 190). Sheridan to Sherman, March 30, 1878, ibid. (frame 460). Telegram, Sherman to CIA, August 6, 1878, RG 75 BIA LR Montana Superintendency, NARA (M234, roll 511, frame 890). Sherman to Sheridan, March 9, 1879, Sherman-Sheridan Letters, vol. 2, Sheridan Papers, Library of Congress. Sherman to Miles, February 9, 1878, vol. 90, pp. 518–19, Sherman Papers, Library of Congress. Miles constantly went around Terry and Sheridan to promote his ambitions directly with Sherman, who just as constantly rebuffed the efforts. In 1873 Col. Ranald S. Mackenzie, with the tacit endorsement of Sheridan, the Secretary of War, and President Grant, had led an expedition into Mexico to punish Kickapoo Indians who raided the Texas frontier. Miles cited this precedent in advocating a similar foray into Canada. But Sherman had not been party to the Mexican adventure, had disapproved it, and emphatically rejected Miles's feelers about repeating it in Canada.

13. SW George W. McCrary to Gen. W. T. Sherman, April 18, 1879, RG 94, AGO LR 1871–80, file 4163 AGO 1876, NARA (M666, roll 286, frame 2). 20 Stat. 145–52 (June 18, 1876). SW, *Annual Report, 1879*, 52.

14. For the Nez Perce mission, see Lt. G. W. Baird to Lt. Col. J. F. Macleod, Fort Walsh, June 21, 1878; and Macleod to Secretary of State R. W. Scott, Fort Walsh, June 26 and July 9 (2), 1878, in *Papers Relating to the Nez Perce Indians of the United States Who Have Taken Refuge in Canadian Territory*. Printed confidentially for the use of the Ministers of the Crown, n.d. RG 7, Records of the Governor General's Office, G21, vol. 318, file 2001, pt. 3d NAC (T-1387, frames 151, 153, 164). This source also contains a transcript of a council between Lt. Col. A. G. Irvine and White Bird.

15. Walsh to CO Fort Walsh, Wood Mountain Post, January 25, 1879, *Papers Relating to the Sioux Indians of the United States Who Have Taken Refuge in Canadian Territory*. Printed confidentially for the use of the Ministers of the Crown, n.d. RG 7, Records of the Governor General's Office, G21, vol. 318, file 2001, pt. 3d, NAC (T-1386, frame 129). Irvine to Deputy Secretary of State Frederick White, Fort Walsh, November 10, 1878, ibid. (frame 125). Walsh to CO Fort Walsh, Wood Mountain, December 30, 1878, ibid., vol. 319 (frame 127). Same to same, October 8, 1878, Walsh Papers, Provincial Archives of Manitoba, Winnipeg. See

also P.O. Matthews to USIA W. Bird, Fort Peck Agency, February 10, 1879, RG 94, AGO LR 1871–80, file 4163 AGO 1876, NARA (M666, roll 285, frame 534).

16. Walsh to Assistant Commissioner Fort Walsh, Wood Mountain, March 24, 1879, RG 7, G21, vol. 318, file 2001, pt. 3b, NAC (F-1386, frame 124). Untitled, undated MS in J. M. Walsh Papers, Provincial Archives of Manitoba, Winnipeg.

17. For the agents' list of grievances against the Sioux, see USIA Wellington Bird to CIA, Fort Peck Agency, Poplar River, April 19, 1879, RG 75, BIA LR Montana Superintendency, NARA (M234, roll 513, frame 322); USIA W. L. Lincoln to CIA, Fort Belknap, June 16, 1879, ibid. (roll 514, frame 535); same to same, December 9, 1878, ibid. (roll 511, frame 269), and January 7, 1879, ibid. (roll 514, frame 343). For Terry's orders, see Miles's annual report in SW, *Annual Report, 1879*, 68–75.

18. Huntley's long story appeared in the *Chicago Tribune*, July 5, 1879. He was widely charged with fabricating the Sitting Bull interview, but a letter from Walsh to Huntley, June 1879, in Walsh Papers, Provincial Archives of Manitoba, supports its authenticity. For other confirmation, see *Bismarck Tribune*, June 28, 1879. See also Lewis O. Saum, "Stanley Huntley Interviews Sitting Bull: Event, Pseudo-Event, or Fabrication?" *Montana the Magazine of Western History* 32 (Spring 1982): 2–15. Saum did not have access to the Walsh letter but concluded, rightly, that the interview in fact took place.

19. Norman Marion in *Manitoba Free Press* (Winnipeg), September 20, 1879. A slightly different version was told by Oliver Brisbo, a Nez Perce mixed blood serving with the scouts, in *Bismarck Tribune*, October 31, 1879. Since the fighting at this stage was almost entirely between Indian scouts and the Sioux, military reports lack detail. Two days later Bog Road and other chiefs gave a detailed account to Major Walsh that affords the best view from the Sioux perspective. See Walsh to CO NWMP Fort Walsh, Wood Mountain, July 22, 1879, RG 10, Records of the Indian Affairs Branch, vol. 3652, file 8589, pt. 1, NAC (C-10114). See also Telegram, Miles to AAG Department of Dakota, Camp opposite Frenchman's Creek, July 23, 1879, RG 393, Division of the Missouri Special Files, NARA (M1495, roll 5, frame 305). More detailed is Miles's annual report, September 1879, in SW, *Annual Report, 1879*, 68–75. The most detailed of all accounts was a series of dispatches by correspondent John F. Finerty, who accompanied the expedition, in *Chicago Times*, July 18, 23, and 28, August 2, 8, 9, 19, and 22, 1879. Excerpts were later printed in Finerty's *War-Path and Bivouac; or, The Conquest of the Sioux* (Norman: University of Oklahoma Press, 1961), pt. 2.

20. My version is directly contradicted by three undated, untitled manuscript fragments in the Walsh Papers, Provincial Archives of Manitoba, Winnipeg, and also by brief references in his 1890 letter to daughter Cora. I would much prefer to embrace Walsh's version, probably penned a decade later, for it is more dramatic and exciting. According to Walsh, he too feared that Miles would violate Canadian territory and hastened to the Sioux camp, where he organized the warriors to oppose such an invasion. When the American force halted at the border, "the

warriors became frantic with disappointment and were determined that Miles should not be allowed to escape. [Sitting] Bull favored attacking him and sweeping him, he said, off the prairie." And more in the same vein. Walsh tells the story with beguiling flair and compelling specificity, yet no suggestion of this creeps into any contemporary source, including his own official reports. The interchange between the military camp and the Sioux village was such that belligerence of this magnitude could not have been concealed. One of Miles's own officers, in fact, had just been in the Sioux village with Walsh, searching for stock stolen on the Yellowstone. Walsh's chronology, moreover, does not match contemporary chronology. Sadly, like Walsh's account of the Sioux response to the Nez Perce flight in 1877, this must be regarded as almost pure fabrication. Walsh's contemporary reports and writings stand up well as sources. His retrospection was grossly colored by his romantic temperament. For Walsh's contemporary reports, see Walsh to CO NWMP Fort Walsh, Wood Mountain, July 22, 25, and 31, 1879, RG 10, Records of the Indian Affairs Branch, vol. 3652, file 8589, pt. 1, NAC (C-10114).

21. *Chicago Times*, August 9, 1879.

22. SW, *Annual Report, 1879*, 72. *Chicago Times*, August 9, 1879.

23. SW, *Annual Report, 1879*, 72.

24. *Chicago Times*, August 1, 1879.

CHAPTER 17

Fort Buford

1. Untitled, undated manuscript in Walsh Papers, Provincial Archives of Manitoba, Winnipeg. In this document Walsh described the "tribal law" that governed belonging and seceding, and the consequences for those who did not obey.

2. Old Bull, box 105, notebook 11; Bob Tail Bull, box 105, notebook 16, Campbell Collection.

3. Minutes of a talk at Fort Buford, May 23, 1880, RG 94, AGO LR 1871–80, file 4163 AGO 1876, NARA (M666, roll 288, frame 104). The Indian is here identified as Young Eagle, adopted son of Sitting Bull, but in a newspaper account of the council he is named Young Bull. Clearly the man was One Bull. *Bismarck Tribune*, May 28, 1880.

4. Walsh to Macleod, Wood Mountain Post, June 5, 1880, RG 10, Records of the Indian Affairs Branch, vol. 3652, file 8589, pt. 1, NAC (C-10114). Undated clipping from *Manitoba Free Press* (Winnipeg), reprinting *Chicago Tribune* dispatch from Fort Walsh of June 2. The *Tribune* correspondent clearly was a witness.

5. Report of the Privy Council, June 28, 1879, enclosing Memorandum of Minister of the Interior John A. Macdonald, June 21, 1879, RG 7, Records of the Governor General's Office, G21, vol. 319, file 2001, pt. 3c, NAC (T-1386, frames 4, 5, and 11).

6. This is my interpretation, based on official aspersions on Walsh in the police

records later in 1880. Reasons for the transfer do not appear in the records at the time, possibly because most of the police records were later destroyed by fire, but probably because the move was presented as routine.

7. Walsh to Minister of the Interior, Wood Mountain, July 3, 1880; Walsh to CO Fort Walsh, Wood Mountain, July 14, 1880, RG 10, Records of the Indian Affairs Branch, vol. 3691, file 13,893, NAC (C-10121). Untitled, undated manuscript describing events in 1879–80 in J. M. Walsh Papers, Provincial Archives of Manitoba, Winnipeg.

8. Walsh to Minister of the Interior, Brockville, Ontario, September 11, 1880, RG 10, Records of the Indian Affairs Branch, vol. 3691, file 13,893, NAC (C-10121). The draft is in the Walsh Papers, Provincial Archives of Manitoba, Winnipeg.

9. Crozier's annual report, December 1880, NWMP, *Annual Report, 1880*, 32.

10. Ibid.

11. Ibid. Telegram, Miles to Capt. O. B. Reade at Poplar, Fort Keogh, October 21, 1880, RG 393, LR Camp Poplar River, Box 1, NARA. Telegram, Miles to AAG Department of Dakota, Fort Keogh, October 23 and 31, 1880, RG 94, AGO LR 1871–80, file 4163 AGO 1876, NARA (M666, roll 288, frames 423 and 453). Eli L. Huggins, "Surrender of Rain-in-the-Face," MS, n.d., 5 pp., National Anthropological Archives, Smithsonian Institution. Huggins was the officer who conducted Spotted Eagle and Rain-in-the-Face to Fort Keogh.

12. Crozier to CO Fort Macleod, Wood Mountain, October 14, 1880, RG 10, Records of the Indian Affairs Branch, vol. 3652, file 8589, pt. 1 NAC (C-10114). USIA N. S. Porter to CIA, Fort Peck Agency at Fort Buford, August 12, 1880, RG 75, BIA LR Montana Superintendency, NARA (M234, roll 517, frame 451). *Bismarck Tribune*, September 3, 1880. Telegram, Rice AAAG District of the Yellowstone to Capt. O. B. Read, Fort Keogh, October 1, 1880, RG 393, LR Camp Poplar River, Box 1, NARA. SW, *Annual Report, 1881*, 100. Raymond J. DeMallie, "The Sioux in Dakota and Montana Territories: Cultural and Historical Background of the Ogden B. Read Collection," in *Vestiges of a Proud Nation: The Ogden B. Read Northern Plains Indian Collection* (Burlington, Vt.: Robert Hall Fleming Museum, 1986), 48.

13. Telegram, Terry to Miles, St. Paul, September 22, 1880, RG 94, AGO LR 1871–80, file 4163 AGO 1876, NARA (M666, roll 288, frame 504).

14. Allison wrote a self-congratulatory account of his adventures. Full of errors and claiming more credit than warranted, it still offers an important view of his activities. E. H. Allison, *The Surrender of Sitting Bull, Being a Full and Complete History of the Negotiations Conducted by Scout Allison Which Resulted in the Surrender of Sitting Bull and His Entire Band of Hostile Sioux in 1881 . . .* (Dayton, Ohio: Walker Lithograph and Printing, 1891). This was reprinted as "The Surrender of Sitting Bull," *South Dakota Historical Collections* 6 (1912): 233–70. I have used this edition, and my page citations refer to it. Major Brotherton's reports furnish a useful check on Allison's claims. None has been

found for the first journey, but for the second see telegram, Brotherton to AAG Department of Dakota, Fort Buford, November 7, 1880, RG 94, AGO LR 1871–80, file 4163 AGO 1876, NARA (M666, roll 288, frame 472). A lengthy interview with Allison appeared in the *Army and Navy Register*, November 11, 1880. See also *Bismarck Tribune*, November 19, 1880; and *St. Paul Pioneer Press*, July 20, 1881.

15. Allison, "Surrender of Sitting Bull," 248–49, represents Gall as openly breaking with Sitting Bull and leading two-thirds of his following to Poplar. If so, this is inconsistent with Gall's statements at Poplar and also with the journey of Jumping Bull, Sitting Bull's adopted brother, to Poplar. At the agency they represented themselves simply as advance agents for Sitting Bull, scouting the situation and assessing how he might be received. I think this the more likely. Also, the thirty-eight lodges with these two leaders do not add up to two-thirds of Sitting Bull's following.

16. For the government's stiffening policy, see Macdonald to Dewdney, November 1, 1880; and telegram, Macdonald to Irvine, October 28, 1880, Edgar Dewdney Papers, vol. 3, pp. 382–85, Glenbow Institute, Calgary, Alberta. Irvine to Minister of the Interior, Fort Walsh, November 10, 1880, RG 18, Records of the Royal Canadian Mounted Police, B3, vol. 2185, Fort Walsh LB November 1880 to March 1881, NAC (T-6268, frame 973). This Fort Walsh letter book is among the few early police records to survive the warehouse fire of 1897.

17. Telegram, Brotherton to AAG Department of Dakota, Fort Buford, December 17, 1880, RG 94, AGO LR 1871–80, file 4163 AGO 1876, NARA (M666, roll 289, frame 289). Allison, "Surrender of Sitting Bull," 249–53. NWMP, *Annual Report, 1880*, 32–33.

18. Telegram, Breck AAG Department of Dakota to Ilges, St. Paul, December 14 and 18 (2), 1880; telegram, Whistler to AAG Department of Dakota, Fort Keogh, December 15, 1880; telegram, Ilges to AAG Department of Dakota, Camp Poplar River, December 25, 1880; same to same, January 31, 1881, RG 94, AGO LR 1871–80, file 4163 AGO 1876, NARA (M66, roll 289, frames 97, 103, 113, 121, 142, 144, and 475).

19. Telegram, Brotherton to Terry, Fort Buford, December 25, 1880, RG 94, AGO LR 1871–80, file AGO 1876, NARA (M666, roll 289, frame 150). Allison, "Surrender of Sitting Bull," 255–56.

20. Ilges to AAG Department of Dakota, Camp Poplar River, December 31, 1880, and January 31, 1881, RG 94, AGO LR 1871–80, file 4163 AGO 1876, NARA (M666, roll 289, frame 266 and 475). For Crow King's meeting at Fort Buford, see telegram, Brotherton to AAG Department of Dakota, Fort Buford, January 1, 1881, RG 393, Division of the Missouri Special Files, NARA (M1495, roll 5, frame 465).

21. Telegram, Breck AAG Department of Dakota to Ilges, St. Paul, December 28, 1880; Ilges to Breck, Camp Poplar River, January 31, 1881, RG 94, AGO LR 1871–80, file 4163 AGO 1876, NARA (M666, roll 289, frames 142 and 475). Same

to same, December 31, 1880, RG 393, Division of the Missouri Special Files, NARA (M1495, roll 5, frame 464).

22. J. M. Bell, interview by Walter M. Camp, Walter M. Camp Papers, Lilly Library, Indiana University, copy in box 3, folder, 4, Hammer Collection, Harold B. Lee Library, Brigham Young University.

23. Ilges to AAG Department of Dakota, January 2, 6, and 31, 1881; Brotherton to Terry, Fort Buford, January 10, 1881, RG 94, AGO LR 1871–80, file 4163 1876, NARA (M666, roll 289, frames 166, 215, 229, and 475). The letter of January 31 is Ilges's comprehensive report of his activities from December 15 to January 31 and is accompanied by a map of the battleground of January 2. The text is printed in SW, *Annual Report, 1881*, 101–5.

24. Breck AAG Department of Dakota to Ilges, St. Paul, January 4 and 10, 1881; Terry to Ruger, St. Paul, January 11, 1881, RG 94, AGO LR 1871–80, file 4163 AGO 1876, NARA (M666, roll 289, frames 205, 248, and 254).

25. Allison, "Surrender of Sitting Bull," 264–69. Terry to Sheridan, St. Paul, January 19, 1881; Terry to AGUSA, St. Paul, January 21, 1881, RG 94, AGO LR 1871–80, file 4163 AGO 1876, NARA (M666, roll 289, 311, and 327). Crozier to Irvine, Wood Mountain, February 8, 1881, RG 10, Records of the Indian Affairs Branch, vol. 3652, file 8589, pt. 1, NAC (C-10114).

26. Telegram, Terry to AGUSA, St. Paul, January 21, 1881; telegram, Brotherton to Terry, Fort Buford, February 6, 1881, RG 94, AGO LR 1871–80, file 4163 AGO 1876, NARA (M666, roll 289, frames 327 and 445). Telegram, Ilges to Breck, Camp Poplar River, February 1, 1881, RG 393, Division of the Missouri Special Files, NARA (M1495, roll 5, frame 609). Same to same, February 12, 1881 (2), RG 94, AGO LR 1871–80, file 4163 AGO 1876, NARA (M666, roll 289, frames 440 and 509).

27. Crozier to Irvine, Wood Mountain, April 3, 1881, RG 10, Records of the Indian Affairs Branch, vol. 3691, file 13,893, NAC (C-10121). Telegram, Brotherton to Terry, Fort Buford, February 8 and 21, 1881, RG 393, Division of the Missouri Special Files, NARA (M1495, roll 5, frames 613 and 664). Irvine to Minister of the Interior (confidential), Fort Walsh, March 22, 1881, RG 18, Records of the RCMP, B3, vol. 2185, Fort Walsh LB November 1880–March 1881, NAC (T-6269, frame 224). Telegram, Read to AAG Department of Dakota, Camp Poplar River, March 29, 1881; telegram, Brotherton to Terry, Fort Buford, April 11, 1881, RG 94, AGO LR 1871–80, filed 4163 AGO 1876, NARA (M666, roll 289, frames 555 and 705).

28. Crozier to Irvine, Wood Mountain, April 3, 1881, RG 10, Records of the Indian Affairs Branch, vol. 3691, file 13,893, NAC (C-10121).

29. Crozier to Brotherton, Wood Mountain, April 5, 1881; Brotherton to Crozier, April 11, 1881; Brotherton to Sitting Bull, April 12, 1881, RG 10, Records of the Indian Affairs Branch, vol. 3652, file 8589, pt. 1, NAC (C-10114). Crozier to CO Poplar River, Wood Mountain, April 5, 1881, RG 393, LR Camp Poplar River, box 1, NARA. Read to CO Fort Buford, Camp Poplar River, April 9, 1881, RG

393, LS Camp Poplar River, vol. 1, p. 84, NARA. Telegram, Brotherton to Terry, Fort Buford, April 12, 1881, RG 94, AGO LR 1871–80, file 4163 AGO 1876, NARA (M666, roll 289, frame 595). *Bismarck Tribune*, April 22, 1881. One Bull tells of the mission in MS, "Statement of Henry Oscar One Bull . . . regarding Sitting Bull's Life from the Custer Fight until his Surrender," box 104, folder 10, Campbell Collection.

30. Deposition of Alexander A. Macdonell, April 25, 1888, *Legare v. United States*, Records of the U.S. Court of Claims, General Jurisdiction, no. 15713, RG 123, NARA. Crozier to Irvine, Wood Mountain, April 19, 1881, RG 10, Records of the Indian Affairs Branch, vol. 3652, file 8589, pt. 1, NAC (C-10114).

31. Crozier to Irvine, Wood Mountain, April 19, 1881, encl. to Irvine to White, Fort Walsh, April 25, 1881, RG 10, Records of the Indian Affairs Branch, vol. 3652, file 8589, pt. 1, NAC (C10114). The incident is also reported in *Bismarck Tribune*, May 6, 1881.

32. Crozier to Read, Wood Mountain, April 21, 1881, RG 393, LR Camp Poplar River, box 1, NARA. Crozier to Brotherton, same date, RG 94, AGO LR 1871–80, file 4163 AGO 1876, NARA (M666, roll 290, frame 19).

CHAPTER 18

Jean Louis

1. The best account of Legaré's activities is his own detailed deposition in support of his claim for reimbursement from the United States for expenses incurred in working for surrender. Despite minor inaccuracies of dates, his account, prepared seven years later, checks well with contemporary sources. *Legare v. United States*, Records of the U.S. Court of Claims, General Jurisdiction, no. 15713, RG 123, NARA.

2. Old Bull, box 105, notebook 12, Campbell Collection. The arrival of the Legaré party, which included sixteen people who surrendered, is noted in telegram, Brotherton to Terry, Fort Buford, May 4, 1881, RG 393, Division of the Missouri Special Files, NARA (M1495, roll 5, frame 751). See also *Legare v. United States.* For Running Antelope's mission, see telegram, Terry to AAG Division of the Missouri, St. Paul, April 24 and 25, May 4 and 5, 1881, RG 393, Division of the Missouri Special Files, NARA (M1495, roll 5, frames 715, 719, 749, and 751).

3. *Toronto Citizen*, c. January 1881, undated clipping in J. M. Walsh Papers, Provincial Archives of Manitoba, Winnipeg. Crozier to Irvine, Wood Mountain, May 1 and 14, 1881, RG 10, Records of the Indian Affairs Branch, vol. 3691, file 13, 893, NAC (C-10121).

4. Brotherton to AAG Department of Dakota, Fort Buford, May 26, 1881, RG 94, AGO LR 1871–80, file 4163 AGO 1876, NARA (M666, roll 290, frame 123). *Bismarck Tribune*, June 3 and August 5, 1881. *Chicago Times*, June 11, 1881.

5. Telegram, Brotherton to AAG Department of Dakota, Fort Buford, May 26 and 29, 1881, RG 393. Division of the Missouri Special Files, NARA (M1495, roll 5, frames 770 and 786). *Legare v. United States. Bismarck Tribune*, June 3, 1881.

6. Telegram, Brotherton to AAG Department of Dakota, Fort Buford, May 26, 1881, RG 94, AGO LR 1871–80, file 4163 AGO 1876, NARA (M666, roll 290, frame 123). *Bismarck Tribune*, June 3 and 17, 1881. An enumeration by the Standing Rock agent early in July gave the following statistics: From Fort Buford there were 133 Oglalas, 169 Miniconjous, 532 Hunkpapas, 176 Sans Arcs, and 111 Blackfeet, for a total of 1,121. This included 307 males over 16 and 219 under, 399 females over 16 and 196 under. From Fort Keogh there were 410 Oglalas, 591 Miniconjous, 172 Brules, 177 Hunkpapas, and 357 Sans Arcs, for a total of 1,707. This included 493 males over 16 and 331 under, 602 females over 16 and 281 under. Total prisoners from both places: 543 Oglalas, 760 Miniconjous, 709 Hunkpapas, 533 Sans Arcs, 111 Blackfeet, 172 Brules, for a total of 2,828, broken down into 800 males over 16, 550 under, 1,001 females over 16,477 under. USIA J.A. Stephan to CIA, SRA, July 15, 1881, RG 75, BIA LR 1881, NARA. The 500 Northern Cheyennes at Fort Keogh were allowed to remain and were ultimately given a reservation on Tongue River.

Fr. Louis Pfaller, biographer of Standing Rock agent James McLaughlin, searched the National Archives for both civil and military records relating to Standing Rock during the McLaughlin reign and deposited them in the James McLaughlin Papers, Assumption Abbey Archives, Richardton, N.D. For much of the official record during this period I have used the Pfaller compilation in the microfilm edition of the McLaughlin Papers, from which the above reference is taken, roll 32. The same documents, of course, appear in the far more extensive National Archives microfilm publications relating to Standing Rock Agency, Fort Yates military post, and the army's Department of Dakota and Department of the Platte.

7. MS, Memoirs of William Morris Graham, n.d., box 1, folder 2B, pp. 267–71, Graham Papers, Glenbow Institute, Calgary, Alberta. "Father Hugounard Gives Interesting Address on Indians of Saskatchewan," undated newspaper clipping, c. 1916, M8097, ibid. *Chicago Times*, June 11, 1881. *St. Paul Pioneer Press*, June 17 and July 13, 1881.

8. Dewdney to Superintendent General of Indian Affairs, Shoal Lake, June 7, 1881, RG 10, Records of the Indian Affairs Branch, vol. 3652, file 8589, pt. 1, NAC (C-10114).

9. *St. Paul Pioneer Press*, June 25, 1881, repeating Winnipeg dispatch of June 24. In the East, according to Major Walsh's later recollections, he brooded over his part in prolonging Sitting Bull's agony. He traveled to New York and Chicago to talk with influential friends and obtained assurances that the government intended no special punishment of Sitting Bull. To Louis Daniels, a friend and former policeman then en route to Fort Qu'Appelle, Walsh wrote asking that Sitting Bull be advised of Walsh's belief that he should surrender. He would

receive the same treatment as Big Road, Spotted Eagle, Gall, and the others who had preceded him. Daniels then delivered the message, which led to Sitting Bull's decision to leave Qu'Appelle and ultimately to surrender. This from an untitled, undated manuscript in the Walsh Papers, Provincial Archives of Manitoba, Winnipeg. According to Colonel Irvine, however, sometime in the week following April 10, a man named Daniels came to Wood Mountain from Qu'Appelle and delivered a message to Sitting Bull that led him to go to Qu'Appelle. Irvine to White, Fort Walsh, August 10, 1881, RG 18, Records of the RCMP, B3, vol. 2185, Fort Walsh LB November 1880–March 1881, NAC (T-6269, frame 584). There is thus substance behind Walsh's recollections, but the result was not what he remembered. What message Daniels delivered, or whether it was garbled in translation, is not known.

10. *Legare v. United States* gives the most detail. Besides Legaré's own deposition, one of his employees, Andre Gandre, provided a deposition containing essential information on the first days of the journey. Legaré's letter to Brotherton, July 12, is in *St. Paul Pioneer Press*, July 18, 1881. Brotherton's reply is in *Legare v. United States*. A significant source for this journey and the surrender is the *St. Paul Pioneer Press*, July 18, 20, and 21, 1881. This was the only newspaper with a correspondent on the scene. See also Brotherton to Terry, Fort Buford, July 14, 1881, RG 94, AGO LR 1871–80, file 4163 AGO 1876, NARA (M666, roll 290, frame 373).

11. For Clifford's account, see *St. Paul Pioneer Press*, August 3, 1881; and *Army and Navy Journal* (quoting *Buffalo Sunday News*), August 13, 1881.

12. Telegram, Whipple AAG Division of the Missouri to AGUSA, Chicago, July 26, 1881, repeating Brotherton telegram, RG 94, AGO LR 1871–80, file 4163 AGO 1876, NARA (M666, roll 290, frame 383).

13. The only extended eyewitness account taken down at the time was that of the St. Paul correspondent. *St. Paul Pioneer Press*, July 21 and 30, August 3, 1881.

14. Brotherton later donated the rifle, together with a sizable collection of Indian artifacts, to the Smithsonian Institution. John C. Ewers, "When Sitting Bull Surrendered His Winchester," in *Indian Life on the Upper Missouri* (Norman: University of Oklahoma Press, 1968), 175–81.

15. Frances Densmore, *Teton Sioux Music*, Smithsonian Institution, Bureau of American Ethnology, Bulletin 61 (Washington, D.C.: Government Printing Office, 1918), 459.

CHAPTER 19

Prisoner of War

1. The week at Buford and the run down to Bismarck and Fort Yates were extensively covered by the *Bismarck Tribune*, August 5, 1881; and *St. Paul Pioneer Press*, August 3, 4, 7, and 14, 1881. These are the principal sources for what follows. See also *Army and Navy Journal*, August 5, 1881.

2. Hedderich worked for Leighton and Jordan, post traders at Fort Buford, who

had a branch store at Wood Mountain, where Sitting Bull traded. Usher L. Burdick, *The Last Days of Sitting Bull, Sioux Medicine Chief* (Baltimore, Md.: Wirth Publishing Co., 1941), 20–21.

3. Lulu's father was not Charles Galpin but Honoré Picotte, the American Fur Company's agent at Fort Pierre in the 1840s. After his retirement to St. Louis, Eagle Woman became the wife of trader Charles Galpin, a respected figure in all the Sioux camps, who died in 1869. His widow remained a power at Standing Rock Agency until her death in 1888. Lulu's husband was William Harmon, an army officer who resigned to become a trader after his marriage in 1870. John S. Gray, "The Story of Mrs. Picotte-Galpin, A Sioux Heroine: Eagle Woman Becomes a Trader and Counsels for Peace, 1868–88," *Montana the Magazine of Western History* 36 (Summer 1986): 2–21. This is the second of a two-part series.

4. *St. Paul Pioneer Press*, August 4 and 7, 1881.

5. I infer this from the fact that Many Horses's name appears as a member of Sitting Bull's immediate family on the roster of people returned from Fort Randall to Standing Rock in May 1883. This means that she must have gone down with him and lived with him for the period of imprisonment.

6. In the recollection of old-timers, Sitting Bull sat for this portrait in Goff's Bismarck studio on July 31 immediately after the banquet at the Merchants Hotel. The newspapers, however, which captured nearly every detail of the day's festivities, make no mention of such a sitting, and the party is said to have gone directly from the hotel to the boat landing because the steamer was preparing to leave. Moreover, while the shirt is possibly the one he wore in Bismarck, his hair is braided in fur rather than flannel, as reported by the newspapers, and he seems to have no paint on his face. I believe it more likely that Goff, whose presence at Fort Yates on August 2 is documented, obtained the portrait there rather than in Bismarck. For the case for Bismarck, see Elmo Scott Watson, "Orlando Scott Goff, Pioneer Dakota Photographer," *North Dakota History* 29 (January–April 1962): 211–15. In an earlier catalog of Sitting Bull photographs, Watson, a fine researcher, identified this picture as taken *either* at Bismarck or Standing Rock. "The Photographs of Sitting Bull," *Westerners Brand Book* (Chicago) 6 (August 1949): 43, 47–48. Sitting Bull's disapproval of the picture is noted in *Bismarck Tribune*, August 26, 1881.

7. Telegram, Drum AGUSA to CG Division of the Missouri, August 22, 1881, RG 393, Division of the Missouri Special Files, NARA (M1495, roll 5, frame 844).

8. Telegram, Breck AAG to CO Fort Yates, Fort Snelling, Minn., September 1, 1881; telegram, Gilbert CO to AAG Department of Dakota, September 10, 1881, RG 393, Division of the Missouri Special Files, NARA (M1495, roll 5, frames 850 and 852). The military reports are cryptically uninformative. The details of what happened at Fort Yates are set forth in *Bismarck Tribune*, September 9, 1881; and *St. Paul Pioneer Press*, September 11, 1881. See also *Army and Navy Journal*, September 17, 1881; and *Army and Navy Register*, September 24, 1881.

9. Andrews to AAG Department of Dakota, Fort Randall, September 19, 1881, RG 393, Fort Randall LS July 1880–December 1881, no. 169, NARA.

10. Andrews to AAG Department of Dakota, Fort Randall, September 26, 1881, RG 393, Fort Randall LS July 1880–December 1881, no. 176, NARA.

11. Rudolf Cronau, "A Red Napoleon," typescript in box 29, folder 3, Orin G. Libby Collection, NDHS. This account is drawn chiefly from Cronau, "My Visit among the Hostile Dakota Indians and How They Became My Friends," *South Dakota Historical Collections* 22 (1946): 410–25. Cronau's painting of Sitting Bull is at the Museum of the American Indian in New York City.

12. M. W. Stirling, *Three Pictographic Autobiographies of Sitting Bull*, Smithsonian Miscellaneous Collections, vol. 97, no. 5 (Washington, D.C.: Smithsonian Institution, 1938).

13. Williamson to Andrews, Fort Randall, December 12, 1881, in ibid., 6–7. See also Andrews to CO Fort Yates, Fort Randall, November 30, 1881, RG 393, Fort Randall LS July 1880–December 1881, no. 212, NARA. In the Stirling compilation, each pictograph is accompanied by the contemporary identification of Surgeon Kimball, who obtained it from Indian and other informants at Fort Buford, and by identifications supplied by Stanley Vestal. The latter are much more specific. Vestal credits his information to an artist named Seth Jones, who is said to have obtained it from Sitting Bull in 1885. The Campbell Collection sheds almost no light on the subject. Several letters show Vestal's effort to obtain specific information from old Indians who might have known, but they provided little of significance. Although I have cited the pictographs as historical sources in earlier chapters, I remain skeptical of Vestal's captions.

The other Four Horns copy came into possession of the Fort Buford commander, Colonel Henry Morrow, who passed it on to his son. It was destroyed in the San Francisco earthquake of 1906.

14. Two of these compilations, known as the Smith and Pettinger drawings, are reproduced and the provenance traced in Stirling, *Three Pictographic Autobiographies of Sitting Bull*, cited above. For the third, the Quimby compilation, see Alexis A. Praus, *A New Pictographic Autobiography of Sitting Bull*, Smithsonian Miscellaneous Collections, vol. 123, no. 6 (Washington, D.C.: Smithsonian Institution, 1955). All these pictographs are currently in the National Anthropological Archives of the Smithsonian Institution, Washington, D.C.

15. Andrews to Marty, Fort Randall, November 11, 1881; Andrews to Hare, Fort Randall, December 23 and 30, 1881, January 5, 1882, RG 393, Fort Randall LS July 1880–December 1881, nos. 205, 231, and 232; and January 1882–July 1883, no. 11, NARA.

16. Andrews to AAG Department of Dakota, Fort Randall, August 27, 1882, RG 393, Fort Randall LS January 1882–July 1883, no. 146, NARA.

17. Andrews to AAG Department of Dakota, Fort Randall, January 6, 1882, RG 393, Fort Randall LS January 1882–July 1883, no. 10, NARA.

18. Andrews to USIA James McLaughlin, Fort Randall, November 21, 1882, RG 393, Fort Randall LS January 1882–July 1883, no. 218, NARA.

19. Sitting Bull to CIA, Fort Randall, August 15, 1882, RG 75, BIA LR 1881, NARA, Pfaller Compilation, McLaughlin Papers, roll 32.

20. Lincoln to SI, December 20, 1882, enclosing Strike-the-Ree to SW, Yankton Agency, December 11, 1882, RG 75, BIA LR 1881, NARA, Pfaller Compilation, McLaughlin Papers, roll 32. See chap. 18, note 6, for explanation of this and subsequent citations to the Pfaller Compilation.

21. McLaughlin to CIA, February 15, 1883; CIA Hiram Price to SI, February 21, 1883; SI Henry M. Teller to SW, February 23, 1883; AGUSA R. C. Drum to CG Division of the Missouri, March 17, 1883, all in RG 393, Fort Yates LR, copies in McLaughlin Papers.

22. *Pierre Signal*, May 9, 1883. The roster of the Indians transferred to Standing Rock is contained in Capt. Henry Howe, "List of Prisoners of War with Sitting Bull's Party, Fort Yates, June 13, 1883, RG 393, Fort Yates LR, NARA, copy in McLaughlin Papers, roll 31.

23. James Creelman, *On the Great Highway: The Wanderings and Adventures of a Special Correspondent* (Boston: Lothrop Publishing Co., 1901), 301.

CHAPTER 20

Standing Rock

1. Though laden with his biases, McLaughlin's autobiography, first published in 1910, is invaluable for understanding the unfolding civilization program at Standing Rock. James McLaughlin, *My Friend the Indian* (Lincoln: University of Nebraska Press, 1989). A competent biography, though uncritical, is Rev. Louis L. Pfaller, O.S.B., *James McLaughlin: The Man with an Indian Heart* (New York: Vantage Press, 1978). The McLaughlin Papers, Assumption Abbey Archives, Richardton, North Dakota, are a prime source.

2. McLaughlin's annual report, August 15, 1883, CIA, *Annual Report, 1883*, 48–49.

3. Higheagle Manuscript, box 104, folder 21, Campbell Collection.

4. Ibid.

5. McLaughlin, *My Friend the Indian*, 134–35.

6. Crow King's death is reported in the *Bismarck Tribune*, April 11, 1884.

7. Higheagle Manuscript, box 104, folder 21, Campbell Collection.

8. *Bismarck Tribune*, February 16, 1883. See especially profile of Running Antelope by missionary Mary C. Collins, in MS, "Sketches of Indian Life," c. 1890, box 2, folder 35, Mary C. Collins Papers, SDHS.

9. White Bull, box 105, notebook 4, Campbell Collection.

10. I have dealt with this subject in *The Indian Frontier of the American West, 1846–1890* (Albuquerque: University of New Mexico Press, 1984), chap. 7; but see

especially Francis Paul Prucha, *American Indian Policy in Crisis: Christian Reformers and the Indian, 1865–1890* (Norman: University of Oklahoma Press, 1977); and Prucha, *The Great Father; The United States Government and the American Indians*, 2 vols. (Lincoln: University of Nebraska Press, 1984). The progress of these institutions at Standing Rock may be followed in McLaughlin's annual reports in CIA, *Annual Reports, 1881–1891*; and his correspondence in the McLaughlin Papers, Assumption Abbey Archives, Richardton, North Dakota.

11. *Bismarck Tribune*, January 11, 1884.

12. The sources are vague on when the move took place, but in 1891 McLaughlin certified Sitting Bull's cabin on Grand River as his residence from the spring of 1884 until his death. McLaughlin [to whom it may concern], SRA, November 1, 1891, Letter Books 1881–90, roll 22, frame 481, McLaughlin Papers.

13. Gray Eagle, box 106, notebook 54; "One Bull's Memoirs," One Bull file, box 104, folder 11, Campbell Collection.

14. McLaughlin to CIA, SRA, April 14, 1886, RG 75, BIA LR 1886, Pfaller Compilation, McLaughlin Papers, roll 32.

15. "One Bull's Memoirs," One Bull file, box 104, folder 11, Campbell Collection.

16. McLaughlin to Bishop Marty, SRA, February 10, 1884, McLaughlin Papers, roll 20, frame 176.

17. MS, Mary C. Collins, "Some Notes on Sitting Bull," n.d., Mary C. Collins Papers, box 2, folder 35, SDHS. See also Richmond L. Clow, ed., "The Autobiography of Mary C. Collins," *South Dakota Historical Collections* 41 (1982): 1–66.

18. McLaughlin reports the incident in his annual report for 1887 in CIA, *Annual Report, 1887*, 52–53, and gives another, slightly different version in *My Friend the Indian*, 232, in which he dates it 1884.

19. McLaughlin's annual report for 1889 in CIA, *Annual Report, 1889*, 166.

20. Senate Reports, 48th Congress, 1st session, no. 283, serial 2164, 65.

21. Ibid., 80–81. This document, the so-called Dawes Report, gives a history of the background as well as a record of the Senate select committee that resulted. The Edmunds Commission Report, which originally appeared as Senate Executive Documents, 48th Congress, 1st session, no. 70, serial 2165, is also reprinted as part of the Dawes Report.

22. Dawes Report, 80–81.

CHAPTER 21

The World Beyond

1. *Bismarck Tribune*, September 7 and 28, 1883. *Harpers Weekly*, September 23, 1883.

2. McLaughlin to J. M. Stevenson, SRA, May 13, 1884, Letter Books 1881–90,

roll 20, McLaughlin Papers. This private letter describes the journey in great detail. See also McLaughlin to CIA, SRA, March 7, 1884, RG 75, BIA LR 1884, NARA, Pfaller Compilation, roll 32, McLaughlin Papers. *Bismarck Tribune*, March 14 and 28, 1884. In the last, the editor observed, "The old villain is a red-handed murderer of the deepest dye, yet he was toadied to as if the laurel wreath of a hero crowned his brow."

3. Allen to Senator D. M. Sabin, St. Paul, March 29, 1884, RG 75, BIA LR 1884, NARA, Pfaller Compilation, roll 32, McLaughlin Papers.

4. McLaughlin to Allen, July 22 and August 26, 1884, Letter Books 1881–90, roll 20, frames 232 and 238, McLaughlin Papers.

5. McLaughlin to Cody, SRA, April 21, 1884, Letter Books 1881–90, roll 20, frame 201, McLaughlin Papers.

6. Allen to SI Henry M. Teller, St. Paul, September 7, 1884, RG 75, BIA LR 1884, NARA, Pfaller Compilation, roll 32, McLaughlin Papers. *New York Times*, September 12, 15, 16, 25, 28, and October 2, 1884. *Army and Navy Journal*, September 13, 1884. *Bismarck Tribune*, September 19, 1884, quoting *New York Herald*.

7. Luther Standing Bear, *My People the Sioux* (Lincoln: University of Nebraska Press, 1975), 185.

8. *Bismarck Tribune*, October 31, 1884.

9. McLaughlin to Marty, SRA, September 16, 1884, Letter Books 1881–90, roll 20, frame 144, McLaughlin Papers. For CIA's query, see telegram, McLaughlin to Allen, SRA, September 16 and October 13, 1884, ibid., frames 243 and 250.

10. McLaughlin to E. D. Comings, SRA, December 14, 1884, Letter Books 1881–90, roll 20, frame 268, McLaughlin Papers. McLaughlin to McKenzie and Coffin, SRA, December 24 and 26, 1884, ibid., frames 272 and 276.

11. Cody to CIA, c. May 15, 1885, with endorsement by Sherman and Colonel Eugene A. Carr, May 14, RG 75, BIA LR 1885, NARA, Pfaller Compilation, McLaughlin Papers, roll 32. Don Russell, *The Lives and Legends of Buffalo Bill* (Norman: University of Oklahoma Press, 1960), 315–17.

12. Shirl Kasper, *Annie Oakley* (Norman: University of Oklahoma Press, 1992), chap. 4. Also, I am indebted to Paul Fees, senior curator at the Buffalo Bill Historical Center in Cody, Wyoming, for sending me clippings from the London press in 1887 containing Oakley's account of her meeting with Sitting Bull in 1884.

13. Again my thanks to Paul Fees of the Buffalo Bill Historical Center for summarizing in a letter of April 28, 1992, the essence of press clippings and show bills relating to Sitting Bull's role in the show. See also Kasper, *Annie Oakley*, chap. 8.

14. *Washington Post*, June 24, 1885. The *Post* does not mention the White House visit, but the letter itself, duly referred to the Interior Department, implies a meeting, and Sitting Bull later talked of meeting the president. The letter is Sitting Bull "To My Great Father," Washington, D.C., June 23, 1885, RG 75,

BIA LR 1885, NARA, Pfaller Compilation, roll 32, McLaughlin Papers. It is written on stationery of "Buffalo Bill's Wild West, America's National Entertainment."

15. *St. Louis Critic*, October 3, 1885. For other interviews, see *Toronto Globe*, August 24, 1885, and *Detroit Evening Journal*, September 5, 1885.

16. Johnny Baker to Walter S. Campbell, Golden, Colo., July 20, 1929, box 113; Andrew Fox [Sitting Bull's son-in-law], "The Hat Sitting Bull Wears," MS, box 104, folder 20, Campbell Collection.

17. McLaughlin to S. C. Armstrong, SRA, November 9, 1885, Letter Books 1881–90, roll 20, frame 386, McLaughlin Papers.

18. McLaughlin to Nate Salsbury, SRA, March 3, 1886; McLaughlin to John M. Burke, SRA, April 16, 1886, Letter Books 1881–90, roll 20, frames 479 and 516, McLaughlin Papers.

19. Williamson to CIA, Crow Agency, September 27, 1886; Special USIA James R. Howard to CIA, Crow Agency, same date, RG 75, BIA LR 1886, NARA, Pfaller Compilation, roll 32, McLaughlin Papers.

CHAPTER 22

Land

1. CIA, *Annual Report, 1887*, iv–x and 274, reproduces the law and discusses its proposed application in terms of contemporary official thinking.

2. See CIA, *Annual Report, 1888*, 294–301, for the text of the act.

3. McLaughlin to Paul C. Blum, April 9, 1888, Letter Books 1881–90, roll 20, frame 745, McLaughlin Papers. McLaughlin to CIA, October 1, 1890, RG 75, BIA LR 1890, NARA, Pfaller Compilation, roll 32, McLaughlin Papers.

4. Notes by Mary C. Collins, n.d., box 2, folder 37, Collins Papers, SDHS.

5. Robert Higheagle Manuscript, box 4, folder 21, p. 82, Campbell Collection.

6. Walks Looking's death is noted in *Bismarck Tribune*, June 17, 1887. Her name is not given, but she disappears from the census rolls between 1887 and 1888, leaving Andrew Fox a widower with an infant son.

7. The Sitting Bull genealogy is difficult to untangle. Family recollections, scraps of fugitive information incidental to other subjects, and even census records give vague and conflicting data. Most informants seem to favor five wives: Light Hair, the contemporaneous Red Woman and Snow-on-Her, and the contemporaneous Four Robes and Seen-by-the-Nation. Light Hair and a son died in childbirth. A son by Red Woman is either the one kicked in the head by a horse in 1876, just before Slim Buttes, or the one who died on the eve of the Fort Walsh council in 1877; I cannot identify the other. Finally, there are the two sets of twins, 1876 and 1880, the first born to Four Robes, the second unknown, and the

daughter, Standing Holy, in 1878. In addition, there were the two stepsons brought into the marriage by Seen-by-the-Nation, identified in early years as Little Soldier and Blue Mountain, among other names, but known in reservation years as Louis Sitting Bull and William Sitting Bull. William was the deaf-mute. The Standing Rock census rolls for 1885–93 are in RG 75, NARA (M596, rolls 547 and 548).

8. Higheagle, "Note on Crowfoot," in Stanley Vestal, *New Sources of Indian History, 1850–1891* (Norman: University of Oklahoma Press, 1934), 55–56.

9. It is possible that these infants were grandchildren or other family offspring mistakenly identified by the census taker, although the son is listed as "Sitting Bull, Jr." As previously noted, the census of 1890 cut several years from the ages given Sitting Bull's wives in earlier enumerations. At forty-two and forty, they would have been twenty-four and twenty-two when Sitting Bull married them, ages that seem more appropriate for marriageable women.

10. McLaughlin to CIA, SRA, December 17, 1888, RG 75, BIA LR SRA 1888, roll 33, Pfaller Compilation, McLaughlin Papers.

11. *New York Sun*, reprinted in *Bismarck Tribune*, January 13, 1888.

12. McLaughlin explained his position in a letter to Bishop Marty, February 23, 1889, Letter Book 1881–90, roll 20, frame 813, McLaughlin Papers.

13. McLaughlin to Paul C. Blum, SRA, April 9, 1888, Letter Books 1881–90, roll 20, frame 745, McLaughlin Papers. *Bismarck Tribune*, July 27, 1888.

14. The council transcript and report of the commission were published as Senate Executive Documents, 50th Congress, 2d session, no. 17, serial 2610. A Bismarck reporter covered the proceedings from beginning to end, and his dispatches are essential for understanding the mood of the Indians and the deliberations of their nighttime councils. *Bismarck Tribune*, July 27, August 3 and 10, 1888. McLaughlin's version is in *My Friend the Indian* (Lincoln: University of Nebraska Press, 1989), 273–76.

15. *Bismarck Tribune*, August 3, 1888.

16. Ibid.

17. Commission report, 108, 116.

18. *Bismarck Tribune*, August 10, 1888.

19. Commission report, 20–21. See also interview at Carlisle repeated in *Bismarck Tribune*, September 21, 1888, in which Pratt tortured precedent, including the Treaty of 1868, to justify ignoring Indian views.

20. *Washington Post*, October 13, 1888. The *Post* gave detailed coverage to the visit of the Sioux, in the issues of October 13, 14, 15, 16, 17, and 20, 1888, from which my account is taken. See also McLaughlin, *My Friend the Indian*, 276–80.

21. *Washington Post*, October 15, 1888.

22. Ibid., October 17, 1888.

23. Ibid., October 21, 1888. See also *Bismarck Tribune*, October 19 and 26, 1888. The majority and minority proposals of the Indians, with the names of signatories, are printed in the Sioux Commission's report, 246–49.

Whether Sitting Bull and the others grasped the bureaucratic implications of the document they signed may be doubted. It was framed by the agents based on the consensus developed in the councils, and the signatories may not have understood it as a statement of acceptable terms rather than simply a critique of the Vilas proposal.

Sitting Bull's speech is reported by the *Washington Post*, October 15, 1888. The reporter said this council was held at night in a big room on the second floor of a cigar store at 237 Pennsylvania Avenue NW, with three open windows looking out on the Botanical Gardens, where a throng of people gathered to watch as one after another the chiefs rose to speak. Clearly obtaining his information from agents or interpreters who were present, the reporter wrote: "Sitting Bull made the opening speech, and every word of it was closely listened to by his hearers. He spoke nearly two hours. His style is, even to a person who cannot understand him, very impressive, and his gestures, though lavish, are graceful." As for the content of his speech: "Sitting Bull favors accepting the terms of the government with an amendment so as to increase the price of the land relinquished to the amount paid by the settlers." Under the homestead laws, settlers paid $1.25 an acre.

24. For the text of the act, see CIA, *Annual Report, 1889*, 449–58.

25. The report of the commission, including transcripts of the councils at all the agencies, was published as Senate Executive Documents, 51st Congress, 1st session, No. 51, serial 2682.

26. Lone Man, "Sitting Bull's Address to the Silent Eaters Protesting the Treaty of 1889," box 104, Campbell Collection. Sitting Bull attempted to enlist Robert Higheagle to take notes, but he was too shy. Higheagle Manuscript, 82–83.

27. McLaughlin, *My Friend the Indian*, 284–86.

28. Martin F. Schmitt, ed., *General George Crook, His Autobiography* (Norman: University of Oklahoma Press, 1946), 288. McLaughlin, *My Friend the Indian*, 286–88.

29. Collins to My Dear Friends, Fort Yates, December 1889, box 1, folder 13, Collins Papers, SDHS.

30. A transcript of the councils is in the commission report, 218–33.

31. The sources are conflicting on whether there was starvation. A complete statistical breakdown on the ration situation is in CIA to SI, January 5, 1891, CIA, *Annual Report, 1891*, 1191–95. It purports to show food issues well above the starvation level. Other persuasive evidence points to an opposite conclusion. That the Sioux were very hungry is plain. For disease, see especially "Rev. William J. Cleveland's Investigation of the Causes of the Sioux Trouble," Indian Rights Association, *Ninth Annual Report, 1891*, 39, 57.

32. James D. Richardson, ed., *A Compilation of Messages and Papers of the Presidents, 1789–1897* (Washington, D.C.: Government Printing Office, 1898), vol. 8, pp. 94–97.

33. Quoted in John G. Bourke, *On the Border with Crook* (New York: Charles Scribner's Sons, 1891), 486.

34. To Rev. William J. Cleveland, in Indian Rights Association, *Ninth Annual Report, 1891*, 29.

CHAPTER 23

Messiah

1. McLaughlin to CIA, SRA, June 18, 1890, CIA, *Annual Report, 1891*, 328.

2. Aside from some newspaper articles of dubious reliability, most of what is known of Mrs. Weldon comes from her own emotional letters, many of which were found in Sitting Bull's cabin after his death. They are printed in Stanley Vestal, *New Sources of Indian History, 1850–1891* (Norman: University of Oklahoma Press, 1934), 92–115.

3. Weldon to CIA, Cannonball, August 7, 1890, RG 75, BIA LR 1890, NARA, Pfaller Compilation, roll 34, McLaughlin Papers.

4. The quotation is from Weldon to McLaughlin, April 4, 1890, in Vestal, *New Sources*, 98–100. McLaughlin's denial is in *Bismarck Tribune*, December 25, 1890. See also McLaughlin to CIA, SRA, October 17, 1890, in CIA, *Annual Report, 1891*, 328–29.

5. The entire sermon is quoted in James McLaughlin, *My Friend the Indian* (Lincoln: University of Nebraska Press, 1989), 185–89. It was paraphrased in McLaughlin to CIA, SRA, October 17, 1890, CIA, *Annual Report, 1891*, 328.

6. McLaughlin to CIA, SRA, October 17, 1890, CIA, *Annual Report, 1891*, 328–30. McLaughlin, *My Friend the Indian*, 191. One Bull is the authority for his inclusion in the police detachment, box 104, folder 11, Campbell Collection.

7. Narrative of teacher John M. Carignan in Frank B. Fiske, *Life and Death of Sitting Bull* (Fort Yates, N.D.: Pioneer-Arrow Press, 1933), 32.

8. McLaughlin's letter of October 17 and Acting CIA R. V. Belt's reply of October 29 are in CIA, *Annual Report, 1891*, 328–30.

9. Weldon to McLaughlin, Cannonball, October 24, 1890; Weldon to Sitting Bull, Kansas City, November 20, 1890, in Vestal, *New Sources*, 102–4. *Bismarck Tribune*, October 28, 1890.

10. Telegram, Royer to Belt, PRA, November 12, 1890; Harrison to SI, November 13, 1890, RG 75, special case 188, drawer 1, NARA.

11. McLaughlin recounts his visit in detail in *My Friend the Indian*, 201–8. He reports on it to the Indian Office in McLaughlin to CIA, SRA, November 19, 1890, CIA, *Annual Report, 1891*, 330–31.

12. Sources give several versions of the origins of the feud, but there can be no doubt that it colored the relations between these three men. Circling Hawk, box 105, notebook 13, Campbell Collection. Frank B. Zahn to Stanley Vestal, September 22 and November 3, 1929, box 107, Zahn folder, Campbell Collection. Fiske, *Life and Death of Sitting Bull*, 50. Fiske's version seems to me most plausible: "There were animosities of long standing, extending from the day that

Sitting Bull called Bullhead an old woman while on a buffalo hunt, to the time when Bullhead saw fit to take some beef tongues away from Catch the Bear. At that time Catch the Bear told Bullhead that he would remember him." The Higheagle characterization is in the Robert Higheagle Manuscript, box 4, folder 21, Campbell Collection.

13. McLaughlin to CIA, SRA, November 19, 1890, CIA, *Annual Report, 1891*, 330–31. *Bismarck Tribune*, November 23 and 25, 1890.

14. One Bull, "Prophesy of Sitting Bull of a Disastrous Year, 1889–90," box 104, folder 11, Campbell Collection. McLaughlin to Herbert Welsh, SRA, November 25, 1890, Letter Books 1881–90, roll 20, McLaughlin Papers. *Bismarck Tribune*, November 25, 1890. The quotation is from Mary Collins, "A Short Autobiography," in Vestal, *New Sources*, 65.

15. One Bull, "Prophesy of Sitting Bull—Would be Killed by His Own People," box 104, folder 20, Campbell Collection.

CHAPTER 24

Death

1. There are several versions, which I have combined: Mary Collins, "A Short Autobiography," in Stanley Vestal, *New Sources of Indian History, 1850–1891* (Norman: University of Oklahoma Press, 1934), 68–69. Collins, "Some Notes on Sitting Bull," n.d., box 2, folder 35, Collins Papers, SDHS. Collins, interview by Walter M. Camp, June 15, 1913, Camp Papers, Lilly Library, Indiana University, copy in box 3, folder 4, Kenneth Hammer Collection, Harold B. Lee Library, Brigham Young University. See also Samuel J. Kirk, "Chief Oihduze of Sisseton-Wahpeton Dakotas," MS, n.d., photocopy in "Sitting Bull-death" folder, SDHS. As Collins's assistant, Kirk was present.

2. Gray Eagle, box 106, notebook 54, Campbell Collection.

3. Lone Man, interview by Walter M. Camp, 1912, Camp Papers, Lilly Library, Indiana University, copy in box 3, folder 5, Kenneth Hammer Papers, Harold B. Lee Library, Brigham Young University.

4. Carignan to McLaughlin, Grand River, November 27, 1890, in Vestal, *New Sources*, 10.

5. Drum to AAG Department of Dakota, Fort Yates, November 30, 1890, RG 393, Fort Yates LS, NARA, copy in roll 31, McLaughlin Papers.

6. Drum's account is in ibid. Indian Office correspondence is in CIA, *Annual Report, 1891*, 331–33. Also, not printed, see McLaughlin to CIA, SRA, December 1, 1890, RG 75, special case 188, drawer 1, NARA; and same to same, December 4, 1890, RG 75, BIA LR 1890, Pfaller Compilation, roll 34, McLaughlin Papers. See also Matthew F. Steele (a Fort Yates officer), "Buffalo Bill's Bluff," *South Dakota Historical Collections* 9 (1918): 475–85; Peter E. Traub (another Fort Yates officer), "The First Act of the Last Sioux Campaign," *Journal*

of the United States Cavalry Association 15 (April 1905): 872–79; Narrative of John M. Carignan in Frank B. Fiske, *Life and Death of Sitting Bull* (Fort Yates, N.D.: Pioneer-Arrow Press, 1933), 37–41; Don Russell, *The Lives and Legends of Buffalo Bill* (Norman: University of Oklahoma Press, 1961), 358–61; and James McLaughlin, *My Friend the Indian* (Lincoln: University of Nebraska Press, 1989), 209–11.

7. The exchange of telegrams, December 5, is in CIA, *Annual Report, 1891*, 333.

8. Telegram (confidential), Miles to Schofield, December 6, 1890; telegram (confidential), Corbin AAG by command of Miles to Ruger, Chicago, December 10, 1890, RG 393, Division of the Missouri LS 1890–91, NARA. Telegram, Barber AAG to CO Fort Yates, St. Paul, December 12, 1890, CIA, *Annual Report, 1891*, 333.

9. McLaughlin's annual report, August 26, 1891, *Annual Report, 1891*, 334. For the special police, see telegram, Gardner Inspector to SI, SRA, December 5, 1890, and SI to CIA, same date, RG 75, special case, 188, drawer 1, NARA.

10. "One Bull's Memoirs," box 104, folder 11, Campbell Collection. Mary Collins reported that One Bull asked McLaughlin to be excused from any police duty aimed at Sitting Bull but was told to do his duty or give up his uniform. He chose to resign. Collins, interview by Walter M. Camp, Camp Papers, Lilly Library, Indiana University, copy in box 3, folder 4, Kenneth Hammer Collection, Harold B. Lee Library, Brigham Young University.

11. McLaughlin included in *My Friend the Indian*, 215–16, those portions he could make sense of. Stanley Vestal, *Sitting Bull, Champion of the Sioux* (Norman: University of Oklahoma Press, 1957), 283–85, gave verbatim both what Sitting Bull dictated and Andrew Fox wrote. The latter is consistent with the McLaughlin excerpts, but where Vestal obtained it is not apparent. A copy was not found in the Campbell Collection. Vestal's rendition of Sitting Bull's dictation seems to have been inferred from the English translation, and it impresses me as a sound inference. My version and Vestal's draw also on Andrew Fox, box 104, notebook 5; and Fox, May 8, 1930, box 104, folder 10, Campbell Collection. In the latter, the questions are in English, the answers in Dakota. I am indebted to Stephen Feraca for the translation, although he says the native orthography is so bad as to present major obstacles to translation.

12. McLaughlin, *My Friend the Indian*, 215. McLaughlin to Mary Collins, SRA, December 26, 1890, LB 1881–90, roll 22, frame 29, McLaughlin Papers. In his book McLaughlin said Bull Ghost arrived at his office at 6 P.M. on December 13, but in the letter, written two weeks after the event, he gave the date as December 12. In a letter cited below, however, dated December 12, Louis Primeau referred to Bull Ghost's mission.

13. McLaughlin to Friend Sitting Bull, SRA, December 13, 1890, LB 1881–90, roll 20, frame 937, McLaughlin Papers.

14. Primeau to Afraid-of-Bear (Bull Head), SRA, December 12, 1890, in Vestal, *New Sources*, 11–12.

15. White Bird, box 105, notebook 12, Campbell Collection. The two men were Young Eagle and Black Bird (not the Black Bird long associated with Sitting Bull). Neither was a policeman, but Young Eagle was one of the four volunteers who accompanied the police in their effort to arrest Sitting Bull.

16. Carignan to McLaughlin, Grand River, December 14, 1890, 12:30 A.M., encl. to McLaughlin to CIA, December 16, 1890, RG 75, special case 188, drawer 2, NARA. Also in Vestal, *New Sources*, 13–14.

17. Photocopies of the original orders to Bull Head, in English and Sioux, appear in Vestal, *Sitting Bull*, 282–83. The text, together with the letter to Carignan, are in Vestal, *New Sources*, 14–16. See also McLaughlin's account in CIA, *Annual Report, 1891*, 334–35; and Drum's in SW, *Annual Report, 1891*, 194–95. See also McLaughlin, *My Friend the Indian*, 216–18.

18. To illustrate the great distances ridden by his men that night, McLaughlin details who went where and why: CIA, *Annual Report, 1891*, 336.

19. Lone Man, as told to Robert P. Higheagle, "The Arrest and Killing of Sitting Bull," in Vestal, *New Sources*, 45–55. Of all the accounts of Indian participants, Lone Man's is the clearest. Others on whom I have drawn for the following story include, from the Campbell Collection: Gray Eagle, box 106, notebook 54; Weasel Bear, box 105, notebook 20; White Bird, box 105, notebook 1; Shoots Walking, box 104, folder 5; from the Walter M. Camp Collection, Lilly Library, Indiana University, copies in the Hammer Collection, Harold B. Lee Library, Brigham Young University: Four Blanket Woman (One Bull's wife), Gray Eagle, and Lone Man, in box 3, folder 5, and One Bull in box 3, folder 6; and deposition of Shoots Walking, January 6, 1925, A1173, box 1, E.D. Mossman Papers, NDHS. Some of these and other firsthand sources appear in John M. Carroll, ed., *The Arrest and Killing of Sitting Bull* (Glendale, Calif.: Arthur H. Clark Co., 1986).

20. Lone Man, interview by Walter M. Camp, 1912, Camp Papers, Lilly Library, Indiana University, copy in box 3, folder 5, Kenneth Hammer Collection, Harold B. Lee Library, Brigham Young University. In his other account, in Vestal, *New Sources*, 48–49, Lone Man does not mention this mission, but Carignan (ibid., 4) names him as one of the four policemen who accompanied him to Bull Head's.

21. Carignan's narrative in Fiske, *Life and Death of Sitting Bull*, 44–46. In his other account (Vestal, *New Sources*, 3–4), Carignan stated that his party did not arrive at Bull Head's until after the main force had left, whereupon the four policemen hurried to catch up while Carignan drove Bull Head's family to the agency. Since Lone Man described the departure of the police from Bull Head's cabin, I have relied on the first citation.

22. Lone Man in Vestal, *New Sources*, 50.

23. Sources, including official rosters, give varying composition of the force. This is from a "roll of honor" prepared by McLaughlin on December 20, 1890, in an effort to gain recognition and reward for the police. LB 1881–90, roll 20, frame 957, McLaughlin Papers.

24. Lone Man in Vestal, *New Sources*, 49–50.

25. Weasel Bear, box 105, notebook 20; and White Bird, box 105, notebook 1, Campbell Collection. There are two interviews with One Bull's wife by Walter M. Camp, in one of which she is named Four-Blanket-Woman and the other Scarlet-Whirlwind-Woman: Camp Papers, Lilly Library, Indiana University, copies in box 3, folders 5 and 6, Kenneth Hammer Collection, Harold B. Lee Library, Brigham Young University. See also Camp interview with One Bull in ibid., box 3, folder 6; and "One Bull's Memoirs," box 104, folder 11, Campbell Collection. Red Whirlwind is the name given in the censuses of 1890–92. In those of 1885–89 Sitting Holy is listed as One Bull's wife, but by 1890 he had replaced her with Red Whirlwind, who was four years younger. One Bull's household also included two adolescent daughters and one infant daughter.

26. My reconstruction rests principally on Lone Man, Weasel Bear, White Bird, and Shoots Walking, all of whom were present, as cited in previous notes.

27. The casualties are listed in CIA, *Annual Report, 1891*, 338. Vestal, *Sitting Bull*, 300–1, wrote that during this melee the gray horse sat on his haunches and began to perform tricks learned in his circus days, which greatly frightened the policemen. The story has been repeated by many writers, including this one in *Last Days of the Sioux Nation* (New Haven: Yale University Press, 1963), 160. No participant mentions it, and I have found nothing in the Campbell Collection to indicate where Vestal got it. Regrettably, for it is a good story, I have to conclude that it probably did not happen.

28. In his account in Vestal, *New Sources*, 53, Lone Man said, "I do not remember who really fired the shot that killed Crow Foot—several fired at once." In his interview with Walter Camp, Lone Man said, "I then struck Crow Foot across the forehead with my gun, knocking him down, and as he lay there we fired three shots into his body." Mary Crawler, daughter of Sitting Bull's close friend Crawler, who was there, is the authority for the tears running down the policemen's cheeks as they killed Crow Foot. Fiske, *Life and Death of Sitting Bull*, 50–51.

29. "One Bull's Memoirs," box 104, folder 11, Campbell Collection.

30. E. G. Frechet, "The True Story of the Death of Sitting Bull," *Proceedings and Collections of the Nebraska State Historical Society* 2 (2d series, 1898): 186. Another version is Fechet's "The Capture of Sitting Bull," *South Dakota Historical Collections* 4 (1908): 185–93, which includes a sketch map of the Sitting Bull settlement. Fechet's official report, December 17, 1890, in SW, *Annual Report, 1891*, 197–99, is also detailed and informative. Another useful first-hand military account is M. F. Steele, "Buffalo Bill's Bluff," *South Dakota Historical Collections* 9 (1918): 475–85. The account of a reporter who accompanied Fechet is in *Bismarck Tribune*, December 18, 1890.

31. Fiske, *Life and Death of Sitting Bull*, 52. White Bird, box 105, notebook 12; and Weasel Bear, box 105, notebook 20, Campbell Collection.

32. Steele, "Buffalo Bill's Bluff," 483. Steele mentions only one person, Sitting Bull's stepson. The correspondent whose account appears in the *Bismarck Tribune*, December 18, 1890, names the two as Looking Horse, Sitting Bull's deaf-mute

"nephew," and Silas, son of Little Assiniboine (Jumping Bull). Other sources also tell of two, including Fechet, "True Story," 188.

33. Steele, "Buffalo Bill's Bluff," 484. Also Steele to Stanley Vestal, October 24, 1919, box 107, Campbell Collection.

34. Fechet, "True Story," 187. Frank Zahn to Stanley Vestal, Fort Yates, N.D., August 6, 1933, box 107, Zahn folder, Campbell Collection. Drum to McLaughlin, February 26, 1891, in Vestal, *New Sources*, 33.

35. McLaughlin, *My Friend the Indian*, 425. Note that this reference is from the University of Nebraska Press edition. In its original form, McLaughlin's book omitted three chapters he had prepared in manuscript. These were later discovered among his papers and published separately. They were included in the edition here cited.

36. Fiske, *Life and Death of Sitting Bull*, 1–2. Fiske mistakenly gave the date as December 15, but the column did not reach the fort until the day after the slaying of Sitting Bull.

37. McLaughlin, *My Friend the Indian*, 433.

38. *Bismarck Tribune*, December 20, 1890.

39. McLaughlin, *My Friend the Indian*, 221–22. Fiske, *Life and Death of Sitting Bull*, 53. Lt. Col. William F. Drum to AAG Department of Dakota, December 18, 1890, RG 393, Fort Yates LS, copy in Major James McLaughlin Papers, Assumption Abbey Archives, Richardton, N.D., roll 31. *Bismarck Tribune*, December 18, 1890. Endorsements of Fort Yates post surgeon and McLaughlin on T. A. Bland to CIA, December 27, 1890, RG 75, special case 188, drawer 3, NARA.

40. Draft by Walsh on stationery of Dominion Coal, Coke & Transportation Co., December 16, 1890, J. M. Walsh Papers, Provincial Archives of Manitoba, Winnipeg.

EPILOGUE

1. Drum to AAG Department of Dakota, Fort Yates, February 27, 1891; and Fechet to Post Adjutant, Fort Yates, December 17, 1890, in SW, *Annual Report, 1891*, 194–98. E. G. Fechet, "The True Story of the Death of Sitting Bull," *Proceedings and Collections of the Nebraska State Historical Society* 2 (2d ser.) (1898): 189. *Bismarck Tribune*, December 18, 1890.

2. Thomas L. Riggs, as told to Mary K. Howard, "Sunset to Sunset: A Lifetime with My Brothers the Sioux," chap. 14, "Sitting Bull and the Ghost Dance," *South Dakota Historical Collections* 24 (1958): 258–69.

3. McLaughlin's annual report, August 26, 1891, in CIA, *Annual Report, 1891*, 334–38.

4. In SW, *Annual Report, 1891*, 195.

5. Casey to CIA, February 14, 1891, RG 75, BIA LR 1891, NARA, Pfaller Compilation, roll 34, McLaughlin Papers.

6. Ibid. McLaughlin [To whom it may concern], SRA, November 1, 1891, LB 1881–90, roll 22, frame 481, McLaughlin Papers.

7. Steele to Stanley Vestal, Fargo, N.D., October 24, 1929, box 107, Sitting Bull folder, Campbell Collection.

8. *Bismarck Tribune*, December 20, 1890. Bland to CIA, December 27, 1890, with endorsements of the post surgeon, January 23, 1891, and McLaughlin, January 25, 1891, RG 75, special case 188, drawer 3, NARA.

9. Kenneth M. Hammer, "Sitting Bull's Bones," English Westerners Society *Brand Book* 23 (Winter 1984): 1–8. Dabney Otis Collins, "The Fight for Sitting Bull's Bones," *American West* 3 (Winter 1966): 72–78. The contemporary press, of course, carried extensive coverage.

10. *Chicago Tribune*, October 8, 1984.

INDEX

About the Author

ROBERT M. UTLEY, a former chief historian of the National Park Service, is the author of many distinguished works of history and biography, including *The Last Days of the Sioux Nation, Cavalier in Buckskin: George Armstrong Custer and the Western Military Frontier,* and *The Indian Frontier of the American West, 1846-1890.*